Classical Theory in International Relations

Classical political theorists such as Thucydides, Kant, Rousseau, Smith, Hegel, Grotius, Mill, Locke and Clausewitz are often employed to explain and justify contemporary international politics and are seen to constitute the different schools of thought in the discipline. However, traditional interpretations frequently ignore the intellectual and historical context in which these thinkers were writing as well as the lineages through which they came to be appropriated in International Relations. This collection of essays provides alternative interpretations sensitive to these political and intellectual contexts and to the trajectory of their appropriation. The political, sociological, anthropological, legal, economic, philosophical and normative dimensions are shown to be constitutive, not just of classical theories, but of international thought and practice in the contemporary world. Moreover, they challenge traditional accounts of timeless debates and schools of thought and provide new conceptions of core issues such as sovereignty, morality, law, property, imperialism and agency.

BEATE JAHN is a Senior Lecturer in International Relations in the Department of International Relations at the University of Sussex. She is the author of *The Cultural Construction of International Relations* (2000) and *Politik und Moral* (1993).

CAMBRIDGE STUDIES IN INTERNATIONAL RELATIONS

Series list continued after index

Classical Theory in
International Relations

Edited by
Beate Jahn

CAMBRIDGE
UNIVERSITY PRESS

CAMBRIDGE UNIVERSITY PRESS
Cambridge, New York, Melbourne, Madrid, Cape Town, Singapore, São Paulo

Cambridge University Press
The Edinburgh Building, Cambridge CB2 2RU, UK

Published in the United States of America by Cambridge University Press,
New York

www.cambridge.org
Information on this title: www.cambridge.org/9780521686020

First published 2006

Printed in the United Kingdom at the University Press, Cambridge

A catalogue record for this publication is available from the British Library

ISBN-13 978-0-521-86685-9 hardback
ISBN-10 0-521-86685-5 hardback

ISBN-13 978-0-521-68602-0 paperback
ISBN-10 0-521-68602-4 paperback

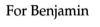
For Benjamin

Contents

Contents

Notes on contributors

Yuichi Aiko is teaching Politics at Nishogakusha University, Tokyo. He wrote his PhD thesis on *The History of Political Theory in International Relations: Seventeenth and Eighteenth-Century Perpetual Peace Projects in Intellectual Context*. His major research interest lies in the historical development of the 'study of international relations' and he is currently working on Kant's international political theory.

David L. Blaney is Associate Professor of Political Science, Macalester College, USA. His research fields include the political and social theory of international relations/international political economy and democratic theory, pedagogy and world politics. He has recently published, with Naeem Inayatullah, *International Relations and the Problem of Difference* (2004). With Inayatullah, he is working on a book about Indians and political economy.

David Boucher is Professorial Fellow in European Studies, Cardiff University, and Adjunct Professor of International Relations at the University of the Sunshine Coast. His most recent publications include *Political Theories of International Relations* (1998), *British Idealism and Political Theory* (with Andrew Vincent, 2000) and *Bob Dylan and Leonard Cohen: Politics, Poetry and Protest* (2004). Among his edited books are: *The British Idealists* (Cambridge University Press, 1997), *Social Justice* (with Paul Kelly, 1998), and *Political Thinkers From Socrates to the Present* (with Paul Kelly, 2003).

Antonio Franceschet is Assistant Professor of Political Science at the University of Calgary, Canada. He has published numerous articles on liberal international thought and is the author of *Kant and Liberal Internationalism: Sovereignty, Justice and Global Reform* (Palgrave 2002).

Naeem Inayatullah is Associate Professor of Politics, Ithaca College, USA. He is currently interested in applying the history of social theory to aspects of popular culture such as music, film, literature and collective memory. He has recently published, with David Blaney, *International Relations and the Problem of Difference* (2004). With Blaney, he is working on a book about Indians and political economy.

Beate Jahn is Senior Lecturer in International Relations at the University of Sussex. Her publications include *Politik und Moral* (1993) and *The Cultural Construction of International Relations* (2000). She is interested in classical and contemporary international and political theory and is currently working on a critical history of liberal internationalism.

Edward Keene is Assistant Professor at the Sam Nunn School of International Affairs at the Georgia Institute of Technology. He is the author of *Beyond the Anarchical Society: Grotius, Colonialism and Order in World Politics* (Cambridge University Press, 2002) and *International Political Thought: A Historical Introduction* (2005).

Michael Loriaux is Associate Professor of Political Science and Co-Director of the French Interdisciplinary Group at Northwestern University. He is interested in European integration, international monetary relations, and philosophical underpinnings of International Relations theory. Among his publications are *France After Hegemony: International Change, Financial Reform and Capital Ungoverned: Liberalizing Finance in Interventionist States* (co-authored). He has recently completed a book manuscript *European Union: Myth and Deconstruction of the Rhineland Frontier.*

John MacMillan is Senior Lecturer in International Relations at Brunel University. His primary area of research is the war/peace proneness of democratic states. Recent publications include articles in *Journal of Peace Research, Review of International Studies* and *International Politics* as well as the co-edited volume, *The Iraq War and Democratic Politics.*

S. Sara Monoson is Associate Professor of Political Science at Northwestern University. She is the author of *Plato's Democratic Entanglements: Athenian Politics and the Practice of Philosophy* (2000) and has written on Athenian democratic thought, Thucydides, and International Relations theory.

Julian Reid is Lecturer in International Relations at the Department of War Studies, King's College, London. His most recent work appears in *Millennium, Alternatives, Space and Culture* and the *Cambridge Review of International Affairs*. He is currently working on two books, *Infinite War* and *The Liberal Way of War* (with Michael Dillon).

Robert Shilliam is Hedley Bull Junior Research Fellow in International Relations at Wadham College, University of Oxford. His research project seeks to integrate Historical Sociology and History of Political Thought approaches. He has published in *Millennium* and *History of Political Thought*.

Michael C. Williams is Professor of International Politics at the University of Wales in Aberystwyth. He is the author of *The Realist Tradition and the Limits of International Relations* (Cambridge University Press, 2005) and 'Words, Images, Enemies: Securitization in international politics' *International Studies Quarterly* (December 2003).

Acknowledgements

While I was developing a new course on Classical Political Theory and International Relations at the University of Sussex, it became clear to me that there were numerous excellent and critical treatments of classical theorists in International Relations, albeit widely dispersed and difficult to get hold of. This state of affairs, I felt, was unsatisfactory not only because it effectively removed this literature from a broader audience but also because it obscured the fact that reflection on the role of classical theory has been an ongoing and systematic concern within the discipline of International Relations. Moreover, as the contributions to this book demonstrate, engagement with classical theory in the discipline is neither reduced to a particular intellectual or political position nor to certain 'issue areas'. It is hoped that this book will help to make this literature more readily available as well as to demonstrate its systematic and quite foundational nature for all areas of international thought.

Indirectly, then, the never-ending processes of restructuring at the University of Sussex have led to the development of this book. Notwithstanding these 'structural' influences, my greatest thanks go to the contributors for the excellent quality of their work as well as for their constructive cooperation in the course of producing this book. The Department for International Relations and Politics at Sussex has generously provided some funding for initial library research. And I am especially grateful to Robert Shilliam who undertook that task with the most astonishing efficiency and intellectual sharpness. Justin Rosenberg has, as usual, patiently listened to my musings on the subject of editing a book, provided feedback on my contributions, and corrected my English. Thanks are also due to the referees of Cambridge University Press who have made some very astute, helpful and generous comments as well as to John Haslam for his support and efficiency.

Chapter 2 is an extensively revised version of S. Sara Monoson and Michael Loriaux, 'The Illusion of Power and the Disruption of Moral Norms: Thucydides' Critique of Periclean Policy' in *American Political Science Review* 92 (1998), 285–297 and is reprinted with the permission of Cambridge University Press; Chapter 3 is an updated version of John MacMillian's 'A Kantian Protest Against the Peculiar Discourse of Inter-Liberal State Peace' in *Millennium* 24 (1995), 549–562 and is reproduced with the permission of the publisher; and a different version of Chapter 8 has first been published as Beate Jahn, 'Kant, Mill, and Illiberal Legacies in International Affairs' in *International Organization* 59 (2005), 177–207. We are grateful to Cambridge University Press and the editors of *Millennium* for permission to reprint these articles here.

Brighton
Beate Jahn

1 Classical theory and international relations in context

Beate Jahn

The contemporary world is widely described as globalized, globalizing or postmodern. Central to these descriptions is the claim of historical change or even rupture. A globalized or globalizing world is juxtaposed to an earlier international world just as the postmodern world has left modernity behind. In the light of these claims of historical change it is remarkable that classical authors[1] reflecting on a modern or even premodern, but certainly international, world still play an important role in International Relations.

Three main uses of classical texts in contemporary International Relations can be identified. First, classical authors are frequently cited as precursors to contemporary theoretical approaches: Realists trace the roots of their thinking back to Thucydides, Machiavelli, Hobbes and Rousseau; Liberals most prominently to Kant; the English School to Grotius; Marxist approaches obviously cite Marx as well as Gramsci; and Nietzsche as well as Hegel play an important role in Postmodernism.

Secondly, classical authors are used for the purpose of explaining contemporary political developments and for the justification or even propagation of specific foreign policies. A case in point is the – academically and politically – influential use of Kant in explaining the data of the Democratic Peace and the implicit or explicit propagation of the spread of democracy and market economy accompanied by a strict legal and political separation of liberal from non-liberal states in contemporary world politics.[2]

---

[1] Classical authors are here understood to have written before the constitution of International Relations as a separate discipline; their work is thus characterized by a relatively holistic approach to social and political life.
[2] See, for the most influential formulation of the Democratic Peace thesis, Michael Doyle, 'Kant, Liberal Legacies, and Foreign Affairs' in Michael E. Brown, Sean M. Lynn-Jones and

Finally, classical authors are used to define and structure contemporary theoretical and political debates. Theoretical debates in International Relations are frequently presented – in the mainstream – as Liberal or Kantian approaches versus Realist or Hobbesian/Machiavellian approaches[3] as well as – from the margins – for instance as Marxist versus Realist approaches.[4] Similarly, contemporary political world views and policies are defined with reference to classical authors and pitched against each other. Most recently and very prominently, for instance, Robert Kagan has characterized the European world view and approach to international affairs as 'Kantian' and the equivalent American position as 'Hobbesian'.[5]

These three different uses of classical authors in contemporary international thought and practice – providing philosophical foundations for contemporary theories, explaining and justifying contemporary policies, and defining and structuring theoretical and political debates – ultimately aim at illuminating contemporary theories, political practices, and theoretical and political debates. It is in order to provide a foundation for contemporary international theories that scholars read Machiavelli; in order to explain the contemporary liberal peace or propagate liberal foreign policies that scholars turn to Kant; in order to classify and specify competing contemporary world views and policies that scholars refer to Kant and Hobbes. This motivation to explain

Steven E. Miller (eds.), *Debating the Democratic Peace* (Cambridge MA: MIT Press, 1996), pp. 3–57. The article was first published in two parts in Philosophy and Public Affairs 12 (1983), 205–235, 323–353. Kant is also prominently used in support of the Cosmopolitan Democracy project heralded by David Held, *Democracy and the Global Order: From the Modern State to Cosmopolitan Governance* (Cambridge: Polity Press, 1995); Daniele Archibugi, 'Models of International Organization in Perpetual Peace Projects' *Review of International Studies* 18 (1992), 295–317; and 'Principles of Cosmopolitan Democracy' in Daniele Archibugi, David Held and Martin Köhler (eds.), *Re-imagining Political Community: Studies in Cosmopolitan Democracy* (Cambridge: Polity Press, 1998), pp. 198–228; as well as Andrew Linklater, 'Citizenship and Sovereignty in the Post-Westphalian State' *European Journal of International Relations* 2 (1996), 77–103; and *The Transformation of Political Community: Ethical Foundations of the Post-Westphalian Era* (Cambridge: Polity Press, 1998).

[3] After E. H. Carr, *The Twenty Years' Crisis 1919–1939* (Basingstoke: Macmillan, 1981) had famously introduced this distinction at the end of the 1930s, there is hardly a textbook in International Relations which does not reproduce it – notwithstanding variations in the authors aligned with each of these positions as well as different strands of thought within them.

[4] See, for example, Justin Rosenberg, *The Empire of Civil Society* (London: Verso, 1994).

[5] Robert Kagan, 'Power and Weakness' *Policy Review* 113 (2002). This classification is widely reproduced not just in academic literature; see William Pfaff, 'Kant and Hobbes. Look Who's Part of the Harsh Disorder' *International Herald Tribune* (1 August 2002).

and understand the contemporary world, implicitly or explicitly, recognizes the necessarily historical location of our own motivations for scholarly enquiry. And yet, it also relies on the assumption of historical and intellectual continuity. These approaches to classical texts posit a significant historical continuity in the development of individual theoretical approaches to International Relations, in the development of international politics as well as in the structure of the theoretical debates and political struggles between them.

Hence, we are confronted with a puzzling tension between widespread claims of more or less radical historical change and widespread uses of classical authors based on the assumption of historical continuity. And it is not the case that only those theories that deny radical historical change in the nature of international politics – most prominently Realist approaches[6] – rely on the continuing relevance of classical authors; in most cases, the contradiction is located within rather than between theoretical approaches. Postmodernists are inspired by Nietzsche and even Clausewitz as are Globalization theorists by Kant. In theory, this contradiction is easily resolved by the recognition that both historical continuity and change mark European intellectual and political development. And, indeed, contemporary theorists generally accept the existence of both to varying degrees.[7]

Such a theoretical recognition of a mixture of continuity and change, however, does not answer the question of which aspects in any given classical text can be considered continuous with the contemporary world and its problems and which fall into the category of change. In the following pages I will first argue that a fruitful use of classical texts for International Relations theory and practice today requires the specification of elements of both historical continuity and change. And I will show that much of the contemporary use of classical authors is characterized by presentism; that is, it does not live up to this requirement with the result that contemporary assumptions are read back into

---

[6] See, for example, Kenneth N. Waltz, *Man, the State, and War* (New York: Columbia University Press, 1959), pp. 235f; and R. B. J. Walker, *Inside/Outside: International Relations as Political Theory* (Cambridge: Cambridge University Press, 1993), p. 7.

[7] Ian Clark 'Traditions of Thought and Classical Theories of International Relations' in Ian Clark and Iver B. Neumann (eds.), *Classical Theories of International Relations* (Basingstoke: Macmillan, 1996), p. 1; Chris Brown, Terry Nardin and Nicholas Rengger (eds.), *International Relations in Political Thought: Texts From the Ancient Greeks to the First World War* (Cambridge: Cambridge University Press, 2002), p. 5.

classical authors instead of being opened up for reflection through the use of classical authors.

In the course of this discussion I will identify three areas – the intellectual context, the political context and lineages of reception – in which such historical specificity can be established. These three contextual dimensions of inquiry provide the structure of this book which I will set out in the final section of this introduction. The individual chapters in the main part of this volume all reconstruct the intellectual and/or political context of classical texts or the trajectory by which these texts have been included – or excluded – from International Relations theory and practice. They demonstrate in a variety of cases that the reconstruction of these contexts unlocks the rich potential of classical authors for illuminating and developing further contemporary international thought and practice.

Continuity and discontinuity

A lack of continuity in actors, issues and concepts between the reflections of classical authors and contemporary international thought and practice would render the former insignificant for the study of international relations today. And, obviously, there exists some continuity between European classical authors and contemporary international theory and practice: classical authors reflected on social and political developments which provide the historical bases of the contemporary European – and through European expansion also to some extent non-European – world; moreover, classical theories have shaped the conceptual framework for our reflections on this world over time. Such continuity or 'points of contact between one period and another' undoubtedly needs to be established for any fruitful use of classical authors in International Relations.[8] It may exist, for instance, in certain social and political phenomena which the contemporary world shares with classical times. If Hobbes discussed the problem of civil war – and 'his' civil wars have something concrete in common with contemporary civil wars – his writings can contribute to an analysis of contemporary civil wars. And yet, it may also be the case that the necessary 'point of contact' between Hobbes' and contemporary civil wars consists mainly in the use of the same term for historically very different social and political phenomena. In this case, Hobbes' discussion of civil wars raises questions about the nature and

[8] Brown et al. (eds.), *International Relations*, p. 5.

extent of historical change – rather than to provide possible solutions for contemporary problems.

This example demonstrates two things. Firstly, both historical continuity and historical discontinuity may provide the basis for insights into contemporary international affairs. Yet, they do so in different ways. The greater the similarities between historical cases, the more we can build on classical analyses – or their shortcomings. Moreover, if it turns out that a classical analysis is satisfactorily applicable to contemporary cases, the solution provided by classical analysts can also be discussed as a possible solution for today. And even if the analysis is convincing but the solution – with historical hindsight – found wanting, it can at least be excluded from the range of contemporary options.

In contrast, discontinuities between classical and contemporary cases do not allow us to follow in the footsteps of the classics with regard to analysis or solution. Instead, they throw into relief areas of historical contingency in social and political life. The identification of such areas of contingency are valuable for their specification of what is open to social and political change. Furthermore, they guide research into the causes and consequences of historical change and thus lead to a better understanding of contemporary phenomena. And, finally, such social and political discontinuity coupled with conceptual continuity firmly puts the question of the relationship between theory and practice – and their historical development – on the agenda.

Secondly, given that historical continuity and discontinuity provide different kinds of insight and call for different applications to contemporary cases – one based on identity, the other on difference – the elements of continuity and discontinuity in any given text have to be specified. That is, the attempt to apply Hobbes' solution to contemporary civil wars if the latter were radically different from the former could at best prove futile, at worst disastrous. Moreover, inasmuch as we must assume that every classical text contains a mixture of continuity and change in comparison with the contemporary world, the relevance of the totality of these theories must be assessed in the light of the specific form this mixture takes. That is, those elements which are similar to the contemporary world may not be the core ones for either a classical author's analysis of the problem or the basis of the proposed solutions. Alternatively, a classical theory may appear to deal with phenomena alien to the modern world, or utterly outdated concepts, and yet – beneath the level of appearance – it may turn out to be based on very similar social and political forces or theoretical meanings.

Moreover, it can be argued that the element of discontinuity is at least as important as the element of continuity. This may be so, firstly, because a mixture of both in a classical text makes it likely that the argument as a whole has to be relativized in the light of significant discontinuities. But, secondly, and more importantly, elements of discontinuity allow potentially for greater insights than elements of continuity. On the one hand, as I will show presently for the use of classical authors in Interntional Relations, 'the continuities . . . are so omnipresent that they have made it all too easy to conceive of the past as a mirror, and the value of studying it as a means of reflecting back at ourselves our own assumptions and prejudice'.[9] In this situation, paying particular attention to the discontinuities can help illuminate aspects of the contemporary world which are otherwise generally overlooked. While in this instance the importance of studying discontinuities stands and falls in relation to the dominant practice, it may also be argued to have an independent value. And this value lies in the fact that the discontinuities point the social scientist towards those aspects of social and political life which are historically contingent and therefore open to social and political change. And, hence, it is the identification of discontinuities which indicates the areas of necessary further research into the conditions of change.

Nonetheless, the assumption of some element of continuity provides the basis for engaging with classical authors in the first place. And, indeed, this assumption is prominent in much of the reception of classical texts in International Relations. Unfortunately, however, more often than not it lacks historical specification with the result that its overwhelming function is to 'mirror' back to us contemporary assumptions and prejudices. The consequences of this presentism are, at best, the irrelevance of classical texts for a better understanding of the contemporary world. At worst, however, this approach entails an unreflected misrepresentation of classical texts as well as of the political issues and intellectual debates at stake in them. And such misrepresentation, since it functions to underline contemporary assumptions, entrenches contemporary debates rather than deepens or broadens them, and it buries – albeit unconsciously – a more constructive reading of classical authors under layers of 'authoritative' interpretations. Finally, the overwhelming prominence of continuities – real or imagined – stands in contradiction to recent claims of historical change.

---

[9] Quentin Skinner, *Liberty Before Liberalism* (Cambridge: Cambridge University Press, 1998), p. 111.

6

Intellectual contexts

Historical continuity is clearly the operative assumption in inventing traditions of international thought. It is argued that Realism can trace its roots back to Thucydides, Machiavelli, Hobbes and Rousseau, Liberalism to Kant, the English School to Grotius and so on, because the discipline of International Relations addresses certain fairly 'timeless' issues – such as war and peace – which have been reflected upon by scholars over time.[10] The construction of traditions of thought on these issues, then, identifies 'certain permanent normative orientations'.[11] Stressing such continuity is seen 'as a potent safeguard against the *hubris* of the present'. It also provides 'a constant point of reference against which change can be measured' and an opening for the question why certain traditions have developed and become important.[12]

And yet, it is precisely the present intellectual and political context which provides the starting point for establishing such traditions. That is, the disciplinary definition of International Relations and its concerns – war and peace, for instance – acts as a guide for selecting certain authors and texts as relevant. It is the issue of war which unites Thucydides, Machiavelli, Hobbes and contemporary Realists over time just as it is the search for a road to peace which makes Kant attractive to Liberals. A closer look at the use of these classical authors in Realism and Liberalism, however, reveals a curious contradiction. On the one hand, the issues of war and peace provide a basis for continuity while, on the other, these authors are used to furnish contemporary theories with philosophical roots that lie outside the definition of the discipline. That is, Hobbes provides a theory of human nature and the state which underpin contemporary theories of power politics between states. Similarly, Liberals use the work of Kant to underline the domestic bases of international conflict and cooperation. In both cases, the attraction of the classics seems to lie in their holistic – or interdisciplinary – approach to social and political life which denotes a fundamental difference in the intellectual context of classical and contemporary theory.

The significance of this difference, however, is not specified and explored. The search for dimensions of social and political life which fall outside the purview of the discipline of International Relations implicitly or explicitly acknowledges that the modern division of knowledge has bequeathed to each of the resultant disciplines a common legacy: the

---

[10] Michael Doyle, *Ways of War and Peace* (New York: W. W. Norton, 1997), p. 9.
[11] Clark, 'Traditions', p. 6.   [12] Clark, 'Traditions', p. 7.

need for philosophical reflection. The much invoked but rarely practised interdisciplinarity is itself an expression of this need – the recognition of the ultimate totality of social life inaccessible to individual modern disciplines. Since, however, contemporary philosophy is as much a victim of this legacy as are the other social and political sciences and since all of them operate according to specific and at times seemingly incompatible methods, simply adding up different disciplines proves not only very difficult but, arguably, does not address the problem. This is not to say that different disciplines cannot enrich or even inspire each other. But reflection on the totality of social and political life is characterized by theorizing the nature of the relationship between its constitutive parts. However, if the reflection on the nature of these relationships is what is lacking in the contemporary social and political sciences, it can still be found in classical authors who wrote either before or during that (in)famous revolution of the sciences.

Arguably, it is this quality of classical writings – more than the assumed continuities – which makes them attractive to contemporary social and political thought and which explains why there is no modern discipline which does not provide, to a greater or lesser extent, an account of its own 'origins' in classical theory as well as some 'applications' of classical writers to its contemporary problems. Indeed, providing the necessary 'non-international' foundations for contemporary theories – the way in which 'descriptive claims about human nature, domestic politics, and world politics are related to one another'[13] – is precisely the function of Hobbes and Kant in contemporary theories of International Relations.

And yet, the philosophical and domestic reflections of Kant and Hobbes are just added onto the contemporary definition of International Relations. Hobbes provides a basis for Realist thought in human nature and Kant's republican constitutions underpin peace. The different spheres of social and political life are here constructed in a hierarchical and linear way; the discipline of International Relations is simply conceived as the study of a specific level or 'image' of social and political life, as Waltz famously put it.[14] What is lacking here is an analysis of the historically specific way in which Kant and Hobbes reflected on the interaction and mutual constitution of different spheres of social and political life. Instead, contemporary definitions of the international, the domestic and their relationship are read back into classical authors

---

[13] Doyle, *War and Peace*, p. 36.   [14] Waltz, *Man, the State, and War*.

8

thus excluding from the pantheon of relevant authors and texts those which do not readily appear to address international issues as defined by the contemporary discipline and precluding the opportunity to overcome the disciplinary distinctions shaping contemporary debates which appeared to provide the attraction of reading Kant and Hobbes in the first place. Last, but by no means least, due to the 'contemporary' construction of the relationship between different spheres of social and political life, Kant's and Hobbes' conception of peace and war are in danger of being misrepresented.

Establishing the concrete nature of the intellectual context of classical texts is, thus, important for any conscious reflection on the limits and possibilities of the definition of International Relations and its core concerns. Beyond this, however, the recovery of the intellectual context can also illuminate the internal structure of the discipline. And here again we find that the invention and use of classical traditions for the purpose of defining and structuring contemporary theoretical as well as political debates is often characterized by a lack of attention to specific historical continuities and discontinuities. To stick with the examples of Hobbes and Kant, by tracing Realism back to the former and Liberalism to the latter, contemporary theoretical debates between these approaches are themselves presented as 'timeless'. Equally, the characterization of a contemporary European approach to international politics as 'Kantian' and an equivalent American position as 'Hobbesian' stresses the permanency of normative and political orientations without regard to the fact that these categories do not appropriately grasp the intellectual debates and political contexts in which Hobbes and Kant wrote. Is it irrelevant for International Relations scholars that outside the discipline Hobbes is often included into – or even presented as a founder of – the 'liberal' tradition while Kant based his theory on the Hobbesian state of nature?[15]

Hence, if this primacy of contemporary classifications and juxtapositions is not relativized by a more thorough recovery of the intellectual context of the classical texts themselves, it entails the danger of a selective reading of the classics on the one hand and a waste of their potential on the other. In the first instance, those aspects of a particular author's work which do not fit the paradigm are in danger of being left out or marginalized. And so are authors and texts

---

[15] Andrezj Rapaczynski, *Nature and Politics: Liberalism in the Philosophy of Hobbes, Locke and Rousseau* (Ithaca: Cornell University Press, 1987); and Immanuel Kant, *Perpetual Peace* (New York: Macmillan, 1957), p. 10.

which do not appear to fit the contemporary classifications readily. Furthermore, the relationship between classical authors may be seriously misconstrued. Contemporary theorists recognize the limitations and dangers of reading these divisions back into classical authors. Such procedures are 'insensitive to the nuances of the distinctive ages and concerns', as mentioned above; they also encourage 'intellectual conservatism' and close down the agenda by providing a framework which itself is not open to reflection and revision.[16] And yet, this approach is defended with the argument that such invented traditions provide the foundations of a dialogue between alternative voices in International Relations with the 'potential for creative synthesis' rather than fixed classifications.[17]

This positive potential of inventing traditions nonetheless fails to address the requirements for a constructive role of classical authors in two ways. The shortcomings of these assumptions which Brown, Nardin and Rengger have identified in the case of the 'timelessness' of the Realist approach, also hold for the dialogue between different 'traditions'. Namely that the tenets of a particular theory 'can be illustrated by texts drawn from any period past or present' and that 'all of these texts can be treated as though they were written by our contemporaries'.[18] The dialogue made possible by reading contemporary intellectual and political distinctions back into history is, at best, a contemporary dialogue in which the classical writers might as well be left out. Their inclusion, however, suggests that we are confronted with a worst case scenario, namely a contemporary dialogue in which classical authors are simply coopted in support of the one or the other position. Apart from the fact that in this scenario, just as in the previous one, classical texts do not add anything to our understanding of today's international affairs – after all, they are just made to fit into contemporary preconceptions – this cooptation is almost certainly accompanied by serious misinterpretation and it hides the critical and constructive potential of classical texts.

The selective and instrumental reading necessary for fitting classical authors into contemporary intellectual frameworks hides the breadth and depth of their writings as well as the historical specificity of their and our debates. And the dialogue itself, in whose name this approach

---

[16] Clark, 'Traditions', p. 8.   [17] Clark and Neumann (eds.), *Classical Theories*, p. 257.
[18] Brown et al. (eds.), *International Relations*, p. 3.

of inventing traditions is defended, does not become richer and more varied through such cooptation of classical authors. Rather, it becomes more entrenched and is itself presented as timeless.[19] In contrast, paying attention to the contemporaneous intellectual debates – that is to the differences rather than the similarities – provides alternative viewpoints, conceptions and interpretations. These can be used to question contemporary theories and world views and the faultlines between them. Thus, a reconstruction of the intellectual debates to which the classics themselves contributed is necessary to break the unreflected mould of contemporary debates; it simultaneously provides a basis for an alternative reading of the classics in the light of their contemporaneous debates and the possibility of reflecting on the grounds for the definition of competing contemporary positions.

Political contexts

These shortcomings resulting from an omission to specify concrete areas of continuity and discontinuity can also be identified with regard to the political context of classical writings. The Democratic Peace thesis, for instance, empirically identifies the absence or rarity of wars between contemporary liberal states. And it is this contemporary observation which appears to be explained in Kant's discussion of republican constitutions. And yet, what this starting point overlooks is that Kant's republican constitutions were conceived as solutions to wars between absolutist states – which were fought for entirely different reasons and under entirely different conditions from wars in the contemporary world. Similarly, the fact that today's world is not characterized by formal colonial rule has led contemporary theorists to overlook the relevance of Kant's

---

[19] This does not mean that reflection on these established traditions is not critical in the sense of questioning their definition and usefulness in individual cases. Hence, Martin Wight, *International Theory. The Three Traditions* (London: Leicester University Press, 1994), p. 259, even while developing the notion of a Realist, Rationalist and Revolutionist tradition continuously reflected on the overlaps between them as well as on the difficulties of fitting classical authors into them, thus engaging in an ongoing process of redefinition and relativization. Similarly, the intelligent and thorough analyses provided by the authors in Clark and Neumann (eds.), *Classical Theories*, for instance, suggest that the classical authors with one exception – Friedrich Gentz – do not satisfactorily fit into Wight's traditions. And yet, while these investigations clearly question the definition and usefulness of Wight's traditions they do not systematically investigate alternative conceptions of the discipline or its theoretical debates in the light of these differences.

as well as Mill's discussions of colonialism and its informal roots as relevant for today.[20]

The political context of Kant's republican constitutions may be absolutism – and thus not identical with the contemporary world. Nonetheless, the conceptual continuity coupled with political discontinuity may yet provide a constructive basis for discussing the relevance of republican or liberal constitutions for peace and war in the contemporary world. The political context of republican or liberal constitutions – absolutist states or liberal capitalist states – can provide an answer to the question of which interests are represented through these institutions. Similarly, recovering the political context of Mill's writings – colonialism – can point towards striking parallels in the contemporary world even though policies of colonialism are today not consciously pursued.

In the absence of a thorough recovery of the contemporaneous political context, however, International Relations uses classical texts simply to confirm contemporary assumptions. In the process, it presents rather anachronistic interpretations of classical authors – Kant is represented as a theorist of intervention and Mill as a theorist of non-intervention despite the fact that the former takes a principled stand for non-intervention while the latter's international theory rests on the principle of intervention. Hence, the reconstruction of the concrete political context in which classical authors were writing is crucial for unlocking their potential to actually illuminate aspects of today's international relations.

Lineages

This more or less inevitable interpretation of classical authors in the light of the intellectual and political context provided by the interpreter described above, points towards a final dimension of the use of classical authors which requires explicit reflection. For if it is the case that the contemporary use of classical authors tends to be shaped – to a greater or lesser degree – by contemporary concerns and debates, then classical authors will have gone through such a process of reception many times over before they enter the discipline of International Relations. In the course of this historical trajectory of appropriation,

---

[20] See Beate Jahn, 'Kant, Mill, and Illiberal Legacies in International Affairs' *International Organization* 59 (2005), 177–207; Beate Jahn, 'Barbarian Thoughts: Imperialism in the Philosophy of John Stuart Mill' *Review of International Studies* 31 (2005), 599–618; and Chapter 8 in this volume.

classical texts will have been variously translated, and selectively published and republished, as well as interpreted and reinterpreted. In using classical authors, International Relations scholars must bear in mind this 'ballast' of intellectual and political interests collected in the texts of classical authors over time.

Many classical authors, for instance, have made their way into International Relations via Political Theory. By relying on the general interpretations of classical texts provided by Political Theorists which are then complemented by rereading select pieces deemed particularly relevant in the international context, International Relations again imports the modern disciplinary division of knowledge. For Political Theory has neglected the international dimension of classical thought as much as International Relations has neglected its domestic dimension – and neither discipline provides a satisfactory account of the nature of their respective interrelations.[21]

Moreover, paying attention to the particular trajectory by which classical texts have variously entered the discipline may well uncover intellectual and political concerns as well as interpretations on the side of the 'importers'. Reflection on these motivations and interpretations is necessary on the one hand in order to relativize any single or hegemonic interpretation and to allow for alternatives. On the other hand, these interpretations may have shaped core concepts in the discipline; and in this case a historical recovery of their roots is one way of opening up these concepts for critical reflection.

Another 'role for the intellectual historian is that of acting as a kind of archaeologist, bringing buried intellectual treasure back to the surface'.[22] But this, the recovery of those traditions or authors 'which have not found a voice', is arguably impossible on the basis of a contemporary starting point which does not pay attention to the specific political and intellectual continuities, discontinuities and lineages. For without this historical relativization the contemporary assumptions guide the inclusion and exclusion of authors and texts, issues and concepts, policies and theories on the basis of the established voices.

In sum, traditional interpretations and appropriations of classical authors in the discipline of International Relations have, despite an abstract recognition of the importance of both continuity and change, and despite repeated claims to recent historical change and rupture, prioritized historical continuity. And they have done so not by specifying

---

[21] Brown et al. (eds.), *International Relations*, p. 7.   [22] Skinner, *Liberty*, p. 112.

concrete elements of continuity – which would inevitably also entail an identification of significant discontinuities. Instead, more often than not, these interpretations stop short at the identification of certain continuous political and intellectual issues and debates. And this form of inventing traditions does not actually function as 'a potent safeguard against the *hubris* of the present'. Stressing abstract historical continuities may well be a safeguard against claims for a radically unique present, but it may constitute simultaneously an arguably more serious *hubris* of the present – namely one in which the present is presented as timeless and thus naturalized and absolute.

Likewise, presenting contemporary theoretical or political positions as a dialogue reaching back into the past without reference to the differences does not create a space for creative synthesis. Rather, it entrenches the contemporary positions and buries those dimensions of classical and contemporary thought which either cut across or do not fit the given paradigm. Furthermore, the assumption of political and intellectual continuity without explicit and systematic reference to the discontinuities only provides 'a constant point of reference against which change can be measured'[23] *within* the framework of the contemporary paradigm defining these continuities. This applies to the definition of the discipline itself in terms of its 'timeless' objects of enquiry as much as to the individual approaches within the discipline. That is, insofar as intellectual or political discontinuities between a classical text and the modern world are noted, they are presented as developments or variations within the given framework rather than taken to question the application of the framework to the classical text and, by extension, potentially also the contemporary framework itself.

This widespread lack of reflection on historically specific – rather than general or continuous – political and intellectual interests shaping the production of social and political theory is not surprisingly also extended to the trajectories by which classical authors have entered the discipline of International Relations. That is, the historically specific interests and perceptions of the translators and interpreters of classical texts on their way into the discipline remain likewise unspecified – thus depriving International Relations of the possibility of investigating the various historical transformations of these texts as well as the meanings and contradictions that may have become embedded in them over time.

[23] Clark, 'Traditions', p. 7.

The contributors to this book, thus, consciously set out to recover the intellectual and political context of classical texts and their lineages. But they do so not in the spirit of presenting a 'true' or 'correct' interpretation of classical texts in their own right. Rather, they do so precisely because they recognize that contemporary concerns guide our interest in classical authors. Yet, these contemporary concerns can only be fruitfully illuminated and analyzed in the light of the concrete specification of continuities and change between classical and contemporary concepts, issues and debates. In other words, the widespread claims to radical historical change mentioned at the outset of this discussion, as well as their equally passionately pursued refutation, can only be assessed if the nature and extent of this change can be specified. And in order to achieve this aim, the intellectual and political context of classical texts and their lineages has to be rendered concrete, too.

This approach overlaps with, and distinguishes itself from, two other cognate literatures. Engagement with classical authors in International Relations is sometimes included in the subfield of International Political Theory. This rather disparate field of study, according to Nicholas Rengger, is in danger of gradually becoming more and more 'rationalist' or, in Robert Cox's famous words, 'problem-solving'.[24] That is, it identifies certain pressing problems of the day and mobilizes classical authors, among others, for the purpose of providing solutions. Such an approach, of course, fits the charge of presentism set out above and it is not shared by the authors of this book who insist on contextualization as an antidote to such anachronisms.

And this brings me to the second literature mentioned above. For while 'not all contextualists are Skinnerian',[25] contextualism is famously

---

[24] Robert Cox, 'Social Forces, States, and World Orders: Beyond International Relations Theory' in Robert W. Cox and Timothy J. Sinclair (eds.), *Approaches to World Order* (Cambridge: Cambridge University Press, 1996), p. 88. In his review article, Nicholas Rengger identifies explicitly normative, poststructuralist and intellectual history approaches as part of the field whose common denominator appears to be an opposition to IR as a 'positivist' social science. See 'Political Theory and International Relations: Promised Land or Exit from Eden?' *International Affairs* 76 (2000), 755–770. While this is important common ground which the authors of this book share, there are nevertheless tremendous differences between and even within normative, poststructuralist and intellectual history approaches. Moreover, not all International Political Theory need necessarily engage – or engage directly – with classical authors.

[25] Duncan Bell, 'Political Theory and the Functions of Intellectual History: a Response to Emmanuel Navon' *Review of International Studies* 29 (2003), 153.

associated with the work of Quentin Skinner.[26] There, classical texts are neither treated as 'timeless contributions to a universal philosophical debate, nor can their meanings simply be read off as determined by the economic, political, and social context in which they were written'.[27] Central to Skinner's approach is the reconstruction of authorial intention through the linguistic and intellectual context which includes the contemporaneous social and political background. Its aim is to show 'how the concepts we still invoke were initially defined, what purposes they were intended to serve, what view of public power they were used to underpin';[28] and hence, ultimately, to open up present political discourse to its inherited meanings as well as to alternatives.

There is no space here for a general discussion of the advantages and disadvantages of Skinnerian contextualism for International Relations.[29] However, this book clearly shares with the Skinnerian approach the aim of opening up contemporary political/international discourse through a contextualization of classical works. And yet, it neither propagates nor systematically adheres to the Skinnerian method. The most immediate reason for this is that the authors of this book take their cue from problems they identify with traditional interpretations and uses of classical authors in International Relations. And in doing so they require a more flexible method. For unlike Political Theorists, scholars of International Relations do not necessarily claim to present an authoritative interpretation of classical authors *as such*. Inasmuch as authorial intention can be established, this may certainly be used to debunk traditional interpretations in International Relations.[30] Quite frequently, however, the authors of this book are concerned not with establishing the authorial intention of a classical author but rather with demonstrating that the changed political and social environment circumscribes the applicability of classical 'analyses' or 'solutions' to contemporary problems,[31] or with revealing alternative but neglected influences of classical authors.[32] Hence, the motivation for our investigations are much more 'presentist'

[26] For an overview see James Tully (ed.), *Meaning and Context – Quentin Skinner and his Critics* (Cambridge: Polity Press, 1988); and David Boucher, *Texts in Context – Revisionist Methods for Studying the History of Ideas* (Lancaster: Martin Nijhoff, 1985).
[27] Gerard Holden, 'Who Contextualizes the Contextualizers? Disciplinary History and the Discourse about IR Discourse' *Review of International Studies* 28 (2002), 261.
[28] Skinner, *Liberty*, p. 110.
[29] See Holden, 'Who Contextualizes the Contextualizers', and Bell, 'Political Theory' for a discussion of the use of Skinner in International Relations.
[30] Aiko, Chapter 5 in this volume, applies Skinner's method for this purpose.
[31] See Jahn, Chapter 8 for example.
[32] Reid's Chapter 12 in this volume is a case in point.

than Skinner's – yet not in the manner of the problem-solving tendencies in International Political Theory.

Structure

In accordance with the aim of reconstructing the intellectual and political context of classical theories as well as of their trajectories over time, this book is divided into three parts focusing respectively on the recovery of the intellectual context, the political context and the lineage of classical theories. Before providing a more detailed description of the structure of this book and its individual contributions, it is important to emphasize that these divisions are by no means exclusionary. Since political and intellectual contexts are mutually constitutive in the sense that 'what it is possible to do in politics is generally limited by what it is possible to legitimise' and this, in turn, 'depends on what courses of action you can plausibly range under existing normative principles',[33] the authors who concentrate on the recovery of the intellectual context of classical texts necessarily also touch upon the political context, and vice versa. Similarly, investigating the lineages by which classical texts have entered the discipline of International Relations – or have been excluded from it – entails the recovery of the political and intellectual context of these trajectories. Hence, the structure of this book simply points towards the specific historical dimension each chapter focuses on without excluding any of the others.

Thus, the contributions in the first part of this volume focus on the recovery of the intellectual context missing from contemporary uses of Thucydides, Kant, Saint-Pierre and Rousseau. In Chapter 2, S. Sara Monoson and Michael Loriaux provide a close reading of Thucydides which pays particular attention to the central role of antithetical reasoning in *The History of the Peloponnesian War* as a whole as well as in the treatment of Pericles in particular. Thucydides praises the statesman Pericles even while he continuously demonstrates the disastrous effects of his policies. In this interpretation, Thucydides insists that morality and social norms are a necessary basis for prudent policies or, to put it the other way around, that Pericles' *Realpolitik* proves to be an important source of the Athenian disaster. By integrating Thucydides' intellectual and rhetorical strategy with the historical background, Monoson and Loriaux undermine two of the major Realist claims about Thucydides.

---

[33] Skinner, *Liberty*, p. 105.

Firstly, the separation between domestic and international politics cannot be traced back to Thucydides and the Greeks and, secondly, morality and prudent politics instead of being incompatible actually depend on each other. And it may be argued that the recovery of a necessary connection between domestic and international politics as well as between prudence and morality is highly topical – not least for recent debates about American foreign and domestic policies.

Kant is most prominently used today in the explanation of the Democratic Peace and in the justification of liberal foreign policies. But, as John MacMillan argues in Chapter 3, the justification of contemporary policies of intervention violates two core principles of Kant's work. Firstly, in distinguishing between the rights of liberal and non-liberal states in the international system, it prioritizes the domestic constitution and thus overlooks the mutually constitutive nature of the domestic, international and transnational sources of war in Kant's thought. Secondly, the justification of differential rights and obligations for liberal and non-liberal states in the contemporary international system violates Kant's categorical imperative – the universal nature of rights. MacMillan argues that a more inclusive reading of Kant, in particular attention to the preliminary articles of *Perpetual Peace*, contradicts the Democratic Peace interpretation and it recovers the critical potential of Kant for judging contemporary international politics.

The same concern underlies Antonio Franceschet's investigation of the use of Kant in contemporary international law in Chapter 4. Here, it is argued that the attempt to reform international law and to accord unequal rights of sovereignty and non-intervention to liberal and non-liberal states can only be supported with reference to Kant on the basis of a highly selective reading. In contrast, Franceschet provides a more inclusive reading which shows that powerful liberal states arrogating to themselves the right to coerce others into a liberal framework falls squarely into the category of 'private judgment'. In Kantian terms, however, private judgment is a characteristic of the state of nature rather than a route to increased legalization. It is not 'being a liberal state that guarantees good political judgment' but rather 'being in a liberal, law-governed state' which best guarantees legalism. While on the one hand undermining these recent interpretations of Kant in the field of international law, Franceschet on the other recovers Kant's constructive potential for assessing policies which aim at increased legalization.

Yuichi Aiko, in Chapter 5, demonstrates the importance of the contemporaneous intellectual debates for the interpretation of Rousseau.

The characterization of Rousseau as a Realist is generally based on his critique of Saint-Pierre's peace project which, in turn, is seen as a typical example of liberal or utopian thought on international affairs. Aiko shows, however, that the intellectual debate to which Saint-Pierre and Rousseau contributed was concerned with natural law. And in this debate, both Saint-Pierre and Rousseau held, against the dominant position, that man's moral constitution resulted from the political order rather than being predetermined by nature. The reconstruction of this intellectual context allows Aiko to show that, *contra* the conventional reading, Rousseau was greatly inspired by Saint-Pierre and complemented the latter's peace project by working out the necessary domestic constitution for it in the *Social Contract*. In this reading, Rousseau contributes to an understanding of sovereignty as justice rather than independence and, thus, to a normative dimension of the core concept of sovereignty which is inaccessible to the discipline as long as it interprets Rousseau within the framework of the Realist/Liberal debate.

All four chapters respectively recover the rhetorical and theoretical context and the contemporaneous intellectual debates of Thucydides, Kant and Rousseau. The reconstruction of this intellectual context demonstrates in each case that contemporary distinctions between domestic and international politics do not apply to the classical texts. Consequently, the integration of these spheres of social and political life in the classical texts leads in all four cases to a reintegration of morality and power. Thucydides' prudent international policies are doomed without a firm basis in social norms and Rousseau's concept of sovereignty is based on justice rather than independence while Kant's pursuit of perpetual peace can only be the result of the employment of universally just and legal means.

These interpretations undermine widely accepted uses of Thucydides', Kant's and Rousseau's theories in International Relations as well as challenging established traditions of thought. If Thucydides and Rousseau integrate the domestic and the international as well as being crucially concerned with the mutually constitutive nature of power and morality, the question arises on what grounds they may be incorporated into the contemporary Realist school of thought. And if a central element of Kant's pursuit of peace consists in the recognition of state sovereignty and international law, the grounds on which he is juxtaposed to Thucydides and Rousseau, or Realism more generally, have to be reassessed. Most importantly, all four chapters contribute constructively to contemporary political and theoretical issues. Aiko's interpretation of Rousseau opens up the defining concept of the discipline of International Relations – sovereignty – to rethinking, while it is almost impossible not to associate the Thucydides interpretation of Monoson and Loriaux with contemporary attempts to separate power and morality in general and in American foreign policy in particular. MacMillan and Franceschet, on the basis of their Kant interpretation, explicitly and critically challenge contemporary theory and practice of liberal foreign policies while simultaneously indicating more promising avenues for such policies.

The chapters in the second part focus on the investigation of the political context of classical texts. David Blaney and Naeem Inayatullah argue in Chapter 6 that the encounter with, and ethnographic work on, the Amerindians plays a crucial role in Adam Smith's theory of Political Economy. They provide the necessary basis for Smith's theory of human progress and they are used to 'insulate a commercial society from moral critique'. And yet, a closer look at the political and ethnological context clearly shows that this use of the Amerindians also introduces a number of contradictions into Smith's theory – and by extension into the views of the Scottish Enlightenment as well as contemporary International Political Economy itself. Blaney and Inayatullah thus disrupt the substantive narrative of International Political Economy and the definition of the discipline by introducing an ethnological context. They also demonstrate that such a contextual reading of Smith recovers an ethical dimension which allows for a critical judgment of contemporary capitalism.

This theme is also taken up by David Boucher in Chapter 7. He argues that John Locke's influential theory of property in the *Second Treatise of Government* is rooted in the attempt to justify colonialism. Despite this international political background, Locke is generally seen as a domestic political theorist and hence widely ignored in International Relations. Boucher shows that with Locke himself, International Relations excludes the centrality of theories of property for the constitution of the modern international order. The chapter, thus, challenges the disciplinary divide between Political Theory and International Relations as well as providing the basis for a constructive investigation into the role of property in the constitution of contemporary international relations.

Beate Jahn reconstructs, in Chapter 8, the political context of Kant's *Perpetual Peace* and argues – in line with MacMillan and

Franceschet – that Kant cannot be used in support of the Democratic Peace thesis or contemporary liberal foreign policies. Kant's republican constitutions were conceived as a solution to wars pursued by absolutist rather than liberal capitalist states. Liberal capitalist states and their foreign policies, however, have been theorized by John Stuart Mill, whose writings are widely neglected in contemporary International Relations or so selectively appropriated that his justification of imperialism – which perfectly mirrors contemporary liberal thought – is not discussed at all. Attention to the political context of Kant's and Mill's work demonstrates that both have been coopted in support of contemporary assumptions and this, in turn, implies the lack of a discussion of the shortcomings of liberalism domestically and internationally as well as the continuing importance of imperialism in contemporary international affairs.

The contributions to this part recover the political context of classical texts for the purpose of illuminating generally neglected dimensions of contemporary international relations. Contemporary assumptions and disciplinary divides have led to the marginalization of Smith, Locke and Mill in the pantheon of classical authors with which the discipline engages. The common themes of these authors, interestingly, all turn out to revolve around issues of property and political and economic inequality in the international system – in other words, around colonialism and imperialism. The relationship between European states and Amerindians or non-Europeans more generally played a constitutive role in the development of the modern international system as well as international theory. It lies at the roots of developmentalist philosophies of history represented in Locke's conception of property as well as in the Scottish Enlightenment and John Stuart Mill. Despite variations on this theme over time, the historical continuity of those conceptions as well as of their exclusion from explicit reflection constitutes a serious challenge to the discipline of International Relations. For despite the claim to investigate the link between politics and economy present in the name, traditional International Political Economy (IPE) approaches not only fail to engage in depth with classics such as Locke, Smith and Mill – whose work constitutes IPE in the first place – they also fail to engage with the important role of culture, power, politics and ethics in the constitution of an 'economic' international order. By reconstructing the political context in which these theories have first been developed, all three chapters open up the possibility of a constructive engagement with contemporary political and economic inequality.

In the third part of this volume, the authors investigate hegemonic as well as marginalized lineages of classical theory in International Relations. In Chapter 9, Robert Shilliam reconstructs Kant's and Hegel's reaction to the French Revolution and argues that both developed their understanding of 'the modern political subject' from a position of comparative 'backwardness'. And both subsumed this actual multilinear – or international – starting point under a unilinear (universalizing) philosophy of history in order to retain the possibility of Germany catching up with its more advanced neighbour. In this reading, Hegel is not the proponent of an ethical pluralism which can be juxtaposed to Kantian universalism – an arrangement which provides the classical foundations of the cosmopolitan/communitarian debate. Moreover, this reinterpretation also challenges poststructural and postcolonial positions. For it shows, firstly, that the European 'self' is an internally fractured rather than an undivided entity opposed to a non-European 'other'; and, secondly, that both Kant and Hegel engage in 'othering' – but from a 'backward' rather than a hegemonic position. On the basis of this argument, International Relations is not confronted with the problem of choosing between a universalist and a particularist ethical position, but rather with the challenge of developing an ethical position towards 'difference' in the first place.

Edward Keene, in Chapter 10, reconstructs the way in which Grotius has turned from a jurisprudential theorist to a political philosopher of international society in contemporary International Relations. The roots of the latter interpretation, argues Keene, lie in the European reactions to the French Revolution. In their search for a 'counter-revolutionary' international law, legal textbooks were rewritten and based on prerevolutionary literature which insisted on sovereignty as the internal independence of states. In this context, Grotius was read as having anticipated the Westphalian concept of sovereignty and legal equality of states which gradually developed into the modern states-system. Contemporary reliance on this 'narrative' leads to a twofold impoverishment of International Relations. On the one hand, it marginalizes a whole body of jurisprudential thought which could provide a much more varied and rich picture of the – not always so natural, gradual and inevitable – development of the modern states-system. The focus on the Westphalian system, on the other hand, displaces alternative dimensions of political thought and practice like republicanism and imperialism – leaving the contemporary discipline firmly in the grasp of the ideological origins of the conventional understanding of Grotius.

Michael Williams investigates a Hobbes revival in Weimar Germany by authors such as Carl Schmitt and Leo Strauss who profoundly influenced Hans Morgenthau, in Chapter 11. In accordance with these authors, Williams develops an interpretation of Hobbes which stands in contradiction to the dominant Realist readings of this author either as a rational choice theorist or as a theorist of international society. The 'evil' nature of human beings does not provide the starting point for Hobbes' conception of politics but rather its solution. The exploration of this neglected lineage does not only turn up an alternative interpretation of Hobbes; it also allows for a better understanding of contemporary neoconservatism which owes a lot in particular to Leo Strauss.

Finally, in Chapter 12, Julian Reid introduces a neglected lineage of the interpretation of Clausewitz. Clausewitz has been central to International Relations as a strategic thinker. Reid shows, however, that Clausewitz plays an equally important role in the development of modern counter-strategic thought. Foucault as well as Deleuze and Guattari have taken Clausewitz's concept of war and tied it to the development of modern power not restricted to the state. And as such, war becomes a 'condition of possibility for the development of new forms of political subjectivity' which undermines the traditional disciplinary control of the state. This account, apart from opening up the possibility of an alternative reading of Clausewitz and its potential application to the analysis of contemporary non-state actors and political movements, also disrupts the traditional disciplinary definition by delinking power and war from the state; in other words, by seriously questioning the inside/outside distinction so prominent in International Relations.

By investigating the historical and political context of the lineages of classical thought, the chapters in this part demonstrate the limitations and historical burdens International Relations has unconsciously taken on. Among these are the universalizing ethical responses of Kant and Hegel to the French Revolution and the counter-revolutionary conception of sovereignty produced by nineteenth-century interpretations of Grotius. In both cases, the inclusion of these particular conceptions simultaneously implies the exclusion of alternatives – either in the form of an ethical position towards difference or in the form of more varied legal, historical and political discourses reflecting and shaping European development. Similar results are also achieved by focusing on lineages outside the discipline of International Relations. The Hobbes interpretation in Weimar Germany does not only provide an alternative understanding of Hobbes but also the basis for an analysis of contemporary neoconservatism while Clausewitz's role in counter-strategic thought highlights the limitations of his interpretation in disciplinary strategic terms as well as his potential for a constructive grasp of non-state actors in International Relations. Hence, the analysis of lineages of classical thought opens up the possibility of alternative interpretations of Grotius, Hobbes, Kant, Hegel and Clausewitz and of the inclusion of hitherto neglected authors. More importantly, however, it squarely puts such core concepts as sovereignty, difference and war back on the agenda and points towards the possibility of their radical reinterpretation. And such reinterpretation clearly entails the potential to transform the nature and definition of the discipline itself.

This collection of interpretations of classical authors based on the analysis of their intellectual and political context as well as on the trajectories of their appropriation in the discipline aims to demonstrate the rich potential of classical texts for the study of international relations. And this potential lies in three different but interrelated areas. Firstly, the analyses presented here all contribute to a broader conception of the discipline itself based on the recovery of the predisciplinary intellectual context of classical thought. They show that – and how – political, economic, ethnological, philosophical, sociological, normative and legal dimensions are constitutive of international thought and practice even in the present-day world. Secondly, the chapters unanimously challenge traditional accounts of timeless debates and schools of thought and recover a contextual understanding of classical authors which truly provides the basis for 'potential creative synthesis'. Finally, the contextual interpretations throw a new and different light on such core concepts and issues of contemporary international thought and practice as sovereignty, morality, law, property, imperialism and agency, and thus provide the basis for further constructive research into these areas.

Part I
Intellectual contexts

2 Pericles, realism and the normative conditions of deliberate action

S. Sara Monoson and Michael Loriaux

Thucydides' *History of the Peloponnesian War* has lost none of its power to fascinate. We are excited by the keen analysis, the apparent accessibility of the actors to rational interpretation, the ring of familiarity in the events the historian recounts. Above all, we are excited by Thucydides' claims to have written a work that will become 'a possession for all time', a work that we will 'judge useful' (I.22.4).[1] But useful how? As good counsel, a theory, an example to avoid (if so, how)? Having treated Thucydides as a forerunner of modern realism,[2] International Relations scholars today better appreciate the complexity of his text and often challenge the Realist reading.[3] Political Theorists have also turned to the text in growing numbers, interrogating its pessimism,[4] its pervasive humanity,[5] its subtle critique of

[1] Unless otherwise noted, all translations are from the revised Crawley edition: Robert B. Strassler, *The Landmark Thucydides, A Newly Revised Edition of the Crawley Translation with Maps, Annotations, Appendices and Encyclopedic Index* (New York: Free Press, 1996). An earlier version of this chapter, 'The Illusion of Power and the Disruption of Moral Norms: Thucydides' Critique of Periclean Policy', appeared in the *American Political Science Review* (June 1998). Extensive revisions explain the change in title.

[2] James E. Dougherty and Robert L. Pfaltzgraff, Jr., *Contending Theories of International Relations* (New York: Harper and Row, 3rd edn, 1990).

[3] Laurie M. Johnson Bagby, 'The Use and Abuse of Thucydides in International Relations' *International Organization* 48 (Winter, 1994), 131–153; Michael Doyle, 'Thucydides: A Realist?' in Richard Ned Lebow and Barry Strauss (eds.), *Hegemonic Rivalry: From Thucydides to the Nuclear Age* (Boulder CO: Westview, 1991). Steven Forde, 'International Realism and the Science of Politics: Thucydides, Machiavelli, and Neorealism' *International Studies Quarterly* 39 (1995), 141–161; Daniel Garst, 'Thucydides and Neorealism' *International Studies Quarterly* 33 (1989), 3–27; Richard Ned Lebow, 'Thucydides, Power Transition Theory, and the Causes of War' in *Hegemonic Rivalry*.

[4] Peter R. Pouncey, *The Necessities of War: A Study of Thucydides' Pessimism* (New York: Columbia University Press, 1980).

[5] Clifford Orwin, *The Humanity of Thucydides* (Princeton NJ: Princeton University Press, 1994).

democracy,[6] its account of the fragility of political unity[7] or its analysis of the tension between love of glory and commitment to the common good.[8]

The variety of reactions and interpretations elicited by the text confirms the observation of a leading classicist that Thucydides forever proves resistant to paraphrase and summation.[9] That resistance owes much to Thucydides' pervasive use of antithesis as a tool of analysis. Antithesis in the form of paired speeches (e.g. Cleon and Diodotus) and dramatic juxtapositions (e.g. the Periclean funeral oration and the plague narrative) is well known. But the presence of antithesis in the treatment of Pericles, a part of the text usually thought to exhibit a more straightforward teaching, has commanded less attention. Although Thucydides presents Pericles as singularly praiseworthy (e.g. II.65), we believe that the progress of his narrative, perhaps unbeknownst to the author, interrogates that glowing assessment. The fuller, more subtle treatment of Pericles as it emerges from the text as a whole, suggests tension between two antithetical yet complementary attitudes regarding the possibility of conducting ourselves wisely. The first is a relentless scepticism about humanity's capacity to assure its welfare by relying on a kind of strategic brilliance that is exercised in either ignorance or defiance of moral norms. The second is a conviction that moral norms must be buttressed by the effective application of coercive power. Thucydides' driving attention to both these views goes to the heart of much contemporary theorizing in International Relations regarding the appropriateness of moral or strategic action.

Thucydides' use of antithesis

The view of the *History* as an 'objective' account of the war and its author as a 'scientific' historian has been dead in the literature for some

[6] Cynthia Farrar, '"Gyges" Ring: Reflections on the Boundaries of Democratic Citizenship'. Paper delivered at the Colloque International: Démocratie Athénienne et Culture, sponsored by UNESCO and the Academy of Athens, 1993; Josiah Ober, 'Thucydides' Criticism of Democratic Knowledge' in Ralph Rosen and Joseph Farrell (eds.), *Nomodeiktes: Greek Studies in Honor of Martin Ostwald* (Ann Arbor: University of Michigan Press, 1993); Arlene Saxonhouse, *Athenian Democracy: Modern Mythmakers and Ancient Theorists* (Notre Dame IN: University of Notre Dame Press, 1996).

[7] J. Peter Euben, *The Tragedy of Political Theory: The Road Not Taken* (Princeton NJ: Princeton University Press, 1990).

[8] Michael Palmer, *Love of Glory and the Common Good: Aspects of the Political Thought of Thucydides* (Lanham MD: Rowman & Littlefield, 1992).

[9] W. Robert Connor, *Thucydides* (Princeton NJ: Princeton University Press, 1984), p. 231.

time. Scholars today focus more on the artistry of the work and the intensity of the experiences it elicits, and express little confidence that the author's 'teaching' can be found in some specific episode, such as the Melian conference, or in some isolated albeit strongly worded first-person commentary, such as the praise of Periclean leadership at II.65.[10] Scholars prefer to examine the text as a whole and specifically how the interrelations of different aspects of the text (speeches, narrative, various episodes, language patterns and literary devices) work to arouse the emotions and intellect of the reader.

As stated above, much of the power of Thucydides' style derives from his use of antithesis, that is, the contraposition of claim and counterclaim in close and rhetorically effective order. This 'most instinctive, necessary clothing of [Thucydides'] thought' extends from the paired speeches to the very structure of the work – the juxtaposition of phrase to phrase, chapter to chapter, book to book of starkly contrasting images, such that expectations nurtured at one point are dashed at another.[11] Thucydides dresses the images up rhetorically as matters of fact. But in the ensuing narrative he reveals them to be social and intellectual constructs, which the protagonists of the drama, through ambition, fear and conceit, proceed to dash or erode.

Awareness of the importance of antithesis helps us not only appreciate his style but understand his political philosophy. Antithesis, when wielded with the skill and relentlessness of Thucydides, nourishes scepticism, doubt regarding anything and everything that one may have previously accepted as knowledge, wisdom or truth.[12] In Thucydides' era, Athenian cultural life was marked by antidogmatic, sceptical and relentlessly critical practices. The corrosive power of such scepticism may be what moved some Athenians, as represented by Plato's Thrasymachus and Callicles, to doubt the possibility of moral conduct and succumb to a kind of 'realism', that is, to the idea that the prevailing notion of the Good must simply embody the interests of powerful people. This is

[10] See, e.g. Raymond Aron, 'Thucydides and the Historical Narrative' in Miriam Bernheim Conant (ed.), *Politics in History: Selected Essays of Raymond Aron* (New York: Free Press, 1978); W. Robert Connor, 'A Post Modernist Thucydides?' *The Classical Journal* 72 (1977), 289–298; Virginia Hunter, *Thucydides: The Artful Reporter* (Toronto: Hackert, 1973); Orwin, *The Humanity of Thucydides*.

[11] John H. Finley, *Thucydides* (Cambridge MA: Harvard University Press, 1942), p. 46; see also W. Robert Connor, 'Polarization in Thucydides' in *Hegemonic Rivalry*, p. 67.

[12] On his antithetical style, see Jacqueline de Romilly, *Les grands sophistes dans l'Athenes de Pericles* (Paris: Fallois, 1988), pp. 86–87, 97–99; Finley, *Thucydides*, p. 44; Simon Hornblower, *Thucydides* (Baltimore: Johns Hopkins University Press, 1987), pp. 45–52, 60–62; and Connor, *Thucydides*, pp. 27–28.

the argument that Thucydides lends to the Athenian generals at Melos, which Realists receive as a kind of 'Realist manifesto'.

Antithesis in Thucydides' treatment of Pericles

We reopen the file on Pericles because he comes across as the only actor of the *History* who is 'on top of things'. Thucydides' attitude toward Pericles seems to be one of 'reverent admiration'.[13] He is, after all, the only speaker of the *History* whose words are never disputed by those of an adversary. The text thus invites us to believe that good politics must be Periclean politics. Alert to Thucydides' use of the antithesis, however, we suspect that on closer reading the text may be inviting us to search for good politics in the critical examination of Pericles.

Thucydides' catalogue of Pericles' virtues is well known. Suffice it to recall that, according to Thucydides, 'for as long as [Pericles] was at the head of the state during the peace, he pursued a moderate and conservative policy; and in his time its greatness was at its height' (II.65.5). Among the virtues displayed by Pericles are his skills as a military leader (I.111.5, 114.5, 116.3, 117.2; II.31.12), his appreciation of and excellence in reasoned deliberation regarding political and strategic issues (II.40.2–3, 62.5), his integrity (II.13.1, 65.8), his grasp of human psychology (II.59.3ff) and his generally accurate estimate of Athenian military strengths and weaknesses (II.65.5). Moreover, he is a master of the art of persuasion. He draws on his oratorical skills to stoke Athenian patriotism and self-confidence (II.40.1–41.5) and to win approval of his ideas even as his popularity flags (II.59.2ff). In sum, his grasp of human psychology, his power to persuade and his military skill all contribute to his ascendance among the Athenians and his ability 'to lead them instead of being led by them' (II.65.8).

Nevertheless, we detect in the *History* as a whole a subtle interrogation of this glowing appraisal. While opposing the people on difficult occasions, Pericles unwaveringly supports their desire for empire; while extolling Athenian virtues, he undermines the norms of social cohesion; while advocating a prudent course of action, he engages Athens in an adventure that produces momentous turns of fortune.

Thucydides unquestionably attributes to Pericles a unique ability to persuade citizens to adopt a strategy that involves hardship and self-discipline, and to speak frankly to the Assembly to the point of

---

[13] F. M. Cornford, *Thucydides Mythistoricus* (London: Edward Arnold, 1907), p. 50.

contradicting the wishes (or whims) of the multitude. During the period of Pericles' prominence, 'what was nominally a democracy [became] in his hands government by the first citizen' (II.65.9). Each of Pericles' three speeches turns public opinion in a particular direction. And indeed Thucydides explicitly distinguishes Pericles from all subsequent leaders precisely on this point. But although Pericles is quite unlike the crop of leaders that succeed him, he does not differ from his successors as regards his attachment to empire. During his leadership, the Athenians boldly transfer the treasury of the Delian League from Delos to Athens and use it to finance the adornment of the city. The alliance becomes an *archê*, an empire. As crisis unfolds, Pericles positions himself as the leader most capable of protecting the empire. He calls for only temporary restraint in adding to it: '[Do not] combine schemes of fresh conquest with the conduct of the war' (I.144.1). He does not rule out enlarging it once the crisis has passed.

Thucydides seems to acknowledge this underlying continuity between Pericles and his successors by Pericles' and Cleon's shared application of the term *tyranny* to Athens' empire (II.63.2 and III.37.2).[14] The term 'tyranny' connotes much more than the extralegal seizure of power. It conveys the violent abuse of power and the disregard or outright rejection of customary Greek norms of conduct. Pericles uses the term to exhort Athenians to maintain their resolve. 'To take [the empire]', he says, 'perhaps was wrong, but to let it go is unsafe' (II.63.3). Cleon uses the term to convince the Athenians to punish rebellion severely, and he does not concede, as does Pericles, that taking the empire 'perhaps was wrong'. Cleon defends its justice and warns the Athenians that showing mercy 'will . . . pass sentence upon yourselves. For if they were right in rebelling, you must be wrong in ruling' (III.40.4).

Although Thucydides praises Pericles, the 'first citizen' (II.65.9), and disparages Cleon, the 'most violent man in Athens' (III.36.6), Thucydides' narrative highlights their shared attachment to empire. Both claim realistically to assess what that attachment requires in terms of policy and action. Both counsel steadfast resolve in carrying out policies once

---

[14] Pericles says: 'What you already hold is like a tyranny' (*hos tyrannida gar ede echete auten* [2.63.2]). Cleon says: 'You don't appreciate that what you hold, the empire, is a tyranny' (*ou skopountes hoti tyrannida echete ten archen* [3.37.2]). To preserve the important parallel with Pericles' language, we depart from Strassler's rendering of Cleon's use of 'tyrannida' as 'despotism'. For sustained analysis of these passages, see W. Robert Connor, 'Tyrannis Polis' in John D'Arms and John W. Eadie (eds.), *Ancient and Modern: Essays in Honor of Gerald F. Else* (Ann Arbor: University of Michigan Press, 1977). For other parallels between the speeches of Pericles and Cleon, see Connor, *Thucydides*, p. 79, n. 1.

they are adopted. Both urge assemblies not to reopen debate on policies simply because their execution proves difficult.[15] For Euben, 'given Thucydides' singularly explicit castigation of Cleon and his equally explicit praise of Pericles, it is disconcerting to find so many similarities between them'.[16]

In the turmoil following the debacle at Syracuse, Athens itself falls victim to the violence of tyranny. Athenian readers would have remembered how, towards the end of the war, the oligarchs behaved so brutally that they earned the epithet the 'thirty tyrants'.[17] But when this happens, the city is victimized not only by the actions of tyrannical leaders but also by the harsh moral character that the people of Athens themselves acquired through their dealings with their empire and now display in their dealings with one another. The disconcerting similarities between Pericles and Cleon nurture suspicion that Periclean policies, too, may bear some responsibility for the dissolution of Athenian political life in factionalism, mistrust and violence.

Indeed, though Pericles exhorted the Athenians to remain true to the 'old ways', to Athens' foundational norms, he may not have promoted normative cohesion among the Athenians as effectively as we are first led to think. On the contrary, he may have accelerated the disintegration of Athenian solidarity and contributed to defeat. The one issue on which the narrative is thoroughly consistent is the attribution of that defeat to 'intestine disorders' (II.65.12), factionalism and growing atomization. For Athenians, affective attachment to the *polis* – their sense of democratic citizenship – pivoted on a norm of reciprocity between individuals and the city. They imagined democratic citizenship to be characterized by mutual benefactions by citizens and *polis*. Civic devotion did not require adopting a slavish, self-sacrificing posture. Instead, a thriving democracy required the cultivation of practices that provided multiple opportunities both for citizens (regardless of social and economic standing) to perform benefactions for the *polis* and for the city to perform benefactions for the citizens. The Athenians extolled devotion to the common good, but they also represented private interests and

---

[15] This is the position of Cleon in the Mytilenean debate and of Pericles regarding the Megaran Decree and the strategy of collecting behind the walls.

[16] Euben, *Tragedy*, p. 178. See also Hornblower, *Thucydides*, pp. 122ff, and Edward Hussey, 'Thucydidean History and Democritean Theory' in P. A. Cartledge and F. D. Harvey (eds.), *CRUX: Essays in Greek History* presented to G. E. M. de Ste. Croix on his 75th Birthday (London: Duckworth, 1985). Plato explicitly criticizes Pericles for pandering to the Athenians in this way. See *Gorgias*, 515eff.

[17] Connor, *Thucydides*, pp. 179–180.

public interests as mutually obtainable. This is not to suggest that real citizens never encountered conflicts between private and public interests. Thucydides' *History*, as well as tragedy and many other literary sources, indicate that such conflict was frequent. Nevertheless, the ideal of citizenship as reciprocal exchange both defined a powerful political norm and acted as a force for social cohesion.[18]

Thucydides' Pericles claims to uphold this ideal. He says, 'I am of the opinion that national greatness is more for the advantage of private citizens than any individual well-being coupled with public humiliation' (II.60.2). In the funeral oration, Pericles praises this aspect of the Athenian way of life.[19] Yet, Pericles' policies require that the Athenians behave in ways that depart from this ideal. As he relates the effects of those policies, Thucydides invites us to observe how Pericles' policies produce a growing tension between the civic ideal and actual conduct, and to speculate how those policies threaten a normative understanding that had functioned powerfully to nurture Athenian solidarity.

Pericles' call to the citizens to collect behind the city walls is strategically brilliant but socially corrosive. The policy does not reward the Athenians for the suffering they must endure in the same way that the city traditionally rewards them for the more common sacrifice of the body in combat. In Athenian practice, dying honorably in battle – contributing one's body to the *polis* (II.43.1) – is rewarded by the *polis*. The soldier knows beforehand that, if he perishes, the *polis* will reward his 'contribution' to the collectivity by attaching honour to his memory, by burying him with pomp at public expense and by assuming certain responsibilities for his family, such as educating his orphaned children and supporting his elderly parents.[20] Pericles' policy, in contrast, does not require the city to express any explicit gratitude toward the

---

[18] The centrality of reciprocity in Athenian democratic ideology is increasingly noted in recent scholarship. See Cynthia Farrar, '"Gyges" Ring'; Leslie Kurke, *The Traffic in Praise: Pindar and the Poetry of Social Economy* (Ithaca NY: Cornell University Press, 1991); Paul Millet, *Lending and Borrowing in Ancient Athens* (New York: Cambridge University Press, 1991); S. Sara Monoson, 'Citizen as *Erastes*: Erotic Imagery and The Idea of Reciprocity in the Periclean Funeral Oration' *Political Theory* 22 (1994), 253–276; Josiah Ober, *Mass and Elite in Democratic Athens* (Princeton NJ: Princeton University Press, 1989); Richard Seaford, *Reciprocity and Ritual* (New York: Oxford University Press, 1994). See also S. Sara Monoson, *Plato's Democratic Entanglements* (Princeton NJ: Princeton University Press, 2000), for sustained discussion of reciprocity in the Athenian democratic imaginary.

[19] Monoson, 'Citizen as *Erastes*'.

[20] The Athenian *polis* celebrated and displayed the generous way in which the city met these responsibilities toward orphans in the 'preperformance rituals' that opened the dramatic competitions on the occasion of the grandest civic festival of the year, the City Dionysia. See Simon Goldhill, 'The Great Dionysia and Civic Ideology' *Journal of Hellenic*

individuals who sacrifice their *property* rather than their bodies. Instead, Pericles exhorts citizens to subordinate their private interests to a future public good. 'Cease . . . to grieve for your private afflictions and address yourselves instead to the safety of the commonwealth', he urges (II.61.4). Pericles not only enjoins the citizens to make extraordinary sacrifices but also minimizes their importance: 'You may think it a great privation to lose the use of your land and houses [but] you should really regard them in the light of the gardens and other accessories that embellish a great fortune and as, in comparison, of little moment' (II.62.3).

In defence of his policies, Pericles makes no attempt at all to fit the citizens' acceptance of property loss into a model of reciprocal exchange. He may promise participation in the enduring glory and pleasures that attend citizenship in a dominant *polis*, but he does not stress any 'exchange'. Rather, he uses his rhetorical skills to shore up the citizens' resolution and their tolerance of 'private afflictions' (II.61.4), offering himself as an example. He is resolute, though he, too, has lost property. He admonishes the Athenians to be strong like him: 'I am the same man and do not alter; it is you who change . . . the apparent error of my policy lies in the infirmity of your resolution' (II.61.2). But he fails to appreciate that the Athenians have only himself, an extraordinary charismatic leader, to help them achieve such resolve.[21] Their daily activity – camping out, often in deplorable conditions, behind the walls – does not provide them with the customary symbolic reinforcements and expiations that would make self-sacrifice on this scale tolerable. Though Pericles succeeds in assuaging the anger and frustration of the Athenians, Thucydides reports that 'still, as private individuals they could not help smarting under their sufferings, the common people having been deprived of the little that they ever possessed, while the higher orders had lost fine properties with costly establishments and buildings in the country and, worst of all, [had] war instead of peace' (II.65.2). Only when Pericles helps them vent their anger by accepting a fine do they

---

Studies 107 (1987), 58–76; and J. Winkler, 'The Ephebes' Song: *Tragoidia* and *Polis'* Representations 11 (1985), 26–62.

[21] Perhaps the success of Pericles' policies was thereby predicated on the subversion of normal institutions of Athenian democracy. This is one way to read Thucydides' famous comment regarding Pericles' relation to democratic institutions: 'What was nominally a democracy became in his hands government by the first citizen' (II.65.9). Pericles' ability 'at once [to] restore them [the multitude] to confidence' (II.65.9) regarding a previously chosen policy was also a capacity to oppose the democratic impulse to rethink, reconsider, reflect and possibly decide anew. As Saxonhouse argues in *Athenian Democracy*, steadfast devotion to a policy is a stance uncharacteristic of democratic assemblies – their distinguishing mark is the tentative, reversible status of all decisions.

finally 'become less sensitive to their private and domestic afflictions' (II.65.4).

After Pericles' death the Athenians lose the ability to subordinate private concerns to the pursuit of victory. The new leaders do not supply the model and the rhetorical reinforcements to achieve this subordination. The Athenians lost the war because they 'allowed their private ambitions and private interests . . . to lead them into [unwise] projects' (II.65.7). Pericles' policy contributes to that development by departing from dominant normative understandings of citizen rights and obligations.

Pericles and the power of chance: the plague

Pericles is an extraordinary leader acting in unusual circumstances. But aspects of Thucydides' narrative invite us to ask if the exceptional circumstances are not to an appreciable extent of Pericles' own making. This is not to diminish the effect of events more or less beyond Athenian control, particularly the eruption of conflict between Corinth and Corcyra. But we must recognize that Pericles' response to the events leading up to the war – abandonment of the countryside and engagement in a potentially protracted war of attrition – is an uncommon one.[22] Thus, when the high mortality suffered by the Athenians crowded behind the city walls during the plague – an unforeseen consequence of Pericles' uncommon policy – takes away the sole leader who might have held the *polis* together under exceptional circumstances, we are forced by Thucydides' narrative (if not by any explicit first-person authorial pronouncements) to question the wisdom of Pericles' strategically brilliant and apparently prudent course of action. Aspects of Thucydides' narrative style, moreover, lend rhetorical emphasis to those interrogations. Thucydides may not in his own voice 'blame' Pericles for the ensuing problems but the 'factual' narrative begs the reader to consider that terrible possibility.

Recall that Pericles recommends in his first speech that the Athenians fight a war of attrition, confident that, because of their strategic skill, exceptional wealth and naval supremacy, they will outlast the Peloponnesians. Pericles' recommendation that the Athenians forsake the countryside is a startling one. But he makes it sound reasonable and the Athenians support it. They are confident of victory and, the reader is invited to think, with good reason. For the modern reader, Pericles'

---

[22] During the Persian Wars, the Athenians were compelled to abandon the city by the press of combat. No such compulsion obtains at the time of Pericles' proposal.

policies embody a prudent realism: he diminishes the city's vulnerability to attack by land and invests in its advantage at sea. But in order to find Pericles' strategy credible one must discount the eruption of chance (*tychê*). Thucydides does not suggest that Pericles ignores *tychê*. He refers to it explicitly in his first speech (I.140.1). But Thucydides does suggest that Pericles may not appreciate its full import. Pericles sees chance as the source of possible sufferings that could threaten public resolve, but he is apparently unaware that it can be the source of deeper and more enduring effects.[23]

The plague provides the most devastating example of the eruption of *tychê* in the entire *History*. Thucydides emphasizes its importance by placing it, with almost no transition, after Pericles' funeral oration. The brutal juxtaposition swiftly contrasts the idealized image of Athenian life in Pericles' speech with the actual behaviour of the Athenians during the plague. Pericles portrays the Athenians as enjoying, among other things, 'ease in our private relations' (II.37.3); '[lawfulness], particularly such as regards the protection of the injured, whether actually on the statute book or belong[ing] to that code which, although unwritten, cannot be broken without acknowledged disgrace' (II.37.3); mutual trust among citizens; and confidence in their good judgment, public spiritedness and courage. Several times he praises the Athenians for their ability to endure ordeals with dignity: 'We are still willing to encounter danger; we have the double advantage of escaping the experience of hardships in anticipation and of facing them in the hour of need as fearlessly as those who are never free from them' (II.39.4). He boasts: 'I doubt if the world can produce a man, who where he has only himself to depend upon, is equal to so many emergencies and graced by so happy a versatility as the Athenian' (II.41.1).

When the plague hits, the Athenians initially struggle to nurse the sick and dying but often end up succumbing to the illness themselves (II.51.2). The majority soon collapses under the strain of the disease

---

[23] See Lowell Edmunds, *Chance and Intelligence in Thucydides* (Cambridge MA: Harvard University Press, 1975); and Orwin, *Humanity*, p. 25, n. 28. Orwin's position is closer to the one we defend here. Cornford, in *Thucydides Mythistoricus*, pp. 82–109, discusses the contrast between chance (*tychê*) and foresight (*gnomê*) in the narration of the events at Pylos. We focus here on the plague because it receives such extensive treatment in the text and because it assumes such importance in Thucydides' narrative of the rapid decay of social norms. Connor, *Thucydides*, p. 51, provides other instances of Pericles' possible lack of foresight. George Cawkwell, *Thucydides and the Peloponnesian War* (New York: Routledge, 1997), pp. 44–45, suggests that insofar as Pericles' policy succeeds, it does so only accidentally.

(II.52.2–4). The plague causes social customs (*nomoi*) to break down and give way to multiple forms of 'lawless extravagance' (*epi pleon anomias*) (II.53.1). In dramatic contrast to the orderly and elaborate public funeral at which Pericles delivered his speech, the Athenians now neglect to perform proper burial rites for their dead: 'The bodies of dying men lay one upon another. The sacred places in which they had quartered themselves were full of corpses of persons that had died there, just as they were' (II.52.3). The Athenians panic, giving the lie to Pericles' boast about their steadfastness in an emergency. They lose confidence in their judgment and act not as self-reliant and responsible citizens but, Pericles chides them, under the influence of slavish thoughts (II.61.3). The rebuke is ironic, for Pericles earlier used the threat of enslavement to justify resistance to Sparta and the adoption of his extraordinary strategy (I.141.1). Athens, in other words, took up that resistance but then failed to elude the servile condition that resistance was supposed to prevent. Fear and the absence of manly virtue drive the Athenians slave-like to pursue immediate personal pleasures for as long as their health permits in utter disregard for the law and social norms. 'Perseverance in what men called honor was popular with none. . . . Fear of gods or law of man there was none to restrain them' (II.53.3). Far removed from the idealized Athens of the funeral oration, we now see the despair of a people besieged, casting aside its recollection of virtue and obligation. 'The plague offers the most violent challenge to the Periclean attempt to exert some kind of rational control over the historical process.'[24]

Pericles' strategy of abandoning the countryside intensifies the trials of the plague. 'An aggravation of the existing calamity', Thucydides notes, 'was the influx from the country into the city, and this was especially felt by the new arrivals. As there were no houses to receive them, they had to be lodged at the hot season of the year in stifling cabins, where the mortality raged without restraint' (II.52.1–2). Plague struck just as the Spartans invaded. Athenians, gathered behind the walls, struggled to accept that their fields, livestock, orchards and homes were, at that very moment, being ravaged by an enemy no less invisible than the plague. To underscore Athens' misfortune, Thucydides matter of factly reports that the plague never entered the Peloponnesus (II.54.5). Even though 'it was actually asserted that the departure of the

---

[24] Adam Parry, 'The Language of Thucydides' Description of the Plague' *Bulletin of the Institute of Classical Studies*, 16 (1969), 106–118. Citation at p. 116.

Peloponnesians [who enjoy the luxury of mobility] was hastened by the fear of the [plague]', Thucydides writes, 'in this invasion they remained longer than in any other, and ravaged the whole country, for they were about forty days in Attica' (II.57.1–2). One wonders if Pericles' strategy is not flawed. His embarrassment is obvious in the more defensive tone and rhetoric of the third speech. As spokesman for civic values in the funeral oration, he speaks of 'we' and 'us', but in his third and final speech he belabours the contrast between 'me' and 'you'. References to 'us' disappear.[25]

Thucydides never suggests that Pericles himself is not equal to the emergency. In his third speech, 'He succeeded in convincing them; they not only gave up all idea of sending to Sparta but also applied themselves with increased energy to the war' (II.65.2). But while describing the positive effects of his third speech, Thucydides almost casually informs us that Pericles, too, has perished. 'He outlived [the war's] commencement two years and six months' (II.65.6). Pericles might have helped the Athenians negotiate unforeseen misfortune, but chance disrupts the anticipated course of events. Pericles is dead. Thucydides might have included some narrative account of the year that separates Pericles' third speech from his death. He might have included some description of the circumstances of that death, and, in so doing, eased the reader into the knowledge of Pericles' loss. Instead, Thucydides leaves the reader asking: 'Wait a minute, did Pericles just die?' Thucydides makes us experience vicariously the shock and confusion that the Athenians felt. We live the power of chance not only intellectually but emotionally. Through the antithetical encounter of praise and disappointment, Thucydides' treatment of Pericles, the most gifted of Athenians, has nourished a corrosive scepticism regarding humanity's capacity to master its destiny through strategic brilliance.

Humanity's dependence on norms of moral conduct

It would be hasty to conclude that the scepticism in Thucydides' treatment of Pericles expressed 'mere tragedy', mere pessimism regarding

---

[25] Connor, *Thucydides*, p. 65. Alcibiades will later exhort the Spartans to occupy the Attic hinterland permanently. The vulnerability of the countryside is, he explains, Athens' greatest vulnerability and the surest means of compelling the Athenians to sue for peace. Subsequent events will prove Alcibiades correct.

humankind's power to master its destiny.[26] Thucydides does not doubt the power of human intelligence but rather the ability of that intelligence to chart a prudent course of action while disregarding norms of moral conduct. The reader appreciates how Pericles' overweening confidence, both in his own talent and in the wealth of his city, breeds in him and his compatriots the illusion that power has made them immune from the sanctions of moral norms, which, in Pericles own words, 'although unwritten, cannot be broken without acknowledged disgrace' (II.37.3). Impressed by Pericles' judgment and capacity for leadership yet suspicious of his abundant self-confidence, Thucydides invites us to observe how prudent action relies on the guidance and restraint provided by moral norms.

The most important discussion of conditions under which deliberate and prudent conduct is possible is found in the passage on the Corcyraean civil war, or *stasis* (III.70–83). Thucydides describes how factional conflict besets Corcyra as a result of war. The opposing factions, each emboldened by the prospect of reinforcement by an invading power, become increasingly 'harsh' toward one another until normal political interaction is no longer possible. Violence ensues, and 'the Corcyraeans engaged in butchering those of their fellow-citizens whom they regarded as enemies' (III.81.4). Under such conditions, Thucydides explains, it became increasingly difficult, and finally impossible, for both 'states and individuals' (*poleis and idiotai*; III.82.2) to conduct themselves prudently, moderately and deliberately. Instead, *stasis* drove them to extremes, to behave with 'reckless abandon' (*tolma gar alogistos*; III.82.4) and 'frantically' (*emplektos*; III.82.4). Thucydides characterizes the situation as one in which actors are unable to practise any measure of 'hesitation' (*mellesis promethes*; III.82.4), 'moderation' (*to sophron*; III.82.4) and 'practical intelligence' (*to pros hapan xuneton*; III.82.4).[27]

---

[26] See Euben, *Tragedy*, p. 194, n. 52, for an accounting of the camps (pessimist versus modernist) into which fall many interpreters of Thucydides' treatment of Pericles.

[27] We depart from Strasser's translation of *xuneton*, 'ability to see all sides of a question', by proposing 'practical intelligence', which conveys the notion of commonly understood virtue. See 1.79.2, where the term is used to describe the Spartan leader Archidamus, who uses the term himself (1.84.3) to designate a characteristic virtue of the Spartans and a reason for their stability and success in war. It appears again (II.IS.1) in reference to Theseus, the mythic founder of Athens as a unified *polis*. Thucydides applies the term, always positively, to a handful of revered historical Greek figures, including Themistocles (1.74.1 and 1.138.2–3) and the Peisistratids (VI.54.5). He also applies it to actors of his history who cut a good and often brilliant figure, such as Brasidas (IV.81.2) and Hermocrates (VI.72.2), as well as in discussing the oligarchs of 411 (VIII.58.4) and by implication Pericles (II.34.6, 8). See A. W. Gomme, *A Historical Commentary on Thucydides*, revised by A. Andrewes and K. J. Dover, (Oxford: Oxford University Press, 1945–81), II.49.377.

For Thucydides, war encourages actors to expect help from foreign sympathizers, freeing them from the need to treat their adversaries with consideration (III.82.2). As it disrupts normal human commerce, war spawns desperation because it 'takes away the easy supply of daily wants'; 'plunges' cities and individuals into dire necessity;[28] and ushers in a situation in which words have no stable meaning (III.82.4). Sincere good naturedness (*to euethes*) is laughed out of court (III.83.1), and there is no trust (III.83.2).[29] War disrupts the norms on which we rely for some measure of predictability and civility in daily life, which are the conditions of rational, deliberate, prudent action.

Thucydides' precise words at III.82.1 help us appreciate the subtlety of his insight. He pauses in his narration to note that revolution at Corcyra, being one of the first revolutions to occur, made a strong impression. 'Later on, one may say, the whole Hellenic world (*pan to Hellenikon*) was convulsed (*ekinethe*).' What kind of convulsion did the whole Hellenic world suffer and with what consequences? The verb *ekinethe* (a form of *kineo*, the root of 'kinetic') suggests movement and instability. The image is one of chaos, flux, a destructive kind of motion. Thucydides introduces the term as a noun, *kinesis*, in the first lines of the *History* (I.1.2), and reintroduces the word into the narrative repeatedly, in some form or other, like a Wagnerian *leitmotif*.[30]

By the time of the Corcyrean *stasis*, kinesis has placed in motion not only men and navies, but the discursive environment of norms and laws that make deliberate action possible. People and cities are losing their reserve, the power to check their motion. They are acting on impulse and fear. The things that war is now setting in motion, or stirring up, are not only men, money, resources and ships but also the very customary understandings of what constitute 'normal' human values and relationships. War is causing 'the distortion of morality and values'.[31] The breakdown of the norms that undergird social relations, captured in Thucydides' observation that even words lose their ordinary meanings, is leading to chaos, violence and the pursuit of immediate wants

---

[28] Thomas Hobbes offers 'plunges' in translation of *piptein*. See David Grene (ed.), *The Peloponnesian War, Thucydides, The Complete Hobbes Translation* (Chicago: University of Chicago Press, 1989).

[29] To *euethes* combines 'eu' (good) and 'ethos' (custom or habit), and it thus designates etymologically the moral virtue of being good as a matter not of calculation but of habit.

[30] Connor, *Thucydides*, p. 21, n. 4, observes that kinesis 'is an unusual word at this point in the development of Greek, clear enough in general meaning but obscure and surprising in this [I.1.2] context'. The inference is, therefore, that it was not lightly or casually employed by the author.

[31] Hornblower, *Thucydides*, p. 156; see also Connor, *Thucydides*, p. 102, n. 57.

without regard to their moral value (*pleonexia*). When those norms are 'convulsed', as they are at Corcyra, one cannot expect reason to provide a useful guide to action. Reason requires that words convey meaning, that the norms to which we commonly refer in judging the actions, intentions, moral character and trustworthiness of others are still generally employed.

The Corcyraean *stasis* has the same effect as the Athenian plague on humankind's capacity to act reasonably. At Athens, when physicians found themselves unable to stem the tide of plague, reason (*logos*) 'was overpowered'.[32] The same condition obtains in Corcyra. For Thucydides, war is a 'violent teacher' (*biaios didaskalos*; III.82.2, translation modified) because it instructs by setting in motion that which in times of peace is *at rest*. Thucydides opposes this *kinesis* of social norms antithetically to *hesychia*, his term for peace. (*Hesychia* literally means quiet or tranquility; the more common term for peace is *eirene*.)[33] Thucydides employs the *kinesis/hesychia* antithesis to highlight the parallel between *stasis* at Corcyra and plague at Athens. In both instances he opposes an image of *kinesis* with an antithetical image of *hesychia*. In the case of the plague, the image of *hesychia* is developed in the funeral oration. In the case of the Corcyraean *stasis*, it is developed in the description of the Athenian purification of the island of Delos, with its long excerpt from Homer's *Hymn to Apollo* (III.104.1–6). In both instances, Thucydides' use of antithesis compels the reader to ponder the contrast.

Pericles and the *kinesis* of customary norms

War and *stasis* destabilize norms and meanings and render reasonable, prudent conduct difficult if not impossible to achieve. But it would belie the complexity of Thucydides' text to call war and *stasis* the cause of that destabilization. Indeed, war and *stasis* themselves can, to a considerable extent, be seen as the consequence of a prior subversion of moral norms. Thucydides, at V.25.1, inverts the variables. The Peace of Nicias

---

[32] Connor, *Thucydides*, p. 100.
[33] Thucydides generally uses the term *eirene* to designate formal peace treaties between cities (as well as the absence of war that results) and *hesychia* to designate the absence of turmoil, both within the city and in relations among cities. At VI.38.3 he explicitly contrasts *hesychia* with stasis and the condition in which fellow countrymen behave toward one another as toward an enemy (*polemios*). Note that the application of *hesychia* is not limited to domestic peace (V.55.1–2). For *eirene*, see 1.29.4 and V.13.2, 14.1, and 26.2; for *hesychia* see 1.70.9, II.22.1, and V.22.2 and 53.

obtains, but Corinth and other Peloponnesian cities are trying mightily to 'disturb' the arrangement. The verb employed here is *diekinoun* (which appends the prefix *dia* [thoroughly] to *kineo*, discussed above). The episode invites us to take a longer view, to ask if the peace that obtained before the outbreak of war was not similarly being 'disturbed'. We recall the broad indictment of Athens by the Corinthians (I.70.19). There we find the 'daring, dynamism, innovation, audacity, immoderation, presentism, and frenetic motion' characteristic of *stasis* being applied to the conduct of Athens in peacetime: 'They were born into the world to take no rest (*hesychian*) themselves and to give none to others' (I.70.9).[34]

The corrosive effect of 'frenetic motion' saps the capacity of the Athenians as well as other Greeks to act with prudence and deliberation. Early in the *History*, moral argument causes Athens to hesitate before entering into the fateful alliance with Corcyra (I.31–44). Moral scruples cause the Athenians to rethink their policy toward the rebellious Mytilenians. They still possess the power to pause, to listen to argument, to reconsider, to check their motion and moderate their conduct. Yet, the hold of norms has begun to weaken. As Euben points out, Diodotus, the advocate of restraint and decency, is compelled by the press of argument and the hubris of imperialism to 'defend the more moderate human policy in relentlessly realistic terms that anticipate the Athenian arguments at Melos'.[35] This argument is self-defeating in the long run. Diodotus' feigned realism saves the Mytilenians but legitimates the idea that imperialist rule is of necessity instrumental, a matter of expedience, beyond the application of moral argument, as oppressive as it is ineluctable, and in so doing subverts confidence in the legitimacy and value of moral discourse. Diodotus thus unwittingly invites those Athenians who may still be willing to subject action to rational examination to shed their regard for norms of decency in favour of a normatively disembodied strategic calculus. By the time of the Melian dialogue, 'a travesty of dialectic',[36] the process of decay is complete. 'Athens is left with self-interest alone, the desire for power without a culture to give it bounds and meaning.

---

[34] Euben, *Tragedy*, p. 190.
[35] Euben, *Tragedy*, p. 180; See Bagby, 'Use and Abuse'; Saxonhouse, *Athenian Democracy*.
[36] Hornblower, *Thucydides*, p. 62; See Connor's treatment of the Melian dialogue in *Thucydides*, pp. 147–155: 'Whatever our reactions to what happens to the Melians, it is hard to escape a feeling of horror at what is happening to the Athenians.' Quoted at p. 154. See also Connor, *Thucydides*, pp. 87–88; Euben, *Tragedy*, p. 198.

Not only is ambition of this sort unlimited, it is incoherent and irrational; for without a comprehensible world there can be no way of reasoning about it or acting within it.'[37]

The norms and understandings that provide guidance to everyday social intercourse are subverted not only by violence but by 'peacetime' politics and political discourse. Pericles plays no mean role in this history of subversion. He is 'not only at home in wartime, and tolerate[s] its climate of aggression, but even foster[s] it'.[38] At 1.127.3, Pericles 'urges' (*horma*) the Athenians to war. The verb *hormao* (cf. English 'hormone') means to set in motion or to rush at something or someone, as in battle. Pericles is a source of *kinesis*. He takes pride in making 'every land and every sea . . . the highway of our daring' (II.41.4). In a passage that is particularly suggestive of Thucydides' complex attitude toward Pericles (VIII.97.2), the historian offers the following judgment on Athens' short-lived experiment with a mixed constitution: 'For the first time in my experience the Athenians appear to have governed themselves well.'[39] The judgment includes Pericles' rule and 'implies censure of Pericles' management of affairs'.[40] It further stokes suspicion regarding Pericles' statecraft. By pandering to the population, by challenging the customary understandings of the bond between citizen and *polis*, by implementing an extraordinarily bold war strategy that uprooted established patterns of life, by offending the allies' reverence for *autonomia* (political autonomy), Pericles is a source of *kinesis* and contributes significantly, though perhaps unwittingly, to the deterioration of norms of social conduct. Not only does he pander to Athenian *pleonexia*, or desire for more power and wealth, but, by making Athens invulnerable to external assault, he tries to free it from the need to cultivate 'normal' relations with other Greek cities. He also tries to free the conduct of the war from the need to secure the customary way of life of the majority of Athenian citizens, who are

---

[37] James Boyd White, *When Words Lose Their Meaning* (Chicago: University of Chicago Press, 1984), p. 79.

[38] Peter R. Pouncey, *The Necessities of War: A Study of Thucydides' Pessimism* (New York: Columbia University Press, 1980), p. 36.

[39] Translation from Connor, *Thucydides*, p. 228 and n. 34, emphasis added (in conformity with the text, which stresses 'my experience' with the enclitic particle *ge*). See the discussion of translation problems in Hornblower, *Thucydides*, p. 160, who also (pp. 166–168) gives a critical examination of Pericles' stewardship, as do Richard Ned Lebow, *The Tragic Vision of Politics: Ethics, Interests and Orders* (Cambridge: Cambridge University Press, 2003), pp. 254–259; and Michael Palmer, *Love of Glory and the Common Good: Aspects of the Political Thought of Thucydides* (Lanham MD: Rowman & Littlefield, 1992), p. 113.

[40] Hornblower, *Thucydides*, p. 160.

compelled to abandon that way of life to seek refuge behind the city walls.[41]

But as Pericles and the Athenians undermine the legitimacy and influence of moral norms through rhetorical flair, brazen strategy and raw violence, they not only create a revolutionary world that loses its moral compass but also prove quite incapable of flourishing in the world they create. In the end, the Athenians suffer as much as anyone from the collapse of political order throughout Greece and the concomitant decay of 'those general laws to which all alike can look for salvation in adversity' (III.84.3; cf. Pericles at II.37.3).[42] The tragic lament of Nicias following the defeat at Syracuse (VII.77.1–7), with its ironic use of language previously employed at the Melian conference, makes this point with pathos.

The *History* offers a sustained exposition of humanity's dependence on moral norms – not for philosophically transcendent reasons but because they are the necessary support of prudent conduct. When those norms are in shambles, the protagonists of the *History* find it virtually impossible to chart a rational course of action. 'Thucydides' history is unquestionably aimed at an audience that values cleverness, sophistication, intellect and self-interest, but it does not simply affirm and reinforce those values.'[43] *Gnomê* (foresight or rational calculation) trips on *tychê* (chance) or is coopted by *orgê* (passion).[44] In some instances, 'sound calculation leads to a poor outcome';[45] in others, carelessly concocted schemes, such as Cleon's assault on Pylos (IV.27–41), succeed beyond hope. We see the actors of the *History* treat morality and prudence as if they were rival terms. Thucydides invites us to consider the cost of doing so.

What are the norms, and how free was Pericles to respect them? The first question challenges us to identify specifically 'international' norms, since we have already discussed the importance of norms such as reciprocity in domestic political life. This is an important issue for International Relations scholarship, because 'international norms' are at the core of one of the most abiding claims of Realist theory: morality is unachievable without first securing 'political order' through the

---

[41] See Josiah Ober, 'National Ideology and Strategic Defense of the Population, from Athens to Star Wars' in *Hegemonic Rivalry*, pp. 254–259, on the development of a defensive ideology in Athens.

[42] Though the authenticity of III.84 is disputed, we are convinced by Connor's defence of the passage in *Thucydides* p. 102, n. 60.

[43] Connor, *Thucydides*, p. 15.   [44] Connor, *Thucydides*, pp. 55–59, esp. 58, n. 18.

[45] Mark V. Kauppi, 'Contemporary International Relations Theory and the Peloponnesian War' in *Hegemonic Rivalry*, p. 18; cf. Connor, *Thucydides*, p. 118.

exercise of power.[46] It follows from this claim that we can discuss morality meaningfully only as it obtains 'inside' states. It is not meaningful 'outside' states, in the anarchical realm of international politics and war.

G. E. M. de Ste. Croix offers a reading of Thucydides that lends some support to the Realist argument.[47] But in general the stark dichotomization between 'inside' and 'outside' does not hold up well in Thucydides' text. It is beyond the bounds of this chapter to explore in any depth the norms that regulated relations among Greek *poleis*, but it is important to verify the existence of such norms in the text. Indeed, Thucydides' claim, advanced in his analysis of the Corcyraean *stasis*, that both private persons (*idiotai*) and states (*poleis*) found prudent action increasingly difficult to achieve constitutes a rather explicit rejection of the 'inside/outside' dichotomy. The text reveals that norms of war and diplomacy regulated the exchange of the dead (III.113.1–5; IV.97.2–98.8), the treatment of prisoners and refugees, Olympic truces, diplomacy through proxenies, the obligations of allies and so on.[48] Perlman shows how the term *archê* evolved to become synonymous with *dynamis*, *despoteia*, and even *tyrannis*, precisely because Athens showed such disregard for the norms of *eleutheria* (freedom) and *autonomia*, which, like sovereignty and *cuius regio* in the Westphalian system, were constitutive of the Greek system of city-states.[49] Indeed, Thucydides seems to experience the war as a kind of civil war within a normatively unified space. Hermocrates' efforts to forge cohesion among Sicilians, a people who 'go by the same name' (*onoma hen keklemenous*; IV.64.3), serve as a foil to the civil war that is raging on the mainland among people who are also designated by a single name, 'Hellenes'.[50] Within this unified normative space, the actors in the drama, as well as the reader, are clearly able to form judgments of the moral character of leaders of opposing cities, that is, across political frontiers, on the basis of shared understandings of such goods as justice, honour, mercy and other common virtues – at least until those norms lose sway under the combined blows of an

---

[46] E. H. Carr, *The Twenty Years' Crisis* (New York: Harper and Row, 1964), Chapter 9; Hans Morgenthau, *Scientific Man vs. Power Politics* (Chicago: University of Chicago Press, 1946).

[47] G. E. M. de Ste. Croix, *The Origins of the Peloponnesian War* (Ithaca NY: Cornell University Press, 1972).

[48] At IV.97–8 is an interesting debate regarding what should be seen as custom (nomos) and what should not. See Hornblower, *Thucydides*, p. 180, Connor, *Thucydides*, on Mytilene, p. 91, and on Nicias, p. 163; and Pierre Ducrey, *Warfare in Ancient Greece* (New York: Schocken Books, 1986), Chapter 9, on treatment of prisoners of war.

[49] Shalom Perlman, 'Hegemony and *Arkhe* in Greece: Fourth Century B.C. Views' in *Hegemonic Rivalry*.

[50] See Connor, *Thucydides*, p. 126, n. 42.

overweening self – self-sufficiency, war and *stasis*. It is only when those norms become inoperative that the reader finds it difficult to develop a firm grasp of the moral character of such figures as Alcibiades and Phrynichus, who dominate the final books of the *History*.

Do we really mean to argue, then, that Pericles ignored opportunities to legitimate, reaffirm and defend such norms of moral conduct by adopting the policy course he did? The claim gives pause because scholarship in International Relations, goaded by Thucydides' claim that the war was 'inevitable' (I.23.6),[51] is accustomed to searching for 'necessary outcomes', treating Pericles as an extraordinary leader confronting the great forces of history. But, in addition to Lebow's well-argued complaint that the popular 'power transition' reading of 'necessity' is not well supported by the text, it is simply impossible to identify any recurring set of factors in the *History* that render some pattern of outcomes 'necessary'.[52] It is true that 'the Archeology' (I.2–23) seems to suggest such a theme by alerting the reader to the role of 'historical forces' in the genesis of the *History*. But Thucydides' interest in 'historical forces' all but vanishes in the narrative of the war. 'There is, in Thucydides, no systematic treatment of Spartan and Athenian weaknesses other than those of character.'[53] As the narrative unfolds, the attention paid to individual moral character grows rather than diminishes. In the final books, the historian's attention is absorbed by the moral character of two figures. Thucydides' analysis of moral character suggests that it matters to history, that 'individual human action can change the course of history'.[54]

Hermocrates at Gela: realism, prudence, and moral norms

Thucydides' demonstration of our dependence on moral norms dilutes his Realist credentials. In a provocative article, Forde argued that Thucydides even counsels us to 'resist' Realism.[55] But our alertness to Thucydides' use of antithesis makes us pause before advancing

---

[51] The use of 'inevitable' to translate *anangkasai* is controversial. See Connor, *Thucydides*, p. 32, n. 31.
[52] Lebow, 'Power Transition Theory'.   [53] Hornblower, *Thucydides*, p. 33.
[54] Hornblower, *Thucydides*, p. 146; see also Kauppi, 'Contemporary International Relations Theory', p. 112.
[55] Forde, 'International Realism', p. 154.

categorical statements. Nicias, after all, resists Realism, and the outcome is less than impressive. Recall, moreover, the Archeology's account of the mastery and accumulation of political and military power by the Greeks, the devolution of that power on Athens as set out in the *Pentekontaetia* (I.88–118.2), and Thucydides' amazement at the dimensions of the *kinesis* with which he introduces the *History*. How could we expect normative restraints to operate effectively when history confers such an overwhelming advantage on a people? The claim that power politics is ineluctable pervades the *History*. In the words of Diodotus, 'it is impossible to prevent, and only great simplicity [*euetheias*] can hope to prevent, human nature [*tes anthropeias physeos*] doing what it has once set its mind upon [*hormomenes*], by force of law [*nomon ischyi*] or by any other deterrent force whatsoever' (III.45.7). The difficulty with Thucydides is finding a coherent rule or prescription in the relentless succession of antithetical claims. How does one reconcile the claim that prudent politics requires guidance by moral norms with the claim that power politics is inevitable? The text provides a hint in the remarkable speech delivered by Hermocrates.

Hermocrates wants to promote reconciliation between two feuding Sicilian cities, Gela and Camarina, to fend off Athenian intervention. He begins by making clear Athenian interest in the feud. Athens, he claims, seeks to ally itself with certain Sicilian cities only as a first step towards subjugating the entire island. Moreover, those ambitions are, he states in a realist sounding utterance, 'very excusable', since 'it is just as much in men's nature to rule those who submit to them as it is to resist those who molest them' (IV.61.5). Hermocrates urges the two cities to settle their differences so that Sicily can unite to dispel the Athenian threat. But why should the cities of Sicily prefer the collective defence of their island to the Athenian alliance? Realism counsels only the course of action that is most likely to succeed at acceptable cost. Hermocrates, however, evokes the sentiment of Sicilian identity: 'We are neighbors, live in the same country, are girt by the same sea, and go by the same name of Sicilians' (IV.64.3). His sentiment of Sicilian unity is not grounded in some nationalist sympathy or solidarity. Indeed, national sentiment is held in check by the more ancient rivalry between Dorians and Ionians. The idea of Sicily, for Hermocrates, refers rather to a geographical space in which shared norms have emerged in time to facilitate interaction, deliberation and the settlement of grievances. 'Do you not think that the good which you have', he asks, 'and the ills that you complain of, would be better preserved and cured by quiet [*hesychia*] than by war' (IV.62.2)?

Hermocrates greets with scepticism the self-assurance that is bred of power and strategic cleverness. He asks his listeners not to fall prey to the illusion that strength is sure merely because it brings confidence (*euelpi*) (IV.62.4). Given that scepticism, he equates prudent action with the defence of Sicily as a space unified by shared norms. He likens war among Sicilian cities to civil war. He evokes civil war using the forceful term *oikeios polemos* (IV.64.5) rather than the more common *stasis*. The expression produces a powerful image of war in the household (*oikos*). He invites his listeners to be terrified, frightened out of their wits (*ekplagentes*), not only in the presence of the Athenians but also before 'the undefined fear of this unknown future' (IV.63.1). The image of civil war, that is, the destruction of a normative space that enables reasoned action and negotiation (with friends as well as enemies) should inspire terror. Terror, in turn, should inspire concessions on the part of the feuding cities in order to preserve that normative space. Hermocrates' argument recalls with irony the words of Pericles, who sought not only to stir confidence in Athenian power and strategic skill but also to inspire *disdain* for the adversary: 'Disdain [*hyperphron*]', Pericles states, 'is the privilege of those who, like us, have been assured by reflection of their superiority to their adversary' (II.62.4). In this same vein, Hermocrates' invitation to make concessions contrasts sharply with Pericles' principled rejection of any meaningful negotiation.

Against Pericles, Hermocrates asserts that power can cause people to 'confuse their strength with their hopes' (IV.65.4). He realizes that the temptation to test one's power is strong. The defence of Sicily as a normative space will therefore probably require the countervailing application of military power. Hermocrates is not a peace activist. He is trying to forge an alliance. He admits, as does the Realist, that violence is inevitable or 'natural' in human affairs. He admits that Sicily's cities will probably wage war on one another again (IV.64.3). But prudence dictates participation in the violent struggle for Sicily's independence, with the goal of preserving the social norms that make deliberate action and prudence possible. He does not invite us to resist Realism but to apply the Realist's alertness to the permanence of power and violence in human affairs in defence of norms of moral conduct. Pericles, in contrast, knows how to acquire and apply power, and Thucydides values that mastery. But what is missing in Pericles is a full appreciation of what one might do with power such that the normative conditions for its intelligent and prudent application can be sustained. To state the argument more boldly, Realism, that is, the deliberate cultivation and application of power, depends on the prior existence of a normative space in which to be deployed. If that condition is not met, Realism is a futile exercise in shooting blindly.

Hermocrates' speech and policy are antithetical to Pericles' earlier speeches and policies. It does not engage Periclean policy directly, but at the level of theory. We submit that the antithesis between Pericles and Hermocrates contains a prescriptive lesson. At the same time, however, we acknowledge how difficult it is to pin Thucydides down. Hermocrates, in another passage, uses the language of ethnic solidarity (VI.80.3). Nevertheless, Thucydides employs all his rhetorical skills to concentrate our minds on Hermocrates' words at IV.59–64 and lend those words centrality. The scene provides us with our first introduction to Sicily and Syracuse, the principal instruments of Athens's defeat, and to Hermocrates, a central figure in that defeat. At Gela, moreover, Hermocrates gives the only speech, a privilege that compels the comparison with Pericles. Finally, his speech follows immediately and antithetically on the Athenian triumph at Pylos, an unexpected victory and the highwater mark of Athens' fortunes.

Thucydides and contemporary theory

Thucydides' scepticism, as conveyed by his antithetical style of analysis, invites us to revisit Realism, whose ties to scepticism have been noted but not systematically explored.[56] Scepticism regarding humanity's aptitude for moral improvement justifies the focus on power politics and self-help. Pericles, by this definition, is a Realist. The label fits not only his attitude toward policymaking but also the philosophical premises underlying that attitude. Pericles, like Thucydides, had ties to the Sophists. He was closely linked with Protagoras, and his consort

[56] See Charles R. Beitz, *Political Theory and International Relations* (Princeton NJ: Princeton University Press, 1979), Chapter 1; Marshall Cohen, 'Moral Skepticism and International Relations' in Charles R. Beitz, Marshall Cohen, Thomas Scanlon and A. John Simmons (eds.), *International Ethics* (Princeton NJ: Princeton University Press, 1985); Michael Loriaux, 'The Realists and Saint Augustine: Skepticism, Psychology, and Moral Action in International Relations Thought' *International Studies Quarterly* 36 (1992), 401–420; R. B. J. Walker, *Inside/Outside: International Relations as Political Theory* (Cambridge: Cambridge University Press, 1993).

Aspasia animated a lively intellectual 'salon' in which Sophistic thought flourished. Pericles may have drawn more or less self-consciously on Sophistic scepticism in order to 'clear the decks' of received wisdom and thus make room for his strategic innovations.

But Thucydides' subtle critique of Pericles questions the Realists' ability to ground their political philosophy in sceptical premises. Scepticism in Thucydides spreads from doubt regarding humanity's capacity for moral deliberation and action to doubt regarding humanity's capacity to deploy Realist policy in defiance of moral norms. Thucydides excites such scepticism even when statecraft is, as in Pericles' case, brilliantly conceived. It is difficult to think of a Realist argument that might stave off this metastasis of scepticism from doubt regarding human morality to doubt regarding the human intellect's self-sufficiency. Thucydides, in any event, 'makes it clear where he stood: it is not with the sophists who denied the validity of any principle of morality but a short-sighted self-interest'.[57]

Thucydides' invitation to appreciate how norms function as a condition for deliberate action intersects with constructivist literature on norms and law.[58] The *History* shows how norms provide guidance in a non-determinist manner. Thucydides' reliance on a sceptical outlook suggests a way that proponents of constructivism might philosophize about the foundations of that perspective.[59] Inversely, his acknowledgment of the inevitability of power relations should inspire caution in constructivists as they mount their assault on Realist Theory. His account of politics in extraordinary times suggests that we can, and should, assess how material struggle supports or unsettles norms.

---

[57] Hornblower, *Thucydides*, p. 185, citing Gomme, *Historical Commentary*, revised by A. Andrewes and K. J. Dover (Oxford: Oxford University Press, 1945–81), p. 81.

[58] Martha Finnemore, *National Interests in International Society* (Ithaca NY: Cornell University Press, 1996); Peter J. Katzenstein (ed.), *The Culture of National Security: Norms and Identity in World Politics* (New York: Columbia University Press, 1996); Audie Klotz, *Norms in International Relations: the Struggle Against Apartheid* (Ithaca NY: Cornell University Press, 1995); Friedrich Kratochwil, *The Humean Perspective on International Relations* (Princeton NJ: Center of International Studies, Princeton University, 1981); Friedrich Kratochwil, *Rules, Norms, and Decisions: On the Conditions of Practical and Legal Reasoning in International Relations and Domestic Affairs* (Cambridge: Cambridge University Press, 1989); Cecelia Lynch, *Beyond Appeasement: Interpreting Interwar Peace Movements in World Politics* (Ithaca NY: Cornell University Press, 1999); Alexander Wendt, 'Anarchy Is What States Make of It' *International Organization* 46 (1992), 391–425; Lebow, *The Tragic Vision of Politics*.

[59] Kratochwil, *Humean Perspective*, sets out from David Hume. There is a parallel between the argument developed here and Hume's own rediscovery of the norms of the 'common life' through the exploration of sceptical premises. Compare Terry Nardin's discussion of Michael Oakshott in Nardin, *Law, Morality, and the Relations of States* (Princeton NJ: Princeton University Press, 1983).

We cannot develop these ideas here, but we raise them to recall Thucydides' capacity to confront each generation's particular theoretical enthusiasm with challenging and even deadly objections. In our view, his capacity to resist encapsulation – not his putative status as the founder of one or another school of thought – remains the reason his work stands as a 'possession for all time'.

3 Immanuel Kant and the democratic peace[1]

John MacMillan

One of modernity's central puzzles has been whether global politics can be organized so as to improve on the seemingly limited and contingent possibilities of human freedom available in a sovereign states system. That is to say, the corollary of state sovereignty, established to provide security and freedom within the state, was international anarchy, which delimited and threatened that very security and freedom through recreating the state of nature – which for Hobbes and Kant was a state of war – in relations between states. A vital reason for Kant's enduring influence among scholars of International Relations, and the basis for his status as a classic thinker in this field, is that he addressed this conundrum in such a way as to promise both security *and* freedom.

Whilst his seminal essay 'Perpetual Peace' (1795) did not offer any guarantees (beyond the unsatisfying recourse to nature's irresistible will),[2] his schema can at least muster sufficient empirical support in the form of the Democratic Peace and related research agendas to have taken it beyond the realm of political philosophy into that of empirical enquiry and practical politics. Indeed, the Democratic Peace has emerged as the major 'Kantian' research agenda in the contemporary study of International Relations and it is for this reason that this chapter concentrates upon the reading of Kant that it has produced.

---

[1] *Millennium: Journal of International Studies.* This chapter is an updated and expanded version of John MacMillan, 'A Kantian Protest Against the Peculiar Discourse of Inter-Liberal State Peace' which first appeared in *Millennium*, [Vol. 24, 1995] and is reproduced with the permission of the publisher.
[2] See the 'First Supplement: on the guarantee of a perpetual peace' in 'Perpetual Peace', in Hans Reiss (ed.), *Kant: Political Writings* (Cambridge: Cambridge University Press, 1991), pp. 108–114.

Kant was introduced into the current debate upon liberal states and peace by Michael Doyle in 1983 and is widely held to be the political philosopher best suited to explain why liberal states appear to be able to maintain peace among themselves, but not in relations with non-liberal states.[3] Since then, Kant's work continues to feature prominently in this literature and David Forsythe, Francis Fukuyama, Jack Levy, Bruce Russett and Georg Sørensen have all accepted Doyle's reading of Kant.[4] Elsewhere, Kant's association with the liberal peace debate is readily observable in the titles of journal articles, such as 'Kant or Cant: The Myth of the Democratic Peace', 'Neorealism and Kant: No Pacific Union', to name but two.[5] Kant's authority has even extended beyond the academic world.[6] Given the special authority Kant commands as a representative of the liberal tradition in International Relations, and especially given the influence he wields in debates on the relationship between democracy and peace, a careful examination of his writings is required.

In this chapter, I will contest the predominant interpretation of Kant's political writings in this debate, and argue that his unique authority as a liberal philosopher has been exploited to establish a new series

[3] Michael Doyle, 'Kant, Liberal Legacies, and Foreign Affairs, Part 1' *Philosophy and Public Affairs* 12 (1983), 205–235; 'Kant, Liberal Legacies, and Foreign Affairs, Part 2' *Philosophy and Public Affairs* 12 (1983), 323–353. See also Michael Doyle, 'Liberalism and World Politics' *American Political Science Review* 80 (1986), 1151–1169; and Doyle, 'Liberalism and International Relations' in Ronald Beiner and William J. Booth, *Kant and Political Philosophy: The Contemporary Legacy* (London: Yale University Press, 1993), pp. 173–203.

[4] David Forsythe, *Human Rights and Peace: International and National Dimensions* (London: University of Nebraska Press, 1993), pp. 50, 156; Jack Levy, 'Domestic Politics and War' *Journal of Interdisciplinary History* 18 (1988), 653–673; Georg Sørensen, 'Kant and Processes of Democratization: Consequences for Neorealist Thought' *Journal of Peace Research* 29 (1992), 397–414. Although Fukuyama's thesis is rooted in his interpretation of Hegel's philosophy, significant here is his explicit reference to Doyle in the text, and the immediate context which draws upon liberal writers including Kant. See Francis Fukuyama, 'The End of History?' *The National Interest* 16 (1989), 18. Bruce Russett does not explicitly acknowledge Doyle's reading of Kant, although there do not seem to be any significant differences between their respective interpretations. See Bruce Russett, *Grasping the Democratic Peace: Principles for a Post-Cold War Order* (Princeton NJ: Princeton University Press, 1993). But, see also Cecelia Lynch, 'Kant, the Republican Peace, and Moral Guidance in International Law' *Ethics and International Affairs* 8 (1994), 39–58.

[5] Christopher Layne, 'Kant or Cant: The Myth of Democratic Peace' *International Security* 19 (1994), 5–49, and Denny Roy, 'Neorealism and Kant: No Pacific Union' *Journal of Peace Research* 30 (1993), 451–454; Michael C. Williams, 'The Discipline of the Democratic Peace: Kant, Liberalism and the Social Construction of Security Communities' *European Journal of International Relations* 7 (2001), 525–553; Bruce Buchan, 'Explaining War and Peace: Kant and Liberal IR Theory' *Alternatives* 27 (2002), 407–428; see also Daniele Archibugi, 'Immanuel Kant, Cosmopolitan Law and Peace' *European Journal of International Relations* 1 (1995), 429–456.

[6] Benjamin Netanyahu, *A Place among the Nations: Israel and the World* (London: Bantam Press, 1993).

of exclusionary practices by liberal against non-liberal states. I begin by identifying the main features of the predominant interpretation of Kant's political writings. Then, I will discuss particularly problematic points of interpretation. Throughout, I seek to offer a more inclusive interpretation of Kant's thought that acknowledges the intertwined fate of liberal and non-liberal states and recalls the importance he attached to justice as a necessary condition of an enduring peace.

The predominant interpretation of Kant's writings

Doyle identifies three features of the political relations of liberal states which, when combined, purport to explain the absence of war between liberal states and the persistence of war between liberal and non-liberal states. At the domestic level, liberalism introduces caution into the affairs of states, since the consent of that same citizenry which will bear the costs of war is required before military action can be undertaken. At the international level, a consensus among liberals upon the rights of states leads to their mutual relations being marked by respect, especially for the principle of non-intervention. At the transnational level, relations are marked by the 'spirit of commerce', which leads states to have a mutual interest in the welfare of other states as trading partners.[7]

It is the international level in particular that holds the key to explaining why liberal pacifism is (according to the orthodox Democratic Peace position) limited to inter-liberal state relations: a 'separate peace'. In a liberal state, relations between the government and populace are assumed to be characterized by consent; whereas, in a non-liberal state, relations between the government and populace are assumed to be characterized by coercion. Liberals will presume other liberal states to be just, and therefore deserving of accommodation; but presume non-liberal states to be unjust, and therefore regard them with deep suspicion. Hence, while 'fellow liberals benefit from a presumption of amity; non-liberals suffer from a presumption of enmity'.[8]

This influential interpretation of Kant's political writings has four significant characteristics. First, the current literature tends to emphasize the differences and, indeed, the opposition between liberal and

[7] Doyle, 'Kant, Liberal Legacies, and Foreign Affairs, Part 1', pp. 229–232; Doyle, 'Liberalism and World Politics', pp. 1160–1162; and Doyle, 'Liberalism and International Relations', pp. 189–192.

[8] Doyle, 'Liberalism and World Politics', p. 1161; 'Liberalism and International Relations', p. 191, and Russett, *Grasping the Democratic Peace*, p. 32.

non-liberal states. These observations have created a potentially danger-
ous climate of assumptions and expectations regarding future patterns
of international relations. As Russett notes, 'social scientists sometimes
create reality as well as analyze it. . . . Repeating the proposition that
democracies [read liberal states[9]] should not fight each other helps reinforce the proposition that democracies will not fight each other.'[10] The
converse, however, is less heartening: by inference, repetition of the
claim that Kant explains why liberal states *do* fight non-liberal states
serves to establish an intellectual climate, in which war between liberal
and non-liberal states is made to appear 'normal'.

Second, calls for reform are projected onto non-liberal states, inhibit-
ing criticism of liberal states themselves. As such, the ideological context
of the research implicitly accords both 'responsibility' and 'absolution'
for that violence that does occur between liberal and non-liberal states.
Regardless of the specific causes of any particular war, the underlying
'problem' is the persistence of non-liberal states, and the 'solution' is
the replication of the liberal democratic political model.[11] The literature
rarely considers that existing liberal states might be in need of critical
self-examination, despite being replete with calls for change on the part
of others. Questions of social justice, the proper domestic civil–military
relationship, the establishment of accountability over the activities of
transnational corporations, the concentration of ownership of the media
and the preservation of civil liberties within liberal democracies do not
appear to have a place.[12] Democracy, in this literature, is sparsely con-
ceptualized and solely for export.

---

[9] Read 'liberal state' in terms of the current usage. See, for example, Hidemi Suganami
who notes that 'the key terms – "liberal", "libertarian", "democratic", "republican", "free",
and "elective", and so on – are sufficiently similar in meaning to warrant the use of
"liberal" to represent them all', Hidemi Suganami, *On the Causes of War* (Oxford: Clarendon
Press, 1996), p. 101. Kant himself was referring, among other things, to the separation of
power between the legislative and executive branches of government. While it is true
that Kant was wary of rule by the *demos*, his reasoning behind the claim that republics
would be pacific indicates that he would be comfortable with a liberal democracy. Chris
Brown, however, questions whether Doyle's 'liberal states' correspond with Kant's notion
of republicanism. Chris Brown, *International Relations Theory: New Normative Approaches*
(London: Harvester Wheatsheaf, 1992), p. 41. Throughout the piece, I refer to liberal states
according to this current usage.
[10] Russett, *Grasping the Democratic Peace*, p. 136.
[11] Doyle, 'Kant, Liberal Legacies and Foreign Affairs, Part 2', p. 344, and Russett, *Grasping
the Democratic Peace*, p. 4.
[12] These concerns are in the spirit of nineteenth-century Anglo-Saxon liberals and radicals
and their twentieth-century heirs. See, for example, Alan J. P. Taylor, *The Troublemakers*
(London: Hamish Hamilton, 1957), and Michael Howard, *War and the Liberal Conscience*
(Oxford: Oxford University Press, 1981).

Third, according to the 'separate peace' school, until the liberal model is universalized the prospects for peace are poor. Russett's view is that 'an international system composed of both democratic and authoritarian states will include both zones of peace (... among the democracies) and zones of war or at best deterrence between democratic and authoritarian states'.[13] Netanyahu projects this claim onto his own political purview: 'here, in a nutshell, is the main problem of achieving peace in the Middle East: except for Israel, there *are no democracies'*. This theme has been elevated by the G. W. Bush White House which has expressed its commitment to the 'global expansion of democracy' and believes that the heart of peace in the Middle East is a 'viable Palestinian democracy'.[14] This view, however, ignores crucial questions regarding cooperation between liberal and non-liberal states *prior* to the homogenization of political forms. Such questions, however, were of crucial importance to Kant.

A fourth feature of the current literature is that, while Kant advocated a confederation of states in order to establish a secure international environment within which states would be better placed to perfect their civil constitutions, membership of this confederation should be restricted to liberal states. Fukuyama, for instance, claims that 'if one wanted to create a league of nations according to Kant's own precepts ... it would have to be a league of truly free states brought together by their common commitment to liberal principles'.[15] Similarly, Netanyahu asserts that Kant advocated a world federation of democracies 'strong enough to compel the arbitration of disputes', and blames the earlier failure of the League of Nations and United Nations on the inclusion of 'dictators'.[16]

However, as the Democratic Peace discovered Kant it also rewrote him, which is to say it provided a fresh interpretation of his thought and his legacy in the light of the research agenda's own core concerns. Indeed, subjectivity of interpretation is not new: Easley has recently analyzed historical trends in the interpretation of Kant's work from a sociology of knowledge perspective and persuasively shows that they have always been coloured by the wider

---

[13] Russett, *Grasping the Democratic Peace*, p. 32.

[14] Netanyahu, *A Place among the Nations*, p. 248. President G. W. Bush, Whitehall speech, 19 November, 2003, http://www.whitehouse.gov/news/releases/2003/11/20031119-1.html

[15] Fukuyama, *The End of History and the Last Man* (Harmondsworth Penguin, 1992), pp. 282–283.

[16] Netanyahu, *A Place among the Nations*, p. 244.

international political conditions and questions of their time.[17] In fact, even as Kant's dead body laid waiting for the Prussian soil to thaw, his legacy was already being contested.[18] In the case of the Democratic Peace a major source of this subjectivity[19] is revealed through examining the function or role that Kant's work has served. Theorists were principally interested to find a thinker or grand idea that could lend support and add weight to the specific empirical finding that liberal states or democracies tended not to go to war against one another. Note, for example, Russett's comment that 'especially in the Vietnam era of US "imperial overreach" . . . both academic observers and policymakers refused to accept even the statement that democracies are peaceful towards each other as a meaningful empirical generalization without some kind of theoretical explanation indicating that it was not merely a coincidence or accident'.[20]

To stress, the academic reading of Kant offered by the Democratic Peace arose first and foremost as an attempt to explain a particular set of empirical phenomena: the removal of the occasion of wars among liberal states and not wars between liberal and non-liberal states. A corollary of this, however, was that the discussion of Kant stressed the significance of the distinction between liberal and non-liberal states, rather than duties to develop global relations as a whole. While both Doyle and Russett are clearly sympathetic to this latter theme,[21] it remains overshadowed

---

[17] Eric Easley, 'The War Over *Perpetual Peace*', unpublished PhD thesis, London School of Economics and Political Science, University of London, (2002).

[18] Manfred Kuehn, *Kant, A Biography*, (Cambridge: Cambridge University Press, 2001), pp. 1–7.

[19] By the subjectivity of the Democratic Peace is here meant that the predominant – or indeed any other – representation of the Democratic Peace is in part a function not only of the 'raw' or unprocessed political-historical subject matter but also of the epistemological and methodological assumptions and techniques of the construction of the Democratic Peace as a 'social scientific' phenomenon. Accordingly, there are a number of possible, actual and potential forms of democratic peace that could develop. For a fuller discussion of these issues see John MacMillan, 'Beyond the Separate Democratic Peace' *Journal of Peace Research* 40 (2003), 233–243; John MacMillan, 'Liberalism and the Democratic Peace' *Review of International Studies* 30 (2004), 179–200; John MacMillan, 'Whose Democracy; Which Peace? Contextualising the Democratic Peace' *International Politics* 41 (2004), 472–493.

[20] Russett, *Grasping the Democratic Peace*, p. 11.

[21] Doyle, 'Kant, Liberal Legacies, and Foreign Affairs, Part 1', p. 230; and the neglected but stimulating discussion of the proper course for a liberal foreign policy in 'Kant, Liberal Legacies, and Foreign Affairs, Part 2', pp. 343–349. In a short discussion entitled 'Democracy and Peace', in Bruce Russett, Harvey Starr and Richard Stoll (eds.), *Choices in World Politics: Sovereignty and Interdependence* (New York: W. H. Freeman, 1989), pp. 245–260, Russett foregrounds the linkage between peace and justice, though in his main (and later) work on the subject, *Grasping the Democratic Peace*, this theme was not prominent.

in the bulk of their work by the emphasis upon homogenization of domestic political systems. This has led to the neglect of other central elements of Kant's political philosophy which would turn the spotlight of responsibilities and reform upon existing liberal states. In this way, the discourse benefits the strong and disadvantages the weak who might benefit from a richer reading of Kantian notions of global justice.

Kant and the relationship between liberal and non-liberal states

Certainly, Kant posited a link between republics and peace. However, and crucially for Kant, those agents concerned to develop his perpetual peace project ought to focus upon the gradual and pacific evolution of global relations according to principles of right, rather than the homogenization of domestic political forms. To focus upon the replication of a particular domestic political system greatly underestimates the scale of Kant's project, and serves to keep from the political agenda serious questions of global justice which Kant and the liberal tradition have long recognized as central to the establishment of peace.

In this section, I will argue that Kant did not sanction a rigid dichotomization of the world between (peaceful) inter-liberal and (warring) liberal/non-liberal zones. For Kant, the distinction between republic and non-republic was frequently a matter of degree rather than kind. Following from this, and contrary to orthodox interpretations, Kant intended that the confederation of states would include non-republics as well as republics. By way of perspective, I share with Lynch the position that 'Kant's understanding of historical development and change cannot be considered apart from his emphasis on ethical action and moral purpose', and that a focus upon the creation of specific kinds of political structures should be avoided.[22] Of those aspects of Kant's thought that have been neglected, his attitudes towards the attainment of perpetual peace and the consequent guidelines for politics and policy are fundamental.

Kant was sceptical about the prospects for the realization of his scheme of perpetual peace. In any case, he was well aware that, even if it were to eventuate, its realization would be a long and difficult task.[23] For this

[22] Lynch, 'Kant, the Republican Peace', p. 42.
[23] Immanuel Kant, 'Metaphysics of Morals', p. 171, and 'Idea for a Universal History with a Cosmopolitan Purpose', pp. 47–48, both in Reiss (ed.), *Kant: Political Writings*,

very reason, Kant was primarily concerned to theorize for contemporary conditions rather than for some, possibly unattainable, future point. He recognized that international society comprised states that are ethically and politically diverse, and was concerned to prescribe guidelines for behaviour *prior* to the establishment of perpetual peace. Accordingly, the burden of Kant's political philosophy is as a guide to the *process* of the evolution of international society. In this respect, the one course of action Kant urged above all else was to recognize international law and avoid recourse to the instrument of war: 'war is not the way in which anyone should pursue his rights', even when in the state of nature.[24] In this vein, I develop below the importance of Kant's six preliminary articles of perpetual peace as a code for state behaviour, while still in the state of nature, to facilitate the evolutionary development of perpetual peace.[25]

Recalling these fundamental aspects of Kant's writings shows that the current concentration upon securing a world in which the liberal state form is the norm is misplaced. Certainly, there is little question that Kant, like most liberals, would prefer other states also to be liberal: it is the only form of constitutional and institutional framework which would permit individuals to exercise full moral choice, and is a necessary condition of Kant's ultimate vision of perpetual peace.[26] For Kant, however, the significant point is that, prior to the attainment of a world of liberal states, states must act according to principles of right. Foremost is to

---

pp. 131–175 and 41–53 respectively. Although Kant was sceptical, he insisted upon a duty to strive towards 'perpetual peace' in the absence of proof that the objective was impossible. For Kant's scheme, see 'Perpetual Peace', also in Reiss (ed.), *Kant: Political Writings*, pp. 93–130.

[24] Kant, 'Metaphysics of Morals', p. 174.

[25] See also Chris Brown, *International Relations Theory*, pp. 34–35. The six preliminary articles are:

(1) 'No conclusion of peace shall be considered valid as such if it was made with a secret reservation of the material for a future war.'
(2) 'No independently existing state, whether it be large or small, may be acquired by another state by inheritance, exchange, purchase or gift.'
(3) 'Standing armies (*miles perpetuus*) will gradually be abolished altogether.'
(4) 'No national debt shall be contracted in connection with the external affairs of the state.'
(5) 'No state shall forcibly interfere in the constitution and government of another state.'
(6) 'No state at war with another shall permit such acts of hostility as would make mutual confidence impossible during a future time of peace. Such acts would include the employment of *assassins (percussores) or poisoners (venefici), breach of agreements, the instigation of treason (perduellio)* within the enemy state, etc.'

See Kant, 'Perpetual Peace', pp. 93–97.

[26] Kant, 'Metaphysics of Morals', p. 174.

act in accordance with the categorical imperative (that is, that practices should be universalizable and persons regarded as ends in themselves) in order to perfect the improvement of one's civil constitution. Due to the anarchic nature of the international system, Kant was at pains to point out that, for the sake of the full realization of moral principles in all states (including those regarded as actually existing republics), it was important to recognize one's obligations to non-republics and to cooperate with them in order to mitigate the detrimental consequences of a lawless international environment.

Although such obligations are incumbent even in the absence of reciprocity, Kant did urge the surrender of sovereign rights and the establishment of contractual relations, in order to foster the development of mutual confidence. In 'Perpetual Peace', for instance, Kant writes that 'it is impossible to understand what justification I can have for placing any confidence in my rights, unless I can rely on some substitute for the union of civil society, i.e. on a free federation'.[27] This combination of non-reciprocal and contractual obligations results in a dual structure of ethics. On the one hand, they oblige the establishment of contractual relations with others; whilst on the other, they maintain an obligation to act morally (according to the categorical imperative) not only in relations with fellow contractors, but with all states, and in the absence of the condition of reciprocity. It would be in keeping with Kant's philosophy of history to regard non-liberal states not as non-contractors, but rather as potential contractors. The current literature on the separate liberal peace emphasizes only those obligations that arise between liberal states, and is virtually silent on the nature and implications of the obligations liberal states hold towards non-liberal states.[28] Uppermost are the duties not to wage war to advance one's rights (as distinct from seeking redress), not to intervene and not to force commerce upon a state.[29] States, for Kant, whether liberal or non-liberal, are subject to obligations arising from moral-practical reason, whether in or out of the state of nature and whether or not others recognize their own obligations.[30]

---

[27] Kant, 'Perpetual Peace', p. 104. Kant actually means a confederation.

[28] On this topic see Christopher Brewin, 'The Duties of Liberal States' in Cornelia Navari (ed.), *The Condition of States* (Milton Keynes: Open University Press, 1991), pp. 197–215.

[29] For an interesting (and pertinent) argument on the rights of states to restrict their involvement in the world economy, see Immanuel Kant, 'On the Common Saying: "This may be True in Theory, but it does not Apply in Practice"', in Reiss (ed.), *Kant: Political Writings*, p. 80n.

[30] Kant, 'Metaphysics of Morals', pp. 164–75.

This interpretation of Kant's political writings can be defended most forcefully through a reexamination of the three 'definitive articles' and, in turn, the preliminary articles of Kant's model peace treaty. The First Definitive Article states that the civil constitution of every state shall be republican, the second that the right of nations shall be based on a federation of free states and the third that cosmopolitan right shall be limited to conditions of universal hospitality.[31] It is important at the outset to clarify the nature of the relationship of these three articles to one another.

The importance of the three should not be ranked as in order of presentation, or depicted as forming three concentric circles with the domestic constitution being primary, an international confederation secondary and then a tertiary notion of cosmopolitan rights and duties. Rather, they should be regarded as of equal status, designed to enshrine the rule of law in their particular realms of jurisdiction. Kant, in the First Supplement of 'Perpetual Peace', identifies the political, international and cosmopolitan as three distinct 'areas of public right'.[32] In writing of them, he acknowledges their own autonomous dynamics which, taken together, will promote the greater agreement over principles that leads in turn to mutual understanding and peace. This interpretation of the relationship of the three fields, marked by contemporaneous and complementary progression rather than a series of three distinct stages, reflects Kant's awareness of the anarchic nature of the international system as an impediment to domestic constitutional development.

In his discussion of the First Definitive Article, Kant outlines one of the mechanisms which is intended to make republics more pacific than non-republics.[33] In a famous passage Kant writes that because in a republic the consent of those citizens who will bear the costs of war in blood and money is required before war can be declared, such action will not be undertaken lightly. By contrast, in a non-republic the head of state will not have to make the slightest sacrifice and hence 'it is the simplest thing in the world to go to war'.[34] However, in practice there is a long record of liberal states circumventing this direct and immediate link between the political classes and war either through the use of a professional

---

[31] Kant, 'Perpetual Peace', pp. 98–108.   [32] Kant, 'Perpetual Peace', p. 112.
[33] It is unfair to regard this as the only reason why Kant thought republics would be more pacific than non-republics, since the principles of right upon which republics are founded are probably the more important restraining influence upon the use of force. However, there is no guarantee that republics will necessarily act according to these principles – as they frequently demonstrate.
[34] Kant, 'Perpetual Peace', p. 100.

army or conscription policies which privilege those groups closest to the centres of power. Hence, claims that this mechanism in practice differentiates liberal from non-liberal states ought to be treated with caution.[35] While this is not evidence of Doyle misrepresenting Kant, it nevertheless suggests that it may be inappropriate to base claims about a Kantian distinction between liberal and non-liberal states solely on the First Definitive Article.

Kant's Second Definitive Article of a 'Perpetual Peace' will be considered in more detail, since it is crucial for establishing whether there is Kantian authority for a confederation comprised solely of liberal states, or whether membership should extend beyond such an exclusive grouping. The second article proclaims that 'the Right of Nations shall be based on a Federation of *Free* States'.[36] Doyle's paraphrase of this article runs 'liberal republics will progressively establish peace among themselves by means of the "pacific union"'.[37] Thus, he appears to interpret 'free' as synonymous with a republican constitution. As such, Doyle's interpretation of the criterion for membership of Kant's confederation is one in which a liberal domestic constitution is a necessary requirement. Implicit in Doyle's view is the assumption that, since republics are likely to be more pacific than other forms of state, only they are able to qualify for what Kant did, after all, say ought to be a 'pacific [con]federation'.[38] However, it is possible to show that Kant intended membership of this confederation to be open to non-liberal as well as other liberal states on two grounds.

First, Kant used the term 'free' to refer to status rather than form: that is, states that are independent or sovereign rather than of a certain regime type. According to Kant, 'freedom' is but one of three principles upon which a republican constitution is founded: therefore, the terms cannot logically be synonymous.[39] Further, Kant's definition of 'external and rightful *freedom*' as 'a warrant to obey no external laws except those to which I have been able to give my own consent'[40] clearly signifies the meaning of sovereignty. This meaning is fundamental to the broader

---

[35] The liberal response to this claim is likely to be a demand for *more* democratization, see Howard, *War and the Liberal Conscience*, p. 76. For the argument that political practices can be made more responsible and humane if decision makers directly face the consequences of their actions (and hence local, regional and global participatory democracy is to be developed), see Robyn Eckersley, *Environmentalism and Political Theory: Towards an Ecocentric Approach* (London: UCL Press, 1992), pp. 170–176.

[36] Kant, 'Perpetual Peace', p. 102, emphasis added.

[37] Doyle, 'Kant, Liberal Legacies, and Foreign Affairs, Part 1', p. 226.

[38] Kant, 'Perpetual Peace', p. 104.   [39] Ibid., p. 99.   [40] Ibid., p. 99n.

Kantian project of maximizing the opportunity for the autonomous *self-development* of each individual or state in accordance with the rights of all.

Second, Kant's illustration of the type of confederation he had in mind clearly indicates the inclusion of non-liberal states. Kant writes that if

> one powerful and enlightened nation can form a republic . . . this will provide a focal point for federal association among other states. These will join up with the first one, thus securing the freedom of each state in accordance with the idea of international right.[41]

It is significant that Kant does not stipulate that the 'other states' ought necessarily also to be republican, which is in keeping with the view that each realm has to an extent its own development dynamic. Moreover, in illustrating such a confederation in the 'Metaphysics of Morals', Kant explicitly refers to states with diverse forms of government. He makes a favourable reference to an assembly of the States General at the Hague in the first half of the eighteenth century, to which 'the ministers of most European *courts* and even of the smallest republics brought their complaints about any aggression suffered by one of their number at the hands of another', and which *'all* neighbouring states' were free to join.[42] Clearly, this was not sufficient to prevent the use of force between states, but it does illustrate that, contrary to Doyle's interpretation, Kant approved of membership in such a confederation extending beyond states with a liberal domestic political system.[43]

When one takes Kant's understanding of the interactive relationship between the nature of the international system and the form of domestic political system into account, it becomes readily apparent that Kant believed republics had a duty to establish a confederation not only with other republics, but also with non-republics. Kant was acutely aware of how the anarchic nature of the international states system not only jeopardized peace by leaving states in the state of nature in relation to one another, but that the system itself also served to limit domestic social and political development. Kant's seventh proposition in 'Idea for a Universal History' explicitly states that 'the problem of establishing a perfect civil constitution is subordinate to the problem of a law-governed *external relationship* with other states, and cannot be solved unless the latter is

---

[41] Ibid., p. 104.   [42] Kant, 'Metaphysics of Morals', p. 171, emphasis added.
[43] Cavallar has recently lent support to this revised interpretation. See Georg Cavallar, *Kant and the Theory and Practice of International Right* (Cardiff: University of Wales Press, 1999) p. 115.

also solved'.[44] Indeed, Kant does in fact sanction an authoritarian constitution as appropriate for a state such as Prussia in order to 'preserve its own existence between powerful neighbours'.[45] That states themselves can operate as agents for the modification of the international system is illustrated by his hope cited above that an enlightened republic would establish a security community.

Thus, not only does Kant recognize that states have obligations to subject their external relations to the rule of law, regardless of their form of civil constitution, but he also acknowledges that a fully developed republican constitution is unattainable outside such a framework. Consequently, it would be not merely immoral, but self-defeating to restrict the membership of a confederation to republican states. It is a point worth emphasizing that, for Kant, given anarchy, no civic constitution can be perfect, and the quality of existing constitutions can be considered as a matter of degree. With reference to the 'separate peace' approach, this aspect of Kant's analysis of international relations renders absurd the notion that 'peace' can wait until the world comprises liberal states. It is only through a delicate process of, on the one hand, mitigating the circumstances of international anarchy and, on the other, constitutional development, that peace *and* republics (in the full Kantian sense) will emerge.

Of course, Kant was also interested in the agencies of political development. While it is true that Kant did identify the long-term mechanism of 'asocial sociability', he also held out hope that states were capable of self-conscious reform and insisted they had a duty to do so. He argues that, even if autocracy and aristocracy, the two constitutional alternatives to democracy, 'are always defective in as much as they leave room for a despotic form of government, it is at least possible that they will be associated with a form of government which accords with the *spirit* of a representative system'.[46] Thus, although it is correct that Kant 'never tires of denouncing the bellicosity of despots',[47] he did not consider all non-republics to be equally despotic. He argues that 'the smaller the number of ruling persons in a state and the greater their powers of representation, the more the constitution will approximate

---

[44] Kant, 'Idea for a Universal History', p. 47. See also Kant, 'Theory and Practice', in Reiss (ed.), *Kant: Political Writings*, p. 92.
[45] Quoted in Georg Cavallar, *Kant and the Theory and Practice of International Right*, p. 5. (Taken from 'The Contest of the Faculties', in *Kant: Political Writings*, pp. 182–183).
[46] Kant, 'Perpetual Peace', p. 101.
[47] Andrew Hurrell, 'Kant and the Kantian Paradigm in International Relations' *Review of International Studies* 16 (1990), p. 195.

to its republican potentiality, which it may hope to realise eventually by gradual reforms'.[48] Support for the process of gradual reform was developed elsewhere, for in the 'Metaphysics of Morals', he writes that 'it is the only means of continually approaching the supreme political good, perpetual peace'.[49]

Two substantive points reinforce these last two paragraphs. First, while Kant does regard republican constitutional forms as being the type best suited to the avoidance of war, he also recognizes that not all non-republics are bellicose, and that anarchy impedes the constitutional development of all states. Hence, both liberal and non-liberal states are faced with a common plight in the transcendence of anarchy. While there undoubtedly are regimes whose leaders deliberately seek personal aggrandizement and military conquest, the majority are more likely to be concerned with the very difficult, yet conventional, political task of providing for the security and welfare of the populace with limited resources and in difficult conditions. Such states, liberal or otherwise, are, in Barry Buzan's terms, engaged primarily in the struggle for 'security' rather than the struggle for 'power'.[50] For Kant, it would be important for the promotion of security *and* the development of liberalism that such states are offered shelter under a liberal security umbrella.

Second, on the question of intervention, despite his belief that republics are more pacific than non-republics, Kant did not believe that regime type was a criterion for the legitimacy of intervention. First, Kant is, in general, a strong non-interventionist, as is evident in the Fifth Preliminary Article of 'Perpetual Peace'.[51] However, there is an apparent exception to this in the 'Metaphysics of Morals', where Kant writes that an 'unjust enemy' can 'be made to accept a new constitution of a nature that is unlikely to encourage their warlike inclinations'.[52] For Kant, though, an 'unjust enemy' is defined as 'someone whose publicly expressed will [in the field of international right], whether expressed in word or in deed, displays a maxim which would make peace among nations impossible and would lead to a perpetual state of nature if it

[48] Kant, 'Perpetual Peace', p. 101.   [49] Kant, 'Metaphysics of Morals', p. 175.
[50] Barry Buzan, *People, States and Fear: The National Security Problem in International Relations* (Brighton: Harvester Press, 1983), pp. 157, 173–213.
[51] 'No state shall forcibly interfere in the constitution and government of another state', Kant, 'Perpetual Peace', p. 96. The legitimacy of humanitarian intervention is not, to my knowledge, an issue that Kant addressed directly and is beyond the reach of this discussion.
[52] Kant, 'Metaphysics of Morals', p. 170.

were made into a general rule'.[53] Hence, such an enemy is defined not by regime type, but by behaviour. As such, Kant's notion of intervention holds similarities to the theory of collective security which penalizes aggression, not regime. Kant's conception of international right, then, was one in which *all* states, not merely liberal states, were under a duty to confederate. This did not legitimate interference in domestic affairs, but did bind states to observe certain common rules in their relations with one another. Kant did not, however, consider this anything but a compromise. In order to manage the tension between the need to coexist with non-republics whilst maintaining the belief that the republican constitution 'is the only perfectly lawful kind',[54] he introduces (but does not use consistently) the distinction between a *legal* and a *lawful* constitution.[55] The distinction is not a comfortable one, but is consistent with the notion that true law can be founded only on right, though we must respect the current system of legal regulation as the best we have for the time being.[56] 'For any *legal* constitution', he writes, 'even if it is only in small measure *lawful*, is better than none at all, and the fate of a premature reform would be anarchy.'[57] Kant, then, was acutely sensitive to the fragility of order in political life. He strongly supported the need to respect existing levels of order as representing a better basis for moral and constitutional development than the chaos that would result from their overthrow.

There are, then, certain tensions within Kant's work deriving from the obligation to act according to the categorical imperative in relations with all; to respect the existence of legal arrangements, even if they do not wholly embody principles of *Recht* ('right'); and the longer-term project of working towards the submission of the rights of persons and states to *Recht*. Although Kant holds a well-defined notion of the good, it is imperative to respect the notion of right; and thus not to attempt to gain the desired ends by unethical means.[58]

Kant was concerned with international relations as an historical, evolutionary *process*. Moving from a lawless condition in the three areas of public right, civil, international and cosmopolitan, Kant did indeed see a gradual evolution in all three spheres marked by an increasing

---

[53] Ibid.   [54] Kant, 'Perpetual Peace', p. 101.   [55] Ibid., p. 118.

[56] For a brief discussion of this aspect of Kant's attitude towards the current system of international law, see Hurrell, 'Kant and the Kantian Paradigm', pp. 187–189.

[57] Kant, 'Perpetual Peace', p. 118n. In the same endnote, Kant also writes that the creation of a lawful constitution based on the principles of freedom is the only one which will last.

[58] This point is particularly pronounced throughout the 'Metaphysics of Morals'.

convergence of principles. Ultimately, if the reign of perpetual peace according to Kantian principles were to commence, then the republican civil constitution would indeed be a necessary (though not sufficient) condition. However, in that Kant was concerned with the processes through which the international system would develop, he emphasized the importance of maintaining peace in order to facilitate this development. In this pursuit, Kant recognized that existing republics were as yet ethically incomplete, and that at least some non-republics were, alongside the deterministic process of asocial sociability, reforming themselves to become republics. In contrast to the 'separate peace' approach, the above reading of Kant stresses his awareness of the moral and political interdependence of liberal and non-liberal states, and his insistence that the strong recognize their obligations and do not abuse their power in relations with the weak.

Sovereignty, the evolution of the international system and the importance of the preliminary articles

Some recent discussion of Kant's work has highlighted the tension that exists between his deference to state sovereignty and his promise of the possibility of international reform. The first of two major arguments is that globalization is rendering the state ineffective as a political authority and hence greater supranational organization is required if one is to achieve the desired levels of representation, regulation and accountability of global forces. The second is that the intrinsic contradictions of the sovereign-state system mean that permanent peace is unattainable in the absence of systemic reform.[59]

However, whilst Franceschet, for example, rightly notes that 'there cannot for Kant be an independent, representative body over and above the contingent will of the sovereigns',[60] the possibility that peoples and states might nevertheless consent to the dispersion of authority in certain areas remains. This does, however, put significantly greater weight on moral and attitudinal developments within states in accordance with Linklater's point that for Kant 'the deeper issue was to enlarge the

---

[59] See Antonio Franceschet, 'Popular Sovereignty or Cosmopolitan Democracy? Liberalism, Kant and International Reform', *European Journal of International Relations* 6 (2000), 277–302; R. B. J. Walker, *Inside/Outside: International Relations as Political Theory* (Cambridge: Cambridge University Press, 1993).
[60] Antonio Franceschet, 'Popular Sovereignty or Cosmopolitan Democracy?', p. 294

moral, as opposed to the political, boundaries of community, so that stronger cosmopolitan sentiments would cancel the tendency of states to act as self-regarding autonomous units'.[61] Whilst this presents many challenges, the weight of the point is only greater if one considers the alternative: some form of supra-state integration *against* the will of the citizenries. That such moral development is, at best, slow is however not only a function of the power of nationalist and patriotic ideologies but also the lack of a clearly articulated and persuasive political vision and moral justification of an alternative global politics.[62]

The willingness of states to develop their moral horizons in a more internationalist and cosmopolitan direction is, then, essential for international political reform. Yet the difficulty of such development remains. Kant himself envisaged two tracks of systemic evolution: that of deliberate political reform and the 'natural' or 'teleological' track. For Kant, the teleological dimension could be taken literally as his faith in reason as an objective, autonomous force enabled him to maintain confidence in the belief that, eventually and after many false starts, humanity would converge upon the principles that he articulated along with their legal–institutional expression as presented in the definitive articles of 'Perpetual Peace' and elsewhere. However, it is this very faith in the autonomous or objective existence of reason – let alone the notion of nature's divine plan – that has been challenged by contemporary social theory and the expansion of international society. As Linklater notes, Kant's 'belief in immutable and universal laws of reason clashes with modern sensibilities which emphasise the social construction of knowledge and the diverse, and changing, cultural conceptions of moral truth'.[63]

However, a modified – if necessarily reduced – working interpretation of this track requires only that actors exercise rational choice in

---

[61] Andrew Linklater, *The Transformation of Political Community* (Cambridge: Polity Press, 1998) pp. 36–37.

[62] See, however, Larry Siedentop, *Democracy in Europe* (London: Penguin, 2001) for an effort to present such an argument for the European context. The Cosmopolitan Democracy project has been at the forefront of putting the case for, in effect, a global multi-layered social democratic world order (see for example David Held, *Democracy and the Global Order* (Stanford: Stanford University Press, 1995). This promising research agenda will become more persuasive when it develops the empirical bases of its argument by showing through a series of case studies how, in practice, the distanciation of social relations negatively influences the possibilities for local democracy and self-determination. It is worth remembering, however, that moral claims for superseding the nation state remain contested within contemporary political theory and that powerful arguments for its defence remain; see for example, David Miller, *On Nationality* (Oxford: Clarendon Press, 1995).

[63] Linklater, *The Transformation of Political Community*, p. 38.

specific contexts that may be developed or weighted to increase the gains and lower the costs of greater international cooperation. Accordingly, whilst this may or may not contribute to greater integration, confederation or even federation, and whilst there is the possibility of unforeseen negative consequences of cooperation, it stands to change the significance of the sovereignty question through modifying the character of inter-state relations such as to increase the prevalence of positive-sum interactions. This line of argument has its roots in the conventional liberal pursuit of internationalism over the narrow pursuit of self-interest or *realpolitik*. Options include but are not restricted to choices between a rules-based international order against one directly determined by relative power capabilities; (just) trade against autarchy; the structure of costs and benefits associated with the use of force; and the wider normative and political attraction or repulsion generated by the character of contemporary liberal regimes and the liberal internationalist project. This structural track, whilst not 'natural' or strictly teleological, does represent the possibility of a normative and institutional evolutionary environment within which increasingly ambitious reform could be undertaken.

It is, then, the interaction between the structural and reformist tracks that presents probably the best hope for the Kantian development of the international political system and for overcoming the reluctance of sovereigns to reform. That this removes any vestiges of faith in a genuinely 'natural' evolution to a liberal international political system, let alone eternal peace, not only renews the challenge to human agency but also raises questions of how one decides upon the processes and principles of such evolution and of who is to be included in this process. The globalist possibilities that this presents is in keeping with the earlier point that Kant recognized the fates of liberal and non-liberal political communities to be intertwined. From this premise, the default position of the Democratic Peace that in relations between liberal and non-liberal states one might rely on prudence or deterrence (therein based on the presumption of ongoing violence) falls well short of what Kant himself envisaged and omits a major and neglected part of his schema.

The problem is not primarily the neglect of the other definitive articles – which *have* attracted greater attention in more recent work[64] – but neglect of the preliminary articles. The function of the definitive

---

[64] See for example Bruce Russett and John Oneal, *Triangulating Peace: Democracy, Interdependence, and International Organizations* (New York: Norton, 2001).

articles was to institutionalize the conditions for the final abolition of war and entrench the development of peace between states. This was to be grounded in law and required, *ultimately*, a high level of solidarism in the international system, if not necessarily the universal adoption of liberal political systems.[65] The preliminary articles, however, have a different emphasis, which is to create the conditions and establish the practices (or culture) of international relations in which states feel sufficiently secure to proceed with confidence not only towards the requirements of the definitive articles but also to the greater objective of establishing the state of peace itself. Cavallar writes that the preliminary articles are 'norms for a semi-juridical condition, after the state of nature has been left, but a juridical condition has not yet been (fully) achieved'.[66]

What radically distinguished the preliminary articles from the maxims developed by the 'sorry comforters' – Grotius, Pufendorf, Vattel – was that they were designed not as a '*justification* for military aggression',[67] but to foster the institutions and culture of peace. Some were to be instituted immediately, others could be deferred, but their character as practical measures pertinent to the actual conditions of eighteenth-century Europe strongly suggests that their exact content may be revised in accordance with the changed historical conditions of the early twenty-first century. Their spirit, however, is akin to the contemporary notion of 'positive peace' and rests on the assumption that aiming only for the absence of war – through for example prudence or deterrence – is likely to fall well short of the mark as peace is something that needs to be actively and deliberately built. At the heart of Kant's preliminary articles, then, one finds such themes as the development of international norms, trust-building measures and the reform of the institutional capacity of the state for militarism, all of which remain highly salient in today's pluralist international society.

Earlier in this discussion the point was made that readings of Kant's work are marked by subjectivity, which in turn implies that interpretations require justification beyond any claims of 'better' textual analysis.

---

[65] Rawls makes clear that liberals need not require other peoples to develop along liberal lines and that there are non-liberal political forms ('decent hierarchical peoples') that liberals do not have the right to try and 'convert' and are obliged to tolerate in the positive sense of being 'equal participating members in good standing of the Society of Peoples'. See John Rawls, *The Law of Peoples* (Cambridge MA: Harvard University Press, 1999) pp. 94, 59.

[66] Cavallar, *Kant and the Theory and Practice of International Right*, p. 53.

[67] 'Perpetual Peace', p. 103.

Whilst the persuasiveness of the reading offered here rests largely on specific textual interpretation of what Kant might have himself meant, it also recognizes the need for justification through an engagement with such contemporary theoretical debates as the standing of liberal claims to universal moral and political truth, the extent and bases of liberal duties and the rightful bases of procedural order and participation in international relations. These issues are central to contemporary liberal normative theory as found in strands of Rawlsian and Habermasian enquiry and politically in the Cosmopolitan Democracy project. Whilst the interpretation offered here may not satisfy all the exponents of these projects I would contend that it embodies and connects with many of their concerns in a way that the orthodox Democratic Peace reading of Kant's work does not. Ethically, a shift towards an updated version of the preliminary articles concerned with the development of a more mature and rule-governed anarchy goes some way to avoid the neo-imperialist connotations of assuming the right to specify the proper constitutional form for others to follow and to open up greater political space for a wider, global dialogue about the normative and institutional require-ments of peace.

In this interpretation, attention to the preliminary articles rebalances the unsatisfactory position of the Democratic Peace on liberal/non-liberal state relations. Neither freedom nor peace can be attained through isolating the democratic realm from wider international society or by neglecting the pressure the international political environment exerts upon domestic constitutional and political development. Thus whilst the absence of war between democracies is the central plank of the Democratic Peace, this is only one aspect of a true, Kantian democratic peace. Pinning hopes on the expansion of democratic regimes, with-out greater effort to tackle the deeper causes of insecurity and to build a culture of peace in international relations, is unlikely to realize this greater vision. Indeed, it is the focus upon the definitive articles and the neglect of the preliminaries that has enabled the Democratic Peace to reproduce the sense of separateness and division between the demo-cratic and non-democratic realms. In neglecting this preliminary stage of Kant's peace project the Democratic Peace risks sanctioning the main-tenance of an unsustainable 'fortress of peace' among a relatively small group of existing liberal democracies, offering its citizenries a peace that is underdeveloped and insecure due to having been severed from a truly global conception of justice.

Finally, if one were developing the preliminary articles for the present day it is worth reflecting on the appropriate scale of ambition and risk given certain long-term historical changes. Kant wrote at the outset of the liberal era in a system characterized by the institutions and culture of the *ancien regime* and in which inter-state war was a common occurrence. There were, at most, two or three states that could plausibly be characterized as 'republics' and these possessed very limited power and influence in the international system at large. Contrast this with the present situation in which liberal democracies are more numerous, powerful and influential than ever before and include the world's only global superpower. Moreover, the international environment too has evolved from a particular 'state of nature' characteristic of the eighteenth century to one in which major areas of international relations, including to some extent the use of force, are governed by a considerable body of law and norms. Given such development, one might reasonably expect liberal states to muster the moral and political resources for a more generous and ambitious, yet at the same time reflective, internationalism, in keeping with contemporary understandings about both the social and political causes of insecurity and underdevelopment in the global system and normative positions on the importance of inclusivity. That such higher expectations are patently not part of regular political discourse, and that the liberal internationalist legacy is itself deeply threatened by the rise of political conservatism and fundamentalism, is telling of the thinness of the Kantian legacy in contemporary international relations, no matter how often his authority is invoked as the underwriter of Democratic Peace.

A starting point from which to respond to this thinness is contained in the Secret Article of 'Perpetual Peace' in which Kant states that 'the maxims of the philosophers on the conditions under which public peace is possible shall be consulted by states which are armed for war'. Implicit in this is a challenge to scholars and intellectuals to actively engage with the causes of violence and the bases of peace in global politics and the ensuing implications for foreign policy. To this end, the chapter closes by taking note of Kant's own relationship to his wider political environment. Besides being a 'classic thinker', Kant was also an intellectual dissident, a so-called 'renegade professor', who at the age of seventy was 'threatened by the King with unpleasant measures for [his] continued obstinacy', possibly including banishment, after having knowingly provoked the Prussian censor.[68]

---

[68] Kuehn, *Kant*, pp. 378–383.

Conclusion

The above discussion highlights the subjectivity of readings of Kant's work in general and that by the Democratic Peace in particular. The analysis suggests that the emphasis upon the homogenization of domestic political systems in the literature upon liberal states and peace has misrepresented the burden of Kant's political philosophy and that the political agenda that has been developed from such an interpretation carries hegemonic implications. This manifests itself through rationalizing and privileging the leadership and separateness of that small group of powerful and developed states from where the discourse has emerged.

The revised interpretation of Kant's thought on the implications of the relationship between liberalism (or democracy) and peace offered here has sought to resituate Kant's support for republics in a broader moral and political context. This is rooted in the assumption that the fate of liberal and non-liberal states is intertwined and that both share the common predicament of how to develop their security from the condition of anarchy. The discussion highlights, among other things, Kant's view that the powerful members of the international system have wider obligations than those acknowledged in the 'separate peace' literature, particularly with regard to the general bases and development of common security measures in the present pluralist international system. In so doing, the emphasis upon the need to rediscover the importance of the preliminary articles of 'Perpetual Peace' seeks to bridge the unnecessary and most likely counter-productive divide between the Democratic Peace and the contiguous research agendas of human security and normative international theory. Finally, the piece notes the importance of active and critical scholarly engagement with contemporary politics and notes that Kant himself was prepared to take risks in this regard.

4 'One powerful and enlightened nation': Kant and the quest for a global rule of law

Antonio Franceschet

'[T]he possession of power inevitably corrupts the free use of reason.'
– Kant[1]

In recent years 'classical' international law as a body of rules, norms and conventions has been assailed by scholars and questioned by world leaders. In particular, the rules concerning sovereign equality and effective power (or control over territory) as the most salient criteria for membership in international society have been challenged. Such rules are problematic because they are supposed to be applied neutrally with regard to regime types, thus ignoring the significant differences between liberal democratic and non-liberal/authoritarian regimes. Classical international law (or right) is indifferent to internal political institutions and thus countenances governments that wield power in a lawless (or rights abusing) fashion. For generations of liberal philosophers and lawyers, this formulation of international law is problematic and contradictory. From Immanuel Kant to the present, critics of classical international law have put forward versions of the following argument: There can be no truly effective global rule of law *among* states if international law permanently acquiesces to the absence of the rule of law *within* states.

This chapter examines the use of Kant's international legal arguments by contemporary scholars. Kant provides genuine inspiration for a critique of classical international law. He is a harsh detractor of traditional international norms and practices among states that simply authorize the illegitimate use of political power. However, I

---

[1] Immanuel Kant, 'Perpetual Peace: A Philosophical Sketch', in *Kant: Political Writings*, ed. Hans Reiss (Cambridge: Cambridge University Press, [1795] 1991), p. 115. Hereafter referred to as PP.

contend that contemporary scholars put forward a view of legal relationships among states that Kant was careful to avoid. Today's self-styled Kantians argue that it is the differences between liberal and non-liberal states that ultimately authorize some states to decide the need for, and to prosecute wars against, non-liberal others. By contrast, Kant worried that *all* states, liberal or otherwise, could continually threaten and limit chances of perpetual peace by exercising unilateral judgments through force.[2]

For Kant, the constant danger is that unilateral, private judgments corrupt and undermine the exercise of political power. This problem is more pronounced for Kant in international politics, which has no effective sovereign to ground the legalism of a political community's general will. In international politics unilateral judgments backed by force are inevitable but not impossible to imagine overcoming, Kant hopes. To the extent that they recur it is to the continued detriment of the realization of an effective and lasting global rule of law. For today's liberal Kantians, however, this danger is not emphasized. Instead, the contemporary concern is with the legal status of liberal and non-liberal states in international society. Fernando Tesón and Anne-Marie Slaughter are two high profile legal scholars who employ Kant to challenge the notion of sovereign equality and universal membership in international society; they particularly reject the notion that liberal and non-liberal states can be bound equally by common legal restraints. However, Tesón and Slaughter each exaggerate the legal supremacy of liberal states in Kant's thought. In contrast to these authors, I argue that for Kant it is not being *a* liberal state that guarantees good political judgment; it is instead being *in* a liberal, law-governed state that is the best guarantee of legalism. In other words, it is the rules or framework of politics rather than the actors (and their virtues) that matter most.

Without a world republic, Kant claimed, there could not be an *enforced* rule of law as it exists within states. Thus his proposed *voluntary* federal union among states (both liberal and non-liberal) is for him a semi-juridical regime aimed at only a negative goal – stopping war. Kant expresses hope that good fortune will enable 'one powerful and enlightened nation' to initiate the first steps to federal union.[3] But he does not believe such a state (or group of enlightened states) have special prerogatives or duties to enforce a global rule of law onto a recalcitrant political

---

[2] See Patrick Capps, 'The Kantian Project in Modern International Legal Theory' *European Journal of International Law* 12, 5 (2001), 1003–1025.
[3] PP, p. 104.

world. Kant's international legal thought is therefore not a doctrine for intervention and preemptive wars, humanitarian or self-defensive.[4] To the extent that Kant allows some latitude for these actions – and he arguably does – it is not because he thinks they will directly bring about true global legalism.[5] He rather indicates that they are yet further and sorry exercises of private judgment in the state of nature, inevitable with the sovereignty that states continually claim.

Kant suggests that perhaps nature can employ such failings and incite *all* states to relinquish their lawless freedom or sovereignty.[6] But the positive actions of the 'one powerful and enlightened republic' are decidedly limited. In contrast to today's 'coercive Kantians', Kant himself is attentive to the risk that political moralism corrupts the judgments of any state, particularly the powerful ones. Additionally, he expressed concern about the existence of self-selected law enforcers using the ideals of global legalism and international right to expediently advance their own power. With such possibilities, he argued that precipitous attempts to go beyond a provisional and pacifistic legalism among all states – both inside and outside his federation – could frustrate and undermine its ultimate end of justice.

This chapter is in two parts. The First part outlines Kant's critique of classical international law and compares it with the arguments that contemporary liberal legalists put forward against today's status quo, particularly the universality and inclusiveness of the United Nations (UN) Charter's legal paradigm. The Second part analyzes the way Kant is employed today by scholars arguing in favour of: strong distinctions between liberal and non-liberal regimes; limited membership in fundamental international legal arrangements; and, most controversially, to authorize coercion. The central argument I put forward is that Kant's international legal legacy does not lend easy support to the simple identification of liberal states' moral concerns with rightful authorization to coerce others into compliance.

---

[4] For an interpretation of Kant's thought as supportive of anticipatory wars (much like the 'Bush Doctrine' found in *The National Security Strategy of the United States of America* of 2002), see Roger Scruton, 'Immanuel Kant and the Iraq War', 19 February 2004, www.opendemocracy.com (accessed June 16, 2004). See also Susan Meld Shell, 'Kant on Just War and "Unjust Enemies": Reflections on a "Pleonism"' *Kantian Review* 10 (2005), 82–111.

[5] See Georg Cavallar, *Kant and the Theory and Practice of International Right* (Cardiff: University of Wales Press, 1999), Chapters 5, 7.

[6] PP, pp. 105, 108–114.

'Sorry comfort': taking aim at classical international law

Kant writes the classic critique of international law. Classical international law is by no means a clear, uncontested entity. It is a construct
used by various waves of liberals, including, retrospectively, Kant, dissatisfied with the immoral and unjust nature and consequences of extant
legal rules among states. Such law is deficient in the light of the superior
standards of the rule of law that putatively prevail *inside* the sovereign
state. For Kant, as discussed below, this is the ideal of the 'original
contract'.

Classical international law is a moving target. This is particularly
the case because many of the reforms and changes advocated by liberals, including Kant, over the centuries have eventually been adopted
in extant practice. In Kant's time, classical international law included
the right of sovereign states to go to war to vindicate their rights.
Today, however, long after the Hague Conventions, the UN Charter
and Nuremberg judgments – all legal steps towards formally outlaw-
ing and criminalizing international aggression – liberals have adopted
a so-called Kantian critique of classical international law. Reexamining
Kant's critique is therefore a useful exercise.

In 'Perpetual Peace' Kant reproaches Grotius, Vattel and Pufendorf
as 'sorry comforters' with misplaced admiration for the law of nations:
'their philosophically and diplomatically formulated codes do not and
cannot have the slightest *legal* force, since states as such are not subject to
a common external constraint'.[7] The classical legal rules among states,
particularly the right to go to war (*jus ad bellum*), are not the mark of
true legality but are only one-sided maxims that engender what Kant
calls 'unrestricted relations'.[8] Kant's critique here has an *a priori* basis.
No action in a structural context of 'unrestricted relations' can be just or
lawful, strictly speaking. It does not matter whether an individual state
has good intentions or not in this context, its actions (its very independent existence) are unjust. It does not matter whether the consequences
of a state's actions are harmless or not, they are unjust for the same
reason. Thus Kant argues that the right to go to war is contradictory.
States can only execute such a 'legally' sanctioned action like war on the
pain of self-contradiction. All other states claim the same right, making it logically impossible to execute the 'right to war' as a universal

[7] Ibid., p, 103.   [8] Ibid.

rule. Rather than civilizing and restraining international conduct, classical international law is sorry comfort *en route* to the 'vast graveyard' of perpetual war.[9]

Contemporary liberal international lawyers draw inspiration from this devastating critique, but they do so from a different historic vantage point. The catastrophic world-historical wars of the early-twentieth century brought states to accept greater legal limits on force and to embrace, at least as aspiration, a collective security pact in the UN Charter. As Gerry Simpson notes, this limited challenge and reform to classical international legality satisfied only one strand of liberal thinkers, those he terms pluralists.[10] This is because the Charter essentially outlaws aggressive wars and authorizes legal sanctions against violators while at the same time preserving sovereign equality and the right of states to maintain their own form of government.

However, the other strand of liberal legalism exemplified by scholars like Tesón and Slaughter has always been unsatisfied with the compromises the Charter makes. The Charter ends up providing 'sorry comfort' of a different type: as a grand bargain among states in 1945, particularly between the ideological adversaries in Moscow and Washington, it acquiesces to classical international law's indifference to *internal* governance or regime type. Although collective security, human rights (and within that context, democratic governance) were inserted into international law through the UN, they were put in a subordinate position to sovereign equality. The Charter is thus viewed as yet another instance of sorry comfort – codes without the slightest legal force.

Tesón states his contemporary 'sorry comfort' accusation as follows: 'An international legal system that *authorizes* individuals to exercise despotic political power (as classical international law does) is morally deficient in a fundamental way.'[11] In his view, the international legal order entrenched in the Charter must be reformed by, among other things, disenfranchising illiberal states from the international community by revoking their sovereignty.[12] Only liberal democracies should be included together in a peace league because only they are genuinely and institutionally committed to the rule of law *both* inside and outside their territorial boundaries.

[9] Ibid., p. 105.
[10] Gerry Simpson, 'Two Liberalisms' *European Journal of International Law* 12, 3 (2001), 537–571.
[11] Fernando Tesón, *A Philosophy of International Law* (Boulder, CO: Westview Press, 1998), p. 15.
[12] Ibid., p. 25.

Slaughter criticizes classical international law's uncritical and dog-matic acceptance of sovereign states as presumptively equal subjects. Under the Charter's rules, it does not seem to matter whether a state is formed through Machiavellian force and fraud or by a legitimate social contract. Slaughter sees the UN Charter era's legal order as less and less relevant (and thus, implicitly as a 'sorry comfort') in the light of the very different way that liberal states actually behave *vis-à-vis* non-liberal states.[13] She also sees sovereign equality and non-interventionism in the Charter paradigm as outmoded in the light of the recent threats posed by unjust, non-liberal states with regard to weapons of mass destruc-tion, terrorism and widespread human rights abuses.[14] The Charter does not provide for meaningful legality because it obfuscates the juridically superior and separate relationships that liberal states enjoy to them-selves, and the juridically inferior relationships between liberal and non-liberal states.[15]

Tesón and Slaughter are by no means alone in making contemporary versions of Kant's 'sorry comfort' critique of classical international law. Thomas Franck and Michael Reisman are other significant critics of the Charter's legal order.[16] For these authors, an international legal order that accommodates as a matter of principle non-liberal governments that violate human rights and resist democracy cannot provide justice. Tesón and Slaughter are significant because, more than any others, they have drawn from Kant's legacy not just to formulate a critique of international law, but also to ground prescriptions for how best to reconstruct and reform the global legal order.

Kant and the global rule of law

The basic premise of Kant's critique of classical international law is rather simple: might (power) cannot alone determine legitimately what is right (lawful). How does one conceive or build a legitimate global

---

[13] Anne-Marie Burley [now Slaughter], 'Law Among Liberal States: Liberal Internation-alism and the Act of State Doctrine' *Columbia Law Review* 92, 8 (1992), 1907–1996.
[14] Lee Feinstein and Anne-Marie Slaughter, 'A Duty to Prevent' *Foreign Affairs* 83, 1 (2004), 136.
[15] Slaughter, 'Law Among Liberal States', p. 1909.
[16] See Thomas M. Franck, 'Legitimacy and Democratic Entitlement', in Gregory H. Fox and Brad R. Roth (eds.), *Democratic Governance and International Law* (Cambridge: Cam-bridge University Press, 2000), pp. 25–47, and W. Michael Reisman, 'Sovereignty and Human Rights in Contemporary International Law', in *Democratic Governance and Inter-national Law*, pp. 239–258.

legalism, then? In this section I outline the way today's liberal legalists appropriate Kant's thought selectively to support plans for reforming today's international legal system. Interestingly, Kant is invoked for the following purposes:

- to make strong distinctions in international law between liberal and non-liberal regimes;
- to limit membership in any pacific federation to liberal states;
- to authorizing or empowering liberal states to use force and intervention to create a more advanced global legal order.

Tesón and to a lesser degree Slaughter misconstrue Kant's thought in ways that overlook the subtlety of his critique of international law, his warnings about power and judgment, and the potential for powerful states to abuse the aspiration of legalism through political moralism.

Distinguishing liberal and non-liberal regimes?

From the early 1980s political scientists such as Michael W. Doyle used Kant to argue that liberal states behave fundamentally differently from others in their foreign policies.[17] They do not engage in war with each other, only with non-liberal regimes. Tesón and Slaughter each endorse the so-called Democratic Peace thesis and argue that it has important implications for international legal order.[18] Just as regime type matters in explaining patterns of foreign policy (*contra* Realism) it also matters for patterns of international legal relations.

Tesón concedes that he puts forward a 'reconstruction' of Kant's position and thereby jettisons the robust commitments to sovereignty and non-interventionism found in Kant's political writings. These are not the essential core of Kant's legacy, Tesón claims, and can be set aside.[19] It is individual rights that are the essential ends of Kant's political thought; all political institutions, domestic and international, are but instruments justified by how well they serve to guarantee rights. 'Normative individualism' is the label Tesón ascribes to this Kantian doctrine and he holds that Kant was the first to argue that international law ought to

---

[17] Michael W. Doyle, 'Kant, Liberal Legacies and Foreign Affairs' (Parts 1 and 2), *Philosophy and Public Affairs* 12 (1983), 205–235 and 323–353.
[18] Tesón, *International Law*, p. 11; Anne-Marie Slaughter, 'Towards an Age of Liberal Nations' *Harvard International Law Journal* 33, 2 (1992), 395 and Slaughter, 'Law Among Liberal States', p. 1909.
[19] Tesón, *International Law*, pp. 2, 19–20.

be ultimately premised on the individual's rights rather than the state's sovereignty.[20] The First Definitive Article of 'Perpetual Peace', 'The civil constitution of every state shall be republican', is cited by Tesón as evidence of the individual's ethical priority in international law. He adds that Kant 'revealed, for the first time, the connection between freedom and the foundations of international law, thus foreseeing the human rights revolution of the twentieth century'.[21]

Slaughter distances herself somewhat from Tesón, and suggests that Kantian liberal internationalism is not captured by 'the alluring simplicity of formulas designed simply to privilege the individual against the state'.[22] But she shares with Tesón the view that the differences between liberal states with constitutional provisions safeguarding individual rights and those without are salient and relevant in international law. And she holds Kant out as the classical exponent of the view that international law need not be based solely on states *qua* states, but on the *superiority of liberal states* with constitutional and institutional restraints on the use of political and military power.[23]

There is a good case to be made in favour of the superiority of liberal regimes based on Kant's thought. But it should not be exaggerated. If liberal regimes are equivalent to those Kant calls republican, that is, they have a division of powers among executive, legislative and judicial authorities, and legislate in the light of the general will or consent of citizens – they are then superior regimes according to Kant's political philosophy. For one thing, these regimes are less likely to engage in war as a means to vindicate rights for a number of reasons (Kant mentions in particular that leaders are restrained and that citizens are prudent and risk averse).[24] However, unlike today's liberals, Kant refrained from easy assumptions that existing states will have already achieved juridical perfection even if they have more or less republican constitutions. Rather than point to the intrinsic virtues of actually existing 'enlightened' republics, Kant argues that the relevant standard for judging is something he calls 'the original contract'.[25] As Tesón and Slaughter are correct to note, Kant believed that an *external* standard based on rights, popular sovereignty and constitutionalism is a legitimate means of judging sovereign states in international law. However, Kant holds

---

[20] Ibid., p. 1, Chapter 2.   [21] Ibid., p. 2.
[22] Slaughter, 'Towards an Age of Liberal Nations', p. 405.
[23] Ibid., p. 395.   [24] PP, p. 100.
[25] Immanuel Kant, *The Metaphysics of Morals*, trans. Mary J. Gregor (Cambridge: Cambridge University Press, 1996), pp. 92–3.

that the 'original contract' is a transcendental ideal that is not just external to non-liberal states: it is *external to all states* qua *states*. Kant's political philosophy thus does not make as categorical a distinction between states in world politics as today's liberal law scholars assume. The often noted tendency of Americans (who are not alone in this regard) to hold their polity as the living embodiment of an external standard for the world is something that Kant would reject.[26]

All states for Kant, whether republican or not, have made *some* progress towards the original contract standard because they have transcended the state of nature, which is a particular deficiency that international political relations (i.e. 'unrestricted relations') have not yet and perhaps can never accomplish. Kant's philosophy thus does not give easy support to separating the world into inherently peace-loving liberal states and intrinsically unjust, violent non-liberal states. Given that all existing states have significant distance from the original contract, and given that within states there is a provisional legality (what he terms as 'legal', if not 'lawful' relationships[27]), Kant actually embraces, at least as a temporary measure, classical international law's accommodation of different regime types. Such a temporary measure does not eliminate the absolute duty that all states have to reform in the light of the 'original contract' – but it would render illegitimate any one state or group of states judging the others as intrinsically deficient and thus not legal equals.

A separate law?

If, as Democratic Peace scholars argue, there is a 'separate peace' among liberal states, is there (should there be) a 'separate law'? Tesón and Slaughter put forward arguments that point to the exclusion of non-liberal states from putatively strengthened, deeper forms of legalism. Both draw on Kant to suggest that a more advanced form of the rule of law among states depends upon non-universal, limited membership. Tesón declares:

> If international law is to be morally legitimate, therefore, it must mandate that states respect human rights as a precondition for joining the international community. Immanuel Kant was the first to defend this thesis. . . . The Kantian thesis, then, is that a morally legitimate

[26] See David P. Forsythe, *Human Rights and International Relations* (Cambridge: Cambridge University Press, 2000), Chapter 6 on American exceptionalism.
[27] PP, p. 118.

82

> international law is founded upon an *alliance of separate free nations,*
> *united by their moral commitment to individual freedom, by their allegiance*
> *to the rule of law, and by the mutual advantages derived from peaceful*
> *intercourse.*[28]

At times Tesón argues that there is also a 'requirement that all states
must be liberal democracies' to join the international peace federation
too, although human rights take pride of place.[29] In any case, he makes
it clear that, from his version of Kantian theory, no legally based peace
alliance can include states that lack the institutional constraints on political power found in liberal states: 'observance of human rights is a
primary requirement to join the community of civilized nations under
international law. It follows that there cannot be a federation or peace
alliance with tyrannical states.'[30]

Slaughter attempts to avoid Tesón's normative language and instead
purports to *explain* the separate legal order that she claims has already
emerged between liberal and non-liberal states. She examines the way
courts in liberal states defer to the actions of non-liberal states by respecting state sovereignty and by letting the political executive in the liberal
state respond to any conflict of laws. But courts in liberal states will
review and interpret the legality of the actions taken by other states'
institutions, thus making legality rather than politics (i.e. bargaining,
diplomacy, negotiation) the basis of a conflict resolution. Like Doyle,
she argues that Kant foresaw and explained an empirical pattern of
separation between liberal and non-liberal states.[31] Whereas

> liberal states operate in a 'zone of law,' in which [for example] domes-
> tic courts regulate transnational relations under domestic law . . .
> Nonliberal states [by contrast] . . . operate in a 'zone of politics,' in
> which domestic courts either play no role in the resolution of transna-
> tional disputes or allow themselves to be guided by the liberal [state's]
> branches.[32]

Slaughter argues that it is non-liberal states themselves that have
decided to jealously guard their sovereignty by resisting internal, liberalizing reforms.[33] It is self-exclusion and the maintenance of sovereignty
at great potential political and economic cost:

> States that openly prefer to follow a non-liberal path may be all too
> willing to keep their sovereignty at any price. But the many states that
> now [in the post-Cold War era] seek to restructure their policies and

---

[28] Tesón, *International Law*, p. 2, emphasis in original.   [29] Ibid., p. 3.   [30] Ibid., p. 7.
[31] Ibid.   [32] Slaughter, 'Law Among Liberal States', p. 1910.   [33] Ibid., p. 1913.

economics in accordance with liberal precepts might be induced to welcome some reforms of judicial review of the validity of their acts by foreign courts.[34]

Slaughter argues here that inclusion in the liberal zone of law is a voluntary choice of states, which at first blush is much closer to Kant's actual view than is Tesón's enforced exclusion. However, she adds that the voluntary nature of this choice is rightly manipulated by liberal states with a view to promoting internal reforms in target, non-liberal states. Slaughter is clear that the purposive normative agenda driving the separation of a liberal zone of law is to provoke changes that otherwise would not occur – to induce choices from non-liberal political leaders that they might not take on their own. Slaughter argues the reluctance of courts within the zone of law to interpret acts of non-liberal states is not '"deference" to non-liberal sovereigns' but rather is 'the ostracism of an outlaw – a state outside the conception of law shared by liberal states'.[35]

Ultimately, both Tesón and Slaughter attribute the justifiability of separate and, as we shall see below, unequal treatment of states as consistent with Kant's view of the creation of a more advanced form of global legality. But this attribution rests on a misreading of 'Perpetual Peace', one that is not uncommon among proponents of the Democratic Peace thesis. Tesón puts it as follows: 'The requirement of a republican form of government [in the First Definitive Article] must be read in conjunction with the Second Article: "The law of nations shall be based on a federation of free states." The first two articles prescribe that international law should be based upon a union of republican states.'[36] Tesón thus interprets Kant's 'free' state as liberal state rather than, as Kant intends, as a 'voluntary' union of states independently choosing to join. Slaughter makes the same interpretation, reading 'free' as liberal.[37] But as Georg Cavallar notes, 'Kant never explicitly contends that all member states of the federation have to be republican'. He adds that Kant could have written the word republic rather than free states if he had wanted this to be the case.[38] *'Each nation'*, Kant makes clear in the Second Definitive Article, 'for the sake of its own security, can and ought to demand of the others that they should enter into a constitution, similar to the civil one, within which the rights of each could be secured.'[39] Certainly Kant

---

[34] Ibid. [35] Ibid. [36] Tesón, *International Law*, p. 3.
[37] Slaughter, 'Towards an Age of Liberal Nations', p. 394.
[38] Cavallar, *Kant*, p. 115. [39] PP, p. 102, emphasis added.

recognized that republican states were more likely to be genuinely oriented towards perpetual peace, but limiting the peace federation to only principled, 'enlightened' states was in his view mistaken. Just as a nation of devils (oriented towards the instrumental satisfaction of selfish ends) can form a lawful state, a federation of differently constituted states can perceive the benefits of security and freedom that a peace alliance can bring.

There is a deeper issue behind Kant's resistance to making the internal characteristics of a state a *precondition* for inclusion into an international peace federation. The exclusions of non-liberal states that Tesón and Slaughter describe are premised in large part on imposing costly or punitive measures against a non-liberal state, thus again bringing into question the problem of unilateral judgments backed by power rather than the force of law. Kant expresses concern that any self-styled peace federation would employ power to forcibly induce compliance, a dynamic he associates entirely with the flaws of the state of nature. He writes:

> This federation does not aim to acquire any power like that of a state, but merely to preserve and secure the *freedom* of each state in itself, along with that of the other confederated states, although this does not mean they need to submit to public laws and to coercive power which enforces them, as do men in the state of nature.[40]

At several points in 'Perpetual Peace' Kant expresses strong misgivings about states using the appearance of legalism, shallow as it is in global politics, as a power resource against weaker states. In particular, Kant describes how the law of nations, as a basis for European states to claim their inherent civilizational superiority compared to other peoples, was used as a basis for slaughtering others outside Europe.[41] In a similar passage he claims Japan is entirely justified, despite its manifest lack of republican institutions, in restricting contact with the far more powerful Europeans.[42] Until a world republic develops, the semi-juridical nature of the law of nations – even Kant's more advanced, critical version – has but provisional, rather than absolute, legitimacy. For this reason he suggests that the law of nations ought to be open, universal and non-instrumental in its treatment of states as ends in themselves, regardless of internal characteristics. Kant does not in any way deny or remove the responsibility of states to reform and perfect their internal institutions

---

[40] Ibid., p. 104.   [41] Ibid., p. 103.   [42] Ibid., pp. 106–7.

in the light of the 'original contract'. However, he believes that states are also notoriously ill-positioned and self-interested in employing their power to uphold their own private interpretations of legal rules.

Authorizing liberal enforcement

For Tesón and Slaughter, liberal states are set apart from others because of their domestic organizing principles. These principles account for liberal states' legitimacy but also for their inclusion in the more advanced legalism of a Kantian peace federation. Does it follow that liberal states, individually and together, also have a right to uphold international law, forcibly, against those states that are excluded from the peace federation? Here I suggest that contemporary liberal legalists tend to exaggerate the role that Kant gives states in international legal relations, thus empowering such states in a way that could only further frustrate the realization of perpetual peace and justice.

Tesón argues that a Kantian international law authorizes liberal states to enforce rules against non-liberal states. Non-liberal states lack this right against all other states, and there is no conceivable reason that liberal states could or would be the target of lawful coercion. Slaughter backs away from linking Kant to coercive enforcement measures, claiming that Kant is a 'libertarian' who eschews supranational legal mechanisms.[43] But she here overlooks the possibility that Tesón puts forward: that there is no contradiction between legitimate international law enforcement and a decentralized legal order lacking supranational mechanisms.[44] Also, Slaughter's position is still clearly that liberal states are authorized legally to use a variety of foreign policy measures against non-liberal regimes in order to promote liberalization, including, as mentioned, exclusion from economic benefits. Significantly, like Tesón, Slaughter assumes that liberal states take the lead and a hierarchical position in the globe in enforcing liberal democratic standards against others. In more recent work she has included a right (if not duty) for liberal states to take anticipatory coercive action against rogue states (but without invoking Kant – for this reason, my chief focus in what follows is Tesón).

It is the fact that liberal states have democratic and rights-respecting institutions that legally authorizes them to engage in humanitarian

---

[43] Slaughter, 'Towards an Age of Liberal Nations', p. 396.
[44] Tesón, *International Law*, pp. 21–22

intervention, according to Tesón.[45] Although one can very plausibly show that Kant authorized humanitarian interventions and anticipatory war, it is a serious misunderstanding of his work to argue that liberal states alone have this licence, and that they will exercise it in a way that enables, rather than frustrates, the development of global legalism.

Throughout this chapter I have been using the concept of 'non-liberal' to describe all states that are not formally democratic and that, principally for this reason, do not guarantee or succeed in protecting human rights. As we have seen, Tesón argues these states should be excluded as equal subjects from international law while Slaughter claims they have self-selected themselves for different, unequal treatment. Although it is possible to invoke Kant as someone who recognized the need for coercion against *a particular* non-liberal state, he did not believe that coercion was authorized against *non-liberal states* per se. As Cavallar notes, 'Paragraph 60 [of *Metaphysics of Morals*] is the only instance where Kant allows for legal coercion in international right.'[46] Keeping in mind that his peace federation is non-coercive, this one exception is worth quoting at length:

> There are no limits to the rights of a state against an *unjust enemy* (no limits with respect to quantity or degree, though there are limits with respect to quality); that is to say, an injured state may not use *any* means *whatever* but may use those means that are allowable to any degree that it is able to, in order to maintain what belongs to it. – But what is an *unjust enemy* in terms of the concepts of the right of nations, in which – as in the case of the state of nature generally – each state is judge in its own case? It is an enemy whose publicly expressed will (whether by word or deed) reveals a maxim which, if it were made a universal rule, any condition of peace among nations would be impossible and, instead, a state of nature would be perpetuated.[47]

Force against non-liberal states cannot be justified simply if they pose what Kant calls a passive injury to others (due to their mere independence in the state of nature). As we see below, he argues that all states have 'outgrown' the need to be coerced into submission under common authority, they have become moral persons in that they are a society of human beings living under common laws.[48] As this passage indicates, it is only states that pose a clear active injury to others that can be lawfully coerced. States *qua* states, not states with non-liberal internal organizing

---

[45] Ibid., pp. 16–19.   [46] Cavallar, *Kant*, p. 109.
[47] Kant, *Metaphysics of Morals*, pp. 118–9.   [48] PP, p. 104.

principles, are judged by their maxims with regard to the overarching goal of perpetual peace.

For Tesón, by contrast, all non-liberal states are judged to have inherently defective forms of sovereignty for which there is no 'equality before the law' provision.[49] Non-member (i.e. non-liberal) states have been attributed with *mens rea* and the liberal state/alliance is in a position to act as a competent judge against it. As Tesón states:

> [T]yrannical governments are outlaws. However, they are not outside the law of nations. Like domestic criminals, they are still bound by elementary principles, such as the rules that prohibit crimes of aggression and war crimes. While outlaw governments do not benefit from the rights conferred by membership in the alliance, they retain some rights [e.g. leaders have individual rights to due process in criminal proceedings].[50]

Also,

> [w]hile war is absolutely banned within the alliance, force will sometimes need to be used by individual states or members of the alliance acting in concert against enemies of the alliance. Therefore, a war of self-defence by a democratic government and its allies against a despotic aggressor is a just war.[51]

Famously, for Kant 'even a nation of devils' can solve the problem of justice, so long as they possess reason.[52] Similarly, morally imperfect states can achieve, in principle, through his perpetual peace project, a provisional rule of law among them. Just as there are limits to morally mandated coercion within states *vis-à-vis* citizens, Kant tries to establish limits to morally mandated coercion among states. (For 'it is certainly not their internal moral attitudes', Kant says, that lead states to seek peace.[53]) In any case, it is certainly true that Kant anticipated the need to use coercion against states that might engage in gross violations of human rights or who harboured designs to acquire and use weapons of mass destruction.[54] But the coercion would be for these reasons and thus for reasons that are *independent from states' internal constitutions*; it is because states behave aggressively and unjustly (that is, make perpetual peace impossible) that they can be coerced, and not because of what they *are*, i.e. non-liberal.

The 'powerful and enlightened nation' is for Kant to set an example and to 'provide a focal point for federal association among other

---

[49] Tesón, *International Law*, p. 6.   [50] Ibid., p. 19.   [51] Ibid., p. 20.
[52] PP, p. 112.   [53] PP, p. 113.   [54] Shell, 'Kant on "Unjust Enemies"', p. 82.

states', not to claim authority over putatively inferior juridical subjects. Certainly Tesón is correct to emphasize that Kant built popular sovereignty and individual rights into the foundations of international law. However, this does not alter Kant's misgivings about including coercive rights by states over others into international right. The key to understanding Kant's concerns is the fundamental distinction he makes (and Tesón overlooks) between morality and legality. This distinction relates directly to the problem Kant has with unilateral judgments and the use of political power.

On the one hand, Kant uses the domestic analogy to suggest that sovereign states, like individuals in the state of nature, have a duty to relinquish their lawless freedom in exchange for law-governed relations. On the other, he is clear that sovereign states cannot be rightfully coerced, as can individual subjects, to enter into a juridical condition. The domestic analogy is of continued importance, however. Neither individuals nor states can be coercively forced to behave morally by an external agent, they can only be forced to behave *in conformity* with morality by being made to obey legal rules.

Within states, legal rules are grounded in the 'general will' rather than each individual's private judgment about what is right and good. Without a competent judge to decide according to rules, there is a state of nature in which each person's judgment about what is moral is asserted with force. There is no way to determine which individual's claim is in true conformity with the categorical imperative (morality). Kant claims that sovereign states (by their mere existence) substitute the private right of individuals with a system of public right; in so doing, states eliminate the legitimacy of (and need for) any unilateral vindication of what is right. But states can mandate only 'legal' obedience on the part of subjects to respect the rules concerning each citizen's outer freedom. And states have a duty to ensure that extant legal rules conform gradually to the 'original contract', an externalized version of the categorical imperative in which the freedom of the individual is made compatible with the freedom of all others.

The domestic analogy is of continued relevance for Kant in separating legality and morality among states. Kant argues that, like individuals, states can only be coerced into performing actions *in conformity* with morality if there is the element of consent. However, here the domestic analogy breaks down. He argues that individuals' consent with the legal order inside a sovereign state can be assumed *a priori* (as the 'general will') because no person could conceivably exercise right without it.

But among states Kant believes that *a priori* arguments do not have the exact same force. Unlike individuals, states have 'outgrown' the need for coercion because they have at the very least transcended the state of nature within.[55] Although they have a moral duty to reform domestically in the light of the original contract, and to join a peace federation *vis-à-vis* their external conduct with other states, such a duty does not for Kant automatically justify a world state that would coerce states. Kant argues that the international peace federation cannot employ coercion precisely because it is not (yet) grounded in a general will of all nations: some states remain outside the federation and, even more significantly, *all* states refuse to rescind their sovereignty or lawless freedom.

Tesón flatly rejects Kant's requirement that lawful coercion be based on a general will, not simply on particular judgments of one group of states asserting what is right and good. He writes,

> Kant himself advocates an international law among separate nations that entails a decentralized system of authority. Judgments of the legality of wars [or the use of coercion] are no different than judgments of legality generally, so if there are no courts for the former there are no courts for the latter.[56]

But Tesón here conflates the assertion of *mere opinions* with regard to what is legally right with the assertion of *lawful authority to coerce*. Certainly *within* sovereign states Kant argued that the gap between these two things had been effectively closed; yet he continually refused to equate these two things *among* sovereign states.

Patrick Capps provides an excellent example of how two states can have conflicting opinions with regard to what is legally right, each grounded upon plausible moral claims with regard to coercive action.[57] The *Nicaragua* case brought before the International Court of Justice (ICJ) in the mid-1980s involved the Nicaraguan and American governments appealing to legality and, simultaneously, the morality each believed was at stake in international law. Nicaragua claimed that the United States' coercive measures taken against it (particularly, the mining of its harbours) were unjustified violations of international law, i.e. aggression. The US claimed that actions against Nicaragua's Sandinista government were legal acts of collective self-defence. It alleged that Nicaragua, linked to the Soviet Union and Cuba, was supplying arms and assistance to rebels in neighbouring El Salvador. Both governments

---

[55] PP, p. 104.   [56] See Tesón, *International Law*, pp. 21–2.
[57] Capps, 'Kantian Project', pp. 1016–1018.

also made arguments that the just use of force was ultimately dependent on democratic self-determination and human rights; and each judged Nicaragua's government in a totally different light. The US interpreted democracy to mean 'political pluralism, human rights, free elections, non-alignment, and a mixed economy', as defined by the Organization of American States.[58] Nicaragua's government, according to Roth, 'interpreted democracy and human rights to require . . . a major redistribution of wealth and power in society in advance of the fixing of permanent institutions'.[59] Now, the ICJ ruled in favour of Nicaragua, but the US famously rejected the ruling. In the absence of judicially enforceable general will, there is a clash of 'moral' perspectives of the legal. As Capps argues, according to Tesón's view of Kantian international law, *both* Nicaragua and the United States could unilaterally *claim* their actions of (collective) self-defence were lawful: 'both states have a justification to use force in support of democracy and human rights'.[60]

Tesón thus misses one of Kant's fundamental points with regard to the global rule of law. International law will lead to war, not perpetual peace, and injustice rather than justice if it is based on clashing unilateral judgments *backed by force*. A situation in which each state's judgment about what is right and good *is* the state of nature, and this is precisely the condition Kant believes makes perpetual peace an impossible to achieve ideal. Unilateral judgments universalized in international politics would lead to 'a war of extermination, in which both parties and all right [i.e. legality] itself might be simultaneously annihilated, [and] would allow perpetual peace only on the vast graveyard of the human race'.[61] When (liberal) states resort to coercion and ultimately justify it in terms of the moral ends of a foreign policy, they put themselves in the position of a juridical superior over inferiors. This is simply not what Kant had in mind with regard to the role of the 'one powerful and enlightened nation'.

Kant's vision of international reform is evolutionary, and his critique of classical international law ought to be viewed in those terms. He rejects the authorization of liberal states to use coercion for moral reasons because a general will among states is (currently) impossible among sovereign states. In the meantime, just as the peace federation he proposes is a surrogate for a world republic, the law of nations he proposes is a provisional, incomplete approximation of true global legalism.

---

[58] Ibid., p. 1017.   [59] Brad Roth, quoted in ibid.   [60] Ibid, p. 1018.   [61] PP, p. 96.

What today's liberal legalists like Tesón misunderstand is that Kant hoped perpetual peace could be approximated through a subtle movement in international law from unilateral judgments to 'omnilateral judgments' to use Capps' expression.[62] A peace federation would move somewhat away from the state of nature and yet fall far short of a world republic – it would be a semi-juridical context in which, in a limited way, right would not be decided through force (of the stronger). Kant writes of the semi-juridical context as follows:

> And this *status juridicus* must be derived from some sort of contract, which unlike that from which the state originates, must not be based on coercive laws, but may at most be a state of *permanent and free association* . . . without some kind of *lawful condition* which actively links together the various physical or moral persons (as in the case of the state of nature), the only possible form of right is a private one.[63]

Should a state resort to coercion, whether liberal or not, and for whatever reason, they will have re-ignited a state of nature situation. It is only *vis-à-vis* the unjust enemy that Kant suggests there is a shared, defensive perspective that many states can and ought to take to protect the limited gains made through the peace federation. The unjust enemy displays

> a maxim by which, if it were made a universal rule, any condition of peace among nations would be impossible and, instead, a state of nature would be perpetuated. Violation of public contracts is an expression of this sort. Since this can be assumed to be a matter of concern to all nations whose freedom is threatened by it, they are called upon to unite against such misconduct in order to deprive the state of its power to do it.[64]

Although this suggests that Kant believed a peace alliance could act to defend their interests together, and in acting, substitute for a genuine public authority in international affairs, he quickly reminds readers that it is indeed *only* a surrogate. He states,

> It is *redundant*, however, to speak of an unjust enemy in a state of nature; for a state of nature is itself a condition of injustice. A just enemy would be one that I would be doing wrong by resisting; but then he would also not be my enemy.[65]

---

[62] Capps, 'Kantian Project', p. 1019.   [63] PP, p. 127.
[64] Kant, *Metaphysics of Morals*, p. 119.   [65] Ibid.

It is not coercive enforcement that enables the possibility of a global rule of law for Kant; it is precisely refraining from coercion that allows *all* states to agree to general principles or rules that could *eventually* be used for public enforcement in a world republic. In that situation, states would settle 'their disputes in a civil way, as if by a lawsuit, rather than in a barbaric way (the way of the savages), namely by war'.[66]

Kant was perfectly aware that a world republic might never come, and for that reason he called perpetual peace 'an unachievable ideal'.[67] He also expressed scepticism about whether a semi-juridical peace federation could last without collapsing, having grown too large and ambitious, into an exhausted empire.[68] Here, too, he acknowledged something that contemporary liberals like Tesón have been perhaps overly sanguine about: the role of power in corrupting or destroying the possibility of justice. The world republic is rejected as an immediate solution by Kant because it would likely be a despotic threat to the freedom of nations and individuals. The peace federation, too, were it to spread too widely or take on coercive powers, even if composed of liberal republics, could become despotic. This would be particularly the case were it to dress up its unilateral judgments through force as if it were authentic public law. Kant argued that a coercive peace federation would in fact simply do what classical international law (as 'sorry comforter') would have authorized, *that might determines what is right.*

Conclusion

Kant's international legacy is a contested and often ambiguous foundation from which different liberals have drawn materials for alternative political and ethical projects.[69] While some readings of Kant are certainly more plausible, there is always the route that Tesón proposes, which is to reconstruct what he takes to be the 'spirit' of Kant for contemporary purposes. There is also the route that Slaughter (following Doyle) takes by converting Kant's highly complex philosophy and forming a stylized hypothesis from certain aspects of it. Both of these ways of using the classical theorist that is Kant will often rest on blatant misreading of certain things, e.g. the fact that Kant did not make a fundamental distinction between liberal and non-liberal states in international law.

[66] Ibid.   [67] Ibid.   [68] Ibid.
[69] See Antonio Franceschet, *Kant and Liberal Internationalism: Sovereignty, Justice, and Global Reform* (New York: Palgrave, 2002).

Kant's classical writings on international law in fact give us many reasons to remain critical of any claims by states, liberal or otherwise, to make force the ultimate basis of their legal authority. Certainly we can judge the justice of international relations from *a priori* principles, as does Kant; but states' actions are never themselves the direct products of pure moral principle. Dangers arise when states present their policies as such. 'Perpetual Peace' diagnoses brilliantly the phenomenon of the political moralist, and not only the unjust enemy, as a significant threat to the prospects of a global rule of law. For the judgment of all states is limited and contaminated; and the unconstrained use of state power can impede the pursuit of justice. Just ends 'cannot be realized by violent or precipitate means, but must be steadily approached as favourable opportunities present themselves'.[70] Today's liberal legalists are correct to believe that Kant would not be entirely satisfied with the legal order of today, i.e. that of the UN Charter. But he would certainly resist the notion that one group of states can unilaterally amend that order *because they are liberal*. To the extent that such states can impose a new world legal order on others it is not because they are liberal but *because they are powerful*.

If massive human rights violations, aggression and terrorism are to be put under lasting legal control and ended it cannot be done through a new doctrine of (liberal) Great Power responsibility. This would be an all too contingent basis for justice and human rights.[71] Kant quotes ironically a Gallic prince's expression, 'Nature has given the strong the prerogative of making the weak obey them.'[72] By the same token 'Perpetual Peace' puts forward the view that justice cannot be simply a matter of the strong having a prerogative to protect the weak. Kant's rejection of classical international law and of the 'sorry comfort' that its proponents have typically provided never leads him to embrace the path of pure expediency. Rather than reject extant legal rules and customs among states altogether (because they lack *force*), then, Kant ends up arguing that we ought to amend classical international law slowly and for as long as it takes to achieve the consent of states *qua* states. Thus, the UN Charter's norms on force (today's 'classical' legal rules)

---

[70] PP, p. 122.
[71] See Thomas W. Pogge, 'Moralizing Humanitarian Intervention: Why Jurying Fails and How Law Can Work', in Terry Nardin and Melissa S. Williams (eds.), *Humanitarian Intervention: Nomos XLVII* (New York: New York University Press, 2005), pp. 158–187.
[72] PP, p. 103.

ought still to be the guideposts, even as they ought to be reformed.[73] As Kant writes, 'It would be contrary to all political expediency, which in this case agrees with morality, to destroy any of the existing bonds of political or cosmopolitan union before a better constitution has been prepared to take their place.'[74]

[73] See Jean L. Cohen, 'Whose Sovereignty? Empire Versus International Law' *Ethics & International Affairs* 18 (2004), 1–24.
[74] PP, p. 118.

5 Rousseau and Saint-Pierre's peace project: a critique of 'history of international relations theory'[1]

Yuichi Aiko

'History of international relations theory' can begin only with the birth of 'International Relations (IR)'. For only when international (or inter-state) relations are conceived as an independent social sphere, can 'international relations theory', and hence its history, exist. Historians in this area have nevertheless neglected this self-evident ontological limit, reading contemporary disciplinary frameworks back into history.[2] Consequently, they overlook the historical context of classical thinkers and miss the opportunity to reflect on the very historicity of modern IR theories themselves.

The purpose of this essay is to bring this fault to light. I do this by challenging the traditional understanding of Jean-Jacques Rousseau (1712–1778) and by developing an alternative 'contextual' interpretation of Rousseau's reading of the peace project written by the Abbé de Saint-Pierre (1658–1743).

In the history of international relations theory, Rousseau is generally seen as a 'realist'.[3] There are many variations of this claim but ultimately it rests on the fact that Rousseau was pessimistic about the prospect for

[1] Special thanks to Professor Martin Shaw, Ms Rhiannon Lambert and in particular the editor, Dr Beate Jahn, for their valuable comments and helpful proofreading. But, of course, I am solely responsible for any errors.
[2] In the category of 'historians of international relations theory' I include the IR scholars who are in one way or another committed to interpreting the classical texts of 'international relations'. This categorization can be unfair to some of those scholars because they may not be 'historians'. I nevertheless use the label with the intention of promoting more awareness for the role of 'history' in interpreting classical texts. Unless IR scholars are explicit that their reading of classical texts is not historical, their interpretations can be criticized as either ahistorical or historically mistaken, as I claim in this essay.
[3] Of course, there are some exceptions to this 'orthodoxy'. The most interesting among those is Michael C. Williams, 'Rousseau, Realism and *Realpolitik*', *Millennium: Journal of International Studies* 18 (1989), 186–189.

fundamental changes in the war-prone 'anarchical' inter-state system. Kenneth N. Waltz, for example, asserts that Rousseau was a typical theorist of 'the third image' who believed that the anarchical international system naturally perpetuates conflicts between states.[4] Ian Clark locates Rousseau's theory within 'a general tradition of despair' because he, although desiring the reform of the inter-state system, eventually 'holds out not a shred of hope that it can be attained'.[5] Howard Williams characterizes Rousseau's IR theory in an identical manner since 'Rousseau's conclusion on the prospects for world peace is a tragic one'.[6] Richard Tuck also concludes that 'Rousseau offered little hope of an end to this state of war between modern states'.[7]

What gives apparent certainty to such a 'Rousseau-realist' thesis are some remarks in his 'review' of Saint-Pierre's peace project, *Extrait du projet de paix perpétuelle de Monsieur l'abbé de Saint Pierre* (1761) and *Jugement sur le projet de paix perpétuelle* (1782). In *Jugement*, for instance, Rousseau states: 'although the project [of Saint-Pierre] is very wise, the means to execute it indicate the simplicity of the author. . . . Let us admit that . . . he saw very well their effects once they are established, but he childishly judged the means to establish them'; and, 'Without doubt perpetual peace is a very absurd project at the moment'.[8] The claim that Rousseau was a 'realist' seems well substantiated here; it appears undoubted that he painted Saint-Pierre as a naive 'idealist'.[9]

My contention is however that this orthodox interpretation of Rousseau's international relations theory is *historically* mistaken. The fundamental problem here is that the idealist-realist dichotomy is uncritically taken as the framework for reading Rousseau's 'review', which

---

[4] Kenneth N. Waltz, *Man, the State and War* (New York: Columbia University Press, 1959), pp. 180–186.
[5] Ian Clark, *Reform and Resistance in the International Order* (Cambridge: Cambridge University Press, 1981), pp. 61, 67.
[6] Howard Williams, *International Relations in Political Theory* (Milton Keynes: Open University Press, 1992), p. 78.
[7] Richard Tuck, *The Rights of War and Peace: Political Thought and the International Order from Grotius to Kant* (Oxford: Oxford University Press, 1999), pp. 205–206.
[8] Jean-Jacques Rousseau, *Oeuvres complètes III: Du contrat social, écrits politiques* (Paris: Gallimard, 1964), pp. 392, 396. Hereafter, I call this work simply *OC*. All quotations from this work are translated by me.
[9] For the argument that Rousseau was a 'realist' critic of an 'idealist' Saint-Pierre, see F. H. Hinsley, *Power and the Pursuit of Peace: Theory and Practice in the History of Relations between States* (Cambridge: Cambridge University Press, 1963), p. 46; F. Parkinson, *The Philosophy of International Relations: A Study in the History of Thought* (London: Sage, 1977), p. 62; Stanley Hoffmann and David Fidler (eds.), *Rousseau on International Relations* (Oxford: Clarendon Press, 1991), pp. liv–lv; Williams, *International Relations*, pp. 74–75; and Tuck, *The Rights of War and Peace*, p. 206.

results in ignoring the meaning of his theory in its time and place.[10] This dichotomous reading is so ingrained in the history of International Relations theory that even critics, such as Torbjørn L. Knutsen, merely present 'idealist elements' in Rousseau's argument as grounds for an alternative reading.[11] And yet, the dichotomy *as conceived by contemporary IR scholars* did not exist for Rousseau and his contemporaries – and neither did IR itself – since it was introduced into IR only in 1939 through the publication of E. H. Carr's *The Twenty Years' Crisis*.[12] It is thus *historically* problematic to use the dichotomy for the interpretation of Rousseau's 'review', or even to understand this work simply as about 'international relations'. Until recently, however, this fatal mistake was largely missed by historians of international relations theory, as a result of their surprisingly ubiquitous lack of reflection about the meaning and activity of 'historians'.[13]

In this chapter I will provide an *historical* interpretation of Rousseau's 'review' by placing it in the intellectual context of mid-eighteenth-century France. This context is neither a discourse on the 'idealist-realist dichotomy' nor 'inter-state relations': rather, a more inclusive intellectual framework that was at stake for Rousseau and his contemporaries, namely, natural-law theory and its transcendence. I will show, firstly, that Saint-Pierre's international relations theory was a source of inspiration for Rousseau's 'political theory of the state' in his contest with natural-lawyers.[14] In this light, secondly, Rousseau's 'review' is read

---

[10] Nicholas Greenwood Onuf, *The Republican Legacy in International Thought* (Cambridge: Cambridge University Press, 1998), p. 6.

[11] Torbjørn L. Knutsen, 'Re-reading Rousseau in the Post-Cold War World' *Journal of Peace Research* 31 (1994), 247–262. David P. Fidler makes a similar argument: 'Desperately Clinging to Grotian and Kantian Sheep: Rousseau's Attempted Escape from the State of War' in Ian Clark and Iver B. Neumann (eds.), *Classical Theories of International Relations* (Basingstoke: Macmillan, 1996), pp. 130–134.

[12] Recent studies reveal that Carr's labelling of 'utopianism (idealism)' is a misrepresentation of what was actually discussed during the inter-war period. See David Long and Peter Wilson (eds.), *Thinkers of the Twenty Years' Crisis: Inter-war Idealism Reassessed* (Oxford: Clarendon Press, 1995).

[13] 'History of political thought' has been aware of this 'anachronism' for a long time. See Quentin Skinner's 'Meaning and Understanding in the History of Ideas' *History and Theory* 8 (1969), 3–53. In IR, on the other hand, this problem began to be recognized only in recent years. See Duncan S. A. Bell, 'International Relations: The Dawn of a Historiographical Turn?' *British Journal of Politics and International Relations* 3 (2001), 116–120.

[14] Merle L. Perkins and Grace G. Roosevelt were well aware of this connection between Saint-Pierre's peace project and Rousseau's social-contract theory, but their contributions have not been sufficiently recognized in IR. See Perkins, *The Moral and Political Philosophy of the Abbé de Saint-Pierre* (Geneva: Librairie E. Droz, 1959), pp. 97–133; and Roosevelt, *Reading Rousseau in the Nuclear Age* (Philadelphia: Temple University Press, 1990), pp. 90–119.

as a document of sympathy with, rather than denouncement of, Saint-Pierre. Thirdly, Rousseau, in agreement with Saint-Pierre, understood sovereignty as the 'moral freedom' of the state. Both thought that the state can be truly 'sovereign' only when it dutifully follows law in its relations with other states, not when it is without constraints (as understood in IR today). And finally, Rousseau criticized Saint-Pierre's peace project as impractical because it did not go far enough; Saint-Pierre had left the problem of absolute rule by princes – the major cause of wars – unresolved.

The argument is developed in four parts. First, I set out the historical development of Rousseau's political theory and its connection with his study of Saint-Pierre's works. Second, I read Rousseau's 'review' in a new light, focusing particularly upon the commonalities between Saint-Pierre's peace project and Rousseau's social contract theory. Third, I shed light on some new aspects of Rousseau's international relations theory that are largely unrecognized in IR. And finally, I will draw out some more general implications of this case study for the history of international relations theory.

The historical context

Rousseau's social-contract theory was one of the first significant challenges to the orthodoxy of modern natural-law theory in mid-eighteenth-century France. Taking this context as a starting point, it is interesting to see that Rousseau was developing the alternative to natural-law theory while studying Saint-Pierre's works intensively. I argue that Saint-Pierre's model for perpetual peace provided Rousseau with a crucial inspiration for the idea of the social contract. This 'debt' is suggested primarily by the fact that Rousseau in *Economie politique* and the *Geneva Manuscript* called the association of the social contract a 'confederation'.

Rousseau's opposition to modern natural-law theory

According to his autobiography, *Les confessions*, Rousseau's concern for politics began between 1743 and 1744. Working at the French Embassy in Venice then, he observed all the defects of this prosperous but quite corrupted republic, and was convinced that 'everything is rooted in politics and . . . no people would ever be other than the nature of their government made them'.[15] This discovery led Rousseau to plan to write *Institutions politiques*, in which he wanted to discuss the relationship between man's moral state and political constitutions. In fact he never completed the project but published 'the least worthless part' of what he managed to write.[16] This part we know today as *Du contrat social* (1762).

A dominant theory was however taking a quite different stance on the subject of politics and morality then. In France this theory – modern natural-law theory – was extremely popular among French *philosophes* as a result of Jean Barbeyrac's very successful translations of Samuel Pufendorf in 1706–1707.[17]

The basic assumption of modern natural-lawyers is that man is essentially a social being. This is based upon an 'instrumental' understanding of human society that man, while being an animal which seeks satisfaction of his self-interests, realizes empirically that society is the best means to fulfil this desire. Two leading natural-lawyers at the time in France expressed this as follows: 'men were moved by want to gather into states, to the end that they might render more civilized and rich a life' (Pufendorf); and 'Avarice is after all the principal instrument with which one built society' (Voltaire).[18] 'Natural law', the fundamental moral law for all human beings, was also derived from this idea of man's instrumental sociality. Pufendorf, for instance, states as the first principle of this law that 'Every man ought to do as much as he can to cultivate and preserve sociality'.[19] French *philosophes* basically agreed; Montesquieu for example counted 'the desire to live in society' as a principle of the concept of natural law.[20]

---

[15] Jean-Jacques Rousseau, *The Confessions* trans. J. M. Cohen (London: Penguin, 1953), p. 377.
[16] *OC*, p. 349.
[17] On the popularity of the Pufendorfian natural-law theory among French *philosophes*, see Robert Derathé, *Jean-Jacques Rousseau et la science politique de son temps* (Paris: Librairie Philosophique J. Vrin, 1970), pp. 28–30. On the impact of Barbeyrac's translations on the development of the French natural-law theory, see Tim Hochstrasser, 'Conscience and Reason: The Natural Law Theory of Jean Barbeyrac' *Historical Journal* 36 (1993), 289–90.
[18] Samuel Pufendorf, *De jure naturae et gentium libri octo: Book II* trans. C. H. Oldfather and W. A. Oldfather (New York: Oceana, 1964), p. 958; and Voltaire, 'Traité de métaphysique' in *Oeuvres complètes de Voltaire: Tome XX*, nouvelle edition (Paris: Garnier Frères, Libraires-Editeur, 1879), p. 222. The translation is mine. About the claim that Pufendorf had an 'instrumental' understanding of society, see J. B. Schneewind, 'Pufendorf's Place in the History of Ethics' *Synthèse* 72 (1987), 134–136.
[19] Samuel Pufendorf, *On the Duty of Man and Citizen*, ed. J. Tully, trans. Michael Silverthorne (Cambridge: Cambridge University Press, 1991), p. 35.
[20] Montesquieu, *The Spirits of the Laws*, trans. and eds. Anne M. Coher, Basia Carolyn Miller and Harold Samuel Stone (Cambridge: Cambridge University Press, 1989), pp. 6–7.

We find the same 'instrumentalism' also in the view of modern natural-lawyers on political authority. They believed that the mere existence of men's sociality cannot guarantee peaceful coexistence in reality, so political authority, or the state, needs to be established in order to ensure security and justice in society. Taking Pufendorf's argument as an example, 'respect for [natural] law cannot guarantee a life in natural liberty with fair security'; therefore, 'Truly the effective remedy for suppressing evil desires, the remedy perfectly fitted to the nature of man, is found in states.'[21] Among the French *philosophes*, Jean-Jacques Burlamaqui argues that it is 'by far wiser' to have a government because some men should abuse their natural freedom in the state of nature.[22] For Montesquieu, 'A society could not continue to exist without a government' because men readily fall into 'the state of war' as soon as they form a society.[23]

Of great importance is that this theoretical conception of the relationship between morality and politics is at odds with Rousseau's Venice discovery. While the dominant theory of the age holds that man's natural sociality leads to the establishment of a government/state, Rousseau's newly attained conviction supports the opposite formulation: that it is government that forms man's (moral) nature. The implications of this difference are most clearly demonstrated in the judgment of absolute monarchy. Pufendorf and many 'progressive' French *philosophes*, such as Voltaire, had no objection to the government of absolute monarchy because, as long as the government functions as the means to secure people's lives and justice, its form, logically speaking, does not matter. For Rousseau, on the other hand, absolute monarchy was undoubtedly the worst kind of government because it deprives men of their freedom, that is, of the very basis of their morality. Rousseau therefore had to attack the dominant natural-law theory and attempted to offer an alternative in his project on *Institutions politiques*.[24]

---

[21] Pufendorf, *On the Duty*, p. 134.
[22] J. J. Burlamaqui, *The Principles of Natural and Politic Law: Volume II*, trans. Thomas Nugent, second edition (London: J. Nourse, 1763), esp. p. 14.
[23] Montesquieu, *The Spirits of the Laws*, pp. 7–8.
[24] Many scholars have pointed out that Rousseau was a critic of the natural-law theory, especially that of Pufendorf. See René Hubert, *Rousseau et l'Encyclopédie: essai sur la formation des idées politiques de Rousseau* (Paris: Gamber, 1928), pp. 31–49; C. E. Vaughan, Introduction to *The Political Writings of Jean Jacques Rousseau: Volume I* (Oxford: Basil Blackwell, 1915), pp. 16–18; and, Robert Wokler, 'Rousseau's Pufendorf: Natural Law and the Foundations of Commercial Society' *History of Political Thought* 15 (1994), 373–402. Derathé however stresses the continuities, rather than discrepancies, of Rousseau's political theory with the natural-law theory. See his *Jean-Jacques Rousseau et la science politique de son temps*.

The development of Rousseau's social-contract theory and his study of Saint-Pierre

Rousseau began to engage with the project of *Institutions politiques* around 1750, but this made a marked progress only after the spring of 1756.[25] His conviction about the Venetian discovery was however strengthened throughout the early 1750s since debates on his *Discours sur les sciences et les arts* (1751) more and more persuaded him that 'all our vices stem ultimately not from our nature but from the ways in which we have been badly governed'.[26] On the basis of this Rousseau launched his open attack on the natural-law theory in *Discours sur l'inégalité* in early 1754. His criticism is directed at the confusion of law in society and 'natural law', and especially at an inadequate understanding of the state of nature as a basis for natural law. Modern society is morally so corrupted that the 'law' based on this society cannot but reflect this corruption. The existing natural-law theory, which mistakenly derives the notion of natural law from man's social state, thus cannot be a proper signpost for man's morality. It does not answer the question of what kind of government/state is the best from a moral point of view.

Rousseau's *Du contrat social* (1762) was meant to fill this gap; it aimed to provide the model of a political constitution in which justice is guaranteed and the freedom of each member is secured. When composing *Discours sur l'inégalité* in early 1754, however, Rousseau had not yet developed this new theory.

> Without entering now the researches that are still to be done on the nature of the fundamental pact of every Government, I constrain myself, following the common opinion, to consider here the establishment of the political Body as the contract between the people and the magistrate that it chooses.[27]

Here Rousseau certainly indicates his dissatisfaction with 'the common opinion', but still accepts this theory of the 'contract of submission'. This theory is based on the notion that the people are subjected to the sovereign (usually a single monarch) in exchange for the provision of

---

[25] Rousseau, *The Confessions*, p. 377.
[26] Robert Wokler, 'The *Discours sur les sciences et les arts* and its Offspring: Rousseau in reply to his Critics', in Simon Harvey, Marian Hobson, David Kelly and Samuel S. B. Taylor (eds.), *Reappraisals of Rousseau: Studies in Honour of R. A. Leigh* (Manchester: Manchester University Press, 1980), p. 267.
[27] *OC*, p. 184.

security and welfare, which was, indeed, a common type of contract theory that natural-lawyers relied upon. The acceptance of absolute monarchy by some lawyers stemmed partly from this contract theory; when the 'enlightened' monarch ensures the safety and welfare of the people, he fulfils the contract and must be considered legitimate. In *Du contrat social*, however, Rousseau neither accepts absolute monarchy nor endorses this 'unequal' contract theory. It follows from this that his critique of the natural-law theory was not yet fully developed when he wrote *Discours sur l'inégalité*.[28]

The first sign of Rousseau's discovery of the social-contract theory appears in *Economie politique* published in November 1755. This work refers to one of the key concepts of the theory – the general will – for the first time, and the notion of 'natural equality of men' is also placed as a condition of what he conceived as a just political constitution.

> It is no more unbelievable that the general will consents that a member of the State, whatever he is, harms or destroys another, than that the fingers of a reasonable man scratch his eyes out. The security of the individual is truly founded upon the public confederation [*la confédération publique*]; . . . this convention will be dissolved by right if the one who can be otherwise saved dies in the State. . . . For, when the fundamental convention is broken, one can no longer see what right or interest can hold the people together in the social union, unless it is kept by force, which causes the dissolution of the civil state.[29]

It is clear that Rousseau rejects the unequal treatment of a citizen within the state here. He argues that, if even a single person is permitted somehow lawfully to 'destroy' another in this 'public *confederation* = civil state', the political association can no longer stand as just. In terms of precision and comprehensiveness the 'social-contract theory' in *Economie politique* is not yet fully developed, but it constitutes an advance in that Rousseau saw the equal treatment of all men as a necessary condition for a moral state.[30]

Comparing Rousseau's discussion of private property and natural law in *Economie politique* and *Discours sur l'inégalité*, some scholars hold that the argument of the latter is more advanced and therefore postdates

---

[28] About this development of the contract theory, see for instance, J. W. Gough, *The Social Contract: A Critical Study of its Development*, second edition (Oxford: Clarendon Press, 1957), esp. pp. 1–7.

[29] *OC*, p. 256.

[30] Vaughan holds that the idea of the social contract was still underdeveloped in *Economie politique*. See *The Political Writings*, pp. 230–231.

Economie politique.[31] However, Helena Rosenblatt's convincing argument shows that Rousseau was closely involved in the political conflict between the aristocrats and the *bourgeois* during his short stay in Geneva in summer 1754 and that *Economie politique* was subsequently written for the purpose of presenting his support for the *bourgeois* demands.[32] This implies that Rousseau composed the work not before *Discours sur l'inégalité* but some time between his return to Paris from Geneva and the publication of the work, that is, between autumn 1754 and summer 1755. It is presumed that during this period he developed his social-contract theory or, at least, its prototype.

Interestingly, it is during this period that Rousseau studied Saint-Pierre's works intensively. Returning from Geneva in autumn 1754, he was commissioned to make 'a selection from the works of the Abbé de Saint-Pierre by the Abbé de Mably'.[33] Without having read the works of Saint-Pierre before, Rousseau accepted this task. He most probably began to work in late 1754.[34]

It may appear a pure coincidence that Rousseau came up with the idea of the social contract while he was abridging Saint-Pierre's works. Rousseau's use of the term 'confederation' however suggests a crucial link between these two seemingly unrelated events. He used this term in *Extrait* and *Jugement* for Saint-Pierre's inter-state alliance for perpetual peace.[35] On the other hand, he used it in *Economie politique* and *The Geneva Manuscript* (the earlier draft of *Du contrat social*), in this case for the political association, or the state, of the social contract.[36] The term appears four times altogether in *Economie politique* but only once in *The Geneva Manuscript*.[37] The latter is nevertheless the clearest expression outside *Extrait* and *Jugement* of what Rousseau meant by 'confederation':

---

[31] See John Hope Mason, *The Indispensable Rousseau* (London: Quartet Books, 1979), p. 74; and Hubert, *Rousseau et l'Encyclopédie*, pp. 62–63.

[32] Helena Rosenblatt, *Rousseau and Geneva: From the* First Discourse *to the* Social Contract *1749–1762* (Cambridge: Cambridge University Press, 1997), p. 198.

[33] Rousseau, *The Confessions*, p. 379.

[34] Rousseau reminisced this episode later in a letter on 5 December 1760, saying that 'Six years ago when Mr. the Comte of Saint-Pierre gave me the manuscripts of the late Mr. the Abbé, his uncle, I started abridging his writings'. See, *Correspondance complète de Jean Jacques Rousseau: Tome VII* (Geneva: Institut et Musée Voltaire, 1969), pp. 339–340.

[35] Saint-Pierre himself never used the term 'confederation' but *'union'*, *'société permanente'* or *'alliance générale'*.

[36] Rousseau used the term 'confederation' in one of his political fragments, too. He says that 'The first object that the people proposed in the civil confederation [*confédération civile*] was their mutual assurance, that is, the guarantee of the life and freedom of each by the whole community' (*OC*, p. 486). According to Derathé, the content of this fragment corresponds to Rousseau's discussion in *Economie politique*. See *OC*, p. 1520.

[37] *OC*, pp. 246, 256, 270, 271.

[T]he act of the primitive confederation [*confédération primitive*] includes a reciprocal engagement of the public with individuals, and ... each individual, contracting with himself, as it were, finds himself in double relations, namely, as a member of the Sovereign to each individual, and as a member of the State to the Sovereign.[38]

This remark is an excellent synopsis of the idea of the social contract; it concisely explains that equal individuals contracting with each other constitute together the single sovereign that relates itself, in return, to each of these individuals as the enforcer of the general will. Perhaps satisfied with the precision and compactness of this remark, Rousseau consequently re-used it in *Du contrat social* but for a single alteration: he replaced the term '*confédération primitive*' with '*association*'.[39]

Of course, one cannot deduce Saint-Pierre's influence on Rousseau's social-contract theory from the use of 'confederation' in *Economie politique* and *The Geneva Manuscript* alone. Indeed, it is not unusual in French that '*confédération*' stands for associations other than a 'confederation of *states*' (for instance, *Confédération générale du travail*), so Rousseau may have just followed the normal use of the term when calling the social-contract association of *individuals* a 'confederation'. And yet, there are reasons to believe that Rousseau's model of a just political constitution was 'inspired' by Saint-Pierre's 'confederation'.[40] In addition to the fact that Rousseau's preparation for *Extrait* and *Jugement* on the one hand and his composition of *The Geneva Manuscript* on the other were made almost simultaneously, Saint-Pierre's confederation of peace and Rousseau's social-contract association resemble each other considerably in terms of their foundational ideas (I will show this resemblance in the following section).[41] We cannot know today why Rousseau decided to replace the term '*confédération*' with '*association*' in *Du contrat social*. A probable explanation is that he intended to avoid terminological confusion; in this work the term was intended only to

[38] Ibid., p. 290.   [39] Ibid., p. 362.
[40] This is also the view of Murray Forsyth. See *Union of States: The History and Practice of Confederation* (Leicester: Leicester University Press, 1981), p. 92.
[41] For Derathé, Rousseau wrote the majority of the *Manuscript* between 1758 and 1760 (based on the Introduction in *OC*, pp. lxxxiii–lxxxiv). Vaughan's speculation is that the composition was made during 1761 (*The Political Writings*, p. 434). The question of when Rousseau composed *Extrait* and *Jugement* is more controversial. While Vaughan and Charles William Hendel think that it was around 1756 (Vaughan, *The Political Writings*, p. 360; and Hendel, *Jean-Jacques Rousseau Moralist: Volume I* (Oxford: Oxford University Press, 1934), p. 198); Sven Stelling-Michaud argues that it was some time between 1758–1759 (Introduction to *OC*, pp. cxxiii and cxxxii.). Stelling-Michaud's conclusion seems more convincing because it is based on wider sources.

mean the alliance of small republican states.[42] In any case, the initial use of the term to denote the social-contract association strongly suggests Saint-Pierre's influence on Rousseau. His 'review' of Saint-Pierre's peace project now has to be reinterpreted in light of this intellectual 'debt'.

Rousseau's 'review' of Saint-Pierre: a document of sympathy

While Rousseau regarded Saint-Pierre's peace project as 'impractical', it is striking how much Rousseau's theoretical position had in common with Saint-Pierre's in the context of eighteenth-century French political discourse; much more, indeed, than is usually recognized in IR literature. I therefore argue that his 'review' of Saint-Pierre should be read as a document of sympathy with, rather than criticism of, the argument of his predecessor. Rousseau was dissatisfied with Saint-Pierre's theoretical inconsistency, without doubt; he nevertheless 'learned' a lot from Saint-Pierre's political theory.

One of the main reasons for the impression that Rousseau was a 'critic' of Saint-Pierre is that he professed his dislike of Saint-Pierre's writings many times. He describes Saint-Pierre's manuscripts as 'twenty-three diffuse and muddled volumes full of boring passages, repetitions, and false or short-sighted views', and says that 'a thorough examination of his [Saint-Pierre's] political works showed me only superficial views'.[43] The task of abridging thus became a 'painful labour', and Rousseau came close to giving up the entire project. Yet, he persisted because he felt indebted to the Comte de Saint-Pierre, the nephew of the Abbé, who had kindly given him the manuscripts for this project.[44] In any case, this trouble made it inevitable for Rousseau to scale down his original plan to produce an abridgement of all the works of Saint-Pierre and to write a short biography of the author. What he produced were only two pairs of 'reviews' on Saint-Pierre's *Polysynodie* and peace project towards the end of the 1750s, four pieces altogether. Judging from this evidence alone, Rousseau is not a follower of Saint-Pierre's argument; indeed, he appears as a critic, even mocking Saint-Pierre, as most IR students believe.

---

[42] About this use, see *OC*, p. 431.   [43] Rousseau, *The Confessions*, pp. 380, 393.
[44] Ibid, p. 393.

And yet, what needs to be stressed is that this general repugnance to Saint-Pierre's works did not prevent Rousseau from realizing 'that the manuscripts which the Count de Saint-Pierre had given me were so many treasures'.[45] On Saint-Pierre's peace project especially, Rousseau states in *Jugement* that, contrary to its appearance, it is a work of great importance and should be taken very seriously: 'the work of the Abbé de Saint-Pierre on perpetual peace may seem at first glance ineffectual for creating it and unnecessary for maintaining it; "it is therefore a vain speculation", said some impatient reader. No. It is a solid and thoughtful book, and it is very important that it exists'.[46] These words are significant; for they suggest that, in contrast to the common understanding in IR, Rousseau sympathized with Saint-Pierre's work in general and his peace project in particular. Of course, this remark may have been mere lip-service or a formality; I nevertheless argue that, confronted with the natural-lawyers at the time, Rousseau indeed found 'treasures' in Saint-Pierre's writings. Among them the most crucial is Saint-Pierre's approach to the issue of politics and morality, which proved very useful for dismantling the dominant natural-law theory. Although Rousseau was unhappy with the general quality of Saint-Pierre's works, he still thought that Saint-Pierre had been moving in the right direction regarding an alternative to the orthodox theory of the age.

Rousseau's moral and theoretical agreements with Saint-Pierre

More than anything else, the very foundation of Rousseau's sympathy with Saint-Pierre lay in the latter's selfless devotion to the cause of morality. *Les confessions* reveal that reading Saint-Pierre's moral writings 'confirmed me [Rousseau] in the opinion I had formed on some of his letters . . . that he had much more intelligence than I had previously imagined'.[47] Indeed, Saint-Pierre began to ponder the means for perpetual peace because he was so shocked by all the moral 'evils' that wars bring about.[48] Rousseau, full of respect for this noble concern of his predecessor, says in *Extrait* that 'no author deserves public attention better than the one who proposes the means to put the project [for perpetual peace among states] in execution'.[49] Rousseau also noted that Saint-Pierre had been very outspoken about the French government,

---

[45] Ibid.   [46] *OC*, p. 591.   [47] Rousseau, *The Confessions*, p. 393.
[48] Abbé de Saint-Pierre, *Projet pour rendre la paix perpétuelle en Europe* (Tours: Fayard, 1986), edited by Simone Goyard-Fabre, pp. 9–10. All the translations from this below are mine.
[49] *OC*, p. 563.

running considerable risks. Although Saint-Pierre only faced expulsion from the French Academy, Rousseau still admired his courage for the sake of enhancing morality in society.[50] For Rousseau 'the truth' was always 'not so much metaphysical as moral'.[51] In this sense Saint-Pierre was, as Rousseau says in *Jugement*, a truly praiseworthy figure who was sincerely devoted to 'the public good' without seeking his 'personal interest'.[52]

Rousseau's sympathy with Saint-Pierre's (international) political theory was however not limited to the level of moral motivation. The more important reason for Rousseau's sympathy lies in the fact that his *theoretical* view on the relationship between morality and politics was quite close to that of Saint-Pierre.

Throughout his intellectual career, Saint-Pierre wrote a number of 'projects' that were, he thought, very useful for augmenting the public good. The most well-known of these is his project for perpetual peace but he also developed other plans, including 'the eradication of barbaric pirate ships', 'roads usable in winter' and 'perfecting the governments of states'. Behind this we find Saint-Pierre's conviction that man's nature is not predetermined by birth and can hence be altered. Although it was accepted that man's actions are always underpinned by *amour-propre*, the passionate desire to fulfil self-interests, Saint-Pierre held the view that this desire does not determine man's moral propensity: '*amour-propre* makes both all vices and all moral goods, depending upon whether it is rightly or badly understood'.[53] It is this conviction that led him to believe the following formula: 'men can be curbed only by the laws of society'.[54]

Saint-Pierre thus started his peace project by posing the following rhetorical question: 'whether this evil [war] is so truly attached to the *nature* of sovereignties and sovereigns that there is absolutely no remedy'.[55] He answered this question in the negative and argued that it is actually *the political constitution among sovereigns* that had long caused the wars that occurred so frequently in Europe: 'The present *constitution* of Europe can never produce anything other than almost continual

---

[50] Rousseau, *The Confessions*, p. 394.
[51] Rousseau à Dom Léger-Marie Deschamps, à Montmorenci le 25 juin 1761, in *Correspondance complète de Jean Jacques Rousseau: Tome IX*, p. 28. The translation is mine.
[52] *OC*, p. 591.
[53] Merle L. Perkins, 'Unpublished Maxims of the Abbé de Saint-Pierre' *French Review* 31 (1958), p. 499. The translation is mine.
[54] Perkins, *The Moral and Political Philosophy of the Abbé de Saint-Pierre*, p. 45.
[55] Saint-Pierre, *Projet*, p. 10. Emphasis added.

wars; this is because it can never procure any sufficient certainty for the execution of treaties.'[56] How can one then prevent this problem of wars from occurring? Only by transforming the present political constitution of Europe into the one that provides a 'sufficient certainty for the execution of treaties'. Saint-Pierre submitted a model for an alternative inter-state system – confederation – in his project; it is, he thought, the only system that can force each sovereign member-state to act morally.

Notice here that Saint-Pierre's argument that the moral 'evil' of war is caused by the form of political constitutions is identical with the principle that Rousseau discovered in Venice. Therefore, when he read Saint-Pierre's works for the first time during his open confrontation with the natural-lawyers in the mid-1750s, he would have thought that he 'unearthed a buried treasure' – a conception of the relationship between morality and politics similar to his own. Naturally then, Rousseau did not object to Saint-Pierre's conclusion about the cause of inter-state wars. He points out in *Extrait* that 'if the present system is indestructible, it is constantly in a stormy state; this is because, between the powers of Europe, there are the action and reaction which, without overthrowing them altogether, kept them in continual agitation'.[57] Rousseau also agreed with Saint-Pierre on the means to solve this problem. Since he accepted the establishment of Saint-Pierre's model for an alternative inter-state system – a 'confederation' – as reasonable, he said in *Jugement* (if somewhat ironically): 'Let us not say any longer that his [Saint-Pierre's] system was not adopted because it was not good; let us say instead that it was too good to be adopted'.[58] In the light of these agreements it is plausible that Rousseau, overall, found Saint-Pierre's peace project solid and convincing. In relation to the dominant paradigm of the modern natural-law theory at the time, Saint-Pierre and Rousseau in fact shared a similar alternative.

On the basis of this fundamental (if largely tacit) agreement, Rousseau saw Saint-Pierre's pacific confederation as a generalizable model for a just political constitution; it could be applied not only to the inter-state sphere but also to domestic society, in order to make men moral. This is probably the reason for Rousseau's use of the term 'confederation' in *Economie politique* and *The Geneva Manuscript*. He discovered the idea of the social contract underlying the *constitution of the state* in Saint-Pierre's *inter-state* model for perpetual peace.

---

[56] Ibid., p. 11. Emphasis added.   [57] *OC*, p. 572.   [58] Ibid., p. 599.

The correspondence between Rousseau's social-contract association and Saint-Pierre's confederation

In order to substantiate the thesis that Rousseau 'imported' the model of a just political constitution from Saint-Pierre's inter-state confederation, we must compare the social-contract association in *Du contrat social* with it. The social-contract association has two core features: first, this constitution consists of free and equal individuals alone; and second, in this constitution, only 'the general will' expressed as law has ultimate authority over its members. In Rousseau's *Extrait*, both features are directly and indirectly stated as the key components of Saint-Pierre's model for perpetual peace; and, of course, they can be traced in Saint-Pierre's peace project itself.

The first core feature of Rousseau's 'social-contract' constitution is that it consists of free and equal individuals only. In *Du contrat social* he categorically rejects, as the principal condition of the social contract, that even a single figure is treated differently from all the rest. This marked the emergence of a new contract theory in history because it rejected the traditional idea of the 'contract of submission'. Entering into an unequal contract with a superior is nothing but a renunciation of freedom, the essence of humanity, and makes one a slave. He therefore severely attacked preceding contract theories, most notably Grotius', that contain this idea of the contract between the ruler and the ruled.[59] For Rousseau, every single member of the constitution must be equally bound by the same rule all the time; even the monarch must not be exempted from this.

Turning to Saint-Pierre's peace project, we find repeated emphasis on the 'mutuality' and 'equality' of states in the 'confederation'. First, searching for means to terminate all wars, Saint-Pierre 'found that all those means are reduced to making *mutual* promises'.[60] He also says that 'I intended to show only one thing, namely, that it is infinitely more advantageous for every man to be in a *permanent society* with his equals, or with those that are almost his equals, than not to be there; and from this I have concluded that the Christian sovereigns will always lack infinite happiness unless they make a *permanent society* among themselves'.[61] Once the confederation is formed, commercial exchanges between states should be promoted under conditions of equality: 'the chief point in commerce is that no nation is to be preferred to another, and all to be

[59] Ibid., pp. 355–358.   [60] Saint-Pierre, *Projet*, p. 10. Emphasis added.
[61] Ibid., pp. 34–35.

equally free to come to sell and buy merchandises'.[62] To put these points the other way around, allowing even a single member to receive special treatment would be disastrous for the confederation: 'if the sovereigns reserved the least pretensions one upon the other, there would be but a chaos of new rights contradicting each other . . . and there would be almost no certain principle for decisions.'[63]

In the *Extrait*, Rousseau did not particularly emphasize the 'mutuality' and 'equality' of states as a key component of the model of the pacific confederation. There is, however, no doubt that he recognized the importance of this principle when he explained that each state is to be almost equal in power in order for this confederation to last: 'for forming a solid and durable confederation, it is necessary to put all the members of it in such mutual dependence that no one is singly in a position to resist all the others'.[64] Rousseau also says in *Extrait* that a 'confederate government' is the government that treats each member equally: 'a form of confederate government, which, uniting the peoples by the bonds similar to those that already unite individuals, places *equally* one another under the authority of law'.[65] Equality among members is the necessary condition for states to form a confederation and to be in peace for ever.

Interestingly, Rousseau indicates in the last quotation that treating every member equally is a condition required for both the union of 'peoples', or states, and the union of 'individuals'. This suggests that Rousseau was quite aware that this feature of Saint-Pierre's pacific confederation could be transferred to his theory of the state. Moreover, the same remark also indicates that Rousseau recognized the purpose of Saint-Pierre's confederation as establishing the rule of law; each member state, joining in this inter-state constitution, is put equally 'under the rule of law'. This is actually the idea that forms the second core feature of Rousseau's 'social-contract' constitution. Entering into the social contract, all free and equal individuals are, like all states in Saint-Pierre's confederation, to be placed under the rule of law expressed as 'the general will'.

In *Du contrat social*, Rousseau vigorously rejects that any individual will is prioritized over the will of the whole. This is because every individual will, whether of the ruler or anyone else, seeks only his own interests and not the common interest.[66] In place of the rule of the individual

---

[62] Ibid., p. 180.   [63] Ibid., p. 175.   [64] *OC*, p. 573.   [65] Ibid., p. 564. Emphasis added.
[66] Ibid., p. 371.

will, the rule of 'the general will' is to be established; and this rule is the same as the rule of law because 'when the matter on which one decides is general, so is the will that decides. This is the act that I call law'.[67] What can produce this rule of law, then? Rousseau maintains that 'force produces no law'.[68] Although force, especially the ruler's, can physically compel people to be obedient, it never creates the law that makes men truly moral. It is the social contract alone that can produce law. When this contract is concluded, all contractors have to agree that they cease to live in the state of war, and that they live together in 'the civil state in which all rights are fixed by law'.[69]

Remarkably, Saint-Pierre presents the same contrast between the lawful state and the state in which force dominates. And, like Rousseau, he holds that his pacific confederation (or 'permanent society' in his own terms) establishes the rule of law in place of the rule of the jungle.

> What means do they [different sovereigns] have to end their differences, and to put limits to their pretensions? We know all the means; there are only two sorts, according to the two sorts of the pretenders; either force or law. For either the two pretenders make a part and are members of some permanent society, or they do not make a part of it. If they do not make a part of it, their differences can be terminated neither by laws nor, consequently, by the judges or interpreters of laws. As they have the misfortune of being deprived of the advantage of a perpetual commerce and of a permanent society, they also have the misfortune of being deprived of the advantage of laws that distribute to each what belongs to him legitimately. . . . Since they [present European sovereigns] have had no permanent society among them yet, they have no law whereby to decide their differences without war . . .[70]

Further, Saint-Pierre says that law must be for the general interest of every member: 'they [sovereigns] would not consent to it [law] if, in that law that they wish to impose upon themselves for utility and common security, some were worse treated than others, namely, if the law were not equal for all'.[71] This also echoes Rousseau's understanding of the law expressed as 'the general will'.

Rousseau does not fail to mention these points in *Extrait*. He recognizes that the purpose of Saint-Pierre's confederation is to place each state 'equally under the authority of law', and refers to the contrast of this rule with the current state of Europe by calling it 'the state of war'.[72] This unlawful state is based on the rule of the selfish individual will:

[67] Ibid., p. 379.　[68] Ibid., p. 355.　[69] Ibid., p. 378.　[70] Saint-Pierre, *Projet*, p. 23.
[71] Ibid., p. 170.　[72] *OC*, pp. 564, 587.

the public law of Europe 'is full of contradictory regulations that are in harmony only with the right of the stronger; so that, reason . . . always turns to the personal interest even in doubtful cases, which makes war inevitable'.[73] Rousseau therefore explains that Saint-Pierre's confederation 'gives the group of states the perfection that it has lacked . . . by forcing all the parties to co-operate for the common good'.[74] One must prevent that 'members depart [from the confederation] at their own pleasure as soon as they believe that their private interests are clashing with the general interest.'[75] All of these statements indicate that Rousseau correctly grasped the core ideas of Saint-Pierre's project. It is very likely that Rousseau found crucial ideas for his social-contract theory in Saint-Pierre's peace project.

In summary, Rousseau left various 'signs' in *Extrait, Jugement* and elsewhere indicating his basic sympathy with Saint-Pierre's peace project. The source of this agreement lies in Saint-Pierre's approach to politics and morality which echoed Rousseau's Venice discovery. Saint-Pierre's concept of a 'confederation' for peace, moreover, looked to Rousseau like the very prototype of a just political constitution; he therefore used it in his social-contract theory.

Rousseau's 'international relations theory' must now be re-assessed in light of this interpretation.

Reassessing Rousseau's theory of international relations

Historians of international relations theory have long regarded Rousseau as a 'realist'. Taking into account that Rousseau found the model of a just political constitution in Saint-Pierre's 'confederation', however, the more plausible conclusion is that he longed for the establishment of the 'social-contract' between states as much as Saint-Pierre had done before him. In fact, for Rousseau, tackling injustice in interstate relations is an indispensible condition for attaining justice within the state: 'between man and man we live in a civil state and are subjected to laws; between people and people we each enjoy natural liberty. . . . Because living simultaneously in the social order and in the state of nature, we are subjected to the inconveniences of both, without finding certainty in either'.[76] The need for the establishment of the confederation between states is therefore beyond controversy; in this respect

---

[73] Ibid., pp. 568–569.   [74] Ibid., p. 574.   [75] Ibid.   [76] Ibid., p. 610.

Saint-Pierre's project for peace is certainly 'solid' and 'thoughtful' for Rousseau.[77]

Objections to this interpretation may entail the argument that, even if there was no 'realism' as such in Rousseau's time, his international relations theory was still anticipating the emergence of what we today in IR call a realist theory. This claim would emphasize that Rousseau's concept of sovereignty sanctified the 'independence' of each sovereign or that in the end he rejected Saint-Pierre's peace plan as impractical. There is, however, no clear textual basis in the 'review' for such claims. On the contrary, the work provides a very different explanation of Rousseau's concept of sovereignty as well as of the meaning of 'impracticality' with regard to Saint-Pierre's project.

Rousseau's concept of sovereignty as moral freedom

In IR Rousseau's concept of sovereignty has often been seen as one of the earliest formulations of 'external sovereignty'. External sovereignty – independence from any other external political authority – is the notion that the discipline has placed at the centre of its theorization of 'international relations'; and this concept has been regarded as an ideological barrier to any attempt to create an overarching political authority above 'sovereign' states. In *Du contrat social* Rousseau called sovereignty 'indivisible' and 'inalienable', which has been read as clear support both for the 'unity' of the nation and the principle of 'non-intervention' as the minimum denominator of sovereign statehood.[78] Jens Bartelson, for instance, claims that Rousseau understood sovereignty for the first time as the representation of 'the inside/outside' – the fundamental idea that demarcates 'domestic politics' and 'international politics' – and thus pre-empted its subsequent emergence in IR.[79]

However, in Rousseau's 'review' of Saint-Pierre's peace project, a very different understanding of the concept of sovereignty emerges. Saint-Pierre defined it not as 'independence' but as 'moral freedom' which removes the incompatibility between remaining a sovereign and joining a confederation with other sovereigns. If the 'review' is a document that indicates Rousseau's sympathy with, rather than opposition to, Saint-Pierre's argument, we must assume that Rousseau accepted this concept of sovereignty as moral freedom.

---

[77] Ibid., p. 591.   [78] *OC*, pp. 368–369.
[79] Jens Bartelson, *A Genealogy of Sovereignty* (Cambridge: Cambridge University Press, 1995), pp. 212–213.

In his peace project Saint-Pierre responds to many probable 'objections' to his proposal. One of those objections is that he 'does not pay sufficient attention to the prerogative of independence, the prerogative essential to sovereignty'.[80] By way of response, Saint-Pierre first defines 'freedom' in the following way: 'the more one can do what pleases one without opposition, without needing to fear its results, namely, *without offending anybody*, the more freedom one has'.[81] Saint-Pierre then rhetorically asks whether one can be truly free if one is allowed to kill and to benefit from booties. Saint-Pierre's answer is negative. He concludes that:

> diminishing their [the sovereigns'] dependence and as a consequence augmenting their independence are achieved by making use of permanent Arbitration, namely, by using the same invention that a long time ago formed the primitive, permanent Society between the chiefs of families . . . which brought them trust, security, communication, arts, sciences, wealth, religions, justice, charity, esteem, friendship, indulgence and all the qualities and talents that contributed to make men more virtuous and happier.[82]

In short, for Saint-Pierre, full 'independence' of a sovereign is attained only in society with others where trust, security, justice and so on are guaranteed. In other words, when no sovereign is able to offend the common interests, each can be 'free' as well as 'independent'. Accordingly, that a sovereign joins a pacific confederation with other sovereigns actually matches the requirement for 'true' sovereignty (or independence) rather than to indicate its loss.

Rousseau of course did not fail to mention Saint-Pierre's formulation of the concept of sovereignty in *Extrait*. He states that, in the pacific confederation, every member state can strengthen its sovereignty rather than weaken or lose it: 'it is very clear that it [the judicial tribunal of confederation] does not at all diminish the rights of sovereignty, but, on the contrary, affirms them'.[83] The reason for this is that, within this confederation, each sovereign gains the guarantee of security, by being able to keep 'not only his state against foreign invasion, but also his authority against all the rebellions of his subjects'.[84] After all, 'there is all the difference between dependence upon others . . . and belonging to the polity [confederation] in which each member is a chief by turns. For, in the latter, one's freedom is assured by the pledges one gives the

---

[80] Saint-Pierre, *Projet*, p. 451. [81] Ibid., p. 497. [82] Ibid., p. 523. [83] *OC*, p. 583.
[84] Ibid.

polity'.[85] Elsewhere, Rousseau points out that the 'absolute independence' of sovereigns is the corollary of continual wars among them: 'the state of disorder and war, which necessarily engenders the mutually absolute independence of all the sovereigns in the imperfect society that rules them in Europe today'.[86] Sovereignty is thus neither the right of 'absolute independence' nor the right to do whatever one wants to do; it is rather the right of freedom in Saint-Pierre's sense, the right to submit oneself to the rule of the pacific confederation. In Rousseau's international relations theory, therefore, sovereignty does not only go hand in hand with joining the confederation, but actually requires it. The confederation affirms the sovereignty of each member and, after all, its freedom.

Interestingly, Saint-Pierre's definition of sovereignty is almost identical with the way in which Rousseau explains the concept of 'civil and moral freedom' in *Du contrat social*. This concept is what he presented as the truly human concept of freedom, the fundamental concept that lies in his social-contract theory. Not only did Rousseau find Saint-Pierre's formulation of sovereignty very persuasive; it might even be the case that he took this concept of moral freedom also from Saint-Pierre's understanding of sovereignty. Here is Rousseau's discussion of the concept of freedom in *Du contrat social*.

In the 'normal' sense of the term 'freedom', men become inevitably 'unfree' once they enter into the social-contract with others. For, as a result of this contract, the actions of the contractors are put under the restrictions of laws or 'the general will', and thus they no longer act free of constraints. However, Rousseau argues that this is no more than men losing their vulgar and barbaric 'natural freedom', instead of which they acquire genuinely human freedom, namely, 'civil (social) freedom' and 'moral freedom'. By 'natural freedom' Rousseau means the freedom that can be limited by its possessor alone; this is a 'crude' freedom because it allows a man to do whatever he wants. 'Civil freedom', however, is the freedom to acknowledge that men possess only what they can possess rightly in society; 'moral freedom', which alone makes a man truly his own master, is the freedom to obey the moral law that men enforce upon themselves by themselves.[87] Rousseau understands the transition from natural freedom to civil and moral freedom as 'a remarkable change, which substitutes instinct with justice in his conduct and gives his actions the morality that has been lacking so

[85] Ibid., p. 584.   [86] Ibid., p. 587.   [87] Ibid., p. 365.

far'.[88] The social contract is therefore the means, and the only legitimate means according to Rousseau, for men, who are free by definition, to become free in the true sense of the term.

This is the same formulation that Saint-Pierre used for the relationship between sovereignty and confederation. Whereas in Rousseau men can be truly free only in the political association of the social contract, for Saint-Pierre sovereigns can be truly free, that is 'sovereign', only in the pacific confederation. Similarly, men lose their 'natural freedom' with lawful restraints, and sovereigns lose their 'absolute independence' with lawful restraints. On the basis of this correspondence it is unlikely that Rousseau rejected Saint-Pierre's understanding of sovereignty; rather, it seems that he inherited it and even used it in his explanation of civil and moral freedom in *Du contrat social*.

In contrast to the common belief in IR, accordingly, Rousseau was not the theorist of 'sovereignty as absolute independence'. He was the theorist of 'sovereignty as moral freedom', the concept that morally obliges all sovereigns to form a pacific confederation and to act lawfully towards each other. Rousseau's international relations theory aimed, after all, at the construction of an inter-state system in which each sovereign becomes truly free. His concept of sovereignty was not an obstacle to this purpose.

Rousseau's critique of Saint-Pierre's peace project

There is one more question to be answered. Why did Rousseau reject Saint-Pierre's peace project as impractical in the end? Was he, after all, an early 'realist'?

Rousseau's real intention in criticizing Saint-Pierre's project as impractical is, I submit, to argue that his predecessor was not consistent enough. Saint-Pierre was 'naive', not because his project itself was utopian, but because he believed that absolute monarchs would agree on the usefulness and necessity of a confederation.[89] Rousseau had no such confidence in princes. '[A]ll the occupation of kings . . . is related to only two objects: to extend their domination externally and to make it more absolute internally'.[90] Princes do not wish to realize perpetual peace between states; their interests lie in an unstable and insecure inter-state system.

---

[88] Ibid., p. 364.
[89] David Boucher, *Political Theories of International Relations: From Thucydides to the Present* (Oxford: Oxford University Press, 1998), p. 302.
[90] *OC*, p. 592.

Rousseau's distrust of princes is consistent with his social-contract theory which defines the monarch as an administrator who merely executes what the sovereign decides. And the sovereign is not the monarch but the collective of individual citizens, the people, who are tied together by the social contract. At the end of *Jugement*, Rousseau claims that a confederation can be established only by 'revolutions'.[91] The scale of this political transformation should, indeed, be 'revolutions' since all domestic societies need to be reconstituted on the basis of the social contract (which also means, in Rousseau's view, that all societies are to be turned into small states) before they can unite under a confederation.[92] Because these 'revolutions' are a precondition for perpetual peace, its achievement should take a painfully long time; and it 'would perhaps do more harm in a moment than it would prevent it for centuries'.[93]

In Rousseau's view, Saint-Pierre failed to recognize the necessity for establishing a just political constitution at the domestic level. Although providing the right solution to men's immorality at the inter-state level, his predecessor was naive enough to trust the good will of princes, despite the fact that their absolute rule is one of the main causes of men's moral corruptions, wars. As long as this moral wrong is left unchanged, the emergence of a pacific confederation is simply an unrealistic dream. A confederation between states has to be built for achieving perpetual peace, to be sure, but this can occur only when each domestic society is based on the social contract.

For Rousseau, the transformation of 'internal' as well as 'external' politics is a single, inseparable agenda for making men moral. It is this recognition that led him to demolish Saint-Pierre's project as impractical eventually; and it is this recognition that distinguishes his international relations theory radically from that of modern IR.

Conclusion

Historically Rousseau's (international) political theory did not differ much from that of Saint-Pierre. Their approach to politics – to regard man's morality as a product of the political constitution – was identical in their own intellectual context in that it cast significant doubts

[91] Ibid., p. 600. About the meaning of Rousseau's 'revolution', see Forsyth, *Unions of States*, pp. 91–92.
[92] J.-L. Windenberger, *Essai sur le système de politique étrangère de J.-J. Rousseau: la république confédération des petits états* (Paris: Alphonse Picard et Fils, 1900), pp. 189–236.
[93] *OC*, p. 600.

on the dominant view of the modern natural-law theory that human nature – seeking to fulfil their self-interest – was predetermined and served as the basis of political association. Because of this theoretical affinity, Rousseau realized that Saint-Pierre's peace project contained the model of a just political order. The notion of a pacific confederation suggested to Rousseau a new form of association consisting of only equal members, and then he took full advantage of this idea in his social-contract theory. We can trace Rousseau's inspiration back to Saint-Pierre through the term 'confederation' which he used to depict the 'social-contract' association as well as Saint-Pierre's association of states for peace. Indeed, Saint-Pierre's pacific confederation and Rousseau's 'social-contract' political constitution resemble each other considerably in their key aspects.

It is therefore misleading to regard Rousseau's international relations theory as 'realist'. This interpretation rests on Rousseau's rejection of Saint-Pierre's peace project in terms of its practicality, but, in the light of their theoretical affinity, it is more plausible to assume that Rousseau felt great sympathy with Saint-Pierre's theory in general and his peace project in particular. In this respect Rousseau's concept of sovereignty is the most prominent indicator that his international political theory differs in a crucial sense from the so-called realist theory while demonstrating theoretical continuity with Saint-Pierre's. As opposed to the realist notion of 'sovereignty as absolute independence', both Rousseau and Saint-Pierre argued for the notion of 'sovereignty as moral freedom', the concept that regards 'true' sovereigns as those who form a 'social-contract' association with each other in order to become truly free and independent. Rousseau denounced Saint-Pierre's peace project as impractical, but it was only because it did not tackle the injustice of absolute monarchy as a precondition for perpetual peace. He saw domestic and international injustices as inseparable. This reading of Rousseau's 'review' of Saint-Pierre's peace project thus challenges the claim that he is a 'realist' thinker.

Yet, this case has more general implications. It demonstrates, firstly, that 'history of international relations theory' has hitherto failed to appreciate the *historical* meaning of classical texts, which is typically illustrated by the 'Rousseau-realist' thesis that is based on the *contemporary* idealist-realist dichotomy. As an antidote to this 'reading the present back into history', this essay supports the strategy to situate past texts in their historical intellectual context. This context may not be fully recoverable, but any attempt to ascertain it can still prevent the most anachronistic results. In arguing for an historical approach to classical authors, I do not claim that this 'contextual' reading is the only or right way to read classics. But I am arguing that the appreciation of historical contexts is a necessary condition for those who call themselves 'historians' of international relations theory.

This case study secondly suggests that these historians cannot limit their attention to 'International Relations theory', in the narrow contemporary sense of the term. Reading Rousseau's 'review' historically demonstrates that his thinking was not at all circumscribed by a narrow understanding of 'international relations' as such. He did not separate international relations theory from the political theory of the state, and thus he was able to apply Saint-Pierre's pacific confederation of *states* to the model of a just political constitution for *individuals*. To put this the other way around, modern IR interpreters have failed to acknowledge the 'inspirational source' for Rousseau's social-contract theory and hence his basic sympathy with Saint-Pierre's theory in general, because they have not been sufficiently free from the narrow disciplinary definition of 'international relations' in approaching past texts. Historians of international relations theory need to challenge the compartmentalization of disciplines today rather than to read them back into history. After all, the value of classical authors lies precisely in their holistic conception of society and politics.

Part II
Political contexts

6 The Savage Smith and the temporal walls of capitalism[1]

David L. Blaney and Naeem Inayatullah

> Indian kinship economics, which, I . . . understand not as pre-capitalist but as anticapitalist, constitute a powerful *and continuing* critique of the waste of an expansive, acquisitive capitalism that . . . [Europe] could not *afford* to entertain. The loss in social vision was, and is, incalculable.
>
> Eric Cheyfitz[2]

In the standard literature in International Political Economy (IPE), Adam Smith serves as a marker for a 'classical liberal school of economics'. This 'economics' derives from Smith a 'shared and coherent set of assumptions' about the drive to truck and barter as the impetus to inevitable and inexorable human material improvement and the existence of 'inviolable laws' of economic life that mandate free markets internally and free trade internationally.[3] Others within IPE and International Relations (IR) have complicated this view[4] even if their efforts have failed to dislodge the standard reading. Additional readings may be useful for those who embed economics within a richly debated history. In this chapter, we emphasize the role the Amerindians play in Smith's work. Reading Smith against the theme of 'savagery' allows us to: (1) focus on

[1] This chapter represents the beginnings of a larger project. We thank Chuck Green, Xavier Guillaume, Sandra Halperin, Beate Jahn, David P. Levine, Khaldoun Samman and Robert Shilliam for helpful comments and suggestions.
[2] 'Savage Law', in Amy Kaplan and Donald E. Pease (eds.), *Cultures of United States Imperialism* (Durham NC: Duke University Press, 1993), p. 118. Emphasis in original.
[3] Robert A. Isaak, *Managing World Economic Change: International Political Economy* 3rd edn (Upper Saddle River NJ: Prentice Hall, 2000), p. 4, makes the claim about the existence of a liberal 'school'. Most texts begin with this same assumption. The account of liberalism as possessing 'shared and coherent' assumptions can be found in Robert Gilpin, *The Political Economy of International Relations* (Princeton NJ: Princeton University Press, 1987), pp. 26–31, 44, 81.
[4] See especially Craig N. Murphy's interesting use of Smith in *International Organization and Industrial Change: Global Governance Since 1850* (Cambridge: Polity Press, 1994).

an often neglected intellectual influence on Smith – the Jesuit Father Lafitau; (2) critically examine the comparative ethnology that Smith uses to develop a theory of human progress and insulate commercial society from moral critique; and, perhaps most fruitfully, (3) recover potential ethical resources that help us assess the present state of global capitalism.

Linking comparative ethnology and Smith may seem surprising, since neither Smith nor any of the key Scottish social thinkers made the voyage to the New World.[5] Nonetheless, their encounters with the Indians were no less profound than those of earlier adventurers, missionaries and scholars whose reports they inherited. It was in and through these reports that the Scots journeyed. Their travels were, as Anthony Pagden puts it, 'cognitive', a 'travel in the mind's eye'.[6] In their constructions of the Indians' place in human history, the Scots identify the Indians as travellers on a common human path. In the minds of Smith and his fellow Scots, the Indians had embarked on a great journey towards Europe – that is, towards Europe's present.

The need to chart the location of the Indians had a prior history. Since the 'discovery' of the Americas, Europeans had struggled to make sense of continents and peoples both unfamiliar and difficult to situate within the confines of scriptural and classical authority.[7] Many regarded the New World peoples' physical and social distance from the singular moment of Edenic creation as a correlate of their degeneration from Christian faith and civilized behaviour. Reports of cannibalism, human sacrifice and low levels of artistic and scientific development confirmed the distance of the Amerindians from the norms of human (i.e. European) practice. Numerous thinkers sought to contain the disorder the Indians represented by placing them below the threshold of humanity, thereby allowing enslavement or extermination. Or, if their humanity was accepted, the differences the Indians exhibited were translated into a form of infancy or childhood that might be corrected and guided through European tutelage. The pedagogical component of imperialism was thus deployed quite early. Over the next century, others would build on this understanding by designating the North American natives as examples of the earliest state of human existence.

[5] The partial exception is Adam Ferguson who visited the American Colonies in the spring of 1778 as an emissary. He was not allowed behind the American lines.

[6] Anthony Pagden, *European Encounters with the New World: From Renaissance to Romanticism* (New Haven: Yale University Press, 1993), p. 30.

[7] See Naeem Inayatullah and David L. Blaney, *International Relations and the Problem of Difference* (New York: Routledge, 2004), Chapter 2.

By the mid-eighteenth century, the novelty of the Amerindians had worn off and the moral threat of cannibalism and human sacrifice had receded. For most Enlightenment thinkers, the demands of a scientific history of humankind replaced the imperative to preserve scriptural and/or classical authority. The Indians continued to represent difference, but the remaining important marker of the Amerindians – low levels of development – would be incorporated into emerging theories of moral or civic philosophy. The temporal separation of the Indians and Europeans became, in the hands of Smith and the Frenchman Baron de Turgot, a theory of historical development with four ages or stages: hunting and gathering, shepherding, agriculture and commerce.[8] The movement from one stage to another appears internal or immanent to processes at each stage, as, in Smith's words, 'a great, an immense machine, whose regular and harmonious movements produce a thousand agreeable effects'.[9] The temporal distance between Indians and Europeans, previously bridgeable only by the activities of the missionary, could now be understood within an 'abstract and philosophical' scheme that locates the American Indian at the very beginnings of human society.[10] The differences suggested by Indian life are rendered benign as superceded ways of existence.

But the past need not appear so agreeably relinquished. Smith was aware of Rousseau's treatment of 'savagery' as a source of critical reflection on emerging commercial societies.[11] Thus, 'cognitive travel' could involve serious reflection on the meanings and purposes constitutive of contemporary societies. 'The past', as Ashis Nandy suggests, is available as 'an open-ended record of the predicaments of our time'. What is required, and perhaps exemplified by Rousseau's civic humanist critique, is 'an attempt to read the past as an essay on human prospects, and ... the ability to live with one's constructions of the past and deploy them creatively'.[12] '[T]ime-travel', thus, potentially 'reshapes the past and the future' by holding 'them up as mirrors to the present'.[13]

---

[8] See Ronald L. Meek, *Social Science and the Ignoble Savage* (Cambridge: Cambridge University Press, 1976), Chapters 3 and 4.
[9] Adam Smith, *The Theory of Moral Sentiments*, eds. D. D. Raphael and A. L. Macfie (Indianapolis IN, Liberty Fund, 1976), p. 316.
[10] Ibid.
[11] See Smith, 'A Letter to the Authors of the *Edinburgh Review*' in W. P. D. Wightman and J. C. Bryce (eds.), *Essays on Philosophical Subjects* (Indianapolis IN: Liberty Fund, 1980), pp. 250–254.
[12] Ashis Nandy, *Time Warps: Silent and Evasive Pasts in Indian Politics and Religion* (New Brunswick NJ: Rutgers University Press, 2002), p. 1.
[13] Ibid., p. 5.

Smith drew much of his knowledge of the Amerindians from Father Joseph François Lafitau's *Customs of the American Indians*. Ronald Meek notes that Lafitau's work was given a 'special role' by Smith and others because it was seen to have 'provided a convincing demonstration of the fact that contemporary American society could be regarded as a living model – conveniently laid out for study, as if in a laboratory – of human society in the "first" or "earliest" stage of its development'.[14] The decisiveness of Lafitau's impact may seem surprising since his principal aim – to reassert a Christian eschatology – was far from the minds of Smith and other Scottish Enlightenment figures. Nonetheless, his work was recognizably scientific by Enlightenment standards and it provided an opportunity for the kind of cognitive travel necessary to the Scots' comparative historical method. And, as we will note, Lafitau's translation of his travels to the Americas as travels in time foreshadows Smith's protective encasement of commercial society behind temporal walls. We examine Lafitau's work in the first section of this chapter.

In the second section, we examine in greater detail the shape of Scottish Enlightenment historiography and the role that encounters with the Indians play in Smith's formulation of a 'conjectural history' and the 'four-stages theory'. If Lafitau is anxious to assert a uniform source of religiosity in the face of religious difference, the Scots control the amazing diversity of forms of human society, both historically and contemporaneously, with the assertion of a uniform and progressive human nature. Progress in Smith's hands takes on the form of a stadial theory of movement through four ascending stages of social and human development. The Amerindians play a crucial role in establishing the content of the earliest stages of humankind, since they are associated with the very infancy of human history. The consequences of this move are that ways of life that differ from Smith's commercial society are relegated to the past. As Smith travels cognitively, not only across space, but also across time, he denies the 'co-evalness' of others, eliminating alternative ways of life as a source of critical reflection on the present. The theory of development separates, thereby, contemporary (therefore relevant) political and ethical concerns from those rendered irrelevant by their association with savagery or barbarism.

Despite Smith's vigorous effort to mute the voices of the savage past, we suggest that he also takes up Ashis Nandy's call for uncovering the critical implications of time travel. While our cognitive travels need to

---

[14] Meek, *Ignoble Savage*, p. 57.

differ markedly from the Scottish Enlightenment's dominant practices, Smith's own work reveals echoes that provide resources for contemporary critiques of global capitalism.

Lafitau: to the Indians and back

Like those before him, Father Joseph François Lafitau's most famous work, *Moeurs des sauvages Ameriquains comparées aux moeurs des premiers temps* [*Customs of the American Indians Compared with the Customs of Primitive Times*] (1724), struggles to reconcile an understanding of the origins of the Americans with scriptural claims of the species' singular origins.[15] For us, what distinguishes Lafitau (1681–1746) from others is that he is recognizably an Enlightenment thinker who has considerable influence on the Scots.[16]

Consistent with this picture of Lafitau as an Enlightenment figure, Fenton and Moore speculate that his early life in the busy port of Bordeaux stimulated his 'dreams of the New World' and spurred interest in missions in North America as well as his later scholarly vocation.[17] In this way, Lafitau is easily associated with a spirit of scientific curiosity akin to that embraced by the Enlightenment. Others paint a different picture, highlighting Lafitau's description of his book as an attempt to refute the work of sceptics like Pierre Bayle, who asserted the mere conventionality of religious belief. This view seems to associate Lafitau more with an earlier period of dogma.[18] The tensions between these views allows us to paint Lafitau as a liminal figure, occupying a pivotal space between religious debate and secular and scientific history. While this characterization accurately captures something about Lafitau, it perhaps anachronistically overdraws the distinction between religious authority and scientific history. Lafitau regards science and religion as overlapping categories so that a move towards a scientifically precise history serves and enhances religious authority.

---

[15] Joseph François Lafitau, *Customs of the American Indians Compared with the Customs of Primitive Times, Volumes I and II*, edited and translated by William N. Fenton and Elizabeth L. Moore (Toronto: The Champlain Society, 1974), pp. 33–34, 327–330. See also Michel de Certeau, 'Writing vs. Time: History and Anthropology in the Works of Lafitau' *Yale French Studies* 59–60 (1980), p. 54.

[16] Meek, *Ignoble Savage*, Chapter 4, makes the strongest case for this influence; See also Anthony Pagden, *The Fall of Natural Man: The American Indians and the Origins of Comparative Ethnology* (Cambridge: Cambridge University Press, 1982), p. 205.

[17] William N. Fenton and Elizabeth L. Moore, 'Introduction', in Lafitau, *Customs of the American Indians*, p. xxix.

[18] See Pagden, *Fall*, pp. 200–5.

By the eighteenth century questions about the status and origins of the Amerindians were far from over, though these controversies flowed along now familiar contours. Deliberations on the origins of the peoples of the Americas usually supported the idea of a single creation and necessarily referred to a migration from Asia to the Americas that had been firmly established in the work of the Jesuit José de Acosta (1540–1600).[19] Acosta's *Historia natural y moral de las Indias* (1590) had shaped the debate by insisting that barbarism existed in multiple forms, that comparisons among peoples be given a firm empirical basis, and 'that all the peoples of the world could be graded for civility'.[20] This final claim spurred argument, including the important late-seventeenth/early eighteenth-century 'Quarrel between the Ancients and the Moderns'. Does the ancient world represent a 'golden age'? Or, does the modern era promise social and scientific advance beyond all other forms of human society, including the ancients? This dispute was at its height when Lafitau studied at seminaries in Pau and Paris.[21] The crucial result of this controversy for his work was the practice of casting '"Antiquity" as a single category'[22] applicable to both Amerindians and ancient peoples. By Lafitau's time, the practice of drawing extensive parallels between ancient and contemporary paganism was well established, preparing the ground for his effort to locate 'conformities' across various 'heathen' peoples.[23]

Lafitau's claims in *Customs of the American Indians* place him at the centre of the monogenist tradition, defending the scriptural account of the unity of creation in the face of the discovery of new lands and peoples. For Lafitau, this defence required translating the myriad differences offered by the peoples of the New World into a recognizable register of similarities and differences.[24] On the one hand, similarities are explained via the process of migratory diffusion, by tracing 'the origins of these peoples in the dark ages of antiquity'.[25] As Pagden puts it, 'new and troubling peoples' can be assimilated to European understanding by treating them as descendents of Eurasian peoples of whom they

---

[19] This is not to ignore the continued existence of various polygenist theories of dual or multiple creations well into the eighteenth century.

[20] Pagden, *Fall*, p. 198.   [21] Fenton and Moore, 'Introduction', pp. xxix and xliii.

[22] Pagden, *European Encounters*, pp. 92–93. See also Certeau, 'Writing vs. Time', pp. 45–46, on the creation of 'antiquity' as a category.

[23] Frank E. Manuel, *The Eighteenth Century Confronts the Gods* (Cambridge MA: Harvard University Press, 1959), p. 19.

[24] See Fenton and Moore, 'Introduction', p. xlvii.

[25] Lafitau, *Customs of the American Indians I*, p. 25.

had knowledge.[26] Identifiable similarities between the Amerindians and ancient peoples are seen as the product of diffusion – of social and linguistic practices moving around the globe along established migratory paths. Thus, the contemporary Huron and Iroquois reflect, in Lafitau's text, vestiges of their origins as Lycians or Spartans. More generally, the various parallels between ancient religiosity, government and marriage practices vindicate the picture of the Old World origins of the Americans.[27] On the other hand, differences are explained with a familiar claim about decay or degeneration.[28] Movement across time and space (and thereby away from the perfection of creation and the centres of revelation) produces a degeneration of religious practice, moral belief and linguistic structures. Thus, the decayed state of the Amerindians is verified principally in relation to Christian moral and religious truths and Eurasian languages. Common origins explain the similarities between Amerindians and the ancients; the dispersal of humans across space accounts for their differences.

Lafitau struggled with a second issue that profoundly shaped his text. More than simply establishing a singular creative episode, he aimed to establish a singular basis for all religious experience in an original revelatory act.[29] His main targets were sceptics who argued that religious belief emerged simply from social convention or perhaps from fear of the unknown.[30] Lafitau's effort to place the universality of religious sentiment on a more secure foundation, one based on God's creation and his acts of revelation, led him to insist that the primitive monotheism of the first human social unit – the family formed by Adam and Eve – be seen as the generative moment for human religiosity.[31] Many ancient and contemporary peoples, without the benefit of continuing revelations, have strayed from the original path, though a careful examination of their religiosity exposes vestiges of that original monotheism imparted at creation. Here, Lafitau de-emphasizes customs and

[26] Pagden, *European Encounters*, p. 29.
[27] On the Hurons and Iroquois, see Lafitau, *Customs of the American Indians I*, pp. 67–69. The entire text is designed to draw 'conjectures' based on comparisons of ancient and Indian practices.
[28] Lafitau, *Customs of the American Indians I*, pp. 30–31, 34–35. See also Inayatullah and Blaney, *International Relations*, pp. 50–57.
[29] The account in Pagden, *Fall*, Chapter 8, is especially good.
[30] Lafitau, *Customs of the American Indians I*, p. 29. See also Pagden, *Fall*, p. 200, and Manuel, *The Eighteenth Century*, p. 146.
[31] It should be noted that this is also the generative moment of human sociality. See Lafitau, *Customs of the American Indians I*, Chapter VI. See also Certeau, 'Writing vs. Time', pp. 54–55.

practices that are particularly vulnerable to degeneration across time and space, and stresses more the commonalities of imagery and myth. He locates the deepest commonalities among peoples – ancient and contemporary, barbarous and civil – in the realm of 'symbolic representation', and uses this realm to demonstrate the single and original inspiration for religious faith.[32] In this way, Lafitau places the human experience in its great variety, across both space and time, within what he calls a 'symbolic theology'.[33]

Enlightenment figures dismissed such 'anti-rationalist' conclusions. Voltaire's tone is especially mocking but Adam Smith also finds many of Lafitau's major conclusions unsound. Though they deride some elements of his method and ignore the sections on religion, Lafitau still inspires the Scots.[34] Lafitau is noteworthy, if for no other reason, than the near exhaustiveness of his sources. He epitomizes the emerging view, as Certeau explains,[35] that far-flung times and places might be available for the contemporary thinker in the form of collections of material artifacts and archives of written reports. Exhaustiveness alone, however, is insufficient to recommend Lafitau to Smith and others. Collections and archives remain silent unless their secrets are voiced; meaning is revealed only when the accumulated vestiges of ancient times and reports of contemporary peoples are systematically compared. Lafitau was not the only thinker who works to establish similarities between the Ancients and the North American Indians. What distinguishes him from contemporaries is the 'wide-ranging character' of the comparisons,[36] his 'scrupulously factual account of the evidence',[37] the 'tabularization of ethnographic knowledge into a systematic and comprehensive form',[38] and that he is the 'most sophisticated and explicit as to his method'.[39]

Lafitau wishes to avoid the errors of previous authors who rely on 'imperfect and superficial records only', resort to 'conjectures [that] are so vague and uncertain that they rather give rise to more doubts than clarifying the existing ones', and claim linguistic connections based on a poor knowledge of the languages involved.[40] He stresses that his

---

[32] The quoted phrase is from Pagden, *Fall*, p. 204. See also Fenton and Moore, 'Introduction', pp. lxxvi–lxxvii.
[33] Lafitau, *Customs of the American Indians I*, pp. 35–36.
[34] Pagden, *Fall*, pp. 205 and 246 fn. 29.   [35] Certeau, 'Writing vs. Time', pp. 43–45.
[36] Meek, *Ignoble Savage*, p. 63.   [37] Pagden, *Fall*, p. 201.
[38] Ter Ellingson, *The Myth of the Noble Savage* (Berkeley: University of California Press, 2001), p. 65.
[39] Fenton and Moore, 'Introduction', p. xlviii.
[40] Lafitau, *Customs of the American Indians I*, p. 26.

knowledge is based on personal experience, knowledge of local languages and reliable eye-witness accounts.[41] But, most importantly, he explains how a comparison of the Ancients and the Indians allows us to understand both much better:

> I have not limited myself to learning the characteristics of the Indian and informing myself about their customs and practices, I have sought in these practices and customs, vestiges of the most remote antiquity. I have read carefully [the works] of the earliest writers who treated the customs, laws and usages of the peoples of whom they had some knowledge. I have made a comparison of these customs with the other. I confess that, if the ancient authors have given me information on which to base happy conjectures about the Indians, the customs of the Indians have given me information on the basis of which I can understand more easily and explain more readily many things in the ancient authors.[42]

The scientific power of this process of comparison comes from the capacity to move back and forth across developmental time. As Anthony Pagden describes it:

> The reflective, informed and 'sensible' being possesses the ability to be, in this [imaginative] way, literally in more places than one. And it is precisely this capacity for cognitive travel which constitutes his power of scientific understanding. For all scientific knowledge, and the power that knowledge brings with it, demands just such movement. And all movement follows the same trajectory. It begins as going out and ends as coming back.[43]

Likewise, Ter Ellingson describes Lafitau's method of comparison as a 'time-shifting' that overcomes geographical distance in order to establish a 'common kinship' among peoples.[44] That is, the collections and archives used to document the practices of the Ancients and the Indians (and establish common origins) are understood 'without recourse to dates or places'.[45] Questions about the historical distance between forms of paganism or barbarism can be set aside where time is apparently erased. As Certeau explains, 'The historical question receives a formalist treatment': Lafitau draws from a 'stock of monuments, piled up without chronological order, elements which are susceptible of being *formally* compared and which fit together *symbolically* as general categories'.[46]

---

[41] Ibid., pp. 26–27.   [42] Ibid., p. 27. See also the description in Pagden, *Fall*, pp. 198–199.
[43] Anthony Pagden, *European Encounters*, p. 30.   [44] Ellingson, *Myth*, p. 77.
[45] Fenton and Moore, 'Introduction', p. xlviii.   [46] Certeau, 'Writing vs. Time', p. 47.

By placing antiquity and contemporary barbarism within a common 'symbolic theology', Lafitau provides a picture of the Amerindians as full members of the human species, '[m]en being everywhere born with the same good or bad qualities'.[47] In this way, he follows in the footsteps of earlier Catholic thinkers, Francisco de Vitoria and Bartolomé de las Casas.[48] He rejects as fanciful or prejudiced descriptions of the Indians as devoid of common features of human society:

> I have seen, with extreme distress, in most of the travel narratives, that those who have written of the customs of primitive peoples have depicted them to us as people without any sentiment of religion, knowledge of a divinity or object to which they rendered any cult, as people without law, social control or any form of government; in a word, as people who have scarcely anything except the appearance of men. This is a mistake made even by missionaries and honest men who, on the one hand, have written too hastily of things with which they were not sufficiently familiar and, on the other, did not foresee the disastrous consequences which could be drawn from the expression of an opinion so unfavourable to religion. For, although these authors have contradicted themselves in their works and, at the same time that they say that these barbarians have neither cult nor a divinity whom they worship, they also say things, as Mr. Bayle himself has observed, which presuppose a divinity and a regulated cult. It results, nevertheless, (from this), that we are prejudiced by the first statement and become accustomed to forming a conception of these Indian and barbarians which scarcely differentiates them from beasts.[49]

Here, Lafitau is far from locating the Amerindians in a golden age, placing them in some privileged place in relation to a natural state of humankind; nor does he characterize the Indians as degenerated or beastly. Indeed, at times Lafitau compares the Indians quite favourably with his contemporary Europeans, especially regarding manly virtues.[50] Lafitau instead achieves a series of careful observations about Indian societies. Some of Lafitau's reports – on age-grades, kinship relations and the position of women in Indian societies – are considered quite acute and unsurpassed by professional anthropologists until the

---

[47] Lafitau, *Customs of the American Indians II*, p. 299. See also *Customs I*, pp. 89–91.
[48] See our discussion of Vitoria in Inayatullah and Blaney, *International Relations*, pp. 58–65, 81–82. On las Casas see Tzvetan Todorov, *The Conquest of America: The Question of the Other* (New York: Harper and Row, 1984), Chapter 3 and pp. 185–193.
[49] Lafitau, *Customs of the American Indians I*, pp. 28–29.
[50] See also Pagden, *Fall*, p. 202; Ellingson, *Myth*, pp. 78–79

nineteenth, or perhaps even twentieth, centuries.[51] However, because Lafitau's project revolves around restoring the original unity of all religious experience and a defence of the possibility of missionary activity, it remains at some distance from the central concerns of his Enlightenment contemporaries, as we shall see.

A second implication of his method extends well beyond his explicit project and better explains Lafitau's role in Enlightenment historiography. Certeau's revealing claim, that Lafitau replaces the Bible with his historical system, gives us an initial hint of that importance.[52] In the Christian worldview, time is given meaning only via the actions of an 'external agent' – God the creator and mover of history towards its final end. Temporal events or secular history necessarily gain meaning only via 'subordination to eschatology'.[53] Nonetheless, this 'millenarian formula' lacks the 'means of explicating the succession of particulars in social and political time' and the emerging imperative is to fill that gap with a natural philosophy rooted in careful observation of human experience.[54] Lafitau might be seen as a transitional figure in relation to that imperative. Despite his ostensive religious motivations, he makes a 'scientific gesture', setting himself apart from 'his social ties and attachments' and placing himself in the position of an autonomous observer and producer of a system of knowledge.[55] In this, Lafitau represents an 'enticing' image of scientific practice, seducing us with its claim to overcome the diversities and discontinuities of time in order thereby 'to produce the formal system of an absolute knowledge'.[56] It is this aspect of Lafitau's work that appeals to the Scots. Though they were likely to distance themselves from his 'immediate polemical intention', they were drawn to the notion that locating the ancients and contemporary primitives at the beginning of time could help explain the patterns of human behaviour, namely, by suggesting 'that all human cultures could be interpreted as the workings out in time of certain known and stable characteristics of the human mind'.[57] Or, as Fenton and Moore explain, though Lafitau 'was neither historical nor evolutionary in the strictest

---

[51] Fenton and Moore, 'Introduction', pp. cvii–cxix; Martha Haroun Foster, 'Lost Women of the Matriarchy: Iroquois Women in the Historical Literature' *American Indians Culture and Research Journal* 19 (1999), pp. 122–124.

[52] Certeau, 'Writing vs. Time', p. 54.

[53] J. G. A. Pocock, *The Machiavellian Moment: Florentine Political Thought and the Atlantic Republican Tradition* (Princeton NJ: Princeton University Press, 1975), pp. 31–32.

[54] Ibid., pp. 47–48.   [55] Certeau, 'Writing vs. Time', pp. 53–54.

[56] Ibid., pp. 59–60. See also Fenton and Moore, 'Introduction', pp. lxiv–lxv.

[57] Pagden, *Fall*, p. 208.

sense of these terms', he contributed 'documentation to substantiate the "law" of progress'.[58]

Though treated as a substantial achievement by the Scots, our reaction to his work foreshadows our response to the historiography of the Scottish Enlightenment. His practice of 'time-shifting' forces an understanding of the Amerindians (and the Ancients) into terms that are his alone.[59] Travel outward to the Indians and the Ancients requires travel back to the self, with considerable damage to his understanding of the particular and distinct histories of both. As Certeau evocatively puts it, Lafitau's comparison 'silences' both the ancients and the savages.[60] If Lafitau travels out and then back, he devalues the goods – the vestiges of antiquity and the reports of the new world – on the way home. More hopefully, we might say, he brings home collections and archives whose secrets wait to be sufficiently voiced.

Smith and the Indians: time, space and moral science

The Scottish Enlightenment is noted for its distinctive variant of the doctrine of progress: Smith's 'conjectural history' and the 'four-stages theory'. Though 'conjectural history' builds on Lafitau's work, Smith's use of this technique diverges in a crucial respect. Where Lafitau embraces a scientific method to give credibility to a particular eschatological scheme, Smith embraces science as a modern calling that sets the modern apart from the superstitions of the past. If God remained a concern, it was as the rather distant 'author' of creation, constructing a natural order the laws of which humankind might discern.[61] In that quest to comprehend the natural order, human beings assumed a central place in the creation (if not quite authorship) of their own world.[62] However, Smith and Lafitau converge at another point. For both, the new peoples and continents 'discovered' and 'explored' by Europeans were sources

---

[58] Fenton and Moore, 'Introduction', p. xliv. See also Meek, *Ignoble Savage*, pp. 54 and 61.
[59] Pagden, *European Encounters*, p. 53.   [60] Certeau, 'Writing vs. Time', p. 63.
[61] Adam Smith, 'The History of Astronomy' in Wightman and Bryce (eds.), *Essays on Philosophical Subjects*, pp. 48–53. See also D. D. Raphael, 'Adam Smith: Philosophy, Science and Social Science' in Stuart C. Brown (ed.), *Philosophers of the Enlightenment* (Atlantic Highlands NJ: Humanities Press, 1979), pp. 77–93, and Andrew Skinner, 'Economics and History – The Scottish Enlightenment' *Scottish Journal of Political Economy* 12 (1965), p. 22.
[62] Robert Wokler, 'Anthropology and Conjectural History in the Enlightenment' in Christopher Fox, Roy Porter and Robert Wokler (eds.), *Inventing Human Science: Eighteenth-Century Domains* (Berkeley: University of California Press, 1995), pp. 33–34.

of some anxiety. The Scots, like Lafitau, needed to make the amazing diversity of peoples and societies consistent with the principles of a natural order.[63] In their minds, managing this diversity required the kinds of travel associated with the scientific practice of comparative or 'conjectual history'.

The Scots imagined themselves living in a scientific age. Newton's knowledge of a world of bodies subject to laws inspired a search for similar laws governing human behaviour and institutions. Francis Bacon, perhaps more than any other, articulated what was also Newton's intuition – that natural and moral science might advance in step. Bacon's mapping of knowledge – rooted in 'the three faculties of Memory, Imagination, and Reason, to which corresponded the three divisions of human learning', namely 'history, poetry and philosophy' – inspired the Scots to create a moral science or a natural philosophy with human beings at its centre. [64]

For the Scots, as for Enlightenment thinking more generally, a 'science of man' was necessarily an empirical science, rooted in experience and evidence. Since the Scots began with the assumption that humans are social beings, the evidence on which to base a science of man might be drawn from numerous sources, reflecting societies far-flung in time and space. The evidence available might be personal, rooted in the thinkers' own experience or it might come to them via Bacon's 'Memory'. The latter made available vast amounts of 'indirect and secondary' material about 'the contemporary "savage" world of the Americas, Asia and Polynesia and the world described by ancient authors'.[65]

What the Scots saw in the recorded evidence of human societies was a complex picture of amazing diversity, but this very diversity potentially stood in opposition to a moral or civic science on a Newtonian plan.[66] Part of the solution was to locate recurring patterns in human societies. Following the example of Montesquieu perhaps, the social thinker would identify the common chains of causes and effects that explained these patterns.[67] The assumption, as we noted above, 'was

---

[63] The importance of the problem of diversity for the Scots is stressed by Christopher J. Berry, *Social Theory of the Scottish Enlightenment* (Edinburgh: Edinburgh University Press, 1997), Chapter 4.

[64] Ibid., pp. 52–53.

[65] We draw here on Berry, *Social Theory*, pp. 52–54, 61; the quotation is from p. 61.

[66] Michael J. Shapiro, *Reading 'Adam Smith': Desire, History, and Value* (Lanham MD: Rowman and Littlefield, 2002), p. 48 and Berry, *Social Theory*, pp. 74– 75, remark on the potentially paradoxical relationship of the evidence and the scientific ambition.

[67] See Berry, *Social Theory*, Chapter 3; David Carrithers, 'The Enlightenment Science of Society', in Fox, Porter and Wokler (eds.), *Inventing Human Science*, pp. 243–244.

that everything in society and history, just like everything in the physical realm, was bound together by an intricate concatenation of causes
and effects which it is the main task of the student of man and society –
i.e. the social scientist – to unravel'.[68]

Thus, for the Scots a science of man required the telling of tales – the
writing of historical narratives and articulating a 'project' of profound
'philosophical speculation, so as to incorporate all this disparate material into a truly philosophical account'.[69] Travel narratives, including
Lafitau's, could serve as no more than 'raw material' or, perhaps, inspiration. Even the noted chains of causes and effects do not alone produce
a moral science of the kind Smith and the other Scots envisioned. Rather,
the social thinker must turn these causal chains to the purpose of telling
a historical story with a clear moral point. Minimally, this requires finding a kind of cause that will explain the great uniformity they see (or
seek) in human societies. As Andrew Skinner notes: 'The key to this
problem was found, as Hume had insisted it must be, in the constant
and universal principles of human nature.'[70] With a given set of characteristics of human nature – 'Hume lists ambition, avarice, self-love,
vanity, friendship, generosity and public spirit' – the Scots could identify patterns that operate regardless of context. In this way, '[a]ll human
behavior, even if it has a "local" character, is explicable because it is
governed by regular springs which have uniform effects'.[71]

However, the evidence still suggested a great variation in forms of
human society. Though these might be *explained* as the consequence of
placing a fixed human nature in varying physical settings (i.e. variations
in climate and fertility of the soil), the Scots resisted the potentially
relativistic implications of such an approach – that the social theorist can
say little beyond that differences in geography produce different forms
of society.[72] For Smith and the Scots, a moral science produces practical
guidance about the direction of human society; about where, reflecting

---

[68] Meek, *Ignoble Savage*, p. 1.   [69] Pagden, *European Encounters*, pp. 84–85.
[70] Skinner, 'Natural History in the Age of Adam Smith' *Political Studies* XV (1967), p. 41.
[71] Berry, *Social Theory*, p. 69.
[72] Montesquieu's employment of physical causes – climate, geography – might well
reduce the clutter of empirical evidence, but the Scots believed that Montesquieu's scheme
failed to provide a clear basis for making moral distinctions. On Montesquieu, see Ernst
Cassirer, *The Philosophy of the Enlightenment* (Boston: Beacon, 1951), pp. 210–215. For the
Scots's reaction, see Fania Oz-Salzberger, 'The Political Theory of the Scottish Enlightenment' in Alexander Broadie (ed.), *The Cambridge Companion to The Scottish Enlightenment*
(Cambridge: Cambridge University Press, 2003), pp. 170–171.

the Scottish Enlightenment's teleological moment, human society must *necessarily* and *appropriately* go.[73]

Thus, the Scots add a crucial second element: the idea that human nature itself contains an impetus to progress. Human beings, as distinct from (other) animals, seek to improve their condition and capabilities – a condition Smith believes 'comes with us from the womb'.[74] The interaction between a common human nature and varying circumstances came to be seen, then, in a much different way. Though variable climate and geography may be of some importance, the key differences in the environment are those humans themselves create. The Scots argued that

> man, following his natural propensities, inevitably produces results well beyond his original intentions; that man, in reacting to a particular situation, must ultimately produce a qualitative change thus creating a new situation within which the same forces must operate.[75]

History takes on a decisively progressive direction and the diversity of social forms can be understood as variations in degrees of progress. In this move, difference is read along a temporal register. Historical and contemporary diversity is no longer understood principally in terms of differences in the character of the spaces they occupy. Rather, differences across societies in the ancient or contemporary world may be thought of as products of uneven development.[76] History is given a new moral reading – as 'a repository of exemplars, for good or for evil'.[77] Thus, barbarism and superstition, whether contemporary or past, may be put safely behind, as superceded time. And Smith, as we will see, regards this temporal register as stadial, involving movement through clearly discernable and ascending stages.

Adam Smith famously describes those stages in his lectures of 1762–3. Smith outlines four stages – '1st, the Age of Hunters; 2dly, the Age of

---

[73] See Donald Winch, *Adam Smith's Politics: An Essay in Historiographic Revision* (Cambridge: Cambridge University Press, 1978); Richard E. Teichgraeber, III, *'Free Trade' and Moral Philosophy: Rethinking the Sources of Adam Smith's Wealth of Nations* (Durham NC: Duke University Press, 1986); and Samuel Fleischacker, *On Adam Smith's Wealth of Nations: A Philosophical Companion* (Princeton NJ: Princeton University Press, 2004).

[74] Adam Smith, *An Inquiry into the Nature and Causes of the Wealth of Nations*, ed. Edwin Cannan (Chicago University of Chicago: Press, 1976), p. 362 [II.iii].

[75] Skinner, 'Economics and History', p. 5.

[76] Pocock, *Machiavellian Moment*, pp. 486–487, notes that this move translates the components of cyclical theories of history into theories of progress.

[77] Knud Haakonssen, *Natural Law and Moral Philosophy: From Grotius to the Scottish Enlightenment* (Cambridge: Cambridge University Press, 1996), p. 6

Shepherds; 3rdly, the Age of Agriculture; and 4thly, the Age of Commerce'[78] – as part of an historical understanding of property rights. He rejects the idea that property is among the 'naturall rights'. Rather, the most powerful 'causes from which property may have its occasion', namely 'Occupation, by which we get any thing into our power that was not the property of one before', varies in its importance depending on the form of society.[79] Smith explains this principle at some length:

> In Tartary, where as we said the support of the inhabitants consist(s) in herds and flocks, *theft* is punished with immediate death; in North America, again, where the age of hunters subsists, theft is not much regarded. As there is almost no property amongst them, the only injury that can be done them is depriving them of their game. Few laws or regulations will [be] requisite in such an age of society, and these will not extend to any length, or be very rigorous in the punishments annexed to any infringements of property. . . . In the age of agriculture, they are not so much exposed to theft and open robbery [as are herds and flocks], but then there are many ways added in which property may be interrupted as the subjects of it are considerably extended. The laws therefore tho perhaps not so rigorous will be of a far greater number than amongst a nation of shepherds. In the age of commerce, as the subjects of property are greatly increased the laws must be proportionately multiplied. The more improved any society is and the greater length the severall means of supporting the inhabitants are carried, the greater will be the number of their laws and regulations necessary to maintain justice, and prevent infringement of the right to property.[80]

In addition, variations in the rules governing occupation of land, ownership of houses, forms of exchange and inheritance practices correspond to the modes of subsistence that characterize the successive 'Ages' of man.[81]

The Scots are hardly the first to deploy the idea of 'ages' of human progress, but the distinctiveness of Smith's 'four-stages theory' is worth emphasizing. First, each stage corresponds to a particular mode of acquiring subsistence or, in a later language, a mode of production. Second, as human societies advance through these successive modes, we can expect corresponding changes (or, generally, improvements) in institutions, laws and manners.[82] Human society gradually loses its

---

[78] Adam Smith, 'Report of 1762–3', in R. L. Meek, D. D. Raphael and P. G. Stein (eds.), *Lectures on Jurisprudence* (Indianapolis IN: Liberty Fund, 1982), p. 14 (para. 27).
[79] Smith, 'Report of 1762–3', p. 13 (paras. 25–26).
[80] Ibid., p. 16 (paras. 33–35).   [81] Ibid., pp. 14–49 (paras. 27–115).
[82] See Meek, *Ignoble Savage*, p. 2; Skinner, 'Natural History', pp. 42–45; Berry, *Social Theory*, pp. 93–99.

rudeness; as the arts and industry advance so are the individuals in society refined.[83] Some, like Ronald Meek, see this formulation as a precursor to Marx's historical materialism,[84] but our current purpose is less to trace out such influences than to examine the logic of 'conjectural history'.

'Conjectural history' rests on a combination of methodological principles: (1) the use of systematic comparison; (2) conjectures, premised on assimilating ancient peoples and contemporary savages as a single coeval category; and (3) the equation of human infancy with savagery. We have noted that careful employment of historical comparisons gave eighteenth-century social thinkers' work the status of science: comparison reveals patterns of commonality and difference that serve as the building blocks in the isolation of causal chains that reveal the orderly character of human society. For Smith and the Scots, human history is a series of social experiments that might be compared.[85] Though comparison might, thereby, facilitate ranking of the relative achievements of societies in various arenas of human endeavour, it does not yet justify the claims of a *stage* theory. Elaborating human history as a series of stages requires recourse to the second and third principles, allowing a series of carefully constructed, albeit 'a priori conjectures'.[86]

The claim that Scottish Enlightenment thinkers deployed 'conjectures' has a long history. It is found first in Dugald Stewart's short biography of Adam Smith (1793).[87] For Stewart, the challenge faced by Smith was to trace the entire history of human progress from its origins to the present. However, the historian faces a seemingly insurmountable constraint: the lack of any direct evidence of the early times of human society. This absence must be filled by conjecture. As Stewart explains:

> In this want of direct evidence, we are under a direct necessity of supplying the place of fact by conjecture; and when we are unable to ascertain how men have actually conducted themselves upon particular occasions, of considering in what manner they are likely to have proceeded, from the principles of their nature, and the circumstances

---

[83] Ibid., pp. 180–181.
[84] Ronald L. Meek, 'The Scottish Contribution to Marxist Sociology' in J. Saville (ed.), *Democracy and the Labour Movement* (London: Lawrence and Wishart, 1954), pp. 84–102.
[85] Berry, *Social Theory*, pp. 62–63, attributes this idea to Hume but notes its influence also on Smith, John Millar, Lord Kames and William Robertson.
[86] Aaron Garrett, 'Anthropology: the "Original" of Human Nature', in Broadie (ed.), *The Cambridge Companion to The Scottish Enlightenment*, p. 81.
[87] Dugald Stewart, 'An Account of the Life and Writings of Adam Smith, L. L. D.' in Wightman and Bryce (eds.), *Essays on Philosophical Subjects*, pp. 269–351.

of their external situation. In such inquiries, the detached facts which travels and voyages afford us, may frequently serve as land-marks to our speculations; and sometimes our conclusions *a priori*, may tend to confirm the credibility of facts, which, on a superficial view, appeared to be doubtful or incredible.[88]

Stewart referred to 'this species of philosophical investigation' as '*Theoretical* or *Conjectural History*'.[89]

This is not to disparage Smith for a cavalier attitude toward evidence, but to examine how Smith was able to translate the amazing diversity of 'facts' available to him into a stadial theory of history. Our discussion of Lafitau suggests part of the answer. Lafitau's assimilation of contemporary Indians with the ancients allowed 'facts' about each to inform an understanding of the other. His example was crucial in Smith's effort to discern the nature of early human societies, and Smith turned directly to Lafitau for evidence about the Amerindians.[90] If the peoples of the ancient world, particularly the various barbarous groups, and the contemporary savages could be placed on the same temporal register, then Smith could begin to delineate a common stage of human progress (or lack thereof) exhibited by barbarians/savages. Thus, the Amerindians became exemplary of the 'savage' and works like Lafitau's became definitive sources on that stage of human development.

Lafitau hints at the possibility that various ancient peoples and current North American Indians might be similarly placed at the very beginnings of human history. There was certainly a precedent for this since Locke had declared: 'in the beginning all the World was America'.[91] Smith himself, as Dugald Stewart noted, provided a philosophical basis for this claim.[92] In 'Considerations Concerning the First Formation of Languages', Smith begins with a thought experiment meant to illustrate the origins of language. Imagine two 'savages', he asks, somehow isolated from society and without language. The savages 'would naturally begin to form that language by which they would endeavor to make their mutual wants intelligible to each other, by uttering certain sounds, whenever they meant to denote certain objects'. Smith prods the reader to follow his surmise (conjecture) that, as with infants, the

---

[88] Ibid., p. 293.   [89] Ibid.

[90] See Berry, *Social Theory*, pp. 62–64; Pocock, *Machiavellian Moment*, p. 501; Meek, *Ignoble Savage*, Chapter 4.

[91] John Locke, *Two Treatises of Government*, ed. Peter Laslett (Cambridge: Cambridge University Press, 1988), II, p. 301.

[92] Stewart, 'An Account', pp. 292–293. The role of conjectural theories of language is discussed by Pagden, *European Encounters*, pp. 129–140.

beginnings of language would be restricted to a process of nomination, a stream of proper names for 'concrete' objects. Only later would our savages begin to learn and apply 'a considerable degree of abstraction and generalization'.[93] The analogy of childhood and savagery was powerful; it allowed Smith and his fellow Scots to treat materials about the Indians as evidence of the 'infancy of society'.[94] Combined with the historical optimism built into the idea of a progressive human nature, barbarism/savagery could be seen as the initial stage in human societies' development from infancy to maturity. Where England, France and, potentially, Scotland serve as exemplary of human maturity, human progress also may be read backwards – from a commercial society to its earlier origins.

For the Scots the savage operates as a 'mirror' against which they assess the progress of their own and other commercial societies. In *The Wealth of Nations*, it is the paltry livelihood of the savage that serves as the basis of comparison when assessing the distributional consequences of a developed division of labour:

> Among the savage nations of hunters and fishers, every individual who is able to work, is more or less employed in useful labour, and endeavors to provide, as well as he can, the necessaries and conveniences of life, for himself, or such of his family or tribe as are either too old, or too young, or too infirm to go a hunting and fishing. Such nations, however, are so miserably poor, that from mere want, they are frequently reduced, or, at least, think themselves reduced, to the necessity sometimes of directly destroying, and sometimes of abandoning their infants, their old people, and those inflicted with lingering disease, to perish with hunger, or to be devoured by wild beasts. Among civilized and thriving nations, on the contrary, though a great number of people do not labor at all, many of whom consume the produce of ten times, frequently of a hundred times more labour than the greater part of those who work; yet the produce of the whole labour of the society is so great, that all are often abundantly supplied, and a workman, even of the lowest and poorest order, if he is frugal and industrious, may enjoy a greater share of the necessaries and conveniences of life than it is possible for any savage to acquire.[95]

---

[93] Adam Smith, 'Considerations Concerning the First Formation of Languages' in Adam Smith, *Lectures on Rhetoric and Belles Lettres*, ed. J. C. Bryce (Indianapolis IN: Liberty Fund, 1985), pp. 203–206.

[94] Berry, *Social Theory*, p. 92.

[95] Adam Smith, *Wealth of Nations*, p. 2 [Introduction]; see also Smith, *Wealth of Nations*, p. 16 [I,I] and 'Report of 1762–3', *Lectures on Jurisprudence*, p. 338 [VI, 19]. Donald Winch, *Riches and Poverty: An Intellectual History of Political Economy in Britain, 1750–1834* (Cambridge:

Where the division of labour distinguishes civilized society, savage society is conceived as 'the *absence* of division of labor'.[96] The rude, the savage, and the barbarous stand in almost polar opposition to the commercial, the civilized. And, we would assert, a stadial account of human development becomes possible because filling in the intermediate steps is easier once you 'know' the beginning and the end.[97]

In this way, Smith and the Scots develop 'conjectural history' as a moral science. Human improvement, though the product of individual action (within the bounds set by human nature), produces social and moral advance. Not only are patterns of social and moral advance visible to scientific inquiry, but scientific inquiry itself is seen to be a product of this process of human development, superceding 'superstition, ignorance and dogma'.[98] A human science diagnoses the mysteries of the past and simultaneously provides an account of its own power to discern those mysteries. This is done without asserting the role of some external agent in history. All that is required is the gradual, but persistent, operation of human nature: moral advance is produced without plan or conscious design. The order that social inquiry discerns is spontaneously generated – the 'harmonious movements' of an 'immense machine'.[99]

Our difficulties with Smith's moral science partly parallel those we locate in Lafitau. Like Lafitau, Smith shifts time, so that the Indians, though contemporaneous, appear instead as exemplary of some initial age of human society. Understood only in contradistinction to modern, civilized society, the Indians do not speak in their own terms; their histories are submerged under the historical constructions of the Enlightenment scientist. Indian self-understandings and their views of European societies are muted. The Indians do not speak, and unlike

Cambridge University Press, 1996), p. 59, comments on this consistent pattern of comparison.

[96] David P. Levine, *Economic Studies: Contributions to the Critique of Economic Theory* (London: Routledge and Kegan Paul, 1977), p. 37.

[97] Perhaps this explains why we find the 'four stages theory' less of a mystery than does Pocock, though he does argue that the 'concept of barbarism' was crucial to the formation of that theory. See J. G. A. Pocock, *Virtue, Commerce, and History: Essays on Political Thought and History, Chiefly in the Eighteenth Century* (Cambridge: Cambridge University Press, 1985), pp. 115–116.

[98] Roger Smith, 'The Language of Human Nature', in Fox, Porter and Wokler (eds.), *Inventing Human Science*, pp. 100–101.

[99] Smith, *Theory of Moral Sentiments*, p. 316 [VII.iii.I.2]. On the Scots' embrace of spontaneous order, see Naeem Inayatullah, 'Theories of Spontaneous Order' *Review of International Political Economy* 4 (1997), 319–348.

Lafitau, Smith does not try to humanize them. While Lafitau incorporates the Indians into the wholeness of human social life, Smith's 'conjectural history' works to position Indians as no more than the foundational bedrock from which he pushes off his universal moral story.

Ernst Cassirer suggests that all Enlightenment thinking struggled with the problem of the relationship between the general and the particular.[100] We have seen the Scots searching for principles that would allow them to reduce the diversity of experience to general patterns. Indeed, for the Scottish Enlightenment, 'the reduction of the diversity of institutions to some intelligible pattern' is precisely 'the hallmark of successful social science'. This reduction serves an essential moral purpose in that it is not the particular but the universal that garners ethical significance.[101] The universal pattern of human history shown in Smith's 'four-stages theory' provides a moral and practical basis for assessing encounters between self and others. Diversity, particularly the diversity of political and ethical views, is contained by temporal displacement; other forms of life become a backward form of contemporary civilization. As Michael Shapiro notes, in Smith the rich diversity of 'the ordinary' is obscured by the emphasis on the 'exemplary'.[102] In this way, the 'exemplary' is given the power to drown out the voices of the diverse particularities of human existence.

In addition, Smith's 'four-stages theory' translates the diversity associated with a geo-cultural mapping of space into developmental time. Smith normally maps these geo-cultural spaces onto what he calls 'nations' – a term describing any social unit from tribes to empires. Adjacent nations in Europe may exist in the same advanced temporal stage or may be separated in time by uneven processes of development. Nations far in physical distance from Europe might lay quite near to Europe temporally (e.g. China), though most of the rest of the world was seen as far-flung both spatially and temporally. However, the paradigmatic case, as seen above, opposes the social space of a developed, civilized Europe to savage or barbarous spaces in Africa, Asia and the Americas. Smith's primary project in *The Wealth of Nations* is to explain the differences in wealth associated with this temporal distance between savage and civilized nations (and, secondarily, those falling in between). What he does not explicitly allow, as we show below, is an overlap of

---

[100] Cassirer, *Enlightenment*, p. 197.   [101] Berry, *Social Theory*, pp. 76, 88.
[102] Shapiro, *Reading 'Adam Smith'*, p. 57.

temporal boundaries. In this way, Smith effects a compartmentalization of time into distinct national units, a Westphalianization of developmental time.

Combining the previous two points, we can begin to understand how Smith barricades modern commercial society within a temporal/ethical fortress. Both time and space operate as a set of boundaries that demarcate 'nations' by developmental level. Where moral judgment is informed by a stage-theory of history, the institutions and practices of the civilized serve as the basis for evaluating those of temporally backward nations. This results in the present, as the height of human historical achievement, being protected from potentially critical values and visions of seemingly past societies. As long as the boundary between the civilized and the savage remains clearly in place, the values of a commercial society automatically take precedence: its values – wealth, social refinement – remain thereby the basis for assessing other (superceded) forms of life as well as for judging its own successes and failures. In this way, a commercial society can only be evaluated as failing or succeeding *in its own terms* – by failing to provide wealth or refinement. Thus, even a critique of the present validates that current forms of societies occupy a superior temporal position.[103]

Like Lafitau, Smith 'believed that traveling in space also meant traveling in time'.[104] This equation of time and space makes sense where the 'four-stages theory' rules the understanding of history. The social theorist moves through the ages of man as he consults contemporary narratives of faraway places. This is conceptual movement, since, as we have noted, Smith did not travel physically to the places he arrayed along a temporal register. As Pagden evocatively puts it, Enlightenment historians traveled from 'text to text', searching for truthful witnesses whose evidence might prove exemplary of the patterns of history.[105] Along the way, Smith places other contemporary societies into a time different from his own. We see this practice as exemplary of the dominant patterns of Enlightenment Modernity, infusing a temporocentrism into much of contemporary social theory and practice.[106] This denial of

---

[103] Shapiro, *Reading 'Adam Smith'*, p. 52; See also Oz-Salzberger, 'Political Theory', pp. 169–170.

[104] Christopher Fox, 'Introduction. How to Prepare a Noble Savage: The Spectacle of Human Science', in Fox, Porter and Wokler (eds.), *Inventing Human Science*, p. 16.

[105] Pagden, *European Encounters*, p. 86

[106] See Inayatullah and Blaney, *International Relations*, pp. 99–102. We draw on Johannes Fabian, *Time and the Other: How Anthropology Makes its Object* (New York: Columbia University Press, 1983).

the 'co-presence' of others serves to shield modern society from external criticism. It also purges all versions of global democracy that resist assimilation to a distinctly modern pattern. Those who exemplify the pinnacle of human history comprise a chronocratic elite; their travels, whether real or conceptual, serve to confirm their status as scientists and purveyors of practical wisdom. However, this is only one aspect of the story, since, as we suggest in the next section, 'co-presence' is the 'real' of travel – something that the traveller both avoids and desires. Travel anxiety produces a double effect: it is what the traveller avoids in order to contain co-presence's potential criticism; and it is what the traveller seeks so that co-presence can catalyze critical self-consciousness.[107]

The Savage within the walls of political economy

Such critical consciousness hardly seems germane for Smith, for whom history tends to assume a 'providentialist' guise.[108] Smith's quietism is due, in part, to the influence of the Stoics, who he describes approvingly:

> The Stoics were of the opinion, that as the world was governed by the all-ruling providence of a wise, powerful, and good God, every single event ought to be regarded, as making a necessary part of the plan of the universe, and as tending to promote the general order and happiness of the whole: that the vices and follies of mankind, therefore, made as necessary a part of this plan as their wisdom or their virtue; and by that eternal art which educes good from ill, were made to tend equally to the prosperity and perfection of the great system of nature.[109]

As Smith moves from the events of the cosmos to those of society, the theological hue of this passage shifts to a kind of mystic science. Smith attests that '[h]uman society, when we contemplate it in a certain abstract and philosophical light, appears like a great, an immense

---

[107] We draw on Bruce Fink, *The Lacanian Subject: Between Language and Jouissance* (Princeton NJ: Princeton University Press, 1995), pp. 24–25; Slavoj Zizek, *Tarrying with the Negative: Kant, Hegel, and the Critique of Ideology* (Durham NC: Duke University Press, 1993), p. 31; and Mary Louise Pratt, *Imperial Eyes: Travel Writing and Transculturation* (New York: Routledge, 1992), pp. 6–7.

[108] Skinner, 'Economics and History', p. 22 and Shapiro, *Reading 'Adam Smith'*, pp. xix–xxx, 50. But see also the contrary view of Fleischacker, *On Adam Smith's Wealth of Nations*, pp. 44–45.

[109] Smith, *Theory of Moral Sentiments*, p. 36 [I,ii,3,4]. Smith's view has been described as a kind of Christian stoicism by Ingrid A. Merikoski, 'The Challenge of Material Progress: The Scottish Enlightenment and Christian Stoicism' *The Journal of the Historical Society* II (2002), 60–65.

machine, whose regular and harmonious movements produce a thousand agreeable effects'.[110] Despite this confidence in the beneficial effects of history, Smith is 'haunted', as Richard Teichgraeber describes it, by the 'moral shortcomings in commercial society'.[111]

Haunted as he might be, and despite the fact that Smith gives substantial play to the failings of commercial society, we see Smith working to restore the dominance of the salutary historical narrative after every notably critical discussion. The transition from savagery to civilization is not always a complete progression; at numerous points, the time of the other disturbs the temporal confidence and security of commercial society, though commercial society is consistently vindicated in direct comparison. In particular, Smith recognizes that commercial society is weakest in its impact on the great masses of common labourers. Nonetheless, he goes to great lengths to show that a commercial society improves the lives of common people. In the end, simple reforms readily meliorate the weakness; commercial society is always vindicated. Still, as we shall see, some of Smith's comparisons leave open greater space for a critical treatment of modern capitalism than he admits.

These rather serious cracks in his temporal fortress are necessarily present. If a benign God rules the world, and human society runs like a beneficial machine, then even the sinful and unnatural are parts of a grand design. The difficulty associated with the Amerindians becomes not so much that they sin against God and conscience, as was the case for many prominent thinkers of earlier centuries, but how to account for their appearance within the historical machine. The problem is not what to do about the Indians in a practical sense, but how to account for them philosophically. Smith verges on tautology here. If even folly and vice produce agreeable effects, can there be anything that does not somehow produce order? Are there events or actions whose difference the machine cannot assimilate? Verging on tautology, as we shall see, is not the same as producing a tautological system; despite our intentions, something always escapes our desire and capacity to tame. Indeed, Smith falls short of meeting the full requirements of his Stoic leanings: his time travel highlights some advantages held by the savages and he implies that the past and the future are underspecified and therefore more open-ended than supposed by his explicit commitments.

---

[110] Smith, *Theory of Moral Sentiments*, p. 316 [VII.iii.1.2].
[111] Teichgraeber, *'Free Trade'*, p. 128.

Though Smith assumes that nations may be placed easily along a temporal hierarchy of development, the overlap of spatial and temporal boundaries disallows an easily manageable and predictable moral cartography. The simplest example is that of the Scottish Highlanders who are European spatially but can be equated with the Amerindians temporally. Lacking in division of labour, wealth and refinement,[112] the Highlands appear as an 'ethnological hinterland'[113] or 'sociological museum'.[114] Though seemingly incorporated within the schema of 'conjectural history', the 'backwardness' of the Scottish Highlands is more troubling because of its spatial and psychological closeness. Scottish universities had flourished for a century or more. The union with England helped spur economic advancement in lowland cities to the extent that Scottish Enlightenment figures would think of lowland Scotland as a commercial society. Most important, Scottish thinking had likely surpassed that of England in its importance. Nevertheless, speaking an odd English and living among a less than refined populace, the Scots could not quite shake the sense of themselves as provincial.[115] If the Highlanders could be equated with a savage state of mankind, they were an other painfully near.[116] These perhaps internal others also offered examples of the kind of generosity, martial spirit and sense of honour that seemed eclipsed by commercial society.

The overlapping of temporal boundaries is seen most forcefully when Smith blurs the analogy between infancy and savagery that informs his own stage theory. Despite his tendency to oppose the sentiments of the savage and the (civilized) moral philosopher, as we saw above, Smith also suggests their overlap:

> A Child caresses the fruit that is agreeable to it, as it beats the stone that hurts it. The notions of a savage are not very different. The ancient Athenians, who solemnly punished the axe which had accidentally been the cause of the death of a man, erected altars, and offered sacrifices to the rainbow. Sentiments not unlike these, may sometimes,

---

[112] Smith, 'Report of 1762–3', *Lectures on Jurisprudence*, pp. 107, 146, 380; 'Report Dated 1766', *Lectures on Jurisprudence*, pp. 540–41; *Wealth of Nations*, pp. 21–22 [I, iii], 88–89 [I, viii].

[113] Jerry A Muller, *Adam Smith, in His Time and Ours* (Cambridge: Cambridge University Press, 1999) pp. 22–23.

[114] Andrew Skinner, 'Natural History', p. 37.

[115] We draw on Berry, *Social Theory*, Chapter 1; Muller, *Adam Smith*, Chapter 1; and Roger Emerson, 'The Contexts of the Scottish Enlightenment' in Broadie (ed.), *The Cambridge Companion to the Scottish Enlightenment*, pp. 9–30.

[116] Robert Shillam refers to this as a 'psychology of backwardness'. See his Chapter 9 in this book.

upon such occasions, begin to be felt *even* in the breasts of the most civilized, but are presently checked by the reflection, that the things are not their proper objects.[117]

Here Smith duplicates Lafitau's method of equating savages and ancients and reinforces the analogy to infancy. Simultaneously, however, Smith provides a moment where the sentiments of the child, the savage and the ancient are co-present 'in the breasts of the most civilized'. Overlaps between self and other, inside and outside, developed and developing ages/stages erupt within Westphalianized time. Here we have a problem that engages Smith's energies; he seems anxious about whether such trespassing sentiments will be smoothed by the social machine.

Despite this disclosure, Smith equivocates; he claims that a refinement of manners naturally accompanies the advance of human society. Commercial society's normal operations should promote a balance among the passions, thereby generating the qualities of self-command: moderation, generosity, humility and frugality.[118] And yet, because he seems less than confident that the smoothing effect of the social machine will extend to all within society, Smith devotes considerable energy to making sure that the passions will indeed be balanced and that his preferred virtues will in fact emerge.

For example, he worries about religious zealotry and factionalism. In early stages of development factions do not consolidate because people are divided into hundreds and thousands of sects. In modern societies, however, the state must consider that

> [t]he interested and active zeal of religious teachers can be dangerous and troublesome only where there is, either but one sect tolerated in the society, or where the whole of a larger society is divided into two or three great sects; the teachers of each acting by concert, and under regular discipline and subordination.[119]

To ameliorate the problems of 'faction and fanaticism', which 'have always been by far the greatest corrupters',[120] Smith turns to the *visible hand* of political intervention. He pins his hopes on public education and public entertainment. The most important intervention is the promotion of 'the study of science and philosophy'. For Smith, '[s]cience is

---

[117] Smith, 'History of Astronomy', pp. 48–49 [III.2]. Emphasis added.
[118] Muller, *Adam Smith*, p. 95 and Teichgraeber, *'Free Trade'*, pp. 13–14.
[119] Smith, *Wealth of Nations*, p. 314 [V.I.iii].
[120] Smith, *Theory of Moral Sentiments*, p. 156 [III, 3, 43].

the great antidote to the poison of enthusiasm and superstition'. Where the cool and abstract light of philosophical reflection fails, which it will for many, Smith turns to a less studious remedy: 'the frequency and gaiety of the publick diversions'. The state should encourage those, 'who for their own interest would attempt, without scandal or indecency, to amuse and divert the people by painting and poetry, musick, dancing'.[121] While Smith's enlightened age had supposed that the era of superstition was long past, a fear of religious fanaticism and factionalism still seems apparent.

Despite this moment of doubt, Smith is quick to restore civilized society to its position on the summit of human achievement. Savages and barbarians, though not without some desirable traits, lack much that we associate with humanity:

> Barbarians . . . being obliged to smother and conceal the appearance of every passion, necessarily acquire the habits of falsehood and dissimulation. It is observed by all those who have been conversant with savage nations, whether in Asia, Africa, or America, that they are all equally impenetrable, and that, when they have a mind to conceal the truth, no examination is capable of drawing it from them . . . The torture itself is incapable of making them confess. . . . The passions of the savage . . . are . . . mounted to the highest pitch of fury. Though he seldom shows any symptoms of anger, yet his vengeance, when he comes to give way to it, is always sanguinary and dreadful. The least affront drives him to despair. His countenance and discourse indeed are still sober and composed, and express nothing but the most perfect tranquility of mind: but his actions are often the most furious and violent.[122]

So 'ignoble' does the savage appear that we cannot but appreciate the great changes that history has wrought.

Nevertheless two issues in particular, namely the corrupting effect of specialization and the problem of poverty, demonstrate how Smith's ambiguity may be productive for contemporary debates in political economy. First in Smith's mind are the problems associated with specialization. In *Lectures on Jurisprudence*, we find a powerful set of passages concerning what Smith calls the 'inconveniences' of the division of labour.[123] These concerns are replicated quite famously in Book V of *Wealth of Nations*:

---

[121] Smith, *Wealth of Nations*, p. 318 [V.I iii]
[122] Smith, *Theory of Moral Sentiments*, p. 208 [V.2.11]
[123] Smith, 'Report Dated 1766', pp. 539–541.

In the progress of the division of labor, the employment of the far greater part of those who live by labor, that is, of the great body of the people, comes to be confined to a few very simple operations, frequently to one or two. But the understandings of the greater part of men are necessarily formed by their ordinary employments. The man whose whole life is spent in performing a few simple operations, the effects of which too are, always the same, or very nearly the same, has no occasion to exert his understanding, or to exercise his invention in finding out expedients for removing difficulties which never occur. He naturally loses, therefore, the habit of such exertion, and generally becomes as stupid and ignorant as it is possible for a human creature to become. The torpor of his mind renders him, not only incapable of relishing or bearing a part of any rational conversation, but of conceiving any generous, noble, or tender sentiment, and consequently of forming any just judgment concerning many even of the ordinary duties of private life. Of the great and extensive interests of his country, he is altogether incapable of judging; and unless very particular pains have been taken to render him otherwise, he is equally incapable of defending his country in war. The uniformity of his stationary life naturally corrupts the courage of his mind, and makes him regard with abhorrence the irregular, uncertain, and adventurous life of a soldier. It corrupts even the activity of his body, and renders him incapable of exerting his strength with vigor and perseverance, in any other employment than that to which he has been bred.[124]

Turning the common labourer into a specialist has a number of negative consequences: it makes him 'stupid', incapable of 'rational conversation', unable to 'conceive any generous, noble, or tender sentiment' and therefore inept at forming judgments concerning the 'duties of private life'. The worker becomes unqualified to ascertain the 'interests of his country', and powerless in 'defending his country in war'. In direct contrast, the absence of a division of labour in savage and barbarous societies means that: there exist 'varied occupations'; inventiveness is 'kept alive'; 'every man is a warrior'; every man is a 'statesman' and each is able to 'form a tolerable judgment concerning the interest of society'.[125] While specialization provides a material plenty unavailable to savage and barbarous societies, this advantage is 'acquired at the expense of [the labourer's] intellectual, social and martial virtues'. The sober consequence is that, 'in every improved and civilized society this is the state into which the laboring poor, that is, the great body of the people, must necessarily fall'. From these passages it is difficult to tell

---

[124] Smith, *Wealth of Nations*, pp. 302–303 [V.i. iii.i].   [125] Ibid., pp. 303–304 [V.i.iii.ii]

if Smith believes, as he asserted earlier, that the working classes are better off than savages. Indeed, so worried is Smith about the fate of the workers that he again invokes the visible hand of the state. If the state does not provide countermeasures, warns Smith, 'all the nobler parts of the human character may be, in a great measure, obliterated and extinguished in the great body of the people'.[126]

In stark contrast to his quietist sensibilities, Smith advocates government intervention, lest commercial society destroy the very thing it advances – namely, ennobling and civilizing wealth. Here, savage society seems to provide a mirror reflecting the moral failings of a commercial society. In case we think that Smith has become a romantic, he reasserts his dominant theme: a more limited division of labour is not an alternative for the present. Savage and barbarous societies, though useful as a foil, are temporally superceded and can not offer additional insight about how we might live today. Instead, a reformed commercial society – one that combines wealth creation with a state sponsored programme of character refinement – must extend itself to 'the greater part of men'. Smith argues for a commercial society, but one in which the state must act to reverse the morally degrading effects of wealth creation. How much state reform of capitalism seems necessary is, of course, a question that continues to spark debate. Thus, Smith opens and sustains a tension precisely where his name is often summoned to close debate on claims associated with the Washington Consensus that free markets and free trade guarantee a path to a future Eden.

Beyond this gesture towards liberal reform, Smith's treatment of poverty suggests a more radical direction. In line with his dominant theme, Smith asserts again and again that a commercial society produces greater material well-being for common people than previous forms of society. Indeed, this is the key criterion by which to assess contemporary society:

> No society can surely be flourishing and happy, of which the far greater part of the members are poor and miserable. It is but equity, besides, that they who feed, cloath and lodge the whole body of the people, should have such a share of the produce of their own labour as to be themselves tolerably well fed, cloathed and lodged.[127]

He promises earlier in the text that, in a 'well-governed society', the 'universal opulence extends itself to the lowest ranks of the people'.[128]

---

[126] Ibid., p. 303 [V.i.ii.ii].   [127] Ibid. p. 88 [I. viii].   [128] Ibid., p. 15 [I.i].

Recall, additionally, his claim that the poorest in commercial society were far wealthier than savage kings. However, such comparisons are not entirely favourable to commercial society, where, Smith admits, we will find 'indigence': 'Wherever there is great property, there is great inequality. For one very rich man, there must be at least five hundred poor, and the affluence of the few supposes the indigence of the many.'[129]

Unsurprisingly Stoic, Smith turns this gap into one of the major advantages of a commercial society. The relative well-being of the 'ordinary day-labourer' is linked to the role of law in maintaining 'the rich in the possession of their wealth against the violence and rapacity of the poor, and by that means preserve that usefull inequality in the fortunes of mankind which naturally and necessarily arises from the various degrees of capacity, industry, and diligence in the different individuals'.[130] Similarly, Smith, in his parable of the 'unfeeling landlord', explains that the wealth of the landlord, though spent only on his selfish desires, employs vast numbers of people, spreading subsistence to many. Thus the 'vain and insatiable desires' of the rich lead them, as if 'led by an invisible hand', to 'divide with the poor the produce of all their improvements' and 'without intending it, without knowing it, advance the interest of the society'.[131] Inequality, even where opulence and indigence stand in striking opposition, proves not the stark weakness that Smith seemed to indicate. Nonetheless, as our discussion below of the damage done by relative poverty will indicate, Smith himself provides resources for challenging this sanguine conclusion.

A deeper tension may be read from the juxtaposition of rather puzzling comments about savage society. Smith suggests that 'extremities of hunger' impose on the savage a kind of 'Spartan discipline'.[132] It is precisely this condition of scarcity that Smith believes a commercial society brings to an end. However, Smith also presents savages as possessed of the leisure to pursue music and dancing:

> It seems even to be amongst the most barbarous nations that the use and practice of them is both most frequent and most universal, as among the negroes of Africa and the savage tribes of America. In civilized nations, the inferior ranks of people have very little leisure. . . . Among savage

---

[129] Ibid., p. 232 [V.i.b]

[130] Smith, 'Report of 1762–3', *Lectures on Jurisprudence*, p. 338 [vi.19].

[131] Smith, *Theory of Moral Sentiments*, pp. 184–185 [IV.i.10–11].   [132] Ibid., p. 205 [V.2.9].

nations, the great body of the people have frequently great intervals of leisure, and they have scarce any other amusement; they naturally, therefore, spend a great part of their time in almost the only one they have.[133]

This abundance of leisure for savages is quite damaging to Smith's claim about the nature of their poverty. They cannot 'spend a great part of their time' in music and dancing unless they can readily meet their minimum requirements as biological beings, a requirement that would seem to belie claims about their poverty.[134]

What might seem puzzling given Smith's historical narrative is perfectly consistent with the way of life of hunters and gatherers according to Marshall Sahlins.[135] It is precisely the presence of abundant leisure that justifies treating hunters and gatherers as 'affluent'. Hunters and gatherers combine a low level of needs and wants with relatively abundant means to meet those needs, leaving them abundant free time. Turning the tables on the economist quite convincingly, Sahlins concludes that scarcity, rather than being nature-given, is in fact produced by 'market-industrial society'.[136] It is this society that shrinks leisure time by expanding needs and wants beyond the capacity of the society to readily produce them. Hegel, drawing on the work of Scottish Enlightenment figures, noted similarly that the emergence of a modern market society itself promotes individual expression and self-seeking. And while that society generates wealth to support individualization and self-seeking, it also creates poverty that subjugates the least advantaged such that the working classes suffer a loss of the 'feeling of right, integrity and honor' that makes them part of society.[137]

Though we have perhaps tread into an area where Smith might claim that 'absolute', not 'relative', poverty is his concern, Smith's own language of 'tolerably well' indicates that 'necessities and conveniences' are both involved in understanding poverty. He recognizes quite well the social stigma and alienation accompanying relative poverty. 'The poor man', as Smith writes, 'is ashamed of his poverty'. This is hardly

---

[133] Adam Smith, 'Of the Nature of that Imitation which Takes Place in What are Called the Imitative Arts' in Wightman and Bryce (eds.), *Essays on Philosophical Subjects*, p. 187 [II.i].

[134] See Levine, *Economic Studies*, Chapter 2, and Naeem Inayatullah, 'Theories of Spontaneous Order'.

[135] Marshall Sahlins, *Stone Age Economics* (New York: Aldine, 1972).   [136] Ibid., p. 4.

[137] Georg Hegel, *Elements of the Philosophy of Right*, ed. Allen G. Wood (Cambridge, Cambridge University Press, 1991), pp. 182–183, 187, 241–244. See also Schlomo Avineri, *Hegel's Theory of the Modern State* (Cambridge: Cambridge University Press, 1972), Chapter 7.

surprising since indigence produces a kind of social invisibility: 'The poor man goes out and comes in unheeded, and when in the midst of a crowd is in the same obscurity as if shut up in his own hovel.'[138]

If this is so, even assuming Smith's most optimistic assumptions about a commercial society, we cannot sustain the claim that poverty is a condition distinct to savage societies. Rather, poverty is strikingly associated with, perhaps even tied to the emergence of, commercial society. Poverty cannot be assumed as an original condition for which commercial society is the antidote.

Like irrational sentiments and violent factionalism, poverty cannot be relegated to the past. Nor can our cognitive travels so readily ignore the moral resources offered by 'superceded' forms of society. Nevertheless, as we have seen, Smith's dominant mode of relating to poverty (and other realities of commercial society) is either to relocate them to the past or to dilute their potency by pointing to the advantages of the age of commerce relative to past ages. Smith's stance indicates that poverty and moral corruption serve as the 'real' of a wealthy commercial society – something a commercial society can neither solve, nor avoid.

In contrast to his dominant practice, we can see that there is a part of Smith that engages the 'real' of travel. He creates a horizon within which engaging the other of commercial society – what Cheyfitz in the opening epigram calls the *kinship economics* of the Indians, what Sahlins calls the *original affluent society* of hunters and gatherers, or what Smith himself alludes to as the *singing and dancing economy of savages* – serves as a potential learning experience for his European commercial society and for those of us who remain immersed in modern capitalism.

Conclusion

Ashis Nandy notes that where political and ethical recourse to various 'pasts' (including those now being lived) is foreclosed, it impairs our capacity to imagine alternative 'visions of the future'.[139] Our claim is not that Smith and the Scottish Enlightenment offer us nothing of value. Rather, Smith's engagement with the Amerindians, however quaint, is a key part of the historical record theorizing capitalist society. The importance of these past sets of cognitive travels, in Quentin Skinner's terms, is that they offer us a 'repository of values we no longer endorse, of

---

[138] Smith, *Theory of Moral Sentiments*, p. 51 [I.iii.2.2.].
[139] Nandy, *Time Warps*, p. 5.

questions we no longer ask'. The challenge is to recover this moment so that we might be able 'to stand back from, and perhaps even to reappraise, some of our current assumptions and beliefs'.[140] Though we resist the temptation to move across space/time like the Scots, we nevertheless can learn much from their travels. Seeing how Smith constructs a temporal fortress around commercial society alerts us, as Skinner might suggest, to contemporary constructions that deploy similar ethical barriers. Such awareness may allow us, as Nandy recommends, to consult the experiences of an outmoded past – including the savages Smith displaces from the present – as resources in our reflections on the shape of the present and future.

Despite the temporal walls and spatial boundaries Smith builds in order to protect liberal capitalism, we can also retrieve alternative moments and recessive spaces that restore the co-presence of others as critical ethical resources. An encounter with Adam Smith requires a more careful engagement with his texts and context than is characteristic of much of contemporary political economy. Equally, an encounter with those societies that various theories relegate to dead history might require contemporary political economy to receive and absorb their criticisms.

---

[140] Quentin Skinner, *Liberty Before Liberalism* (Cambridge: Cambridge University Press, 1998), p. 112.

7 Property and propriety in international relations: the case of John Locke

David Boucher

Introduction

It is a common assumption, although not undisputed, that Locke's *Two Treatises of Government* considerably influenced the framers of both the 'Virginian Declaration of Rights' (1776), and shortly afterwards, in the same year, 'The Declaration of Independence'. The second declaration informs us that our Creator has bestowed upon us certain 'unalienable Rights', among which are Life, Liberty and the pursuit of Happiness. In the former declaration all men are acknowledged to have inherent rights, including 'the means of acquiring and possessing property'.[1] It is this right of acquiring and of possessing property, acknowledged in 'The Declaration of Independence', that had in fact been central to discussions about the relations of Europeans to non-Europeans in International Relations. And it is the importance of property in such discussions that I want to explore in this chapter, with specific reference to John Locke, but also with a wider frame of reference to the classic thinkers in International Relations. I use the case of Locke in order to illustrate the importance of theories of property in discussions of International Relations. It is, I think, another instance of extending domestic considerations and conceptions to the international sphere. It is not surprising that property rights have such a significant place. Property was central in late medieval and early modern European history in defining the political person. Property was the qualification for entry into the public arena. It brought with it political rights that non-property holders, and those with little property, did not have. This is why Mary Wollstonecraft wished to establish the equality of women to the rights

---

[1] The claim is made, for example, in A. I. Meldon, *Human Rights* (Belmont CA: Wadsworth, 1970), p. 10. The Declarations are reproduced as Appendices I and II.

of private ownership, and not just because she thought it would make them economically independent. They would become political persons in their own right.

Each European state, of course, had its own settled property laws, and how you acquired and exchanged property was legally defined. Among states in the European arena territorial disputes arose, but the issue of ownership and acquisition was not by and large addressed in this context. It was in the context of colonialism that such issues became contested. In America, Africa and Australia there was land that may with just title become occupied and owned by nationals of European states, and it was important that these states acknowledged that title. In some cases the prior ownership of the land by indigenous populations was acknowledged, and the title to that land passed by means of exchange, a transactional relationship. More controversially, however, was the prevalent contention that indigenous peoples had no claim to ownership because they lacked some essential qualification to give them just title, such as in Locke's case failure to cultivate, that is, mix their labour with, the land. In addition, it could be claimed, as it was for parts of America and the whole of Australia, that the land was empty, unoccupied, unused. This is the infamous doctrine of *terra nullius*. The doctrine of *terra nullius* denied both that native peoples were owners of lands, in Vattel's famous phrase they simply 'ranged through' rather than 'inhabited them', and also it denied that native peoples possessed sovereignty, because they did not constitute political societies.[2] Thus the land was there for the taking and title to it could be claimed by displaying the conventional signs of ownership, such as occupancy and possession.

In a discipline obsessed with contemporary relevance and imbued with a utilitarian, or consequentialist attitude to scholarship – that it must be useful or it cannot be any good – it may be wondered of what relevance are such antiquated disputes about property? In the first place, at the macro level, they serve to explain how the world in which we live came to be what it is. The world's only superpower is a product of this European expansionism. In the second place, the doctrine of *terra nullius* and its denial of sovereignty to indigenous peoples has served permanently to exclude such nations within nations from the international sphere; they are diplomatically, in bilateral and multilateral relations

---

[2] Emmerich de Vattel, *The Law of Nations or the Principles of Natural Law* (1758), Book One, Chapter 7, Section 81.

among states, and by international organizations such as The League of Nations and the United Nations, denied direct representation, and are deemed to be virtually represented (to use Burke's phrase) by the dominant culture.

Locke's chapter on property

The chapter on 'Property' in Locke's *Second Treatise* is justifiably famous, but it is by no means clear why it appears at all. Most of the rest of the *Second Treatise* is addressed to justifying obligations to the state, and determining the conditions when those obligations may be disregarded, that is, giving magistrates the right to resist arbitrary government. It is not concerned with the broader conception of property that Locke uses elsewhere in the treatise to refer to self-ownership, and the implied ownership of natural rights. The chapter is more often than not discussed in isolation from the rest of the argument.[3] Indeed, stylistically it differs from the rest of the *Second Treatise*, and there is evidence that it may have been composed at a different time.[4] Richard Tuck suggests that Locke's chapter on property in the *Second Treatise* was very likely composed about 1681 or after.[5] The chapter on property conceivably had a different purpose from the rest of the *Two Treatises*, and may indeed have a different context as a referent by which to illuminate its meaning. It is often suggested that The Glorious and Bloodless Revolution of 1688, when James II was replaced on the throne by William of Orange and Mary, the daughter of the deposed king, because of his attempt to re-Catholicize England, provides the context in which the *Two Treatises* may be best interpreted, offering as it does a justification for rebellion – the famous appeal to heaven. To place it in this context raises a significant puzzle. Given that Robert Filmer had long been dead, and that his arguments for the patriarchal authority of the king played no part in the arguments of those who opposed the depositon of James II, why did Locke devote the whole of the *First Treatise* to distinguishing between

---

[3] D. A. Lloyd Thomas, *Locke On Government* (London: Routledge, 1995), pp. 89–90.
[4] See Richard Ashcraft, *Revolutionary Politics and Locke's 'Two Treatises of Government'* (London: Unwin Hyman, 1986), p. 463, fn 251. Ross Harrison suggests that: 'its importance is independent of the value of Locke's thoughts about the foundation and dissolution of government.' Harrison, *Hobbes, Locke and Confusions's Masterpiece* (Cambridge: Cambridge University Press, 2003), p. 219.
[5] Richard Tuck, *The Rights of War and Peace: Political Thought and the International Order from Grotius to Kant* (Oxford: Oxford University Press, 1999), pp. 169–170.

paternal and political power and its implications with direct and continuous reference to Filmer?

It is quite plausible that Locke meant his *Two Treatises* to be a contribution to the Exclusion Crisis during which time Filmer's *Patriarcha* was resurrected in defence of the right of Prince James, Duke of York, to accede to the throne. Indeed, Locke himself was a casualty of the Royalist backlash in the aftermath of the Exclusion Crisis. He strongly supported Lord Shaftesbury's attempt to change the constitution, by opportunistically using the scare over the Popish Plot, to press for the Exclusion Bill.[6] When in 1881 the King moved Parliament to Oxford, the Whigs appear to have been resolved to resort to military resistance if the Exclusion Bill was defeated for a second time. Locke took an active part in soliciting accommodation for members of Shaftesbury's entourage. When military resistance evaporated on the defeat of the Exclusion Bill the government went on the offensive, Shaftesbury escaped to Holland, and after the failure of the Rye House Plot to kidnap Charles II and James Duke of York on their way back from the Newmarket races, Algenon Sidney, Lord William Russell and the Earl of Essex were arrested in June 1883. Essex committed suicide and Sidney and Russell were hanged. Later that summer the government had Locke in its sights, and he fled to Rotterdam fearing the same fate as Sidney, who at his trial had his criticisms of Sir Robert Filmer cited as evidence of his sedition.

At Oxford University Locke did not read any radical writers such as Lilburne and the other Levellers. There is no evidence that he would have wished to implement any of their radical programmes, including extending the right to vote. Neither the arguments of the Levellers nor the Diggers constituted a significant threat against the Whigs of Locke's

---

[6] Because of the fear of Catholicism and of arbitrary government, the two went hand in hand for opponents of Catholicism, a Test Act was passed in 1673 in order to differentiate between Anglicans and Catholics. Office holders were required to swear an oath of allegiance acknowledging the monarch as head of the Church of England. Its purpose was to exclude Catholics from public office. James Duke of York, Charles II's brother, was forced to give up his public office of admiral because of his refusal to take the oath in 1678. In the same year Titas Oates, an activist protestant opponent of Catholicism disingenuously swore in court that there was a French and Catholic plot to depose the King. Although the claim had no foundation, it created enough hysteria to precipitate the second Test Act which demanded of all members of parliament, Commons and Lords, the swearing of an oath of allegiance and endorsement of an anti-Catholic declaration. The Duke of York was exempted from the terms of reference of the second Test Act. The Exclusion Crisis (1680–81) refers to the attempt by the House of Commons to exclude James, Duke of York, from succession to the throne because of his known Catholic sympathies. The Commons also demanded the expulsion from office of all those who supported James' succession.

day. There is little evidence that the rights of private property were being seriously questioned at the time he wrote the *Two Treatises*. Indeed, the original title to property in a state of nature is significantly qualified with the invention of money, that is, the consenting to attribute an exchange value to scarce metals that have no intrinsic value, and the terms of holding property are allowed by Locke to be determined by each political society and its government.

On Locke's account governments are instituted to protect property. Pursuing its obligation, a government enacts laws that regulate property from that time on. Property now becomes what the rules say it is, and no man can own property without consenting to those rules. To accept property implies accepting the rules and acknowledging the legally constituted sovereign.[7] Regarding the internal arrangements of European states that had well-established property laws it is difficult to see why Locke would have wanted to establish claims that applied prior to their existence. Indeed, he explicitly excludes the possibility of labour being the sole or most common legitimate claim to private property in civil society. It is, he argues, the 'original Law of Nature for the *beginning of Property*' (*Second Treatise*, 30).[8] It is conceivable, as D. A. Lloyd Thomas suggests, that the theory was in fact an assault upon the arbitrary and expedient raising of funds by Charles II without the consent of Parliament.[9] On this interpretation Locke would have had a stronger case had he made reference to the property laws of England. The theory may, of course, have multiple purposes. Among its purposes was one, relating not so much to the internal arrangements of the state, with which the *Two Treatises* are predominantly concerned, but to relations among states, and between states and areas of the world that had not yet established a recognizable (on European standards) political society. European states were in competition with each other for these extra-European territories, and once having acquired them, were under pressure to establish by what right they owned or exercised dominion over them. Establishing this right was not so much to satisfy those dispossessed of propriety by such acquisition, but to lay title against competitors who may have similar designs, and to discredit those settlers whose dealings with the

---

[7] See John Dunn, 'Consent in the Political Theory of John Locke' in John Dunn, *Political Obligation in Its Historical Context* (Cambridge: Cambridge University Press, 1980), p. 37.
[8] Cf. Thomas L. Pangle, *The Spirit of Modern Republicanism* (Chicago: University of Chicago Press, 1988), p. 161.
[9] Lloyd Thomas, *Locke On Government*, p. 91.

Indians were based upon acknowledging indigenous peoples' property rights.

The importance of property

Because property defined one's political persona, and qualified one for participation in the public realm, the psychological importance of property was extended to the international sphere, and particularly where there was a lot of it at stake, namely, in the Americas.

Philosophers in relation to rulers, and as stakeholders, were in many respects like artists, dependent upon patrons and often employed to compose philosophical justifications of current political practices. Marsilius of Padua, for example, was employed by Ludwig of Bavaria to support him in his dispute against Pope Clement VI over the independence of secular from spiritual authorities.[10] Hugo Grotius provided a defence for the East India Company, *De Jure Pradae*, the twelfth chapter of which was to become the famous booklet *Mare Liberum* (*Freedom of the Seas*), in order to impress upon the states of Europe that the Dutch had as much right to trade in the East Indies as the Spanish and Portugese.[11] Nor were philosophers indifferent to establishing their own political stake in society through property ownership and trade. Grotius' aristocratic family had extensive interests in the Indies trade, and both Hobbes and Locke, for example, had property interests in the Americas. Thomas Hobbes, while secretary to Lord Cavendish in June 1622, before the dissolution of the Virginia Company in 1624, was given by his employer a share in the company in order to stack the cards in Cavendish's favour in the court of the company. Locke's interests in north America are impeccable. Locke had a direct involvement with colonialism through his patron Lord Shaftesbury, and both were responsible for justifying the settlement of Carolina against the charge that such a policy would enfeeble England. Locke's knowledge of America was in fact extensive. He read books on its exploration and discovery, had investments there, and was practically involved with the administration of aspects of its affairs.[12] During the 1660s and 1670s, while in the employ of the Earl

---

[10] David Boucher, *Political Theories of International Relations: From Thucydides to the Present* (Oxford: Oxford University Press, 1998), p. 119.
[11] Barbara Arneil, 'John Locke, Natural Law and Colonialism' *History of Political Thought* XIII (1992), p. 588.
[12] Herman Lebovics, 'The Uses of America in Locke's *Second Treatise of Government*' *Journal of the History of Ideas* XLVII (1986), pp. 575–6.

of Shaftesbury, Locke was secretary to the Lord Proprietors of Carolina and Secretary to the Council of Trade and Plantations. Locke believed that a properly managed colonial policy in America would be the key to England's economic success.[13]

If the peoples in the Americas had a title to property, especially the 'vacant' or 'waste' lands, then their political personas also had to be recognized, and European claims to ownership would be tenuous and in contravention of the law of nature and of nations. Should, however, such rights have to be acknowledged, it was not an insurmountable impediment to deprive the American Indians of them. Among the many issues at stake in establishing the right of European states to a title in American lands was first, whether the aboriginal peoples had a prior claim or right, and if so, under what conditions may they be deemed to relinquish it? Answers to these questions varied considerably, and were often swayed by the nationality of the author, and they occupied a central place in discussions of the natural law and the law of nations, and were also integrally related to humanitarian intervention and just war theory in which the issues of property and reparations came into play once a just cause was established.

Spain experienced centuries of fighting against the Moors of Africa. Spanish soldiers were crusaders in their own country and finally defeated the infidel in 1492 with the fall of the last Moorish stronghold of Granada. The newly discovered continent of America now became a considerable attraction to Spanish adventurers in search of fortune. The ascendancy of Spain in Europe throughout the sixteenth century was maintained by its colonial trade and the importation of bullion. The Spanish conquest of the Americas gave prominence to questions that had hitherto not been at the forefront of the minds of theologians, jurists and philosophers. The discovery of new territories raised the question by what right a foreign power could occupy and take possession of lands inhabited by other peoples. To legitimate such acquisition familiar terms of reference had to be invoked. A theory of property needed to be developed in order to justify the occupation of the lands of 'primitive peoples', subject these people as slaves and even massacre them. The question of the justice of acquisition was immensely important. At the heart of the issue was the question of property and the terms of its appropriation and ownership. The violation of such terms could,

---

[13] Barbara Arneil, 'Locke and Colonialism' *Journal of the History of Ideas* 55 (1994), 593–597. Also see Arneil, 'John Locke, Natural Law and Colonialism'.

indeed, provide an additional pretext for the acquisition of territories. A significant degree of talk about just war relates to the violation of property rights and the restitution of the loss. The justice of restitution and reparations gave further justification for dispossessing the Indians of their land.

The right to occupy unoccupied land – the doctrine of *terra nullius*

Alberico Gentili (1552–1608) somewhat disingenuously claimed Tacitus as an authority, and used an idea that Thomas More articulated in his *Utopia*, to conclude from the presupposition that there is a universal human society, that exiles, out of necessity, were entitled to wage offensive wars in their quest for habitable territory, and that vacant lands may be colonized by people who need them for their own use. This justification of appropriation rarely found expression in French or Spanish writers, but was to become increasingly important for Dutch and English apologists for colonizing the new world.[14] The right was to figure prominently in Locke's justification of acquisition, without the requirement of necessity. The fact that the land was deemed empty was justification for occupancy, but occupancy in itself did not in the eyes of many apologists give sufficient grounds for title, or ownership. Occupancy had to be equated with possession. The doctrine of *terra nullius* therefore needed to be supplemented with a theory of property that established a moral title to the ownership of the land. Possession was equated with cultivation. For Locke, the Indians certainly had a natural right to property just like everyone else, they just hadn't exercised it, and what is more they were in dereliction of their duty to God to make the soil as productive as possible by cultivating the land. People had an obligation to cultivate the land (Locke and Vattel), and if they did not they had no right in preventing those who would. Vattel suggests that: 'The cultivation of the soil . . . [is] an obligation imposed by nature on mankind.'[15]

---

[14] Tuck, *Rights of War and Peace*, pp. 47–50.
[15] Vattel, *Law of Nations*, Book One, Chapter 7, 'Of the Cultivation of the Soil', Section 81. Vattel was quite clear that occupancy was not enough: 'The law of nations will, therefore, not acknowledge the property and sovereignty of a nation over any uninhabited countries, except those of which it has really taken actual possession, in which it has formed settlements, or of which it makes actual use'.

With increasing numbers of colonists arriving in Virginia after 1607, in the West Indian Islands, and New England from 1620, Gentili's and More's arguments came to greater prominence. Whereas the seizing of lands effectively constituted conquest, the apologists for the settlers were reluctant to describe their occupation in such terms. To do so would have invoked the laws of war and conquest under natural law and the law of nations, and would have afforded the English Crown a greater degree of authority over the activities of the settlers. Settlement on unoccupied land, on the other hand, entailed the settlers taking with them the laws of their own land. Another implication that was later to become more explicit was that settlers acquired rights over the land they occupied, but not, at least initially, over the peoples of those lands, whereas conquest had the clear corollary of acquiring rights over the inhabitants. While there was some obscurity surrounding this distinction, at least in the practice of the colonists, Hugo Grotius (1583–1645) was clear that the colonists had no political control over the Indians, but on the contrary it was the aboriginals who had a right of control over the colonists. He identified a law of nature that made it permissible for individuals to acquire and retain those things that are useful for life, but excluded injuring others, and taking possession of something that belonged to someone else, that is, the laws of inoffensiveness and abstinence.

Acknowledging that the colonists had an emphatic right to occupy the vacant territories, he nevertheless believed that they should recognize some degree or kind of *imperium* in the indigenous rulers. Silently taking his lead from Gentili, Grotius argued that barren or waste lands that are not deemed to be the property of anyone because they were uncultivated, should be given to strangers on their request, or indeed, may justifiably be occupied by them, acknowledging, however, that jurisdiction continued to reside in the indigenous peoples.[16] There was a distinction to be made between the use of the land by American Indians and ownership. Thomas Hobbes (1588–1679), although less fulsome in his discussion, subscribed to the view of More, Gentili and Grotius that the lands of the Americas were plentiful enough to accommodate a people that was still increasing in population and needed to expand into extra territories. This did not give settlers a right to massacre the natives, but they could constrain them to live closer together.[17]

---

[16] Hugo Grotius, *The Rights of War and Peace*, trans. A. C. Campbell (Westport CN: Hyperion, 1993, reprint of 1901 edition), Book II, Chapter 2, Section 17.
[17] Thomas Hobbes, *Leviathan*, ed. Richard Tuck (Cambridge: Cambridge University Press, 1991), p. 239.

Philosophers did not completely disregard the rights of indigenous peoples, and indeed, refuted claims by foreign governments to dominion in the Americas. Such writers as Vitoria and Grotius were vociferous in acknowledging some basic rights inhering in the American Indians. For example, the Portuguese sought to monopolize trade in the Indian Ocean and in 1605 one of its ships and cargo was captured by a Dutch East India vessel. The services of Grotius were called upon to vindicate the Dutch.[18] Grotius defended Dutch attempts to defeat the Portuguese monopoly in the Indian Ocean. Grotius drew upon Vitoria (1483–1546) to argue that the American Indians had natural rights to public and private property, and could not be deprived of them on religious grounds, nor on the pretext of converting them to Christianity. They were subject to the same natural law as Christians and had to be treated accordingly. No title could be claimed on the grounds of their insanity or irrationality because they were both clever and wise people.

Grotius's theory of property relied upon the condition of occupation. As such it would deprive the Portuguese of their title to property in the Spice Islands, but it was also directed at denying the Portuguese ownership of the seas on the ground that, unlike the land, it could not be occupied.[19] The sea, like the air, was held in common by mankind, and to attempt to occupy it for exclusive use was a violation of the use right of mankind, and could not be justified on the ground that it was necessary to the preservation of peace. The sea is so vast that everyone can share in its benefits including sailing and fishing. Unlike ponds and rivers the sea is not naturally contained, and in fact constitutes more of the earth's surface than land.[20] The idea of the freedom of the seas, like that of free movement and access to markets, benefits those who are capable of taking advantage of these rights. Those who are not, as a result of these freedoms, may find themselves the victims of exploitation, as indeed the American Indians did.

Grotius allows title to private property on the ground that it diminishes conflicts and promotes the preservation of peace. Grotius's theory of property relies upon a common use right in order to generate title

[18] Thomas A. Horne, *Property Rights and Poverty* (Chapel Hill NC: University of North Carolina, 1990), p. 11.
[19] Stephen Buckle, *Natural Law and the Theory of Property: Grotius to Hume* (Oxford: Clarendon Press, 1991), p. 14.
[20] Grotius, *Rights of War and Peace*, Book I, Chapter 2, Section 3. Also see W. E. Butler, 'Grotius and the Law of the Sea' in Hedley Bull, Benedict Kingsbury and Adam Roberts (eds.), *Hugo Grotius and International Relations* (Oxford: Oxford University Press, 1990), pp. 213–214.

165

to ownership by means of possession. The condition of possession was designed to defend Dutch commercial and colonial aspirations. Possession of mobile or moveable property simply meant seizure, whereas fixed or immovable property like land required the marking of boundaries, or construction of some sort.[21]

Land used only by hunters and gatherers was to be deemed vacant because it was uncultivated, and remained common and available for appropriation.[22] European monarchs held great tracts of land in the Americas on behalf of the whole community of their subjects. Such land was a legitimate possession if there was a demonstrable intention to divide it into private sections for cultivation. This justified what in fact both the English and Dutch were practising in the Americas, and demanded that their 'legitimate' claims be respected by other European monarchs.[23] First sighting was not, therefore, a legitimate ground for title to ownership. Occupancy was an important criterion to undermine possible claims to ownership on first sighting. Property claims had to be public. No property rights could be generated by subjective thought because no one could guess at what someone else intended to appropriate. Richard Tuck, for example, remarked in passing that by putting forward this theory of property, 'Grotius had provided a useful ideology for competition over material resources in the non-European world'.[24]

For Grotius sociality basically consisted in respecting one another's rights, and he used the American Indians to illustrate the operation of this principle in the state of nature. Tully has argued that '"Sociableness", for Pufendorf, as for Grotius, is characterised essentially by the negative duty of respecting what belongs to others'.[25] On the contrary, self-preservation and the preservation of society, two principles that were later to constitute for Locke our duty to God, were for Pufendorf (1632–1694) the fundamental laws of nature from which all others followed.[26] Contrary to Grotius, sociality for Pufendorf was not merely a matter

---

[21] Richard Tuck, *Natural Rights Theories: Their Origin and Development* (Cambridge: Cambridge University Press, 1979), pp. 61–62.
[22] Grotius, *Rights of War and Peace*, Book II, Chapter, 2, Sections 4 and 17.
[23] Arneil, 'John Locke, Natural Law and Colonialism', pp. 589 and 593.
[24] Tuck, *Natural Rights Theories*, p. 62.
[25] James Tully, *A Discourse on Property: John Locke and his Adversaries* (Cambridge: Cambridge University Press, 1980), p. 86.
[26] Samuel von Pufendorf, *The Elements of Universal Jurisprudence*, trans. W. A. Oldfather (Oxford: Clarendon Press, 1931), OB. IV, 4. Pufendorf says: 'That each should be zealous so to preserve himself, that society among men be not disturbed.' He was later to give a much more active role to the individual for promoting society.

of respecting other people's property rights. Pufendorf conspicuously departed from Hobbes' position. Self-preservation for Hobbes carried with it no moral duty to preserve others. For Pufendorf our natural sociableness inclines us towards peace, and makes us averse to the war of all against all. Peace is our natural condition whether inside or outside a commonwealth, and 'to undertake a war without provocation, is both improper and unprofitable'.[27]

Grotius' theory of property constituted a justification of colonialism, whereas Pufendorf's is far more protective of the rights of natives. Both authors contend that God gave the earth to men in common. They did not own it collectively, but were granted a right to use it. This did not amount to collective ownership. It is what Pufendorf called a negative community in which no one has property rights. A positive community is one in which property is communally owned.[28] The things of the earth are not infinite in supply, and use by one may prevent use by another. As the population increases competition for use increases. It is as a result of conflict over use rights that private property emerges.[29] Private property, for Pufendorf, is a moral quality that has no 'intrinsic effect upon things themselves, but only produce a moral effect in relation to other men'.[30] Private property, if it is conducive to peace, is consistent with nature, and although it is a human institution, it is nevertheless natural. Proprietorship develops historically in response to circumstances and it is perfectly acceptable that elements of primitive community have been retained by 'backward peoples'.[31]

A use right, for Grotius, gives users exclusive right over that which is used. Agreement is not necessary, because a simple sign of seizure or occupancy will do. Private property is a necessary development out of the original use right as communities become more complex. It becomes imperative that agreements among individuals acknowledge what each

---

[27] Samuel von Pufendorf, *On The Law of Nature and Nations: Eight Books*, trans. C. H. Oldfather and W. A. Oldfather (Oxford: Clarendon Press, 1934), 2, ii, 9. Also see Alfred Dufour, 'Pufendorf' in J. H. Burns (ed.), *The Cambridge History of Political Thought 1450–1700* (Cambridge: Cambridge University Press, 1995) p. 268.

[28] Pufendorf, *Law of Nature*, Book Four, Chapter, iv, Section 2. Arneil argues that Grotius postulates a positive community and thus common ownership of the earth. My own reading accords with that of Stephen Buckle. Arneil, 'John Locke, Natural Law and Colonialism', p. 597; Buckle, *Natural Law*, pp. 36–37. It is significant that Pufendorf took Grotius to be describing a negative community.

[29] Pufendorf, *Law of Nature*, Book Four, Chapter iv, Section 7 and Grotius, *Rights of War and Peace*, Book Two, Chapter ii, Section, 1.

[30] Pufendorf, *Law of Nature*, Book Four, Chapter iv, Section, 1.

[31] Pufendorf, *Law of Nature*, Book Four, Chapter iv, Section, 13.

has appropriated as his or her own. It is then *ex post facto* acknowledge-ment.[32] Pufendorf takes a different view. He argues 'that dominion pre-supposes absolutely an act of man and an agreement, whether tacit or express'.[33] In other words use or occupancy do not in themselves imply private ownership, nor does the expended labour create a title to prop-erty. Property is a moral quality and requires agreement to create the moral effect of obligation. The original division of land among members of communities or nations required an express pact, but at the same time, Pufendorf suggested, agreements were made which allowed first occu-pancy of land, not already designated, to be a sign of ownership.[34] In effect, then, tacit consent is deemed to acknowledge private ownership of those things of which individuals take possession, and which have not already been designated to someone in the original pact.

Pufendorf's theory of property is important for International Rela-tions because it serves considerably to restrict the grounds for colo-nial expansionism. His views on what he calls 'eminent domain' and 'occupancy as a whole' or 'universal dominion' are of particular signif-icance.[35] Unlike Grotius, who distinguished between property owner-ship and jurisdiction, Pufendorf believed that waste lands, while not being the private property of any individual, were nevertheless collec-tively owned by the people as a whole. This he called eminent domain. It is quite different from an individual's title to property, in that it estab-lishes the dominion of the whole group over all things in a particular territory. Whereas the private ownership of the property by an individ-ual may be transferred to a foreigner, 'universal dominion is preserved only in the state'.[36] Here the state is clearly distinct from the person of the monarch, and those rights that are devolved to individuals within the universal domain are decided by the popular will. The commu-nity, or state, as a whole has rights over property that no one outside it has, nor any individual distinct from his capacity as a member of that community. Eminent domain is the power that the whole community has over the property of its citizens, and constrains the use of private property within bounds consistent with the common good. Even the lands and other property of the church fall within this domain and in

---

[32] See Tuck, *Natural Rights Theories*, p. 61; Arneil, 'John Locke, Natural Law and Colonial-ism', p. 598; and Buckle, *Natural Law*, pp. 42–43.
[33] Pufendorf, *Law of Nature*, Book Four, Chapter iv, Section 4.
[34] Pufendorf, *Law of Nature*, Book Four, Chapter iv, Section 9.
[35] Pufendorf, *Law of Nature*, Book Four, Chapter vi, Section 4.
[36] Pufendorf, *Law of Nature*, Book Four, Chapter iv, Section 4.

cases of extreme necessity can be confiscated without compensation or restitution.[37]

No signs of seizure nor cultivation are required for occupancy as a whole, nor, contrary to Grotius, need there be a clear intention to divide the land among individuals. Any land that appears to be unoccupied and without a private owner 'should not at once be regarded as unoccupied and free to be taken by any man as his own, but it will be understood to belong to the whole people'.[38] This, then, is a direct denial of the principle of *terra nullius*. Community rights and eminent domain are not restricted to states, but apply to societies as such. What this means is that even if one takes the American Indians to be living in a state of nature, as Grotius and Locke did, the Indians still exercise property rights of 'occupancy as a whole' and determine its use and distribution by title of eminent dominion.

Pufendorf's theory is nevertheless flawed. In legitimating community property rights, private property and the establishment of a plurality of states he fails adequately to explain how, if property, or at least its initial distribution, requires agreement, can anything less than the whole world community authorize it. Tacit consent can hardly be invoked to cover the whole population of the world, in complete ignorance of particular acts of appropriation in far-flung parts of the globe. If, as Pufendorf believed, all the world was given by God for the use of every individual in common, on whose authority can small groups permanently appropriate portions, especially of immovables like land, for their exclusive common use? If this stage is not completely legitimated the further stages of the creation of the state with universal dominion and eminent domain, that serves to secure private property, cannot be justified.

John Locke – born in the same year as Pufendorf (1632) – offered a solution to the dilemma of how the whole world, given to mankind in common, can be owned by individual property rights without the consent of the whole. His solution legitimated the appropriation of foreign lands that had not yet come under cultivation, such as those of the American Indians. Locke's theory of property incorporates the New World into his philosophical perspective, offering a justification for the appropriation of foreign lands based upon individual property rights.

---

[37] Pufendorf, *Elements*, I, DEF V, 5.
[38] Pufendorf, *Law of Nature*, Book Four, Chapter vi, Section 4.

Locke follows Hobbes and Pufendorf, rather than Grotius, in identifying the law of nature with the law of nations.[39] Locke believed that the human condition was naturally social, and that God gave the earth to men in common. Agreement, or consent, was not however necessary to create private property. If it were, Locke argued, private property would be contrary to God's intention. Private property existed in the state of nature from the outset in that every person had a property in himself over which no one, because of the principle of natural equality, could exercise dominion without consent. God wills that we sustain and protect this property in ourselves by cultivating and appropriating the things of nature.[40] The use of the gifts of nature requires that we first take possession of those things. We do so by means of an instrument inherent in the person, labour. It is labour, and not consent, which creates property in things: 'The *labour* that was mine, removing them out of that common state they were in, hath *fixed* my *Property* in them.'[41]

The state of nature, although primitive, is populated by people who have a sense of justice and injustice. Each has executive power in enforcing the moral code of the law of nature. God has granted us life, a property in the person, and we have an obligation to preserve it, and as far as we can, to preserve the life of others. Preservation of property in the person is enhanced by the efficient use of the resources of the Earth. We are also, therefore, under an obligation to God to make the land and all that lives and grows on it as productive as possible.

Locke begins to establish this moral obligation to labour in the *First Treatise*. There the Biblical basis of his argument is much more evident. Before the Flood, God gave man a mere stewardship of the land, but no right of dominion over the birds and animals. It was Noah and his sons who were first granted 'Liberty to use the Living Creatures for Food'.[42] What God granted was propriety in the living creatures, a liberty to use them, but not private ownership of them. Locke is here, of course, refuting Filmer's claim that Adam and Noah had ownership rights over the world granted to them by God in bestowing upon them patriarchial authority. His point, on the evidence of I. Genesis 28, is that men in general were granted dominion in common over other creatures. It is this use right that the American Indians exercise, and which Locke explicitly

---

[39] Locke, *Two Treatises of Government*, ed. Peter Laslett (Cambridge: Cambridge University Press, 1988) II, p. 276 §14.
[40] Locke, *Two Treatises*, II, §26 and §86.   [41] Locke, *Two Treatises*, II, §28.
[42] Locke, *Two Treatises*, I §38.

relates to the sons of Adam and Noah.[43] Thus: 'The Fruit or Venison, which nourishes the wild Indian, and who knows no Inclosure, and is still a Tenant in common, must be his, and so his, i.e. a part of him, that another can no longer have any right to it, before it can do him any good for the support of his Life.'[44] It is important, however, to see how subtle is the shift from ownership of things, to ownership of land in Locke's theory. The labour expended by hunter-gathers, deep-sea fishermen, bakers or craftsmen entitles them in the state of nature to what they have killed, gathered or made. When it comes to land, however, there is a change of emphasis. In the *First Treatise* Locke excludes certain types of 'labour' from affording a property title. Referring to the Bible, Locke recalls the curse placed upon Adam requiring men to labour because of their impoverished and destitute condition.[45] The earth requires long and sustained labour in order to yield its fruits and make it productive. Mere occupancy or appropriation, that is taking possession, does not qualify.

Ownership and labour is now clearly associated with cultivation. Locke contends that: '*As much Land* as a man Tills, Plants, Improves, Cultivates, and can use the Product of, so much is his *Property*.'[46] The crucial point is this: Locke excludes such activities as roaming over the uncultivated land, hunting and gathering or grazing one's sheep on it, from securing a title to property. What is of more significance is that not only does labour provide a title for the ownership of property in the state of nature, but Locke also wanted to establish the moral obligation to engage in labour. It is not enough to mix one's labour in the land, say by enclosing it and planting trees, but we are obliged to develop it to its greatest productive capacity as industrious and rational creatures. God did, after all, give men the world 'for their benefit. And the greatest Conveniences of Life they were capable to draw from it' (*Second Treatise*, Section 309).[47] By implication, the American Indians, in failing to cultivate the land to its full productive capacity, were rather less than industrious and rational and had no grounds for preventing those who are fulfilling God's destiny for men. Locke's view of the Indians was that they were wretched creatures, barely achieving subsistence levels,

[43] Locke, *Two Treatises*, II, §310–311.   [44] Locke, *Two Treatises*, II, §306.
[45] Locke, *Two Treatises*, I, §144–145.
[46] Locke, *Two Treatises*, II, §32. Cf. Jeremy Waldron, *God, Locke, and Equality: Christian Foundations in Locke's Political Thought* (Cambridge: Cambridge University Press, 2002), pp. 164–170.
[47] Cf. Lebovics, 'The Uses of America', p. 577.

and whose kings were worse off than day labourers. They were ignorant and barely able to raise themselves above the level of the brutes. In his journal entry for 1677 he says that their 'minds are as ill clad as their bodies'.[48] One of the purposes of government is to ensure the productive use of land. Indeed, Locke was later to suggest that the British Government should promote colonization by facilitating the emigration of those who are currently a burden on society to colonies where, because of underpopulation and underproduction, they are a net beneficiary for the resources of the Kingdom of England.

Locke did not believe, however, that appropriated land should be allowed to lie waste.[49] It is not without significance, then, that the American Indians are constantly invoked as examples of people currently living in a state of nature, and subject to the principle of spoilage in the accumulation of property, slightly modified in some instances by a primitive form of money.

England's war against the Dutch was becoming increasingly more difficult to finance with the Great Plague of 1665 and the Fire of London of 1666. For some political commentators colonialism was seen to be the way out of financial difficulties, while for the majority it appeared to exacerbate them. Plantations in particular were seen to be a drain on the realm of England. The accumulation of vast tracts of land if uncultivated was an offence against the law of nature. In this respect Locke shared the sentiments of many supporters and administers of colonialism who were concerned that the accumulation of land be limited to that which had sufficient men to cultivate it. More efficient government in Virginia, for example, and a larger population would make the land more productive and also benefit England, making it an asset rather than a liability. In fact, many landowners in Virginia were in violation of the law of nature because they occupied vast tracts of land, much of which lay uncultivated, and which was technically 'waste'. Locke suggested that such land should be transferred into the hands of the king for redistribution.[50]

Locke does not allow unlimited accumulation of property in the state of nature. Individuals can appropriate without consent only so much as they can use. The principle of spoilage limits accumulation. It would

---

[48] Cited in Richard H. Cox, *Locke on Peace and War* (Oxford: Clarendon Press, 1960), pp. 98–99.

[49] Locke, *Two Treatises*, II, §37 and §42.

[50] Richard Ashcraft, 'Political Theory and Political Reform: John Locke's Essay on Virginia' *The Western Political Quarterly* 22 (1969), pp. 747–9.

be a sin to take goods out of the common sphere and allow them to perish.[51] The principle applies to both the produce of the earth and to the accumulation of land. It is with the invention of money, by agreement to endow with exchange value that which is intrinsically valueless, that the unlimited accumulation of wealth is facilitated. In other words, whereas property does not rest upon consent, the 'disproportionate and unequal Possession of the Earth' does.[52]

The obligations to God of self-preservation and of cultivating the earth in order to make it more productive and conducive to self-preservation are better discharged within a political society. The inconveniences of the state of nature, regulated by a law that is not written down, wilful and innocent misinterpretation of the law with no common superior to arbitrate, and no power to enforce it, make it imperative by agreement to set up political society and government.

The implication of Locke's discussions of the American Indians is that they fall short of adequately discharging their obligations to God. They still live in a state of nature and they fail to add to the common stock of mankind by improving the productivity of the land. In so doing they have no claim on vast territories in the Americas that '*lie waste*'. By this Locke means more than land that is simply left barren. Land that was not efficiently utilized, and whose produce was allowed to rot, regardless of its being enclosed, 'was still to be looked on as Waste, and might be the Possession of any other'.[53]

The lands of the more civilized peoples of the world are protected, first by governments instituted for that purpose and which regulate use, and by agreements among states that explicitly or tacitly renounce claims to the lands of the others. It is by mutual consent that states give up the common natural right which they originally had and establish territorial boundaries in the division of the Earth into 'distinct Parts and parcels'. Those primitive societies that have not taken their place among the civilized society of states are therefore not protected against peoples who settle, mix their labour and make the land their own, because that land is still the common possession of mankind.

Locke's intention to legitimize colonialism, while establishing the principle of European territorial integrity is clear from the following passage:

---

[51] Locke, *Two Treatises*, II, §31.   [52] Locke, *Two Treatises*, II, §50.
[53] Locke, *Two Treatises*, II, §38.

there are still *great Tracts of Ground* to be found, which (the Inhabitants thereof not having joyned with the rest of Mankind, in the consent of the use of their common Money) *lie waste*, and are more than the People, who dwell on it, do, or can make use of, and so still lie in common. Tho' this can scarce happen amongst that part of Mankind, that have consented to the Use of Money.[54]

Locke, then, is a defender of colonial expansionism and justifies it with a theory of property that requires mixing one's labour, or that of one's employees, to create a title to specific tracts of land, or produce, that are otherwise considered vacant and open to all mankind in common. However, his theory would not legitimate colonialism if the inhabitants of occupied territories with a claim to the land were subdued by unjustifiable force. The use of force without right cannot legitimate conquest. Agreements reached under duress are void, and no obligation is incurred. This position is very different from that of Hobbes, who might pronounce the unnecessary use of force dishonorable, but would have no grounds in international relations upon which to pronounce force unjust.

Whereas Grotius made a distinction between property ownership and jurisdiction, where the latter extended to people who inhabit a certain territory, but not the property they occupy, and Pufendorf emphasized that societies exercise eminent domain even over territories with no evident sign of occupancy, Locke realized that such arguments as those of Grotius and Pufendorf undermine claims to European colonial expansionism, and deny the Mother country political authority in those lands. The direct impetus for Locke's attempt to close this loophole may have been William Penn's political experiment in Pennsylvania. Penn was granted a royal charter in 1681 to found his colony and almost immediately began to formulate views at variance with the Whigs with whom he had formerly been associated, including Locke himself. Penn acknowledged the Indians as possessors of rights over the land, and instructed his agents to negotiate with them for the purchase of their property.[55]

[54] Locke, *Two Treatises*, II, §45.
[55] America was not seen by the classic law of nations theorists, nor in fact by Locke, to be homogenous. Even Vattel, who is always invoked as the theorist who justified colonization, was discerning in what he justified. In his view the Spanish conquest of South America was unlawful, whereas parts of North America could be legitimately possessed, on condition that the colonizers confine themselves within 'just bounds'. (Vattel, *Law of Nations*, Book One, Chapter 7, 'Of the Cultivation of the Soil', Section 81). Whereas Vattel provides the basis for the position taken in Australia, he does nevertheless indicate that it is to be commended that Penn and his colony of Quakers purchased their land from the Indians and thus acknowleged their ownership.

Locke, as we saw, not only denied the American Indians ownership of 'waste land', but also of land that was insufficiently cultivated, or on which the produce was under utilized. Locke emphatically rejects Pufendorf's theory of eminent domain in maintaining that only when a tract of land has been cultivated and therefore appropriated can governments exercise authority over it.[56] American chiefs or kings, then, had no jurisdiction over the waste and insufficiently cultivated lands of their country and Europeans need not recognize their authority because they had no rights over such property, except those of use that they share with every other person of humanity.

This is not the place to discuss in detail the centrality of property to just war theory, and how just war allows legitimate seizure of property. It suffices to say that resistance by the American Indians to the appropriation of land to which they had no legitimate claim, because they failed to cultivate it productively, constituted a just cause of war. For Locke Americans are deemed to have no right to defend their traditional ways of life against European encroachment, after all, their way of life is inherently inferior to that of Europeans, and deficient in discharging their obligations to God. We have a natural right to punish Indians and to gather together our kith and kin to gain reparations from the Indians for injuries caused.[57] Locke simply takes for granted the injustice of native resistance to the appropriation of waste lands, and the justice of developers to counter such aggression.[58]

Vattel, writing over ninety years later, reflected the extent to which the State had now become central to international relations. Contrary to Locke, he thought that seizing territories from the civilized nations of Central and South America of dubious legality and praised the English Puritans of New England and Quakers of Pennsylvania for their moderation in purchasing lands from the American savages.[59] This was an acknowledgment of the property rights of American Indians that Locke was reluctant to allow. Vattel's justification of the appropriation of foreign unpossessed lands was based not on individual right, but upon the argument that it was contrary to nature to allow land to go uncultivated that was needed to sustain the world's vastly increased population. Without agricultural communities the world could not sustain its population and therefore agricultural communities have a right

---

[56] Locke, *Two Treatises*, II, §121.   [57] Locke, *Two Treatises*, §9 and §130.

[58] Wayne Glausser, 'Three Approaches to Locke and the Slave Trade' *Journal of the History of Ideas* 51 (1990), p. 209.

[59] Vattel, *Law of Nations*, §81 and §209.

175

to occupy and work land that was not effectively being exploited by others.[60]

Terra nullius and sovereignty

The doctrine of *terra nullius*, then, was extremely important in the colonization process. It was related to what Carole Pateman calls 'the settler contract', a variant of the social contract in so far as it relied upon many of the features of a state of nature central to that doctrine.[61] The denial of sovereignty to indigenous peoples did not depend upon first establishing *terra nullius*. One of the most famous denials, that of Locke, did depend upon the idea of *terra nullius*. As we saw, Locke not only denied the American Indians ownership of 'waste land', but also of land that was insufficiently cultivated, or on which the produce was underutilized.

Even when it was acknowledged that native peoples exercised ownership rights, the colonizing country retained the rights of eminent domain, and denied sovereignty to native peoples. Social Contract theory, in its classic form, was central to theories of sovereignty. The complexity of the contract varies. For Hobbes it is one stage, for Pufendorf three. Whether the theory was absolutist or limited, they both constituted in Pufendorf's view instances of supreme sovereignty. In other words, shared sovereignty was inconceivable. A nation within a nation was undesirable and constituted in Pufendorf's view an unstable monstrosity.

The aboriginal peoples who roamed but did not occupy or possess territories were deemed not to have made such contracts and therefore did not possess sovereignty. Given that sovereignty became the membership card for entry into the international club, this constituted permanent exclusion for minority nations. The legality of such exclusion was put to the test soon after the establishment of the League of Nations. The Six Nations Iroquois Confederacy attempted to gain recognition of their independence, and to resolve their ongoing dispute with Canada. Between 1922 and 1924 they petitioned the League of Nations to accept

---

[60] Thomas Flanagan briefly discusses Vattel's position in 'The Agricultural Argument and Original Appropriation: Indian Lands and Political Philosophy' *Canadian Journal of Political Science* XXII (1989).
[61] I am indebted to discussions with Carole Pateman for distinguishing between the settler contract and the social contract. She is currently working on a book with Charles W. Mills extending her treatment of the Sexual Contract to the idea of the 'Racial Contract'. The settler contract is part of this project.

them as a member and to intervene to prevent further encroachment by the Canadian government on their independence. They argued that the six nations had long been a highly organized self-governing people, whose confederacy of self-governing states had been acknowledged in treaties, and through diplomatic activity with the Dutch, French, Americans and British since at least 1613. The Canadian Government responded to the petition by claiming that there was no provision in the Covenant of the League for discussion of the internal matters of a sovereign state in its dealings with individuals who owe the state allegiance. In other words, the answer presumed what was in dispute. The League did not accept the petition.[62]

Conclusion

I have shown how colonization was integrally related to the development of theories of property that legitimated occupation and possession of foreign lands. This entailed the formulation of the doctrine of *terra nullius* which acknowledged occupation and possession only in terms of specific kinds of labour, namely cultivation. In practice, it was much less costly in terms of money and lives to enter into transactional relations with the Indians that acknowledged their prior ownership, and for the Puritans it was morally more justifiable. The doctrine nevertheless persisted in the colonization of Australia. Whether indigenous peoples were deemed to own the land over which they 'roamed', or whether they merely had a use right in common, they were not deemed to have entered into a social contract among themselves, and therefore they were not deemed to have instituted sovereign political societies (there were, however, exceptions in South America that were acknowledged even by Vattel). The legacy has been the permanent exclusion from the international realm of minority nations within nations, on the grounds that they do not constitute sovereign political communities.

---

[62] See Robert Lee Nichols, 'Realizing the Social Contract: The Case of Colonialism and Indigenous Peoples' *Contemporary Political Theory* 4 (2005), pp. 42–43.

8 Classical smoke, classical mirror: Kant and Mill in liberal international relations theory[1]

Beate Jahn

The Democratic Peace thesis constitutes the most influential use of a classical author – Immanuel Kant – in the contemporary discipline of International Relations. Its central claim that democracies don't fight each other is hailed as coming 'as close as anything we have to an empirical law in international relations'.[2] Innumerable publications from proponents and critics alike fill the discipline's journals; it has given rise to what one might rightly call a whole industry of quantitative and qualitative studies testing and refining, challenging and refuting its central categories and claims.[3]

Moreover, while academic theories are often hotly debated within their disciplines, they rarely play much of a role outside this narrow circle. This, however, is not true for the Democratic Peace thesis, which has risen to extraordinary influence in the justification of Western or liberal foreign policies in the last decades. But even here its importance does not end. The idea that liberal or democratic states are more peaceful than other states has pervaded the public political discourse in the West to such a degree that it can be presented and reproduced as a self-evident truth in the media.[4]

---

[1] A different version of this chapter has first been published as Beate Jahn, 'Kant, Mill, and Illiberal Legacies in International Affairs' in *International Organization* 59 (2005), 177–207.

[2] Jack S. Levy, 'Domestic Politics and War' in Robert I. Rotberg and Theodore K. Rabb (eds). *The Origin and Prevention of Major Wars* (Cambridge: Cambridge University Press, 1989), p. 88.

[3] For a collection of articles on the Democratic Peace thesis, see Michael E. Brown, Sean M. Lynn-Jones and Steven E. Miller (eds.), *Debating the Democratic Peace* (Cambridge MA: MIT Press, 1996); and Tarak Barkawi and Mark Laffey (eds.), *Democracy, Liberalism, and War* (Boulder CO, Lynne Rienner, 2001).

[4] Michael Doyle, 'Liberalism and World Politics' *American Political Science Review* 80 (1986), p. 1151, and *Ways of War and Peace* (New York: W. W. Norton, 1997), p. 205; 'Bush, Blair Address Prospects for Peace' *Los Angeles Times* (12 November 2004).

In the original formulation and argumentation of the Democractic Peace thesis, Kant's 'Perpetual Peace' played a crucial role as offering 'the best guidance' for an explanation of the statistical evidence of a liberal peace.[5] And even much of the later literature in this field – whether or not it explicitly engages with Kant's argument – routinely cites his name.[6] Hence, Kant's arguments in 'Perpetual Peace' play a crucial role in the explanation of a contemporary theory as well as, indirectly, in the justification of liberal foreign policies and the inspiration of contemporary public political discourses.

This prominent use of a classical author requires reflection on the limits and possibilities of their appropriation in contemporary International Relations (IR). There are two obvious disjunctures between classical and contemporary theory. First, the qualitative relevance of the historical differences between the contemporary world and that which Kant, or other classical authors, reflected on has to be established. Second, classical authors wrote before the establishment of IR as a separate discipline; hence their reflection on international politics forms part of a more holistic conception of human social and political life. Contemporary use of classical authors thus has to pay particular attention to the relationship between the domestic and the international sketched in their work.

In the first part of this chapter I will show that Democratic Peace theorists read Kant without reflecting on the implications of the different historical and intellectual context and I will provide an alternative reading which is sensitive to these differences. Kant identified sources

---

[5] Michael Doyle, 'Kant, Liberal Legacies, and Foreign Affairs' in Brown et al. (eds.), *Democratic Peace*, p. 21. The article was first published in two parts in *Philosophy and Public Affairs* 12 (1983), 205–235, 323–353.

[6] See, for example, Bruce Russett, 'The Fact of the Democratic Peace' in Brown et al. (eds.), *Democratic Peace*, pp. 58–81; John M. Owen, 'How Liberalism Produces Democratic Peace', in Brown et al. (eds.), *Democratic Peace*, pp. 116–154; Christopher Layne, 'Kant or Cant: The Myth of Democratic Peace', in Brown et al. (eds.), *Democratic Peace*, pp. 157–201; David E. Spiro, 'The Liberal Peace – And Yet it Squirms', in Brown et al. (eds.), *Democratic Peace*, pp. 202–238; Ido Oren, 'The Subjectivity of the "Democratic" Peace: Changing U.S. Perceptions of Imperial Germany', in Brown et al. (eds.), *Democratic Peace*, pp. 263–300; Tarak Barkawi and Mark Laffey, 'Introduction: The International Relations of Democracy, Liberalism, and War', in Barkawi and Laffey (eds.), *Democracy*, pp. 1–23; David Blaney, 'Realist Spaces/Liberal Bellicosities: Reading the Democratic Peace as World Democratic Theory', in Barkawi and Laffey (eds.), *Democracy*, pp. 25–44; Timothy R. W. Kubik 'Military Professionalism and the Democratic Peace: How German Is It?', in Barkawi and Laffey (eds.), *Democracy*, pp. 87–106; Sven Chojnacki, 'Demokratien und Krieg. Das Konfliktverhalten demokratischer Staaten im Internationalen System 1946–2001' in Christine Schweitzer, Björn Aust and Peter Schlotter (eds.), *Demokratien im Krieg* (Baden-Baden, Nomos, 2004), pp. 72–106.

of international conflict in his time on the domestic, international and transnational levels which he addressed respectively in the three definitive articles. The domestic source of conflict to which the republican constitution was meant to provide a solution was the nature of the absolutist state which is not comparable to contemporary liberal capitalist states. The international and transnational sources of conflict in Kant's time – the security dilemma and the imposition of unequal economic relations on non-European states – however, are perfectly comparable with contemporary international politics. And yet, in its neglect of these historical continuities and discontinuities, the Democratic Peace thesis prioritizes the republican constitution for today's world and radically misinterprets Kant's international and transnational sources of conflict. Hence, the ethico-political implications of the Democratic Peace thesis, namely the principled justification of intervention, stands in direct opposition to Kant's argument.

This insensitivity to the historical context, moreover, prevents contemporary authors from recognizing a much more appropriate classical predecessor for the Democratic Peace thesis, as I will show in the second section. This author is John Stuart Mill. The parallels between contemporary and Mill's arguments demonstrate that an unreflected implication of the former lies in the justification of imperialist policies explicitly spelt out by the latter. Nonetheless, as I will show in the third part of this chapter, Mill's analysis of modern civilization and representative government in a liberal capitalist state undermines the grounds on which these states are accorded more rights than others – then and now – and the contradictions found between Mill's political and his international theory are equally present at the heart of the Democratic Peace thesis. In short, where the non-interventionist Kant is cited in support of interventions, the interventionist Mill is generally seen as a non-interventionist.

In conclusion, I will argue that the ahistorical and acontextual approach to classical authors results, on the one hand, in the reification of contemporary ideological approaches to international relations and, on the other, in an abandonment of the critical analytical potential which an historically and contextually sensitive reading of classical authors can provide. Specifically, the ahistorical reading of Kant functions as a smoke screen which hides his own as well as Mill's potential as a mirror for contemporary liberal theory and foreign policy. The price for this unreflected use of classical authors in the discipline lies ultimately in the abandonment of the very *raison d'être* of a social science which does not lie in the unreflected amplification of the *Zeitgeist* but in its critical examination.

History and the perpetual peace

The Democratic Peace thesis is so widely known in International Relations that I will only briefly summarize its main claims.[7] It identifies the republics of Kant's First Definitive Article with contemporary liberal states. This identification is based on the comparability of the form of government – a representative constitution – on which the relatively peaceful nature of liberal states is based.[8] Accordingly, the source of international conflict is seen to lie in the non-representative constitutions of non-liberal states.[9] Consequently, Kant's Federation of Free states in the Second Definitive Article is identified with a separate liberal peace in the contemporary world – an exclusive club of liberal states.[10] And, finally, Kant's law of hospitality is identified with transnational economic and other interaction in the contemporary world providing the material basis for increased cooperation while simultaneously undermining non-liberal constitutions.[11]

The aim of a liberal foreign policy, hence, lies in the systematic promotion of 'liberal principles abroad', that is, in changing the cultural, economic and political constitution of non-liberal states.[12] This promotion of liberal principles requires a clear distinction between liberal and non-liberal states; there can be no alliance with the latter.[13] The preferred means to this end are economic – sanctions or restricted interaction with non-liberal states and extended aid and trade with liberal or transitional states.[14] Historically, resistance of non-liberal states to such interference has predominantly led to military interventions which in turn often proved counterproductive. Hence, Doyle advocates the extension of the right of military non-intervention to non-liberal governments.[15] This recommendation, however, is not based on the assumption that military interventions constitute a departure from liberal principles; rather they are fundamentally rooted in them. Doyle, therefore, advocates non-military means consistently for reasons of prudence rather than as a

---

[7] My summary rests on Michael Doyle's most influential statement of the Democratic Peace thesis in 'Kant, Liberal Legacies, and International Affairs'. For a more detailed discussion of its claims, see Beate Jahn, 'Kant, Mill, and Illiberal Legacies in International Affairs' *International Organization* 59 (2005), 177–207.

[8] Doyle, 'Kant, Liberal Legacies, and International Affairs' pp. 5f.   [9] Ibid., pp. 31f.
[10] Ibid., p. 26.   [11] Ibid., p. 26.   [12] Ibid., p. 49.   [13] Ibid., p. 50.
[14] Ibid., pp. 48, 50ff.   [15] Ibid., pp. 37, 48ff.

matter of principle.[16] The Democratic Peace thesis, thus, while offering a normative constraint against the use of force between liberal states, does not provide such constraint for the relations between liberal and non-liberal states. And this, of course, implies that consent of the target population – while generally expected but not always forthcoming – is not necessary.

The first defining feature of these policy recommendations, which aim at the spread of democracy and market economy around the world, is the propagation of particularist rather than universal international law.[17] International organization, the Federation of Free States, is not open to non-liberal states. Rights of sovereignty and non-intervention are only conferred on liberal states. A second defining feature of this reading of Kant is the primacy accorded to the domestic sources of international conflict. Just as the source of peacefulness is seen in the domestic representative constitution, the source of aggression is seen in the non-representative constitutions of other states. Consequently, the pursuit of perpetual peace entirely hinges on the transformation of all non-liberal states into liberal states. In line with this logic, the Second and Third Definitive articles are understood as providing the means – international and transnational – to achieve the end of changing the constitution of non-liberal states which is provided in the First Definitive article.

The Democratic Peace thesis, I will suggest first, misconceives the relationship between theory and history in Kant's work and, consequently, the nature of moral laws. Subsequently, I will provide an interpretation of 'Perpetual Peace' based on Kant's historical analyses and demonstrate that contemporary liberal thought, far from just misinterpreting Kant, develops policy recommendations diametrically opposed to those of Kant. In particular, it propagates policies which Kant identified as the source of imperialism in his time and it reifies the security dilemma between liberal and non-liberal states, thus reproducing the very sources of international conflict Kant set out to solve. Moreover, it prioritizes the domestic constitution expecting peace to follow without regard to the mutually constitutive nature of domestic, international and transnational sources of conflict identified by Kant – thus jeopardizing the liberal achievements in the domestic sphere through the pursuit of illiberal policies in the international.

---

[16] Ibid., pp. 41f.
[17] See Chapter 4 by Antonio Franceschet in this volume for a detailed discussion of the exclusion of non-liberal states from international law.

Kant argues that nature and human nature play themselves out in history, so that a survey of this history is necessary in order to ascertain potential goals of human development. Accordingly, he derives the values of individual freedom and equality on which the ideal of the republican constitution is based from a philosophy of history. This philosophy of history is systematically worked out in his *Idea for a Universal History with Cosmopolitan Purpose* on whose basic assumptions the First Definitive Article relies.[18] However, 'reason is not yet sufficiently enlightened to survey the entire series of predetermining causes, and such vision would be necessary for one to be able to foresee with certainty the happy or unhappy effects which follow human actions by the mechanism of nature (though we know enough to have hope that they will accord with our wishes)'.[19]

Essentially, Kant recognizes here the limitations of human interpretations of history. Hence, they are speculative, and do not allow us to extract moral principles from empirical knowledge – though they can establish the possibility of such moral principles. Once established, it is therefore reason and not nature (history) which establishes the rules of moral conduct and 'suffices for attaining the ultimate end'.[20] And the basic principle which reason establishes for moral conduct is the universality entailed in the categorical imperative.[21] Moral laws are by definition universal laws and moral conduct requires the observance of these laws for their own sake 'and without regard to hope of a similar response from others'.[22] Applied to the political sphere, Kant says that this 'should be understood as the obligation of those in power not to limit or to extend anyone's right through sympathy or disfavor'.[23]

---

[18] Immanuel Kant, 'Idea for a Universal History with a Cosmopolitan Purpose' in Hans Reiss (ed.), *Kant: Political Writings* (Cambridge: Cambridge University Press, 1991), pp. 41–53, and 'Perpetual Peace', pp. 11–15. Kant argues that the history of humankind – from barbarians to contemporaneous Europeans – can be interpreted as a gradual development of political organization towards the realization of individual freedom. In principle, this philosophy of history is very similar not only to Mill's, which I will set out below, but to those underlying Enlightenment thought in general. See Beate Jahn, 'IR and the State of Nature: The Cultural Origins of a Ruling Ideology' *Review of International Studies* 25 (1999), 411–434, and *The Cultural Construction of International Relations: the Invention of the State of Nature* (Basingstoke: Palgrave, 2000), pp. 118ff; as well as Ronald L. Meek, *Social Science and the Ignoble Savage* (Cambridge: Cambridge University Press, 1976); Uday Singh Mehta, *Liberalism and Empire. A Study in Nineteenth-Century British Liberal Thought* (Chicago: University of Chicago Press, 1999), pp. 88ff. Since Kant does not rely on this philosophy of history as an authoritative basis for his moral and political thought, its highly questionable contents do not have to concern us here.
[19] Kant, 'Perpetual Peace', p. 36.   [20] Ibid., p. 36.
[21] Ibid., p. 42.   [22] Ibid., pp. 41, 42, 43.   [23] Ibid., p. 44.

The requirement of universality essentially functions as a safeguard against the potential misinterpretation of history (nature), so that Kant does not resolve or transcend the dialectic between nature (history) and reason (morality).[24] While they are not mutually exclusive in theoretical terms, subjectively, for real existing men and women, 'this conflict will always remain. Indeed, it should remain, because it serves as a whetstone of virtue, whose true courage . . . consist[s] . . . in detecting and conquering the crafty and far more dangerously deceitful and treasonable principle of evil in ourselves'.[25] Moral laws, thus, always apply to ourselves rather than to others. It is this reflexivity which makes Kant a *critical* philosopher.[26]

Quite strikingly, the Democratic Peace thesis violates every single one of these principles of moral laws. Where Kant argues that we must observe moral laws for their own sake and apply them to ourselves, contemporary liberals disqualify non-liberals from choosing their own laws. Where Kant argues that we must observe these laws without regard to a similar response from others, in contemporary thought liberalism becomes a precondition for equal rights. Where Kant argues that rights must not be extended on the grounds of sympathy or limited on the grounds of disfavour, contemporary liberals extend rights on the grounds of sympathy to other liberal states and limit them on the grounds of disfavour for non-liberal states. In short, where Kant requires the universality of law, contemporary liberals justify particularist law.

The reason for these contradictions lies in a misunderstanding of the dialectic between nature (history) and reason (theory) in Kant. The Democratic Peace thesis resolves this dialectic in favour of history by empirically identifying contemporary liberal states as embodying the values of freedom and equality. It thus reifies a particular reading of history from which it derives its ideals rather than treating them as regulative. Hence, the ideal is embodied in a particular part of that history which in turn underlies the particularist nature of the laws it justifies. Moreover, a historically sensitive reading of Kant, as I will show presently, undermines the possibility of equating his republican constitutions with contemporary liberal states.

---

[24] Jens Bartelson, 'The Trial of Judgment: A Note on Kant and the Paradoxes of Internationalism' *International Studies Quarterly* 39 (1995), p. 276f.

[25] Kant, 'Perpetual Peace', p. 45.

[26] See Georg Cavallar, 'Kantian Perspectives on Democratic Peace: Alternatives to Doyle' *Review of International Studies* 27 (2001), p. 248; and John MacMillan, 'A Kantian Protest Against the Peculiar Discourse of Inter-Liberal State Peace' *Millennium* 24 (1995), p. 553.

Since Kant's republican constitution – or more generally liberal
ideals – are not unambiguously identifiable in history, they cannot provide the starting point for an attempt to solve the problem of war.
Hence the order of Kant's argument in 'Perpetual Peace': he starts with
an analysis of the wars of his time, proceeds to formulate preliminary
and definitive articles which would make these wars impossible, and
finally ensures their compatibility with the ideal in the two appendices.[27]
He identifies three historically specific elements contributing to wars –
located respectively on the domestic, the international and the transnational level. His solutions, the three Definitive Articles, are therefore
derived from, and substantively linked to, these concrete historical analyses.

Kant clearly characterizes the nature of wars in his time. Rulers are
'insatiable of war'; wars are pursued for the glory of the state, defined
as 'continual aggrandizement'; the state is seen as the property of
rulers which can be 'inherited, exchanged, purchased, or donated', even
'espoused'; and wars are financed by debt, crippling the development
of the domestic economy – in short, Kant refers to wars between absolutist states in Europe.[28] Absolutist states, as Kant rightly points out, are
seen as the property of the rulers, and wars between absolutist states are
generally fought for territorial gains which, in turn, benefit the rulers as
proprietors of the state, and certainly not the population.[29]

This very specific historical situation underlies Kant's central argument in the First Definitive Article: that the civil constitution of every
state should be republican. Democratic Peace approaches pick up this
ideal of the republican state and demonstrate that contemporary liberal
democratic states fulfil Kant's criteria of a republican constitution.[30] This
equation of contemporary liberal states with Kant's republics has been
challenged on empirical grounds. Critics have pointed out that in modern liberal states sections of the population do benefit from wars, that
not all sections of society vote, that liberal states rarely, if at all, hold
referenda on questions of war and peace and that liberal populations
can be shown to have been in favour of war.[31]

---

[27] Kant, 'Perpetual Peace', pp. 35–53.   [28] Ibid., pp. 3–6.
[29] See Benno Teschke's analysis of wars between absolutist states and the defining role of
all the characteristics of war mentioned by Kant in *The Myth of 1648. Class, Geopolitics and
the Making of Modern International Relations* (London: Verso, 2003), pp. 181ff.
[30] See Doyle, 'Kant', pp. 5f; Russett, 'The Fact of the Democratic Peace'; Owen, 'How
Liberalism Produces Democratic Peace'.
[31] See Ernst-Otto Czempiel, 'Kants Theorem und die zeitgenössische Theorie der Internationalen Beziehungen' in Matthias Lutz-Bachmann and James Bohman (eds.), *Frieden durch*

These empirical challenges are not just accidental. They reflect the systematic differences between absolutist and liberal capitalist states. For here the government is not the 'proprietor' of the state; instead private actors may indeed gain from wars, and they *are* represented in government; hence there is no need for referenda on war and peace, and accordingly liberal populations have often supported wars. Hence, the republican constitution is not a solution to war if the interests represented through it may benefit from war. The First Definitive Article is therefore not automatically relevant for the contemporary world. While it may plausibly be argued that there is an institutional 'match' between Kant's republics and contemporary liberal democratic states, this ahistorical institutional comparison misses the core of Kant's argument – peaceful policies will be represented through such institutions only if and when the citizens do not gain from war – and it obscures the presence of specifically liberal interests in war.

In the Second Definitive Article, Kant identifies the security dilemma at the international level as contributing to wars: 'Peoples, as states, like individuals, may be judged to injure one another merely by their coexistence in the state of nature' and he proposes the Federation of Free States as a solution.[32] Liberals understand this federation as an exclusive club of liberal states, or a separate liberal peace, poised against aggressive non-liberal states. This interpretation, again, has been challenged widely. Logically, such a reading contradicts the argument in the First Definitive Article. If citizens tend to avoid war because of its costs, they have to avoid all (costly) wars, not just those against other liberal states.[33]

Historically, Kant established guidelines for behaviour in a diverse international system – prior to worldwide liberalism and peace – and accorded non-liberal Prussia with full rights. He states clearly that the

---

Recht: Kants Friedensidee und das Problem einer neuen Weltordnung (Frankfurt: Suhrkamp, 1996), pp. 300–323; Cavallar, 'Kantian Perspectives', p. 237f; MacMillan, 'A Kantian Protest', p. 556; Scott Gates, Torbjørn L. Knutsen and Jonathan W. Moses, 'Democracy and Peace: A More Sceptical View' *Journal of Peace Research* 33 (1996), p. 2; Antonio Franceschet, 'Popular Sovereignty or Cosmopolitan Democracy? Liberalism, Kant and International Reform' *European Journal of International Relations* 6 (2000), pp. 284f; Kubik, 'Military Professionalism'; Tarak Barkawi, 'War Inside the Free World' in Barkawi and Laffey (eds.), *Democracy*, pp. 107–128; and Mark Rupert, 'Democracy, Peace: What's Not to Love?' in Barkawi and Laffey (eds.), *Democracy*, pp. 153–172.
[32] Kant, 'Perpetual Peace', p. 16.
[33] See Gates et al., 'Democracy and Peace', p. 4; Cavallar, 'Kantian Perspectives', pp. 233f; Layne, 'Kant or Cant'; Henry S. Farber and Joanne Gowa, 'Polities and Peace' in Brown et al. (eds.), *Democratic Peace*, pp. 239–262.

Federation should gradually encompass all states and aims only at 'the maintenance and security of the freedom of the state itself' (not its citizens).[34] While Kant clearly expected a 'powerful and enlightened' republic to assist in setting up this Federation of Free States, the latter is open to all sovereign states, not just to republican or liberal states, and it is designed as a collective security arrangement dealing with aggression rather than regime type.[35]

In this case, because of the prior equation of liberal states with peaceful foreign policies, the ahistorical reading misses the generality of the security dilemma. Ironically, the separate liberal peace does nothing else but to rearrange the parties to this dilemma – which is now played out between liberal and non-liberal states and may even provide peculiarly liberal grounds for aggression against non-liberal states, resulting in more rather than fewer wars.[36] Yet, the Second Definitive Article understood as a response to a general security dilemma is eminently relevant for the contemporary diverse states system.

In the Third Definitive Article Kant turns to transnational sources of war and injustice, that is, to the imperialism of his day. Liberal theorists use this article to underline the pacifying potential of transnational, particularly economic, interaction. And on this basis, they propagate interference in non-liberal states through private actors and by economic means.[37]

And yet, while Kant undoubtedly believed in the pacifying potential of transnational interaction, he clearly identifies the interests of the 'civilized and especially the commercial states' of his time (Britain and the Netherlands) as the source of imperialism.[38] This imperialism was based on the assumed *right* to trade, imposed on others; it constituted, according to Kant, 'an injustice carried to terrifying lengths'[39] and thus a transnational barrier to peace. Consequently, the Third Definitive Article demands that 'The Law of World Citizenship Shall Be *Limited* to Conditions of Universal Hospitality' which requires only that a refusal to

---

[34] Kant, 'Perpetual Peace', p. 18.
[35] See MacMillan, 'A Kantian Protest', pp. 557, 559; Cavallar, 'Kantian Perspectives' pp. 244f; Andrew Hurrell, 'Kant and the Kantian Paradigm in International Relations' *Review of International Studies* 16 (1990), p. 193.
[36] See Hurrell, 'Kantian Paradigm', p. 193; Raymond Cohen, 'Pacific Unions: A Reappraisal of the Theory that "Democracies Do Not Go to War with Each Other"' *Review of International Studies* 20 (1994), 207–223; MacMillan, 'A Kantian Protest', p. 551; Cavallar, 'Kantian Perspectives', p. 244; Franceschet, 'Popular Sovereignty', p. 287; Raymond Duvall and Jutta Weldes, 'The International Relations of Democracy, Liberalism, and War: Directions for Future Research' in Barkawi and Laffey (eds.), *Democracy*, pp. 195–208.
[37] See Doyle, 'Kant', p. 50.   [38] Kant, 'Perpetual Peace', pp. 21–23.   [39] Ibid., p. 21.

interact must not lead to the death of the applicant.[40] Hence, Kant does not establish a *right* to trade but rather *limits* this very right. Accordingly, China and Japan were not just entirely within their rights but also very wise when they refused the Europeans entry.[41] Trade and other forms of transnational interaction can be a means to a moral end only if they are entered into voluntarily by all parties.

The ahistorical reading of liberals picks up on the positive potential of transnational interaction and overlooks the historically specific analysis of imperialism. This results in an interpretation which is diametrically opposed to Kant's Article which identifies the right to trade as a contribution to injustice and wars. This blindness to the historical analysis of imperialism, moreover, obscures its continuing relevance in the contemporary world. For the perpetrators Kant mentions, Britain and the Netherlands, were the most advanced liberal capitalist states at the time – not the absolutist states of the First Definitive Article.

That is, private interests within liberal capitalist states continue to pursue the opening up of markets abroad, and they continue to enlist their governments' support, through multilateral and bilateral arrangements – conditional aid, International Monetary Fund (IMF) and World Trade Organization (WTO). While the latter agreements are formally 'voluntary', in the light of the desperate economic dependence of many Third World states, they are to all intents and purposes 'imposed'. Moreover, the beneficiaries of these agreements – sometimes intentionally so, often unintentionally – turn out to be the rich countries. The Trade Related Intellectual Property Rights (TRIPS) agreement, it has been argued, turned the WTO into a 'royalty collection agency' for the rich countries. The Structural Adjustment Policies (SAPs) connected to IMF loans have proven singularly disastrous for the poor countries but provide huge interest payments to the rich. In both cases, the 'voluntary' signatures of poor states do not signify consent to the details of the agreement, but need. Obviously, trade – with liberal or non-liberal states – is not a moral obligation, yet conditional aid, just as IMF and WTO policies, aims at changing the cultural, economic and political constitution of a target state under conditions which render its formal consent almost meaningless.

In short, all these policies use the economic power differentials in order to impose a particular order on weaker states. The liberal preference for economic means of changing the cultural, economic and

---

[40] Ibid., p. 20 (emphasis added).   [41] Ibid., pp. 22f.

political constitution of non-liberal states, thus falls squarely into the category of activities which Kant intended to rule out as a source of injustice and war. If historical imperialism had to rely more on military means, this is arguably due to the fact that it had to destroy the independent economic basis of non-European societies before it could establish the very dependency on which contemporary 'informal' means rely.

This discussion also suggests that the liberal insistence on a moral distinction between state and private actors lacks a social foundation in liberal capitalist states. Private interests – the East India Company, the Dutch East India Company – often lay at the heart of imperialism, and these were simultaneously represented in the government of liberal states. The same holds for contemporary liberal states so that it is unclear why transnational interaction should be understood to be more beneficial or less interventionist than interaction between states. In short, Kant's Third Definitive Article is eminently relevant for the contemporary world.

Finally, the Democratic Peace reading of Kant gives primacy to the domestic constitution. Yet, the three definitive articles cannot be ranked in order of presentation.[42] Instead, each of the three levels – domestic, international and transnational – provides sources of international conflict, and thus requires a solution in its own right which Kant provides in the three definitive articles. Moreover, progress towards perpetual peace is only possible if the sources of conflict on all three levels are tackled simultaneously. Wars between liberal and non-liberal states, or a war-prone international environment in general, indicate for Kant not just a lack of progress on the international level, but an environment in which a 'fully developed republican constitution is unattainable'.[43] Historically, Kant's insistence on the mutually constitutive nature of all three definitive articles is borne out by the frequent limitation of individual rights in the name of national security – recently, liberal rights are limited in the name of the 'war on terror', just as previously in the name of the Cold War.[44]

---

[42] See MacMillan, 'A Kantian Protest', p. 555; Cavallar, 'Kantian Perspectives', p. 247.

[43] See MacMillan, 'A Kantian Protest', pp. 558, 553; Cavallar, 'Kantian Perspectives', pp. 235, 238, 243; Franceschet, 'Popular Sovereignty', p. 286; Michael Mann, 'Democracy and Ethnic War' in Barkawi and Laffey (eds.), *Democracy*, pp. 67–86; Rupert, 'Democracy, Peace'.

[44] That liberal rights are frequently limited in the name of national security is widely acknowledged yet not consistently theorized in contemporary liberal thought. See Doyle, 'Kant', p. 41.

189

In summary, then, consistent with the dialectic between history and theory, each of Kant's articles is based upon an analysis of the domestic, international and transnational causes of historically specific wars. Yet, the ahistorical reading of liberals reifies and prioritizes the republican or liberal constitution – irrespective of its questionable historical application in the contemporary world. Furthermore, instead of addressing the general security dilemma through the Federation of Free States, liberals propagate a separate liberal peace, thus reconfiguring the security dilemma as one between liberal and non-liberal states. Finally, instead of recognizing the crucial role of private interests and transnational interactions in establishing injustice and, historically, imperialism and war, liberals propagate precisely these means. This ahistorical reading of Kant does not just 'inhibit criticism of liberal states themselves' by removing their particular contributions to international conflict from the analysis;[45] furthermore, it actively promotes the private interests and transnational activities lying at the heart of imperialism, supported by the possibility of state intervention based on the denial of rights of non-intervention to non-liberal states on moral grounds.

This interpretation does not just violate the spirit of 'Perpetual Peace' but also its letter. First, the justification of intervention is contradicted by the Fifth Preliminary Article which states unequivocally that 'no state shall by force interfere with the constitution or government of another state'.[46] Moreover, this principle of non-intervention applies 'regardless of circumstances'[47] and is, thus, explicitly considered a 'perfect duty' by Kant. This reading is further strengthened by the centrality of the categorical imperative establishing the necessary universality of law.[48] International right must be based on the principle of equality and cannot confer rights of intervention on liberal states while denying them to non-liberal states.[49]

Secondly, Kant clearly expected republican constitutions to arise out of an internal political process rather than to be established through outside interference. However, Kant was explicit that constitutional reform is an imperfect duty, allowing for subjective latitude according to the

---

[45] See MacMillan, 'A Kantian Protest', p. 551; Cavallar, 'Kantian Perspectives', p. 244; Franceschet, 'Popular Sovereignty', p. 287; Duvall and Weldes, 'International Relations of Democracy'.
[46] See Kant, 'Perpetual Peace', p. 7; and Hurrell, 'Kantian Paradigm', p. 200.
[47] Kant, 'Perpetual Peace', pp. 7, 8.
[48] See MacMillan, 'A Kantian Protest', p. 554; Cavallar, 'Kantian Perspectives', p. 244; and Hurrell, 'Kantian Paradigm', p. 199.
[49] Cavallar, 'Kantian Perspectives', p. 241.

circumstances, and thus subordinate to the perfect duty, which has to be executed at once, of a state to 'preserve its own existence' as well as to the perfect duty to refrain from intervention; hence, constitutional reform is neither more basic than the principle of non-intervention nor a precondition for international rights and obligations but, if anything, subordinate to them.[50]

Consequently, and thirdly, the use of force for the purpose of spreading liberalism would not only violate the principle of non-intervention but also the principle that republican constitutions must rest on consent. Moreover, a justification of force for the purpose of spreading liberalism, or republican constitutions, directly contradicts the perfect duty of a state to defend itself. Practically, such a reading would imply that liberal states have a right to use force against non-liberal states who, in turn, have a duty to defend themselves – amounting to a vicious circle of wars which would fit rather awkwardly into Kant's goal of perpetual peace.

In conclusion, the ahistorical reading of Kant overlooks the reduced historical relevance of the republican constitution in contemporary liberal capitalist states just as it overlooks the historical continuity and relevance of the general security dilemma and transnational sources of international injustice and war. Moreover, lacking attention to the 'non-disciplinary' thought of Kant leads to a misconception of the relationship between the domestic, international and transnational spheres. For Kant, these spheres are mutually constitutive of each other and of peace – or war – yet the contemporary reading accords primacy to the domestic sphere and relegates Kant's comments on the international and transnational sphere merely to tools for achieving domestic changes. Hence, the Democratic Peace thesis is essentially based on the one and only article in Kant's 'Perpetual Peace' – the First Definitive article requiring republican constitutions – which for reasons of historical change does not straightforwardly apply in the contemporary world. It thus stands in stark opposition to the letter and spirit of 'Perpetual Peace'.

John Stuart Mill and liberalism

The same ahistorical approach to classical authors which mistakenly traces the trajectory of the Democratic Peace thesis back to Kant is, I will

---

[50] See Cavallar, 'Kantian Perspectives', p. 246; and MacMillan, 'A Kantian Protest', p. 558.

argue now, also responsible for overlooking a much more fitting predecessor. John Stuart Mill's defence of imperialism, I will now suggest, provides a perfect match for contemporary liberal thought. Like Kant, Mill derived the liberal ideals of equality and freedom from a philosophy of history. But unlike Kant, Mill was an empiricist; he therefore allowed this history to provide the basis of his political and international theory.[51] A brief look at the contents of this philosophy of history should serve to clarify this point.[52]

Mill identified four stages of development in history. Of these, modern civilization is the highest and 'distinguishes a wealthy and powerful nation from savages or barbarians'.[53] It is characterized by commerce, manufacture and agriculture, cooperation and social intercourse, law, justice and the protection of people and property; and it exists in modern Europe, and especially in Great Britain.[54] Furthermore, the mode of government we find in Britain, representative government, is the 'ideal type of a perfect government' because it best allows for the development of individual liberty.[55]

Mill then proceeded to sketch three earlier stages of development in the history of humankind for each of which a different form of government is best suited for progressing to the next stage. There is, first, the stage of savagery, characterized by personal independence, by the absence of a developed social life, and a lack of discipline either for unexciting work or for submission to laws.[56] Savages must learn to obey, and this is achieved through slavery and despotism as the appropriate form of government.[57] This second stage of development, slavery, requires a government 'which possesses force, but seldom uses it' in order to raise the people 'from a government of will to one of law'.[58] Subsequently we find the third stage of civilizational development, barbarism, which is characterized, above all, by 'mental' shortcomings such as an inveterate spirit of locality, passivity, ignorance, rudeness, attachment to tradition

---

[51] John Stuart Mill, 'Coleridge' in Alan Ryan (ed.), *John Stuart Mill and Jeremy Bentham, Utilitarianism and Other Essays* (London: Penguin, 1987), p. 188.
[52] For a more detailed discussion of Mill's political and international theory, see Beate Jahn, 'Barbarian Thoughts: Imperialism in the Philosophy of John Stuart Mill' *Review of International Studies* 31 (2005), 599–618.
[53] John Stuart Mill, 'Civilization' in John M. Robson (ed.), *The Collected Works of John Stuart Mill* (Toronto: Toronto University Press, 1977), vol. XVIII, p. 119.
[54] Ibid., pp. 120f.
[55] Ibid., p. 122; and 'Considerations on Representative Government' in John Gray (ed.), *On Liberty and Other Essays* (Oxford: Oxford University Press, 1998), p. 256.
[56] Mill, 'Representative Government', pp. 232, 260, and 'Civilization', p. 120.
[57] Mill, 'Representative Government', pp. 232f.   [58] Ibid., pp. 233f.

and general 'positive defects of national character', making representative government impossible.[59]

Mill did not believe that progression from one stage to the next was an automatic process: stagnation and even regression are the order of the day for 'large portions of mankind'.[60] Historically, two different roads to civilizational development can be identified. The first is the exception, namely government through an indigenous leader of extraordinary genius; the second is the rule, namely government through a culturally superior power carrying the people 'rapidly through several stages of progress, and clearing away obstacles to improvement which might have lasted indefinitely if the subject population had been left unassisted to its native tendencies and chances'.[61]

Just like Democratic Peace theorists, Mill identified the highest stage of development empirically with European, and especially British, culture and political organization. This identification necessarily entails the separation of humanity into a civilized and an uncivilized part which provides the basis for two different principles governing international relations.

These 'true principles of international morality' are based on the distinction between culturally superior and inferior peoples.[62] 'To suppose that the same international customs, and the same rules of international morality, can obtain between one civilized nation and another, and between civilized nations and barbarians, is a grave error, and one which no statesman can fall into'.[63] Mill gives two main reasons for this distinction.

> 'In the first place, the rules of ordinary international morality imply reciprocity. But barbarians will not reciprocate. They cannot be depended on for observing any rules. . . . In the next place, nations which are still barbarous have not got beyond the period during which it is likely to be for their benefit that they should be conquered and held in subjection by foreigners'.[64]

Relations among civilized nations should be governed by the principle of equality. Mill supported the principle of free trade. He also suggested that international law and an International Tribunal are 'now one of

---

[59] Ibid., pp. 261–264, 212.   [60] Ibid., pp. 224, 241.   [61] Ibid., pp. 264, 231, 234f.
[62] John Stuart Mill, *Autobiography* (London: Penguin, 1998), p. 195.
[63] John Stuart Mill, 'A Few Words on Non-Intervention' in Robson (ed.), *Collected Works*, vol. XXI, p. 118.
[64] Ibid., p. 118.

the most prominent wants of civilized society'.[65] 'Among civilized peoples, members of an equal community of nations, like Christian Europe' aggressive war, conquest and annexation are out of the question; what needs to be decided in this relationship between civilized nations is the question of interference.[66] In general, Mill argued for a principle of non-intervention because 'a government which needs foreign support to enforce the obedience of its own citizens, is one which ought not to exist'.[67] Similarly, a people whose desire for, and capability of achieving, freedom against its own government is not strong enough, will not be able to retain the freedom given to it by foreign intervention.[68] The same principle applies to the white settler colonies.[69] While Mill preferred a continued international integration through institutions like the Commonwealth he clearly stated that the settler colonies are entitled to the full rights of sovereignty and non-intervention.[70]

In contrast, relations between civilized and barbarian peoples should take the form of a hierarchy. If the culturally inferior population is in the majority, as in India, 'the conquerors and the conquered cannot . . . live together under the same free institutions' because the absorption of a culturally superior people into an inferior civilizational stage would be an evil. The conquered have to be governed by despotism which 'is the ideal rule of a free people over a barbarous or semi-barbarous one'.[71]

And yet, even in Mill's time, military intervention and colonial rule were not the driving force of imperialism. Rather, as Mill clearly states, 'it has been the destiny of the East India Company to suggest the true theory of the government of a semi-barbarous dependency by a civilized country'.[72] That is, the private interests of the East India

[65] Mill, 'Representative Government', p. 441.
[66] Mill, 'Non-Intervention', p. 120.   [67] Ibid., p. 121.
[68] Ibid., p. 122. It is this problem of intervention between sovereign European states to which discussions of John Stuart Mill in International Relations are generally restricted. See Hedley Bull, *The Anarchical Society* (New York: Columbia University Press, 1977), pp. 251f; Charles Beitz, *Political Theory and International Relations* (Princeton NJ: Princeton University Press, 1979), especially Part II, Chs. 2 and 3; R. J. Vincent, *Nonintervention and International Order* (Princeton NJ: Princeton University Press, 1974), pp. 54–56; Michael Walzer, *Just and Unjust Wars* (New York: Basic Books, 1992), pp. 87–96; Robert H. Jackson, *Quasi-states: Sovereignty, International Relations and the Third World* (Cambridge: Cambridge University Press, 1990); Chris Brown, Terry Nardin and Nicholas Rengger (eds.), *International Relations in Political Thought* (Cambridge: Cambridge University Press, 2002). For a recent detailed discussion of the development of Mill's position on non-intervention between European states and its exceptions see Georgios Varouxakis, 'John Stuart Mill on Intervention and Non-Intervention' *Millennium* 26 (1997), 57–76.
[69] Mill, 'Representative Government', p. 449.   [70] Ibid., p. 451.   [71] Ibid., p. 454.
[72] Ibid., pp. 466, 396–398, 406f; and *Autobiography*, p. 182.

Company and their transnational interaction with India led, over time, to the establishment of colonial rule. Even in its nineteenth-century hey-day, imperialism was pursued 'by informal means where possible and formal means where necessary', as Gallagher and Robinson famously pointed out.[73] And the same dynamics are aptly described by Doyle for the contemporary world in which private property and free enter-prise abroad, when it meets with local resistance, calls for protection by the state.[74] Transnational interactions, especially of an economic nature, are of primary importance in both cases and only followed by military intervention or direct colonial rule when necessary.

It is clear, then, that John Stuart Mill did not just utter *A Few Words on Non-Intervention* pertaining to sovereign European states, as his com-mentators in International Relations suggest. Rather, he provided an overall theory of international relations. What governs the selective application of the right to sovereignty is the stage of civilizational devel-opment set out in his philosophy of history. The attempt, therefore, in International Relations to separate *A Few Words on Non-Intervention* from Mill's 'eurocentrism' which Brown, Nardin and Rengger relativize by pointing out that it only expressed the common prejudice of his time[75] overlooks that precisely this 'prejudice' lies at the heart of Mill's philos-ophy of history and provides the principle on which the whole of Mill's theory of International Relations rests.

Moreover, this selective reading also obscures that Mill's arguments for not extending rights of sovereignty and non-intervention to non-civilized peoples are perfectly mirrored in contemporary thought. Firstly, non-liberal states are defined by their refusal to comply with international law – they do not reciprocate – and, thus, have to be denied the right to sovereignty and non-intervention.[76] Secondly, intervention is an appropriate means to speed up the development towards liber-alism in the interests of the target population as well as of humanity at large because the former will benefit from equality and freedom guaranteed by liberal institutions while the latter will be safer once the non-liberal sources of aggression are removed. Thirdly, transna-tional interaction is the preferred means of international communica-tion and followed or accompanied by military means only if and when necessary.

---

[73] J. Gallagher and R. Robinson, 'The Imperialism of Free Trade' *Economic History Review* VI (1953), p. 3.
[74] Doyle, 'Kant', pp. 38, 40.   [75] Brown et al. (eds.), *International Relations*, p. 465.
[76] See Mill, 'Non-Intervention', p. 118; Doyle, 'Kant', p. 31f.

Despite these parallels, there are also some differences between Mill and contemporary liberals. Most obviously, Mill considered formal colonial rule the ideal government of barbarians, while this is certainly not the view of contemporary liberals.[77] However, both historical evidence and Kant's argument for the republican constitution demonstrate that the institutional form which a hierarchical international order takes is not decisive. In terms of justification, Mill and contemporary liberals deny equal rights to non-liberal or non-civilized states on exactly the same grounds: they are defined as aggressive and will benefit from the accelerated development of liberalism or civilization. The realization of such a hierarchical order, on the other hand, depends on the means available and here, as liberals readily point out, the contemporary interdependent world offers a greater and more efficient range of informal means than were available in Mill's time.

Yet, are Mill's 'civilizations' comparable to the contemporary liberal emphasis on 'regime type'? Yes, for Mill identified 'civilization' with representative government theoretically and practically. And while the culturalist version of the Democratic Peace thesis mirrors Mill's argument regarding the mutually constitutive nature of government and cultural development explicitly,[78] implicitly we find such a connection underlies most liberal thought.

In sum, then, Mill and contemporary liberal thought start from the empirical identification of liberal ideals in liberal states, leading to the distinction between liberal and non-liberal, or civilized and non-civilized, peoples. In both cases, liberal or civilized states are defined as peaceful, and non-liberal or uncivilized states are seen as the source of international conflict and aggression. This distinction requires the application of particularist rather than universal rights of sovereignty and non-intervention, justifying the 'implementation of a foreign

---

[77] Formal colonial rule is generally not advocated even in the recent discussions on American Empire. See Michael Cox, 'The Empire's Back in Town: or America's Imperial Temptation – Again' *Millennium* 32 (2003), 1–27; and Andrew J. Bacevich (ed.) *The Imperial Tense. Prospects and Problems of American Empire* (Chicago: Ivan R. Dee, 2003). These debates on American Empire, however, may well be seen as rooted in liberal thought. After all, the defence of unipolarity or primacy advocated by 'neoconservatives' does not constitute a radical alternative to the cooperative security approach of the 'liberal internationalists' and neither do the foreign policies based on them; rather, as Posen and Ross have shown, both remain 'strongly committed to liberal principles'. See Barry R. Posen and Andrew L. Ross, 'Competing Visions for US Grand Strategy' *International Security* 21 (1996/97), pp. 5, 34.

[78] See Bruce Russett, 'Why Democratic Peace?' in Brown et al. (eds.), *Democratic Peace*, pp. 82–115.

policy of intervention' which 'constitutes the fundamental nature of imperialism'.[79]

Hence, if contemporary liberal thought has a classical tradition, it leads back to John Stuart Mill rather than to Immanuel Kant, who may be regarded as 'the last of the Continental republicans' rather than the first liberal.[80] Mill, however, provides a perfect match for contemporary liberal thought – and this not despite, but because of, the fact that he justified imperialism.[81]

It is, hence, precisely the historical continuity between Mill's society and contemporary liberal states – in their constitutional set up as well as in their economic order – which provides the basis for the close 'match' between Mill's argument and that of the Democratic Peace thesis – despite the difference of a world of empires and of sovereign states in terms of their appearance. While this historically sensitive reading of Mill thus uncovers that the Democratic Peace thesis, albeit not intentionally, may contain elements of the justification of imperialism, there is more to be gained from Mill than this. I will argue in the next section that close attention to the relationship between the domestic and the international in Mill can help us test the claims on which the Democratic Peace thesis rests.

Mill's political theory

As we have seen above, the Democratic Peace thesis as well as Mill's international theory rest on the fundamental claim that liberal societies are superior to others – they support the development of individual liberty and they are relatively peaceful and law-abiding members of the international sphere. But unlike contemporary liberals, Mill provides an analysis of modern civilization in his political theory which can serve as a starting point for a critical assessment of this claim.

Mill's domestic political theory reveals a curious and alarming inversion of the claims he made in his philosophy of history and his international theory. The very civilization which represented the highest stage

---

[79] Eddy M. Souffrant, *Formal Transgression: John Stuart Mill's Philosophy of International Affairs* (Lanham: Rowman and Littlefield, 2000), p. 136.
[80] Nicholas Greenwood Onuf, *The Republican Legacy in International Thought* (Cambridge: Cambridge University Press, 1998), p. 250.
[81] Eileen Sullivan, 'Liberalism and Imperialism: J. S. Mill's Defense of the British Empire' *Journal of the History of Ideas* 44 (1983), p. 599. For a detailed discussion of the claim that contemporary Democratic Peace theory, and liberal thought more generally, implies the justification of imperialism, see Jahn, 'Kant, Mill'.

of the development of individual liberty in the latter is here depicted as a form of society 'which in its uncorrected influence ... has ... a tendency to destroy' the highest goods, namely individual liberty.[82] Modern civilization is characterized by a loss of 'individual energy and courage', pride and self-reliance, 'slavery' to artificial wants, 'the dull unexciting monotony' of life, absence of individuality, 'great inequalities in wealth and social rank'; the wants of 'the great mass of the people of civilized countries ... are scarcely better provided for than those of the savage, while they are bound by a thousand fetters in lieu of the freedom and excitement which are his compensations'.[83]

Mill insists that all the inventions of which civilization is so proud have not 'lightened the day's toil of any human being'.[84] Civilization, in his analysis, has neither initiated material progress *for the benefit of human beings*, nor achieved the development of individual liberty. Mill comes to the conclusion that in the highest form of modern civilization, Britain, 'society is itself the tyrant – society collectively over the separate individuals who compose it – its means of tyrannising are not restricted to the acts which it may do by the hands of its political functionaries'.[85]

While this analysis of modern civilization clearly removes the basis of Mill's claim that modern civilization uniquely and successfully realizes the ideals of individual freedom and equality, it also provides a fundamental challenge for contemporary liberal thought. For Mill demonstrates that constitutional liberalism does not as such guarantee individual freedom and equality – on the contrary, it jeopardizes them. Hence, unless it can be shown that the particularly liberal forms of 'unfreedom' which Mill identifies as integral tendencies of modern civilization have been overcome in contemporary liberal states, there is no ground for according these states more rights than others.

Yet, Mill certainly believed that modern civilization was superior to other stages of development and that higher goods 'may yet coexist with civilization'.[86] And this hope motivated Mill to work out remedies for these 'vices and miseries of civilization'.[87] Since Mill's remedies have a

---

[82] Mill, 'Civilization', p. 135.   [83] Mill, 'Coleridge', p. 182.

[84] John Stuart Mill, *Principles of Political Economy* (Oxford: Oxford University Press, 1998), p. 129.

[85] See John Stuart Mill, *On Liberty* (New York: W. W. Norton, 1975), p. 6, and 'Coleridge', p. 182.

[86] Mill, 'Civilization', p. 135.

[87] Ibid., p. 119. Mill develops the theoretical argument for the integral tendencies of civilization to suppress individuality mainly in 'Civilization' while *On Liberty* is devoted to propagating the countermeasures society should adopt.

parallel in the means which Democratic Peace theorists employ for the spread of liberalism internationally, their discussion will serve to test the claim that they can overcome the shortcomings of modern civilization or spread liberalism.

In the domestic sphere, Mill argues for the protection of the private sphere from the pressures of public opinion; the freedom of thought and discussion; the development of individual genius and mental superiority; the promotion of free trade; support for different forms of education, including elite education; and weighted suffrage.[88] In addition, in order to diversify and enrich the narrow and limited tendencies of modern civilization, he prescribes the study of the 'opinions of mankind in all ages and nations', the study of the noble manifestations of the cultures of 'Athens, Sparta, Rome; nay, even barbarians, as the Germans, or still more unmitigated savages, the wild Indians, and again the Chinese, the Egyptians, the Arabs'.[89] Furthermore, in order to counteract the unlimited increase of wealth and population resulting in the destruction of the earth's 'pleasantness' for the mere purpose of supporting a larger 'but not a better or happier population', he recommends the abandonment of economic growth in favour of the stationary state.[90]

Thus, Mill's remedy for the 'vices and miseries of civilization' is the introduction of as much plurality as possible in society, which can only be ensured if no community 'has a right to force another to be civilised'.[91] Not even in the name of the necessary defence against barbarism can this right be established since it would mean the degeneration of civilization to such an extent that it were better to be 'destroyed and regenerated (like the Western Empire) by energetic barbarians'.[92]

Mill supports policies such as weighted suffrage and elite education which themselves violate the liberal ideals of freedom and equality. This contradiction has historically and theoretically been part and parcel of liberal thought and practice. Whereas all human beings were supposed to be 'born equal, free, and rational' this birthright, from Locke onwards, has never been enough; liberal 'political inclusion is contingent upon a *qualified* capacity to reason'.[93]

[88] See Mill, *On Liberty*, pp. 14, 17ff, 53ff, 88, 98; and 'Representative Government', pp. 335–338.
[89] John Stuart Mill, 'Bentham' in Ryan (ed.) *Utilitarianism*, p. 148, and 'Coleridge', p. 200.
[90] Mill, *Political Economy*, pp. 126, 129.   [91] Mill, *On Liberty*, p. 86.   [92] Ibid., p. 86.
[93] Mehta, *Liberalism*, pp. 49, 60 (emphasis added).

Hence, the use of illiberal methods must be seen as a central feature of liberal political reason distinguishing between those who can be governed through the promotion of liberty and those who cannot. Traditionally, these distinctions have most commonly been made along gendered and developmental lines, excluding women, children, the mentally handicapped, slaves, workers etc. in the domestic sphere, and non-European cultures in the international, from rights of freedom and equality.[94] In the domestic sphere, Mill excluded workers from suffrage on the grounds that their lack of education amounted to a lack of the requisite reason, while internationally non-European cultures were excluded on the same grounds.[95]

These remedies which undermine the liberal ideals themselves have a parallel in contemporary liberal thought. For, as we have seen, it is not actual consent of real existing people which establishes legitimacy. While preferring informal methods for the aim of changing the constitution of non-liberal states, Democratic Peace theorists do not rule out the use of military force in principle and they propagate unequal rights of sovereignty and non-intervention. Thus, in case of resistance by the target population – or parts thereof – to the change of their cultural, economic and political constitution, we have a perfect parallel to Mill's justification of imperialism in which despotic government – here military means – is necessary to prepare the population for the next stage of civilization.[96] And this implies that the rationality with which all human beings are born does not constitute sufficient grounds for equal rights of freedom. Spreading liberal values by illiberal means betrays these values; the means do not serve the ends.

Finally, we can test the logical consistency of Mill's theory by paying attention to the relationship between the domestic and the international in his thought. In the domestic sphere, Mill promotes the stationary state while fighting it in the name of progress in the international; in the domestic sphere, he denies the right to civilize others while supporting the civilizing mission as a moral duty in the international; in the domestic sphere he promotes cultural plurality while demanding assimilation in the international. Confronted with a lack of individuality in modern

[94] Barry Hindess, 'Liberalism – What's in a Name?' in Wendy Larner and William Walters (eds.), *Global Governmentality* (London: Routledge, 2004), pp. 23–39.
[95] Mill, 'Representative Government', pp. 335–338. See Mehta, *Liberalism*, for a discussion of the role of education in raising these groups to the required level of rationality.
[96] Applied to other cases of exclusion from equal rights, the logic of this argument implies that women or, indeed, non-European peoples have only developed the requisite reason for the rights they now enjoy through the forceful denial of these rights in the past.

civilization, Mill imports the characteristics of the international sphere – cultural diversity, coexistence and stationary conditions as a solution; confronted with those same characteristics in the international sphere he exports the characteristics of the domestic – conformism/assimilation, hierarchy, progress.

These contradictions might not present a major problem if the domestic and international spheres can be neatly separated. This, however, is not the case. Mill himself defines civilization as a negation of barbarism, and vice versa. And he imports the cultural plurality of the international sphere in order to rescue the domestic from the pitfalls of cultural assimilation and stagnation. This remedy, however, will be lost in the case of a successful civilizing mission in the international sphere. And, hence, the primacy of the domestic becomes untenable, for the international environment constitutes an integral part of the conditions of domestic development and vice versa. And this conclusion holds equally for Democratic Peace theory, which prioritizes the domestic constitution and expects peace to follow – without reflecting on the detrimental effects of conflictual international relations on the development of domestic liberalism.

In sum, a historically sensitive reading of Mill not only reveals the parallels with contemporary liberal thought; it also undermines every single one of the claims we find in the Democratic Peace thesis. In his political theory, Mill demonstrates that modern civilization and representative government do not as such support the development of individual liberty and equality. Further, Mill shows that transnational interaction undertaken by the East India Company, for instance, has historically been a crucial element of the constitution of imperialism rather than a basis for international justice, cooperation and peace. Further, his work demonstrates that illiberal means – legal inequality – contradict the fundamental principles on which liberal ideals rest in the first place. And, finally, the fundamental contradictions between his international and his domestic political theory in the light of the mutually constitutive nature of these two spheres suggest that neither is tenable without a radical revision of the other, or both.

Conclusion

Democratic Peace authors are motivated to read classical authors for exactly the right reasons – namely in order to illuminate contemporary problems. And yet, they squander the critical potential of the classics for an analysis of the contemporary world by disregarding the very differences between the classics and our world from which this potential arises. And these differences lie in historical distance and non-disciplinary thought. By disregarding the nature of the societies represented through republican constitutions as well as the mutually constitutive nature of domestic, international and transnational sources of peace and war, Democratic Peace theorists use Kant solely in support of contemporary liberal ideologies – and thus fall into the trap identified by Rengger: 'if we focus solely (or even largely) on the problems of the moment we are likely to become prisoners of the assumptions of the moment, some of which may well have created the problems in the first place'.[97] And the assumptions contributing to the problems of the moment are the specifically liberal reasons to go to war: the aim of changing the constitution of non-liberal states because they are perceived as sources of conflict; the attempt to impose transnational economic interaction – for economic and political reasons – without the consent of non-liberal states; the exclusion of non-liberal states from equal access to rights and institutions. In this way, the ahistorical reading of classical authors appears to produce 'timeless truths' which amplify the *Zeitgeist* rather than analyze it.[98]

This ahistorical and disciplinary approach to classical authors is also responsible for the neglect of John Stuart Mill. A historically sensitive reading of Mill would have immensely benefited Democratic Peace theory for the reasons pointed out by Stanley Hoffmann almost fifty years ago: 'philosophers of history have a disarming way of making explicit and even central, assumptions about man, society, and history which are often repressed but nevertheless operating in all social scientists' schemes'.[99] Attention to the historical comparability of Mill's society with contemporary liberal ones as well as to the relationship between the domestic and international spheres in his work could have provided what Max Weber identified as the ultimate task of the social sciences: namely to assist the scientist 'in becoming aware of the ultimate standards of value which he does not make explicit to himself or, which he

---

[97] Nicholas Rengger, 'Political Theory and International Relations: Promised Land or Exit from Eden?' *International Affairs* 76 (2000), p. 770.
[98] Doyle, *War and Peace*, p. 9.
[99] Stanley Hoffmann, 'International Relations: The Long Road to Theory' *World Politics* 11 (1959), p. 355.

must presuppose in order to be logical'.[100] That is, a historically and contextually sensitive reading of Mill would have uncovered the justification of imperialism as an ultimate standard of value in the Democratic Peace thesis – one that it does not make explicit to itself – as well as fundamental contradictions between domestic and international political means and goals which defy logic and explain the failures of liberal foreign policies then and now.

Hence, it is the ahistorical reading of Kant which allows his contemporary use – within and outside the academic discipline of International Relations – for the justification of interventionist policies in direct contradiction to his principled objection to intervention as a means for furthering peace. And it is the ahistorical reading of Mill which establishes his reputation as a non-interventionist irrespective of his principled support of intervention in pursuit of a peaceful development of international affairs. For this game of smoke and mirror the discipline of International Relations pays a high price. Behind the smoke are hidden exactly those aspects of classical texts which could provide a critical assessment of contemporary assumptions while the mirrors only provide support for the latter.

[100] Max Weber, '"Objectivity" in Social Science and Social Policy' in Edward A. Shils and Henry A. Finch (eds.), *The Methodology of the Social Sciences* (New York: Free Press, 1949), pp. 81, 54.

Part III
Lineages

9 The 'other' in classical political theory: re-contextualizing the cosmopolitan/communitarian debate

Robert Shilliam

Introduction[1]

The current debate over the ethics of international relations focuses upon the following issue: can and should political obligation be extended to citizens in other communities?[2] Within this debate, a 'cosmopolitan' position, referring back to Immanuel Kant's notion of the pre-social universal self, holds that a global principle of justice, backed up by an institutionalized system of democratic global governance, is both necessary and desirable in an increasingly interdependent world. Against this, a 'communitarian position', often in some way referring back to Georg Hegel's notion of the socially-constituted self, points out that not only is there no such institutional capacity in world politics to organize global justice, but furthermore, there can be no *a priori* principle of justice because political rights and duties are always embedded in a community-dependent value system.[3] Essentially, then, two classical

[1] This chapter benefited from instructive feedback at this book's panel session at the ISA conference 2005. I must especially thank Beate Jahn and Naeem Inayatullah for their constructive and powerful criticisms. These have compelled me to develop the argument to a position that I would not have reached on my own.
[2] Famously, M. Walzer, *Just and Unjust Wars: A Moral Argument with Historical Illustrations* (Penguin: Harmondsworth, 1980); and Charles R. Beitz, *Political Theory and International Relations* (Princeton NJ. Princeton University Press, 1979). For overviews of the debate see M. Cochran, 'Cosmopolitanism and Communitarianism in a Post-Cold War World', in J. MacMillan and A. Linklater (eds.), *Boundaries in Question – New Directions in International Relations* (London: Pinter Publishers, 1995), pp. 40–53; C. Brown, 'Review Article: Theories of International Justice', *British Journal of Politics* 27 (1997), 273–297; and Nicholas Rengger, 'Political Theory and International Relations: Promised Land or Exit from Eden?' *International Affairs* 76 (2000), 755–770.
[3] For the Cosmopolitan position see, for example, Daniele Archibugi, 'Models of International Organization in Perpetual Peace Projects', *Review of International Studies* 18 (1992), 295–317; David Held, *Democracy and the Global Order: From the Modern State to Cosmopolitan Governance* (Cambridge: Polity Press, 1995); and Andrew Linklater, *The Transformation*

authors, Kant and Hegel, have consistently been mobilized as authorities through which to frame the cosmopolitan/communitarian debate in the following terms: *either* there ought to be a universal justice system, *or* we should accept what is, namely, an array of self-referential value systems.

Some have questioned the framing of the debate around an ethical dichotomy of *either* pursuing what 'ought to be' *or* accepting what 'is'.[4] And such concerns have increasingly become expressed (although by no means exclusively) through a broadly poststructuralist understanding of the relationship between identity and difference. Here, the cosmopolitan/communitarian dichotomy is understood in terms of the philosophical discourse of the 'modern' or 'Western' subject. Granted an authoritative sovereign voice through modern/Western philosophy this subject constantly works to re-produce and occupy a secure, pre-social, centre of being. To retain the authority gained from an objective sense of self, this individualized subject must constantly be reproduced by means of a discourse that separates morality from politics, security from danger, sovereignty from anarchy, the domestic from the international, identity from difference and, ultimately, the 'self' from the 'other'. In short, for the poststructuralist position, the disciplining mechanism of the sovereign nature of modern political identity is what frames the ethical debate in international relations in terms of *either* universal right *or* particular value system.[5]

---

of Political Community: Ethical Foundations of the Post-Westphalian Era (Cambridge: Polity Press, 1998). The Communitarian position is usually taken with some qualification. See Stanley Hoffmann, *Duties Beyond Borders: On the Limits and Possibilities of Ethical International Politics* (Syracuse: Syracuse University Press, 1981); D. Miller, 'Bounded Citizenship' in K. Hutchings and R. Dannreuther, *Cosmopolitan Citizenship* (London: Macmillan, 1999), pp. 60–80; and C. Brown, 'Universal Human Rights: a Critique' in T. Dunne and N. J. Wheeler (eds.), *Human Rights in Global Politics* (Cambridge: Cambridge University Press, 1999), pp. 103–127. For examples of the mobilization of Kant and Hegel as classical authorities in the debate see Chris Brown, *International Relations Theory: New Normative Approaches* (London: Harvester Wheatsheaf, 1992); Linklater, *Transformation of Political Community*, pp. 48–55; and D. Heater, *World Citizenship: Cosmopolitan Thinking and its Opponents* (London: Continuum, 2002), especially pp. 53–54.
[4] For example, Andrew Hurrell, 'Kant and the Kantian Paradigm in International Relations', *Review of International Studies* 16 (1990), 183–205; and especially K. Hutchings, 'The Possibility of Judgment: Moralizing and Theorizing in International Relations', *Review of International Studies* 18 (1992), 51–62.
[5] See in general D. Campbell, *Writing Security: United States Foreign Policy and the Politics of Identity* (Manchester: Manchester University Press, 1992); R. B. J. Walker, *Inside/Outside: International Relations as Political Theory* (Cambridge: Cambridge University Press, 1993); Jens Bartelson, *A Genealogy of Sovereignty* (Cambridge: Cambridge University Press, 1995). On the cosmopolitan/communitarian debate specifically see E. Frazer and N. Lacey, *The*

But perhaps the most powerful criticism of those who internalize this sovereign self in their approach to the ethics of international relations emanates from a post-colonial inspired body of literature.[6] In very general terms, this literature places the origins of the modern dichotomy of self/other as an effect, in the first instance, of the need to legitimize the European conquest of the Americas. Colonization required the distancing of the Amerindian, as a social being, from the European in both time and space. The construction of the European 'self' was achieved by situating the Amerindian 'other' within a pre-social 'state of nature'. The 'other', having being cast out of the ethical universe populated by the European 'self', was then reconciled through narratives that took the European 'self' to be the *Telos* of human history, and thus the future civilized image of the backward 'other'. By cleaving a co-constitutive relationship into 'self' and 'other', and then subsuming the identity of the 'other' under that of the 'self', the very possibility of developing an ethics of international, or inter-cultural, difference is denied.

Approaching the problem of difference from this perspective one would have to say that the cosmopolitan/communitarian debate utilizes an essentially *colonial* separation of 'self' and 'other', and as such possesses a woefully inadequate framework through which to interrogate the ethics of international relations. And in this chapter I take such a position with all due seriousness. Nevertheless, I contend that the poststructural and especially postcolonial inspired critique of the modern/Western sovereign self has difficulty in making sense of the context and content of Kant and Hegel's writings on international relations. In short, I charge that neither the above mainstream nor critical literatures can adequately contextualize the founding 'debate' between Kant and Hegel that is used, today, as an authority with which to frame the dominant investigation of ethics in the International Relations discipline (IR).

Politics of Community – a Feminist Critique of the Liberal-Communitarian Debate (London: Harvester Wheatsheaf, 1993); K. Hutchings, *Kant, Critique and Politics* (London: Routledge, 1995); and R. B. J. Walker, 'Citizenship After the Modern Subject' in Hutchings and Dannreuther, *Cosmopolitan Citizenship*, pp. 171–200.

[6] See especially W. E. Connolly, *Identity/Difference – Democratic Negotiations of Political Paradox* (London: Cornell University Press, 1992); Beate Jahn, *The Cultural Construction of International Relations: the Invention of the State of Nature* (Basingstoke: Palgrave, 2000); and Naeem Inayatullah and David L. Blaney, *International Relations and the Problem of Difference* (London: Routledge, 2004).

In what follows I sympathetically mobilize the language of the postcolonial critique to inform a re-contextualization of this classical 'debate', but I do so with the purpose of opening up a neglected aspect (and legacy of) the development of 'European' or 'Western' thought on the constitution and rights of the modern sovereign self. I argue that a) the 'other' to which both Kant and Hegel addressed their writings on international relations was a novel political subject produced *within* Europe; and b) the process of 'othering' in Kant and Hegel cannot be understood as a disciplining effect of modern sovereign identity but as a *peripheral* and defensive response *to* this identity from *within* Europe. In this context, the 'other' perceived by both Kant and Hegel is, paradoxically, the sovereign political subject encoded in the revolutionary French Constitution. And the process of 'othering' is a disciplining aspect of what might be called a 'consciousness of backwardness'.

The purpose of the chapter is to support, against the mainstream cosmopolitan/communitarian debate, the critical project of orienting ethical debates in international relations towards the problem of difference, but, at the same time, to push the problematization of 'difference' further. I seek to make the case that 'othering' cannot be understood solely as a disciplining effect of the discourse of the modern sovereign subject, whether internalized by either the powerful or the subordinated. Specifically, I aim to dissolve the security of the discursive European/Western/modern self in order to show that the commonly perceived classical tradition of 'liberal' thought is *itself* constructed just as much, if not more, by critical intellectual responses from non-liberal societies. The ultimate point is to show that ethics from the standpoint of the 'periphery' or the 'backward' constitute the subject matter of our classical legacy in normative IR theory far more intimately than is usually supposed.

Before continuing, it might be useful to explain what I mean by a 'consciousness of backwardness'. As a general rule of contextualizing classical political thought, I take the intellectual stratum to hold a liminal position within the ruling strata. The intellectual stratum enjoys an authoritative position by virtue of mentally policing the coherence of political authority. Yet this is no slavish task, for at the same time as they pursue this general purpose, the intellectual stratum also pursues the rights of their own freedom to think against noble, monarchical and/or hierocratic influences and interests. In this respect, the prescriptions that some intellectuals promote with regard to ensuring the coherence of the body politic as a whole may well threaten specific elements within the ruling strata.

An intellectual becomes aware of a specific sense of comparative backwardness through geo-political impingement whether by direct military means, and/or by indirect means. These indirect means might, for example, pertain to the content of a foreign policy that disturbs the legitimacy of the existing domestic form of political authority, especially with regard to the promotion of an alternative set of political rights and duties (for example, the impact of the promotion of free trade on a corporate, hierarchically organized system of social reproduction). Consciousness of comparative backwardness compels the intellectual to take seriously the problematic of international 'difference' to the extent that this difference impacts upon and potentially or actually subverts existing social structures of political authority. This impact is felt by the intellectual stratum not only with regard to the general tasks of reproducing a coherent body politic, but also with regard to the tasks of pursuing the specific interests of knowledge production against other interests in the ruling strata. The point is that a consciousness of backwardness implicates itself in intellectual thought not only in directly political prescriptions, but also by pressing the need for a reordering or reassessment of philosophical and ethical arguments over the particular and universal attributes of the human condition.

While there is no room here to engage in the substantive relationship between Revolutionary France and Kant and Hegel's Prussia-Germany (let alone the rest of the world), it is necessary to at least point out briefly why the Revolution was perceived by many European contemporaries as an alien, indecipherable eruption of both Reason and Terror into the 'civilized' world.[7] Essentially, a political constitution had been enacted that almost overnight (legally) swept away the corporate and personalized rights and duties of absolutist France, and re-encoded the political subject in terms of 'natural rights': a pre-social free and equal individual. Not even the influential American Declaration had dared to proclaim such a radical break with tradition. The Declaration, after all, looked back to English Common Law, haphazardly evolved over centuries through the system of 'precedent', to prove that

---

[7] Most famously, Edmund Burke in *Selected Writings: Four Letters on the Proposals for Peace with the Regicide Directory of France* (Oxford: Clarendon Press, 1875). See additionally, M. P. Thompson, 'Ideas of Europe During the French Revolution and Napoleonic Wars' *Journal of the History of Ideas* 55 (1994), 37–58.

individual freedom was 'self evident'. However, this self-evidential nature of Anglo-American tradition did not exist in the context of the French Revolutionaries: rather, *natural* 'man' had to be made manifest through a *political* artifice.[8] In short, this direct encoding of the political subject as a pre-social individual was a radical departure from the practices of both *ancien régime* Europe and even capitalist Britain.

Taking Kant and Hegel in turn I will now proceed by summarizing the existing IR debate on their ethical stance towards international relations, and then show how this stance was foundationally structured by a consciousness of backwardness towards revolutionary France.

Kant's universal self

Not withstanding Charles Beitz's influential treatment of Rawls' principles of distributive justice[9], the touchstone for the cosmopolitan position in IR is overwhelmingly Kant's *Perpetual Peace,* and specifically Michael Doyle's influential interpretation.[10] The debate over Kant's legacy has focused on the empirical veracity of Doyle's reading of Kant's tract that posits an inevitable universalization of the peaceful liberal state in world affairs. However a growing body of critics charge Doyle et al. with separating Kant's historical-empirical claims from the philosophical schema in which they gain a different meaning. For example, by ignoring Kant's categorical imperative to do unto others as you would do unto yourself, advocates of the Democratic Peace Thesis privilege liberal states over non-liberal states and implicitly justify imperialist policies that would be anathema to Kant's moral sensibilities.[11] In this respect, the debate over *Perpetual Peace* has focused upon how the tripartite ethical relationship Kant constructed between the individual, the state (system) and humanity should be interpreted.

Here I re-contextualize Kant in the following way. Prior to the Revolution, Kant's political philosophy derived from a universal history that

---

[8] On these points see J. Habermas, *Theory and Practice* (London: Heinemann, 1974), pp. 84–102; and F. Furet, *The French Revolution, 1770–1814* (Oxford: Blackwell, 1996), pp. 73–76.

[9] Beitz, *Political Theory and International Relations.*

[10] Michael Doyle, 'Kant, Liberal Legacies, and Foreign Affairs' *Philosophy and Public Affairs* 12 (1983), 205–235, 323–353.

[11] For example, M. Franke, 'Immanuel Kant and the (Im)possibility of International Relations Theory' *Alternatives* 20 (1995), 279–322; John MacMillan, 'A Kantian Protest Against the Peculiar Discourse of Inter-Liberal State Peace' *Millennium* 24 (1995), 549–562; Georg Cavallar, 'Kantian Perspectives on Democratic Peace: Alternatives to Doyle' *Review of International Studies* 27 (2001), 229–248; and Beate Jahn, 'Kant, Mill, and Illiberal Legacies in International Affairs' *International Organization* 59 (2005), 177–207.

sought to regulate behaviour in the experiential world by the tenets of the sovereign individual's Reason so that a reform of absolutist power relations could be pursued. But as a reformist political philosophy, Kant held to the impossibility of manifesting the sovereign individual of Reason within an absolutist, personalized and corporatized experiential realm. Thus, between Reason and experience there existed an unbridgeable divide. The Revolution radically threatened this political philosophy by effectively manifesting the rights of the sovereign individual in a political constitution. With his project of reform now painted in a comparatively backward light, Kant consistently shifted his tripartite ethical relationship between individual, state(s) and humanity in order to subsume the political 'other' of the French Revolution under the philosophical 'self' of the German Enlightenment. Kant's discussion on the ethics of the liberal subject, therefore, was a discussion disciplined by a consciousness of backwardness.

Kant's political philosophy before the French Revolution

At its core, the German Enlightenment – *Aufklärung* - was a philosophical and usually practical project aimed at avoiding the growth of centralized despotism while promoting inter-dependency – an harmonious relative autonomy of various corporate bodies within the Reich.[12] Domestically, the immediate task of *Aufklärung*, by the later half of the eighteenth century, was to secure for the intellectual stratum a secure corporate autonomy from which to promote Reason as a counterweight to the potentially despotic interests of the noble court.[13] Internationally, the enlightenment philosophers (the *Aufklärer*) sought to built an alternative philosophy to those perceived fraternizers of Bourbon despotism, the French *philosophes*.[14] In this respect the *Aufklärer* increasingly turned towards Britain for philosophical inspiration; after all, Britain had helped Prussia in the recent Seven Years War (1756–63) against the French. The *Aufklärer* eagerly accepted Montesquieu's claim that the origins of the Anglo spirit were to be found in the Forests of

---

[12] On this link see P. H. Reill, *The German Enlightenment and the Rise of Historicism* (Los Angeles: University of California Press, 1975), p. 4.

[13] N. Elias, *The Civilizing Process Vol. 1: The History of Manners* (Oxford: Blackwell, 1994), p. 20.

[14] C. E. McClelland, *The German Historians and England: a Study in Nineteenth Century Views* (Cambridge: Cambridge University Press, 1971), pp. 13, 21.

Germany, as well as his assessment of Britain as a reformist monarchical state.[15]

Therefore, British philosophers, especially David Hume, were received enthusiastically by the *Aufklärer,* including Kant, as fellow intellectuals in the battle for Enlightenment. Foundational, in this respect, was Kant's acceptance of Hume's sceptical claim to a discontinuity between reason and experience. Although I cannot go into detail here, it is important to at least note that Hume's scepticism was part of an English philosophical tradition developed to interrogate the rights of the socially unencumbered individual found in 'common law' and made necessary by enclosure and the rise to supremacy of private property. Hume posited an individualized pre-social subject, universal in time and space, that could count on no guidance to his actions from the world at large save the utilitarian principles of his own internal sense perception: the embrace of pleasure and avoidance of pain.[16] Kant agreed with Hume that it was impossible to 'know' the phenomenal world – the objects of experience in and of themselves. But he further claimed that it was eminently possible to produce secure knowledge if one accepted the claim that experience was made sensible through universally held mental categories. In short, Kant agreed that the reasoning of Hume's pre-social, sovereign individual was a universal attribute of humanity, and autonomous from particular experience – a 'Pure' Reason.

A few years before Kant's whole-hearted turn to Hume he had courted Rousseau; and Rousseau had taught him that Reason was not simply a metaphysical riddle, but a *moral* guide with which humanity should actively shape its world.[17] In this sense, Rousseau confirmed to Kant his duty to use the universality and autonomy of Pure Reason to take an active and reformist stance towards despotism in the world.[18] The

---

[15] See N. Vazsonyi, 'Montesquieu, Friedrich Carl von Moser, and the "National Spirit Debate" in Germany' *German Studies Review* 22 (1999), 225–246; and Reill, *German Enlightenment,* p. 4.

[16] D. Hume, *Treatise of Human Nature* (Oxford: Clarendon Press, 1978). See also C. J. Berry, 'Hume on Rationality in History and Social Life', *History and Theory* 21 (1982), 238–241.

[17] Hans S. Reiss, 'Introduction' in Hans S. Reiss (ed.), *Kant: Political Writings* (Cambridge: Cambridge University Press, 1991), p. 4; and F. C. Beiser, 'Kant's Intellectual Development: 1746–1781' in P. Guyer (ed.), *The Cambridge Companion to Kant* (Cambridge: Cambridge University Press, 1998), pp. 43–44. See also, Immanuel Kant, 'Conjectures on the Beginning of Human History' in *Kant: Political Writings,* p. 227.

[18] On Kant and Rousseau see S. Shell, 'Rousseau, Kant, and the Beginning of History', in C. Orwin and N. Tarcov (eds.), *The Legacy of Rousseau* (Chicago: University of Chicago Press, 1997), pp. 45–64.

overarching guide to action, in this respect, was Kant's categorical imperative, a 'Practical' Reason: 'act that the maxim of your will could always hold at the same time as a principle establishing universal law'[19]. So even if Pure Reason could not be directly mapped onto the world of experience inhabited by humanity, human agency should aim to work *as if* this was possible.[20]

To this effect, Kant's 'universal history' acted as the virtual bridge between reason and experience, as a regulative narrative. Specifically, to conjecture on human development was to prescribe the course of actions that would allow humanity to approximate Pure Reason in the experiential realm.[21] The means of this enlightened development, Kant claimed, was the 'unsocial sociability' of men: it was only through social interaction that man's talents could be cultivated towards their ends, even if such activity was, pathologically, self-serving. Through this sociability humanity would condense into a set of civic states, wherein a balance between political mastery and autonomy would be achieved. Furthermore, this balance would lead the way towards a peaceful federation solving the most generally disruptive problem of war. In fact, prior to the French Revolution, Kant believed that the problem of establishing a civic constitution should be subordinated to that of building law-governed relations with other political communities.[22]

In a sense, of course, Kant's utilization of the sovereign self of Reason was dangerously radical in his German context. After all, breaking with the Natural Law of Grotius, Pufendorf and Wolff, Kant posited Pure Reason as the grounds for action rather than providence or nature.[23] But practically, Kant promoted such sovereign individuality only with regard to the distinct corporate body of the intellectual stratum. For example, he famously asserted that one should have freedom to think in a 'public' capacity as a learned man addressing a reading public, but not when acting in a 'private' capacity as a direct functionary of the

---

[19] I. Kant, *Critique of Practical Reason* (Indianapolis: Bobbs-Merrill, 1956), p. 30.

[20] See famously, the 'Appendix to Transcendental Dialectic' in I. Kant, *Critique of Pure Reason* (London: Macmillan, 1950).

[21] The main texts (pre-revolution) are I. Kant, 'Idea for a Universal History with a Cosmopolitan Purpose' in *Kant: Political Writings*, pp. 41–53; and 'Conjectures on the Beginning of Human History', pp. 221–234.

[22] Kant, 'Idea for a Universal History', p. 47.

[23] See F. C. Beiser, *Enlightenment, Revolution, and Romanticism: the Genesis of Modern German Political Thought, 1790–1800* (Cambridge MA: Harvard University Press, 1992), p. 31; and R. Tuck, *The Rights of War and Peace: Political Thought and the International Order from Grotius to Kant* (Oxford: Oxford University Press, 1999), pp. 114–115.

state – as a tax collector, military officer or even as a man of the clergy.[24] Therefore, the sphere of public debate was actually, for Kant, specifically the corporate arena of the intellectual stratum – an arena *inside of which* intellectuals could and should exercise their specific rights and duties to debate, relatively autonomously, and as free thinkers, reform of the absolutist state.

Indeed, even Kant's pre-Revolution comments on war were mobilized towards the possibilities of corporate reform. For example, he believed that the threat of war brought together a closer association of corporate groups within the commonwealth under the banner of promoting the wellbeing of all. The marshal spirit, unlike the selfish and cowardly commercial spirit, forced Reason to act upon the natural world rather than allowing the capriciousness of human nature to act upon Reason.[25] And in Kant's corporate context this was not untrue: Frederick the Great's enlightened absolutism granted all corporate groups from peasants to nobility various rights and duties *through* their contributions to his war machine.

Thus, before the French Revolution, Kant's universal history provided guidelines for humanity to approximate the autonomy and universal applicability of pure Reason in the phenomenal realm and slowly progress away from despotism. Practically, this progress would contribute to a harmonious order of relatively autonomous yet interdependent corporate bodies within which the intellectual stratum itself could be guaranteed freedom of thought as a corporate body. In this task, Kant could imagine Frederick the Great's enlightened absolutism as a vanguard movement against despots, a movement guided by the *Aufklärer*. Having placed such a weighty burden on the shoulders of his political philosophy, Kant asked if there was any phenomenal sign to indicate that his narrative of universal history was worth pursuing. His answer, in 1784, was tentative but affirmative, pointing to the freedom of religious thought in his home state of Prussia, as well as the increased interdependency that trade and commerce produced between nations.[26] His answer by 1798, as I shall now discuss, was to be very different.

---

[24] I. Kant, 'An Answer to the Question: "What is Enlightenment?"' in *Kant: Political Writings*, pp. 55–56.

[25] On these points see Kant 'Conjectures on the Beginning of Human History', p. 232; and I. Kant, *Critique of Judgment* (Cambridge: Hackett, 1987), pp. 122–123. The *Critique of Judgment* was published during the first year of the Revolution. It should therefore be taken as a pre-revolutionary text in Kant's oeuvre.

[26] Kant, 'Idea for a Universal History', p. 50.

Kant's political philosophy after the Revolution

Not only did the announcement of the Rights of Man appear to herald, for the *Aufklärer*, the destruction of old French despotism but the Revolution now allowed for a *comparison* of two paths to liberty: the piecemeal monarchical reform of the Anglo-Germanic 'Volk' versus the clearly delineated and rationally codified obelisk of the French constitution. However, come the Terror and the invasion of the Rhineland, fear of French despotism resurfaced and, moreover, intensified. In fact, the first Revolutionary Wars then proceeded to transform the *Aufklärer's* admiration of the British spirit into infatuation, for Albion was now portrayed as the re-balancer of the scales of European geo-politics. And at the same time, the new Rights of Man were pushed into an ill-fitting absolutist category of 'mechanical' rule, a category opposed to the organically evolving Anglo-Germanic folk.[27] Moreover, the Revolution impacted upon the *Aufklärer* in Prussia in the wake of the death in 1786 of Frederick the Great, the 'philosopher king'. The successor, Frederick William II, preferred the instruction of Rosicrucian Christianity to philosophy. In this respect the return of religion within Prussia, as the preferred regulator of politics, threatened to undermine the *Aufklärer's* project of corporate reform through the guidance of Reason.

In short, the *Aufklärer* came to be uncomfortably caught between a de-enlightenment in Prussia, and a revolution of Reason in France. And the Revolution was therefore internalized by the intellectual stratum in an intensely contradictory fashion: it was, at the same time, potential friend, enlightened superior and definite enemy: friend, because the French bourgeoisie had apparently launched a revolution of Reason sweeping away Bourbon despotism and the ill-deserved supremacy of the nobility; superior, because in so doing, the Revolution had opened up a comparative vista on British freedom and thus problematized the efficacy of monarchical 'reform' as a path towards enlightenment; and enemy, because at the same time the Revolution's regicidal excesses and mobilization of the lower ranks undermined, in most German monarchs, the desire to allow the continuance of corporate reform.

Kant, likewise, internalized the meaning of the Revolution. And this propelled him to find a way to frame the Revolution that would re-legitimate his existing project of corporate reform, and thus save what was left of German Enlightenment. But to do this Kant had to engage directly with this new manifestation of Reason in the experiential realm.

[27] See McClelland, *German Historians and England*, pp. 30–33, 36–7, 44.

For the Declaration of Rights and the following Constitution challenged the very heart of his political philosophy – a regulative universal history that heretofore had formed the *only*, and *virtual*, bridge between Reason and experience. In effect, Kant was compelled to modify his universal history by a growing consciousness of backwardness: the 'other' of the French Revolution had to be tamed in order to save the 'self' of German corporate reform.

The start of this modification is found in Kant's response, in 1793, to Edmund Burke's conservative attempt to de-legitimize rationalism and regicide by calling for a return to tradition.[28] Kant claimed that the regulative principle of social conduct should be derived, even in revolutionary times, from Pure Reason rather than church or tradition. To defend this position, Kant proceeded to enquire into the degree to which Practical Reason could still, in revolutionary times, inform ethical conduct. To answer this question, Kant took three perspectives: the individual, the state and humanity in general.[29] In his discussion of the individual, Kant essentially summarized his existing Critique of Practical Reason; and in his discussion on humanity, he recounted his existing narrative of a universal history. But it is Kant's investigation of the morality of the political realm – the state – that is most interesting.

In fact, unlike in his pre-Revolution writings, Kant now invoked the civil constitution itself as a regulative tool; after all, the political rights that the constitution encoded – freedom, equality and independence – were all qualities of Pure Reason. Kant, therefore, used the design of the Revolutionary constitution to directly criticize the 'post-enlightenment' Prussian Rosicrucian order. Nevertheless, he immediately proceeded to forbid any revolution or resistance against the existing supreme political power as a means to realize the principles of the constitution, for such an act would undermine a core universal tenet of Practical Reason that for each subject to have formal equality and freedom required coercion to be exercised only by the ruler. Rebellion would only encourage the King to fear that the path of Reason led to anarchic licence. Instead, freedom of the pen (of the *Aufklärer*) remained the prime safeguard of the rights of the people.[30]

Yet it was not so much talk of a constitution that eventually led Kant into direct confrontation with his Christian king. It was, instead, an essay

---

[28] Beiser, *Enlightenment, Revolution, and Romanticism*, p. 50. The text is I. Kant, 'On the Common Saying: "This May be True in Theory, But it Does Not Apply in Practice"' in *Kant: Political Writings*, pp. 61–92.
[29] Kant, ibid., pp. 62–63.   [30] Ibid., pp. 84–85.

that had, ironically, been requested by some of the French Deputies – *Religion within the Limits of Reason*. Upon its publication, Johann Christof Wöllner, closest personal advisor to Frederick William II, wrote to Kant expressing dissatisfaction and disappointment. Rosicrucianism now directly threatened to place secular Reason under the moral authority of religion, and faced with such a mortal threat to *Aufklärung*, Kant had no recourse but to bow to the censor. The whole episode worked to intensify Kant's consciousness of backwardness, almost to the point of anxiety.[31] For in effect, all he could now offer fellow *Aufklärer* was a passive hope that the German philosopher king might one day be reincarnated.

But in the aftermath of this controversy, during 1795, Frederick William II signed the Treaty of Basle with France, ensuring Prussian neutrality in the Revolutionary Wars until 1806. And here, Kant saw a glimmer of hope to push for a reform out of Rosicrucian backwardness. For meanwhile, the Prussian war machine had been transformed from a conduit of Reason to a crusader of religious superstition. Therefore, with peace, Kant was presented with a slim opportunity to re-make the case for an enlightened rather than despotic geo-politics. This plea, of course, was *On Perpetual Peace*. In this text, Kant's ethical discussion of the state took the form of an investigation of a federation of such civic states. Again, he pleaded the case for the corporate right of luminaries to 'publicly' discourse on the maxims of warfare and peacemaking:[32] the philosopher would help guide the King through international relations so that actions in the political realm might accord to Practical Reason; and the regulative narrative of his universal history justified this strategy.[33] Nevertheless, with *Perpetual Peace*, the civil constitution had gained in importance as a regulative tool. Its political tenets of freedom, equality and independence were not only a guide for societal relations; they now formed the guide for inter-societal relations too.

But even though the *Perpetual Peace* is Kant's most famous statement on his political philosophy (at least in IR), there is another text that exposes the final resolution that his consciousness of backwardness gave to the tripartite ethical relationship between individual, political realm

[31] G. P. Gooch, *Germany and the French Revolution* (London: Frank Cass, 1965), p. 267.
[32] I. Kant, 'On Perpetual Peace', in *Kant: Political Writings*, pp. 93, 115.
[33] On Kant's plea for political action to accord to Practical Reason see the two appendices, ibid., pp. 116–130. On Kant's justification of *Perpetual Peace* through his universal history see the First Supplement, ibid., pp. 108–114.

and humanity. For in November 1797, Frederick William II died, and his successor Frederick William III, while no great philosopher king, nevertheless proceeded to dismantle the overarching influence of Rosicrucian Christianity. Kant's nemesis, Wöllner, was dismissed and his various commissions closed. Kant immediately proceeded to press the advantage of a possible return to enlightenment, and in 1798 published *Contest of the Faculties*.[34]

The *Contest* included a statement on the relationship between the philosophical and theological faculties, and, most importantly for our purposes, a re-visitation of his narrative of universal history. Back in 1784, Kant had assured the reader that his universal history was not simply a fantasy narrative by tentatively pointing to Prussia's freedom of religious thought and the increased interdependency that trade and commerce produced between nations. But in order to make his regulative history compelling for the readers of revolutionary times, Kant had to replace the sign that pointed towards the application of Pure Reason in the experiential world: *Revolution as a process itself* (and not just its constitutional result) became the new sign of human progress.

But even so, Kant warned that the revolutionary sign was in no way to be confused with the phenomenal transformation of political authority itself. Rather it was to be found in the attitude of the onlookers: disinterested sympathy from non-French onlookers proved the progression of the moral capacity of the human race.[35] To Kant, such disinterested onlookers were 'primitive philosophical historians' who could detach reason from experience. In short, the Revolution proved that there was developing a human faculty through which political action could be judged by the criteria of Kant's regulative universal history. And in this way, Kant managed to separate and isolate the unprecedented experiential developments brought about by the Revolutionary 'other', for example, Terror, Jacobinism, etc., from the 'real' pertinence of the Revolution for human progress – its demonstration of the potentiality for individuals to act according to a regulative universal history.

Let us now recapitulate the argument in order to fully draw out Kant's treatment of the relation between the German 'self' and French 'other'. In Kant's political philosophy before the Revolution, the progress of

[34] Manfred Kuehn, *Kant: a Biography* (Cambridge: Cambridge University Press, 2001), p. 404.
[35] I. Kant, 'The Contest of the Faculties' in *Kant: Political Writings*, pp. 182–183.

humanity through reason was a guide, not an unfolding fact. It was this regulative nature of the narrative that formed the only (virtual) bridge between reason and experience along which the ethical relation between individual, political community and humanity could be organized. Here, humanity's general proclivity towards unsocial sociability was the tool of progress, and a vague growth of commercial interdependency the sign. However, after 1789, Kant mobilized the revolutionary constitution to be the tool of progress, first in its 'domestic' role, and then in its geo-political role. But by 1798, Kant presented revolution itself, as a process, to be the sign of progress. Thus, in his post-Revolutionary writings, Kant's Practical Reason cumulatively relied upon the experiential organization of, and experiential processes of transformation of, political authority. But crucially, at the same time, Kant had to somehow maintain that the machinations of the political realm remained a fiction of a regulative universal history, and not a reality to be directly copied 'on earth'. This was necessary in order to uphold the core philosophical foundation of his corporate Enlightenment project – the separation between reason and experience. The final moment of this incorporation came in *Contest of the Faculties* when Kant made the sign of progress the revolutionary process itself, but at the same time derived the meaning of that process not from its substantive transformations of political authority, but from the sympathy of its onlookers.

This is how Kant's consciousness of backwardness attempted to contain the threat that the French Revolution had created in manifesting the rights of the sovereign individual *within* the experiential world. Ultimately, the more he was compelled to make elements from an experiential world of 'difference' pivotal to his political philosophy of Enlightenment, the more that 'difference' was flattened by his consciousness of backwardness. In order to save the reform project of the German intellectual stratum, Kant had to reconcile the enigmatic effects of the Revolution on political identity to an existing sense of 'self'.[36] In these ways, Kant separated the effects of the Revolution (Terror, Jacobinism, etc.) from its meaning, and then subsumed this meaning under his narrative of universal history. The 'other' – French sovereign individualism – had been disciplined by the 'self' – German enlightened corporatism.

---

[36] Kant's growing concern for the backwardness of the German 'spirit' within this world of difference is evidenced in his turn-of-the-century anthropology of national characteristics; I. Kant, *Anthropology From a Pragmatic Point of View* (The Hague: Martinus Nijhoff, 1974), p. 180.

The question for the Democratic Peace debate, then, is this: through which eyes are we looking at international relations if we approach the ethical relationship between individual, state (system) and humanity through *Perpetual Peace*? From the above contextualization, it would seem that *Perpetual Peace* was an ethical engagement with international relations taken from the standpoint of an intellectual inhabiting a comparatively 'backward', 'peripheral' and non-modern political community.

In contrast to Kant, Hegel believed that an ethical engagement with the new revolutionary world could not be developed by reference to a non-experiential sense of Reason, but to a 'real world' engagement with the effects of the French Revolution.[37] But as we shall now see, albeit in a different way, Hegel also worked to subsume the 'other' encoded in the French Constitution under the 'backward' German philosophical 'self'.

Hegel's constitutive self

Hegel's famous critique of Kant has often been mobilized in the cosmopolitan/communitarian debate to question the cosmopolitan idea of universal rights based on a pre-social sovereign individual.[38] Hegel's alternative 'constitutive' approach, it is said, posits the development and negotiation of rights through interactions between individuals within really existing societies.[39] In this schema, rights are not decided by virtue of their *a priori* value; rather, they are dynamically created through frictional – although institutionalized – processes of recognition.[40] Most

---

[37] See for example G. W. F. Hegel, 'On the Scientific Ways of Treating Natural Law, on its Place in Practical Philosophy, and its Relation to the Positive Sciences of Right' in L. Dickey and H. B. Nisbet, *Hegel: Political Writings* (Cambridge: Cambridge University Press, 1999), pp. 112–114, 123; G. W. F. Hegel, *Phenomenology of Spirit* (Oxford: Oxford University Press, 1977), pp. 1–45; and G. W. F. Hegel, *Elements of the Philosophy of Right* ed. Allen G. Wood (Cambridge: Cambridge University Press, 1991), pp. 25–72.

[38] See D. Morrice, 'The Liberal-Communitarian Debate in Contemporary Political Philosophy and its Significance to International Relations' *Review of International Studies* 26 (2000), p. 234; and Brown, *International Relations Theory*, p. 65.

[39] On the constitutive approach to rights see famously A. Honneth, *The Struggle for Recognition: the Moral Grammar of Social Conflicts* (Cambridge: Polity Press, 1995) in Political Theory; and M. Frost, *Ethics in International Relations: a Constitutive Theory* (Cambridge: Cambridge University Press, 1996) in IR theory.

[40] For example, H. Brod, *Hegel's Philosophy of Politics – Idealism, Identity, and Modernity* (Boulder CO: Westview Press, 1992); J. N. Shklar, *Freedom and Independence: a Study of the Political Ideas of Hegel's Phenomenology of Mind* (Cambridge: Cambridge University Press, 1976); and S. B. Smith, *Hegel's Critique of Liberalism: Rights in Context* (London: University of Chicago Press, 1989).

importantly for IR is the extension of this idea of constitutive right to the arena of international law and rights-based relations between states.[41] Commentators point out that Hegel seemed to attribute a certain ethical nature to war in terms of the (unintentional) impetus it gives to the world-historical progress of individual freedom.[42] But Chris Brown has made the core point: if one is to accept Hegel's argument that war is the 'world's court of judgment', making international relations a constitutive – and thus ethical – arena of social relations, then this requires a metaphysical belief in *Geist* (spirit). For it is the 'world spirit' that for Hegel drives forward the progress of humanity through mechanisms that might not be immediately recognizable as 'progressive'.[43] If we are to approach Hegel from a 'secular' position, then can we really use Hegel's constitutive approach to inform an ethics of international relations?

In what follows, I argue that Hegel sought to make sense of a world of 'difference' within which Germany occupied a backward position *vis-à-vis* revolutionary France. The Terror of the Revolution, which Hegel attributed to the limitless sovereign rights of the individual (encoded in the French Constitution) threatened to destroy the German enlightenment project by forcefully introducing (by way of the Napoleonic army and the civil code) the socio-political infrastructure for Terror into Germany. To address this threat, Hegel promoted a specifically German revolution of Philosophy with which to escape from backwardness. By using the Philosopher's special attribute, the internal cultivation of self-awareness (*Bildung*), this revolution would overcome the destructive egoism of limitless individual rights, thus progressing the social basis of individual freedom to a higher level. *Geist* was the necessary 'institution' through which German Philosophy could reach across political boundaries and graft elements of the French subject onto the German body politic. And through this transnational process, Hegel's political philosophy posited an ethics of universal rapprochement. This, however, obscured his proposition about the foundational importance of

---

[41] For example, E. Ringmar, 'The Relevance of International Law: a Hegelian Interpretation of a Peculiar Seventeenth-Century Preoccupation' *Review of International Studies* 21 (1995), 87–103.

[42] For example, David Boucher, *Political Theories of International Relations: From Thucydides to the Present* (Oxford: Oxford University Press, 1998), pp. 331–345; H. Jaeger, 'Hegel's Reluctant Realism and the Transnationalisation of Civil Society' in *Review of International Studies* 28 (2002), 497–517; T. Brooks, 'Hegel's Theory of International Politics; a Reply to Jaeger' *Review of International Studies* 30 (2004), 149–152; and S. Walt, 'Hegel on War: Another Look' *History of Political Thought* 10 (1989), 113–124.

[43] Brown, *International Relations Theory*, pp. 67–70.

'difference' for the cultivation of an ethical modern life, and in so doing progressively subsumed the 'other' of the French Revolution of Politics under the 'self' of the German Revolution of Philosophy.

Hegel's embrace of 'difference'

Hegel's political philosophy was, in the first instance, informed by the traditional project of *Aufklärung* outlined above, namely, taming the despotic absolutist state (inside and outside Germany), and engineering the organic balance of an array of relatively autonomous corporate bodies.[44] Yet, the French Revolution was the first and greatest challenge to Hegel's political philosophy.[45]

Initially, the French Declaration and Constitution appeared to Hegel as the manifestation of Reason on earth and the inauguration of a new age and set of conditions through which to realize freedom and autonomy for mankind. But at the same time he noticed that something in the encoding of the 'natural' rights of pre-social man worked to corrupt these promises and instead foster an arbitrary and particularistic execution of egoistic will. Through the Constitution, individualized political freedom had turned into factionalism, and factionalism into the Terror of unrestrained sovereign wills.[46] Moreover, by the turn of the century, Napoleon's military advances into Germany highlighted to Hegel the impotence of the Reich's defensive capacity: an ill-fitting set of corporate bodies faced a unified citizen's army from across the Rhine.[47] In essence, the moment of geo-political contest with France had exposed, for Hegel, not only the technical fragility of the emperorship within the Reich; but more so it had exampled this *form* of political unity to be utterly inadequate with regard to the geo-political challenges of the new revolutionary era.[48]

---

[44] On Hegel's initial influences see H. S. Harris, *Hegel's Development: Toward the Sunlight 1770–1801* (Oxford: Clarendon Press, 1972), pp. 3–6,17, 20–21; and T. Pinkard, *Hegel: a Biography* (Cambridge: Cambridge University Press, 2000), pp. 9, 15–16.

[45] The case is made by a number of commentators. See, famously, J. Ritter, 'Hegel and the French Revolution' in *Essays on the Philosophy of Right* (Cambridge MA, MIT Press 1982), pp. 35–89.

[46] On Hegel's intimate following of the Jacobin Republic, see J. Schmidt, 'Cabbage Heads and Gulps of Water – Hegel on the Terror' *Political Theory* 26 (1998), 4–32. For later commentaries see Hegel, *Phenomenology of Spirit*, pp. 355–363; and G. W. F. Hegel, 'Lectures on the Philosophy of History – Part 4: The Germanic World' in L. Dickey and H. B. Nisbet, *Hegel: Political Writings* (Cambridge: Cambridge University Press, 1999), pp. 217–219.

[47] G. W. F. Hegel, 'The German Constitution' in *Hegel: Political Writings*, pp. 6–101

[48] Ibid., pp. 7, 40, 62, 87, 92.

Thus, as it had been for Kant, the Revolution was for Hegel an ally in the enlightened fight against aristocratic despotism, and at the same time, its Terror threatened to destroy enlightened reform and the interests of the German intellectual stratum altogether. Yet if, in this respect, Hegel shared with Kant a consciousness of backwardness, Hegel, in the company of the Romantics, made a virtue of the fact that France and Germany were *different*. Moreover, unlike the Romantics, Hegel also accepted the validity of the 'modern' life of the pre-social individual that the Revolution had presented. Indeed, Hegel started to accept the need to somehow solve the problem of German backwardness, and the specific threat it posed to the German project of Enlightenment, by incorporating the positive aspects of the French constitution into German society. In this respect, Hegel, unlike Kant, not only embraced 'difference', but at the same time sought to resolve the antagonism that difference produced between the German 'self' and the French 'other' by recognizing co-constitution with this 'other' to be a necessary element in the progression of the identity of the 'self'.

In order for this process of mediation to disarm the Terror of the sovereign individual, a sense of ethical life was required that, Hegel believed, could only be found in Germany, specifically within its traditional social bonds of a paternal religion. He considered this original Christianity as a 'civic theology', an internalized communal love emanating from the people themselves.[49] Via a set of mediating institutions, the egoistic freedom of the French individual could be 'grafted on' to this existing ethical life. Furthermore, Hegel claimed that the social force that would power this process of mediation was to be found in Philosophy itself.[50] For Philosophy allowed for a cultivation of self-awareness (*Bildung*), especially regarding the social conditions of one's individuality, and therefore provided the opportunity to inject an ethical content into the amoral form of modern life. Having developed this idea over a number of years, Hegel showed, in the *Philosophy of Right*, how *Bildung* operated through a set of socio-political institutions that progressively

---

[49] On this point see especially, Pinkard, *Hegel*, pp. 61–68; and L. Dickey, *Hegel: Religion, Economics, and the Politics of Spirit 1770–1807* (Cambridge: Cambridge University Press, 1987), pp. 278–281. See also G. W. F. Hegel, *Lectures on the Philosophy of World History: Introduction: Reason in History* (Cambridge: Cambridge University Press, 1975).

[50] This was part of a wider German neo-Humanist project to substitute philosophical revolution for political revolution. See in general S. Kouvelakis, *Philosophy and Revolution* (London: Verso, 2003); Habermas, *Theory and Practice*; and H. Mah, 'The French Revolution and the Problem of German Modernity: Hegel, Heine, and Marx' *New German Critique* 50 (1990), 3–20.

mediated particular interests for the universal good – the family, the corporations in civil society and an impartial bureaucracy. This process would combine corporate German social bonds with French pre-social individual rights, and cultivate an Ethical State fit for modernity. For this State would allow the articulation of an identity that was individually free but also aware of, and respectful to, the social relations that allowed for this freedom.[51]

In effect, then, Hegel was attempting to outline an historical movement conducive to importing the French 'other' (the sovereign individual) into the German 'self' (a corporate and personalized body politic) so as to preserve the good of individual freedom while removing its egoistic bad. This movement was understood as *Aufhebung* – a dialectical development that at the same time raised, preserved and nullified social identity: Hegel wished to *preserve* the old – the ethical life of the traditional *German* corporate community – by *raising* it in the process of grafting on the pre-social individualism of the modern *French* subject; this process, he hoped, would *nullify* the old and produce a *new* German identity that would be equipped to resolve the core problem of modern life emanating from the French Revolution, namely, the pre-social and amoral licence that came with the individualization of rights and duties.[52]

Thus, unlike Kant's, Hegel's political philosophy provided an opportunity to build an ethical stance towards international relations sensitive to 'difference'. But as we shall now see, the felt need for Germany to escape its backward condition *vis-à-vis* revolutionary France also propelled Hegel to collapse the condition of 'difference' within a universal world history.

Hegel's denial of 'difference'

Let us, at this point, return to Hegel's *Philosophy of Right* and specifically the notion of the Ethical State as the highest moment of the mediation of particular interests through universal institutions. In fact, this moment was expressed through (but not reified into) the person of the sovereign; Hegel in this way anthropomorphized the state into an individual.[53] Thus, the degree to which particular interests had found constitutional resolution formed the national being's 'spirit', and this was expressed in

---

[51] Hegel, *Lectures on the Philosophy of World History: Introduction*, p. 95.
[52] On this point see also Pinkard, *Hegel*, p. 196.
[53] Hegel, *Lectures on the Philosophy of World History: Introduction*, pp. 51–53; Hegel, *Philosophy of Right*, p. 359 §321.

a singularity, the sovereign.[54] The question is, what kind of international domain did this spiritual 'individual' inhabit?

Hegel's answer is contradictory. By the logic of one aspect of his argument, the international domain was indeed akin to a 'state of nature'. Ethical life, after all, was produced in the process of mediation which itself presupposed a higher, more universalistic, institution. But there existed, materially, no institution higher than the executive and legislature within the state through which a process of *Aufhebung* could mediate the particularistic collection of national spirits.[55] Yet Hegel at the same time claimed that war itself was an ethical moment, and, moreover, the ultimate process that tested the ethical adequacy of any national spirit. In other words, even if not 'empirically' observable, the international domain had to possess some form of universalistic institution through which the particularities of national spirits could be mediated into a higher ethical life.[56]

Hegel proposed that the geo-political contest played itself out as the expression of an unobservable 'institution', none other than *Geist* – the world spirit.[57] *Geist* manifested itself most forcefully in war, because war tested the resolve and integrity of each individual national 'spirit' with regard to its specific resolution of particular rights with universal duty.[58] So even if all states, just as individuals in civil society, had to recognize each other's independence formally, it was the ethical content of the state that decided which 'individual' would concretely be judged through war as truly independent and thus free.[59] In short, whichever state possessed the higher spirit was *world-historical*: and this 'individual' would set the historical standard by which others were externally pressured to transform internally, else wither and die. Through the working out of this geo-political inter-subjectivity, the kernel of a new stage of development in world spirit would be placed in a 'young' state, and as the current world-historical state decayed, world spirit would move to inhabit this new national spirit. This, incidentally, is why Hegel criticized Kant's purely *formalistic* prescription of 'Perpetual Peace': in effect, it could not

[54] Ibid., p. 367 §331; Hegel, *Lectures on the Philosophy of World History: Introduction*, pp. 51–65.

[55] Hegel, *Philosophy of Right*, p. 275 §258.   [56] Ibid., pp. 359–363 §321–326.

[57] See famously, Hegel, *Lectures on the Philosophy of World History: Introduction*, especially 'General Concept', pp. 26–32; and 'The Course of World History', pp. 124–131.

[58] Hegel, *Philosophy of Right*, pp. 361–365 §324–328. Thomas Mertens lists a number of 'Just War' criteria evident in Hegel's discussion on war; see 'Hegel's Homage to Kant's Perpetual Peace: an Analysis of Hegel's Philosophy of Right §321–340' *Review of Politics* 57 (1995), 680–691.

[59] Hegel, *Philosophy of Right*, pp. 366–367 §330–331.

conceptualize ethical systems as constitutive of the interaction produced by 'difference'.[60] Alternatively, in Hegel's political philosophy, international relations quite literally formed the 'world's court of judgment', and hence an ethical domain rather than a state of nature.

Yet for Hegel, the core of this ethical nature of *Geist* was that, just as particular individuals in civil society found their universality in the state, so did particular states find their universality in world spirit.[61] And just as within the state, particularistic individuals found rapprochement through a higher mediation, so too did particular states find rapprochement through war and the world spirit. This meant that *Geist*, as a movement of mediation, progressively sublated particular national interests into a human ethical whole. To be clear, *Geist*, for Hegel, did not result in an institutional rapprochement of geo-politics into a 'world state'; rather, the rapprochement that *Geist* pursued was one of socio-political forms: through the process of mediation, both domestically and geopolitically, humanity was historically progressing towards the expression of *one* form of political subject – the free, equal and self-conscious individual.

Let us recapitulate the argument so far. In order to escape backwardness and resist the destruction of the German enlightenment project by the French Terror (and its Napoleonic incarnations), Hegel had presented a German revolution of Philosophy as an alternative to the French constitutional version. This German revolution was charged with beating the French Revolution at its own game, so to speak. For to salvage the German intellectual stratum's project of free thought, Hegel required the German revolution not only to institutionalize individual rights in Germany, but, at the same time, to overcome the self-destructive nature of sovereign individualism. Therefore, Hegel had to convince his audience that it was both possible and desirable for the Philosophy faculty to mobilize, for Germany, a historical 'leaping over' of the French constitutional 'stage' through the special energy of *Bildung*. This, however, required an institution within the geo-political arena that did not simply allow for a clash of civilizations, but for a philosophically driven moment of mediation *beyond* the borders of a backward political community. In this respect, the 'dialectical' world-historical movement that Hegel termed *Geist* was necessary if Hegel's revolution of Philosophy was to hold integrity, for only through *Geist* could *Bildung* drive a

---

[60] Ibid., p. 371 §340; Hegel, 'On the Scientific Ways of Treating Natural Law', pp. 140–141.
[61] Hegel, *Philosophy of Right*, p. 324 §362.

world-historical rapprochement of discrete subjectivities. As we shall now see, this requirement, borne of a consciousness of comparative backwardness, worked to close down the challenge of 'difference' in international relations that Hegel's political philosophy had originally been so sensitive to.

To this effect, let us examine Hegel's narrative of world history. The first thing to note is that Hegel had to foreground the 'internal' moment of cultivating self-awareness (*Bildung*) within the process of *Aufhebung*. For although Hegel, contrary to popular opinion, did not conflate this 'idealist' moment with the overriding force of historical development *per se*, it *was* the overriding force for the German present with regard to the tasks of escaping backwardness. However, this privileging of a specifically German condition in world history had to somehow be justified: after all, it was hardly backward Germany that had recently appeared as the leading 'spirit' of the age.

Hegel solved this problem by focusing on his critique of the historical causes of the Terror. In his opinion, the French Constitution manifested a purely 'outward' individual freedom – an encoding of the negative rights of the individual within a political constitution – while ignoring its 'inner' content – the development of self-awareness of the social constitution of this freedom (*Bildung*). Because of this lack, the spiritual soil of France was too poor to facilitate the growth of an Ethical State. But, Hegel pointed out, Luther's Reformation had already produced a rich inner freedom, even if the German polity was woefully lacking in its outward manifestation.[62] By this reasoning, the French Revolution had now passed on the external component of individual freedom – the Constitution – to the German world via the world-historical individual, Napoleon, and his civil code. Germany could therefore indeed conceive of itself as world-historical in solving the problem of the self-destructive nature of the sovereign individual by actualizing its freedom both 'internally' and 'externally'.[63]

But to make this claim of a prior actualization of 'inner' reason in Germany stick, Hegel had to make two historical-sociological propositions. Firstly, he proposed that art, science, religion – in short, all those facets of human life that cultivated inner freedom – were in fact

---

[62] See for example, Hegel, 'Lectures on the Philosophy of History: Part 4', pp. 210,212; and Hegel, *Philosophy of Right*, p. 379 §358.
[63] On Hegel's treatment of the Reformation see L. W. Beck, 'The Reformation, the Revolution, and the Restoration in Hegel's Political Philosophy' *Journal of the History of Philosophy* 14 (1976), 51–61.

moved by an *evolutionary* logic; while politics, the medium of external freedom was open to *rupture*.[64] Secondly, he ascribed this inner evolution to the 'Germanic' people in general – meaning, in fact, most European polities.[65] Thus Hegel was invoking the world of European Christianity as the milieu of modern world development, while at the same time noting that a fracture within this world had appeared: Catholicism had led to the political rupture of the French Revolution, while Protestantism had led to the internal revolution.[66] Crucially, in setting up the problem of the contemporaneous transition of world spirit in this way, Hegel implicitly allowed the specificity of the French Revolution as a political rupture to be superseded by a *general* evolution. And through this argument, Hegel at once separated the 'other' of the French Revolution from German history and then subsumed its historical effect under a universal trajectory of world development defined by the 'self' of the German revolution of Philosophy.

In sum, as a site that possessed no political institution to mediate particular interests, the international domain, for Hegel, was akin to a 'state of nature' – a world of pre-social individualized states. Yet at the same time, as a site of inter-subjective mediation (between these national 'spirits') and ultimately as a site that hosted a process of rapprochement between political forms, the international domain was an expansion of the domestic ethical domain. Thus, borne of a recognition of the co-constitution of 'self' and 'other' in modern world history, but a recognition driven by the attempt to escape a backward and subordinate position within this co-constitution, Hegel's political philosophy at once opened up and shut down a vista on the problem of 'difference' in international relations. One might say that rather than being a religious relic, teleology of the liberal individual or the manifestation of human consciousness in general, *Geist* was a necessary manifestation of Hegel's consciousness of backwardness.

Conclusion

It is usually assumed that the contemporary cosmopolitan/communitarian debate derives from an unproblematically 'Western' or 'modern' intellectual debate on the possibilities of universalizing the

[64] Hegel, *Lectures on the Philosophy of World History: Introduction*, p. 120.
[65] See, for example, Hegel's topography in 'The German Constitution', pp. 62–63; see also the editors note in Hegel, *Philosophy of Right*, p. 379*f*2 §358.
[66] Hegel, 'Lectures on the Philosophy of History: Part 4', p. 220.

liberal condition. But this singularity does not hold, at least according to the re-contextualization presented above. Rather, the (commonly perceived) classical origin of this debate spoke to the concerns of a 'peripheral' intellectual stratum; it interrogated the ethics of international relations through the problem of 'difference', and from the perspective of a comparatively backward partner in the relationship that constructed difference; and it agonized over the ethical challenges of engaging with a potentially progressive, yet at the same time threatening, 'foreign' form of political subjectivity.

Moreover, the re-contextualization presented above also questions the poststructural, especially postcolonial inspired, critique of the cosmopolitan/communitarian debate. For both Kant's and Hegel's ultimate elision of 'difference', the intellectual processes of 'othering' and 'universalizing', was a disciplining effect of a consciousness of backwardness, and one that was not internally *derived from* (critically or otherwise), but *a response to*, what was contemporaneously seen as the imperialistic expansion of the 'modern' sovereign subject. This sovereign subject was itself taken to be the 'other', at least, from the standpoint of intellectuals who sought reform of a non-modern 'self'.

To be clear, while I have here placed the French Revolution in the foreground, this is in no way meant as an attempt to marginalize the colonial moment from European history. Rather, my intention has been to problematize the issue of 'difference' further. It is, of course, true that most postcolonial inspired literature takes the European 'self' as a fiction, an effect of colonial mentality. And positing the sovereign subject of 'Europe' usually proceeds as a heuristic strategy through which to show the co-constitution of European 'self' and colonial 'other'. Nevertheless, there is a point where this fiction becomes an unspoken taken-for-granted, a starting point, whereas this European 'self' should be problematized as *itself* historically saturated with 'difference'.

This line of thought presents two challenges for normative IR theory. Firstly, and specifically regarding the mainstream cosmopolitan/communitarian debate, neither Kant nor Hegel provide an intellectual retreat from the problem of 'difference'. Both developed their ethical standpoints on international relations through a consciousness of backwardness that was itself a direct engagement with inter-societal 'difference'. And secondly, regarding the more general project of critically interrogating the production of identity, the discipline of modern sovereign subjectivity by no means exhausts an understanding of the self/other problematic. For the commonly accepted modern or

'Western' canon of political thought through which we make sense of, and over which we contest, the making of modern subjectivity, is *itself* significantly constituted by the concerns of intellectuals situated in a 'peripheral' and comparatively 'backward' society. It might well be the case that even before we intellectually travel to the non-European world, we are already gazing at international relations through 'peripheral' eyes. If the 'other' to the liberal project is already constitutive of the liberal tradition itself, then both the mainstream of the normative debate in IR and its critics must think more deeply about how, precisely, 'difference' might be recognized.

10   Images of Grotius

Edward Keene

The literature on the history of ideas about international politics is over-whelmingly devoted to a small group of 'great thinkers': Thucydides, Augustine, Machiavelli, Grotius, Hobbes, Rousseau, Burke, Kant, Hegel, Marx and Nietzsche.[1] Even as their works have been reinterpreted in novel ways, these thinkers have retained their position at the centre of historical scholarship, often at the expense of others. Thucydides, for example, no longer enjoys an unquestioned title to be the original author of the theory of the balance of power, but he is still the subject of a flourishing 'cottage industry' in International Relations theory that must be the envy of other ancient historians, such as Herodotus.[2] Machiavelli's satanic reputation as the master of *Realpolitik* may have acquired a more benign aspect as we become more familiar with his republican sympathies, but his ability to overshadow early-modern reason of state theorists such as Francesco Guicciardini has not been

---

[1] There are, of course, some notable exceptions. A few outstanding ones are Carsten Holbraad, *The Concert of Europe: a Study in German and British International Theory, 1815–1914* (London: Longman, 1970); James Muldoon, *Popes, Lawyers, and Infidels: the Church and the Non-Christian World, 1250–1550* (Pennsylvania: University of Pennsylvania Press, 1979); Azar Gat, *The Origins of Military Thought: From the Enlightenment to Clausewitz* (Oxford: Clarendon Press, 1989); and David Long and Peter Wilson (eds.), *Thinkers of the Twenty Years' Crisis: Inter-war Idealism Reassessed* (Oxford: Clarendon Press, 1995). Torbjørn Knutsen, *A History of International Relations Theory* (Manchester: Manchester University Press, 1992) is an unusually wide-ranging textbook.

[2] The idea of a 'cottage industry' on Thucydides is taken from David Welch, 'Why International Relations Theorists Should Stop Reading Thucydides', *Review of International Studies* 29 (2003), p. 307. The literature on Thucydides is too voluminous to quote here (Welch's article offers a useful overview). I do not cite any works on Herodotus for a somewhat different reason: I am unaware of *any* study of Herodotus's place in the history of international political thought, whether an article or a monograph. Considering that Herodotus wrote much more extensively on Greek-Persian relations than did Thucydides, this is a surprising omission, but one that reinforces our sense of the tight grip that the canon exerts on the field.

lessened by the considerable reappraisal of 'Machiavellism' that has taken place from, say, Friedrich Meinecke to R. B. J. Walker.[3] Kant's thought about international relations has undergone any number of new formulations in recent years, but he is still generally acknowledged as one of the pivotal thinkers about international politics in the modern period, while other equally worthy thinkers from his period – Denis Diderot and Johann Gottfried Herder, for instance – languish in relative obscurity.[4]

In these and other examples that might be drawn from the canon, critically-minded scholars have left the *dramatis personae* of the history of international thought largely unchanged, while substantially rewriting the play within which they appear. Hugo Grotius is no exception to this general trend. Over the last couple of decades, thanks in large part to the scholarship of Richard Tuck, a new interpretation of Grotius has acquired something approaching the status of a textbook orthodoxy.[5] The new reading, however, has not for one moment threatened to displace Grotius from the central position he occupies in the his-

---

[3] Friedrich Meinecke, *Machiavellism: the Doctrine of Raison d'État and its Place in Modern History*, trans. Douglas Scott (Boulder CO: Westview Press, 1984); and R. B. J. Walker, *Inside/Outside: International Relations as Political Theory* (Cambridge: Cambridge University Press, 1992). Maurizio Viroli, *From Politics to Reason of State: the Acquisition and Transformation of the Language of Politics, 1250–1600* (Cambridge: Cambridge University Press, 1992) includes an excellent study of Guicciardini's thought. On this topic, see also Kenneth Schellhase, *Tacitus in Renaissance Political Thought* (Chicago: University of Chicago Press, 1976).

[4] See Andrew Hurrell, 'Kant and the Kantian Paradigm in International Relations', *Review of International Studies* 16 (1990), 183–205 for a good overview, and Antonio Franceschet, *Kant and Liberal Internationalism: Sovereignty, Justice, and Global Reform* (Houndmills, Palgrave, 2002) for a more recent study. Again, I can find little to cite on Diderot or Herder within the literature on the history of international political thought. For relevant scholarship, one often needs to go beyond the standard international relations journals: for a good example, see Sankar Muthu, 'Enlightenment anti-imperialism', *Social Research* 66 (1999), 959–1007.

[5] The main works are Richard Tuck, 'The "Modern" Theory of Natural Law' in Anthony Pagden (ed.), *The Languages of Political Theory in Early-modern Europe* (Cambridge: Cambridge University Press, 1987), pp. 99–119; *Philosophy and Government, 1572–1651* (Cambridge: Cambridge University Press, 1993); and *The Rights of War and Peace: Political Thought and the International Order from Grotius to Kant* (Oxford: Oxford University Press, 1999). For a good commentary which relates Tuck's interpretation to contemporary international relations theory, see Benedict Kingsbury, 'Grotius, Law, and Moral Scepticism: Theory and Practice in the Thought of Hedley Bull' in Ian Clark and Iver Neumann (eds.), *Classical Theories of International Relations* (Basingstoke: Macmillan, 1996), pp. 42–70. For the adoption of Tuck's reading of Grotius in a leading textbook, see Chris Brown, Terry Nardin and Nicholas Rengger (eds.), *International Relations in Political Thought: Texts from the Ancient Greeks to the First World War* (Cambridge: Cambridge University Press, 2002), pp. 313–314, although it should be noted that their analysis is not entirely in line with Tuck's reading, especially as presented in *Rights of War and Peace*.

tory of international political and legal thought; indeed, it may even be expected to lead to the inauguration of a new 'cottage industry' in Grotius among International Relations theorists in its own turn. The danger is that scholars will simply latch onto the new interpretation, without thinking properly about the reasons why Grotius enjoys such prominence in the history of ideas about international relations, and without paying sufficient attention to the 'lesser' thinkers who live in his shadow.[6]

This is especially worrying in view of new approaches to the history of ideas, of which Tuck himself is a prominent exponent, that lay particular emphasis on reading 'minor texts' closely in order to understand how ideological conventions are constructed, and so to acquire a better understanding of the significance not only of the intellectual moves carried out by 'major texts', but also to understand the relationship between the theory and practice of politics.[7] In part, the point here is that the most celebrated 'great thinkers' in the history of political thought are often ones who introduced novel ways of thinking about a particular problem, but their innovations can only be appreciated once one has a thorough grasp of the more conventional ways of thinking that they were challenging. Appreciating what the ideological conventions of political thought were in a particular period is thus a crucial part of the study of the history of ideas, and is essential before the ideas of major thinkers can be understood. To the extent that the study of the history of international political thought has concentrated on a select group of great thinkers in isolation, this understanding of the ideological conventions of international politics is sadly lacking.

Another important issue is highlighted by Brian Schmidt's penetrating analysis of the disciplinary roots of twentieth-century ideas about international anarchy in late nineteenth-century political science.[8]

---

[6] My analysis of Grotius's thought in *Beyond the Anarchical Society: Grotius, Colonialism and Order in World Politics* (Cambridge: Cambridge University Press, 2002) may well appear to be guilty of this kind of error. My purpose in that book, however, was not so much to try to set up a new kind of 'Grotian tradition', but rather to show the ideological purposes which Grotius' account of the law of nations was made to serve in subsequent international legal justifications of the practices of colonialism and imperialism, and which have been masked by the subsequent reinterpretation of Grotius in International Relations theory as the 'father' of modern legal thinking in the society of states. In this respect, the analysis in that book is broadly consistent with the argument made here.

[7] See James Tully, 'The Pen is a Mighty Sword: Quentin Skinner's Analysis of Politics', in James (ed.), *Meaning and Context: Quentin Skinner and his Critics* (Princeton: Princeton University Press, 1989), especially pp. 8–16.

[8] Brian Schmidt, *The Political Discourse of Anarchy: a Disciplinary History of International Relations* (Boulder Westview Press, 1998).

Schmidt shows that we should not treat the 'great minds' or 'great tradi-tions' of thought as an unimpeachable source of profound insights into the perennial questions of international affairs, subject only to the need to find the correct interpretive lens with which to view them; rather, we should ask how the academic disciplines of international law and, later, international relations constructed and used particular images of these thinkers for certain purposes. Why were *these* thinkers chosen as representative of the much larger and more diverse body of work which constitutes international political and legal thought? Why have certain interpretations of their ideas acquired the exceptional power that they possess? As the academic disciplines of International Relations and international law have developed, so they have constructed stories of their own intellectual foundations, which need to be interrogated to uncover how they work to support certain ways of thinking about the subject and to marginalize others.

My purpose here is to locate the context within which Grotius' work may be understood; to shed some light on the various 'minor' late six-teenth and early seventeenth-century thinkers who live in his shadow; and to explain how a distorted idea of the 'Grotian tradition' has come to occupy such a central position within International Relations theory today. I will begin with a summary of two current views of Grotius, and then try to trace the origins of the widely-held belief that he is the 'father of modern international law'. Having done that, I will briefly describe three quite distinct literatures on international politics and international law that commanded influence during or shortly after Grotius' lifetime. A crucial point here is that one of these literatures – which mainly con-sisted of commentaries on the negotation and provisions of treaties – has been largely forgotten as a result of the fixation with 'Grotian' inter-national lawyers and theorists of reason of state. Bringing this neglected literature back into focus is essential if we are to understand how the image of Grotius with which we are most familiar today was first constructed.

Two views of Grotius' importance

According to the traditional story, which still has plenty of adherents among experts on international politics and international law,[9] Grotius

---

[9] See, for example, Robert Jackson, *The Global Covenant: Human Conduct in a World of States* (Oxford: Oxford University Press, 2000), pp. 379–380, or Cornelius F. Murphy, 'The

deserves the title of 'father of modern international law' because he was the first to appreciate the extent of the changes taking place in the international order of the seventeenth century, thanks to the breakup of Christendom and the emergence of independent sovereign states, crystallized by one of the principal events of Grotius' later years: the Thirty Years War. Grotius' famously 'eclectic' combination of naturalist and positivist (or 'volitional') jurisprudence provided a sufficiently broad template within which the competing claims of the old and new legal orders could be woven into a more or less coherent whole, albeit one with enduring ambivalences and internal contradictions. Subsequent scholars, such as Emmerich de Vattel, could then use the opening Grotius had created, while sloughing off the medieval residue that still coloured his thought, to produce more comprehensively modern accounts of the sources and content of international law in the context of a society of states.

So the conventional story goes. Tuck's account, by contrast, appeals to what he claims is an even older view of Grotius' importance in the history of ideas, which depicts him as one of the main authors of a new theory of natural law designed to accommodate sceptical or Tacitean objections against the traditional scholastic assertion of a universally binding code. According to Tuck, Grotius 'was generally reckoned by writers at the end of the seventeenth century to have created a new science of morality by inventing a new way of talking about international relations'.[10] His principal innovation in this respect was to ground his conception of natural law not upon revelation or shared religious belief, but upon nothing more than the idea of a natural impulse for self-preservation, itself an integral part of sceptical thought. Thus, as Tuck puts it, 'sceptical ideas could be restated in the language of natural rights and duties'.[11] The content of natural law might be different from that suggested by more traditional scholastic theories, but Grotius' move was essential to the survival of naturalist jurisprudence itself as a vehicle for conceptualizing social and legal order.

Grotius might therefore still be seen as the father of *something* – in this case, a new 'modern' kind of naturalist moral science – but the intellectual context in which he is located is now differently conceived. The old

---

Grotian Vision of World Order' *American Journal of International Law* 76 (1982), 477–498. Much the same point of view on Grotius is also in evidence in A. Claire Cutler, 'The "Grotian Tradition" in International Relations' *Review of International Studies* 17 (1991) 41–65, see especially, pp. 44–49.
[10] Tuck, *Rights of War and Peace*, p. 78.   [11] Tuck, *Philosophy and Government*, p. 347.

view saw him as responding to the practical crisis of the Thirty Years War by advancing broadly humanitarian ideals that ignored the sceptical objections of reason of state theorists, towards whom, as Hirsch Lauterpacht put it, Grotius maintained a dignified silence throughout *De Jure Belli ac Pacis*.[12] Tuck's narrative, on the other hand, begins with the intellectual clash between scholastic natural law and Tacitist ideas about reason of state in early modern thought; and presents Grotius not as someone who ignored the latter, but as a unifier of these diverse strands who paved the way for Hobbes' yet more strongly articulated version of the new natural law theory. The conventional story treats Grotius more narrowly as a purely legal thinker, placing him in a tradition that begins with Vitoria and Suarez, and goes on to include Pufendorf and eventually Vattel; Hobbes is emphatically *not* included in this account of the 'Grotian tradition', but belongs in a quite distinct 'Machiavellian' or realist one.[13] Tuck's interpretation, despite retaining the sense of a connection between Grotius and lawyers like Vitoria, Suarez, Vasquez, Pufendorf and Vattel, also stresses the links between Grotius and more obviously ethical or political philosophers: not only Hobbes, but Rousseau and Kant as well.

My purpose here is not to synthesize these competing interpretations, nor to arbitrate between them, but rather to examine the reasons why the belief that Grotius was the 'father of modern international law' came to exercise such a strong grip on the history of ideas about international politics and international law in the first place. If we grant, for the moment, Tuck's contention that Grotius' contribution was 'generally reckoned by writers at the end of the seventeenth century' in terms of his development of a new moral science that was proof against scepticism, an extraordinary transformation had taken place by the mid-nineteenth century, when the view that Grotius' works should be understood as an eclectic but forward-looking response to the crisis of medieval Christendom and the emergence of the sovereign state was so widely accepted among international lawyers (and by then they were often the only ones to attach importance to Grotius' work), that there are few if any traces

---

[12] Hirsch Lauterpacht, 'The Grotian Tradition in International Law' *British Year Book of International Law* 23 (1946), 1–53. More recently, A. Claire Cutler agrees that Grotius 'rejects the doctrine of the "reason of state"': 'The "Grotian Tradition"', p. 47. The view of Grotius as a humanitarian idealist is also a long-standing one: see, for example, Arthur Nussbaum, *A Concise History of the Law of Nations* (New York: Macmillan, 1947), p. 101.

[13] See, for example, Hedley Bull, 'Martin Wight and the Theory of International Relations' in Martin Wight, *International Theory: the Three Traditions* (New York: Holmes and Meier, 1992), pp. ix–xxiii.

of the alternative interpretation espoused by Tuck to be found during that period.

In comparison with the impressive detail in which his broader interpretive thesis on natural law theory is couched, Tuck only comments very briefly on the reasons for this dramatic change in Grotius' image, and what he has to say on the point is not entirely clear. In *Philosophy and Government*, he points to Kant as the key person who drove the late seventeenth-century reading of Grotius out of the history of moral philosophy, substituting a new narrative within which, by a happy but hardly surprising coincidence, the Kantian statement of the categorical imperative emerged as the pivotal moment in the development of a modern science of morality. In *The Rights of War and Peace*, by contrast, Kant has been included within the new naturalistic moral science created by Grotius and (especially) Hobbes, and the notion that he was primarily responsible for overturning this interpretation within the history of ideas is presumably in question, although Tuck does not explicitly deal with the issue here.[14]

In any event, whether or not Kant was responsible for expelling Grotius from the pantheon of great moral philosophers, Tuck's new reading still poses the question of why international legal thought on Grotius developed as it did, and that is a topic on which Tuck remains virtually silent.[15] He might have rescued Grotius for historians of moral philosophy, but this raises more questions than it answers for historians of international political and legal thought. If Grotius' contemporaries thought of him primarily as a 'moral scientist', whence did the belief that he was the 'father of modern international law' originate? How did Grotius become so inextricably involved with something so apparently divorced from his main intellectual concerns as the Peace of Westphalia? How did he become the animating personality behind an entire tradition of thought about the conditions for maintaining legal order in a society of independent sovereign states?

This enquiry speaks to the concern raised in the opening paragraph: the tendency for debate about the history of international political thought to revolve around a relatively small group of great thinkers, with everything turning on our interpretation or reinterpretation of

[14] Tuck, *Rights of War and Peace*, especially pp. 11–15, 207–25 and 228–31.
[15] His only gesture in this direction is to castigate, in rather a vague manner, the 'generation of scholars . . . funded by the Carnegie Endowment from the time of the First World War onwards, working under the influence of James Brown Scott': Tuck, *Rights of War and Peace*, p. 11.

239

their ideas and the connections or disagreements between them. It is not entirely facetious to say that much of what passes for the history of ideas in International Relations theory today amounts to little more than a discussion about the correct formation in which the 'First XI' should line up: is Grotius to play alongside Hobbes, or should they be placed on opposite wings? Tuck's reading is hugely welcome for having exposed previously neglected themes in Grotius' thought, and for compelling theorists of international politics or international law to reconsider their conventional wisdoms about the relationships between Grotius and Machiavelli, Hobbes, Rousseau and Kant. But it does not help us to understand where those conventional wisdoms came from, or where their power lies.

The development of the traditional image of Grotius

The conventional picture of Grotian eclecticism in international law would have been inconceivable without the broader proposition that European legal thought as a whole can be defined in terms of the dichotomy between naturalism and positivism. It is meaningless to speak of a 'middle way', after all, without first identifying two extremes on either side of it, and Grotius' method only seems eclectic because it cannot be subsumed under either one of these poles.[16] Of course, the distinction between natural and positive law speaks to a long-standing philosophical debate in Western legal thought, but, in the form it assumes in modern textbooks on international law, the divide is usually understood in a *chronological* way, and this is highly significant.

Natural law is presented as the signature of medieval scholarship on the law of nations, animated by the belief that there is a single, universal, eternal and divinely-ordained code that governs, or ought to govern, the conduct of all peoples in the world. It is admitted that this point of view may have made sense in a world where the Pope and the Emperor had plausible claims to universal lordship, but the collapse of the confessional and political unity of Christendom during the wars of the religion, and the rise of absolutist monarchs proclaiming their independent sovereignty over their own dynastic territories, destroyed the

[16] On this point, see David Kennedy, 'Primitive Legal Scholarship' *Harvard International Law Journal* 27 (1986), 1–98.

capacity of natural law to be an effective foundation for the *jus gentium*. It was replaced by positive law, which provided a consent-based theory of the sources of international obligations that was better suited to the voluntaristic climate of the society of states. Thus, as T. J. Lawrence put it, 'Modern International Law, of which Grotius must be considered the father, was in its origin an attempt to find a working substitute for the exploded theory of universal supremacy'.[17]

In other words, the distinction between naturalism and positivism that colours the international legal interpretation of Grotius is interwoven with an historical theory of the origins of the modern international society and legal order. This theory attaches colossal importance to the Peace of Westphalia of 1648 as the dividing moment between the two periods, on the grounds that, to quote Lawrence again,

> The progress of the new principles was clearly shown by the Peace of Westphalia. It was the first of a series of great international instruments which have regulated the state system of Europe down to our own time. It recognised the independence of each separate state, even within the boundaries of the Empire. The principles of the territorial character of sovereignty and the equality of states before the law were involved in the arrangements that it made. . . . Since 1648 International Law has had no rival system to contend with. . . . In spite of modifications and additions, it stands today the same in all essentials as Grotius left it in 1625.[18]

Here, then, we find that 'well-known combination' of the Grotian law of nations and the Westphalian international system.[19] But not for the first time. By the late nineteenth century, the idea was already so deeply ingrained in the minds of international lawyers that Lawrence's version of it is but one among several, in most of which the claim is seen as so commonplace and so well-established that it is seldom presented with any further justificatory argument.[20]

---

[17] T. J. Lawrence, 'The Work of Grotius as a Reformer of International Law', in *Essays on some Disputed Questions in Modern International Law* (Cambridge: Deighton, Bell and Co., 1884), p. 187. For a more recent statement, along similar lines, see Cutler, 'The "Grotian Tradition"', p. 49.

[18] Lawrence, 'The Work of Grotius', pp. 189–190.

[19] C. G. Roelofsen, 'Grotius and the "Grotian Heritage" in International Law and International Relations: the Quarcentenary and its Aftermath (circa. 1980–90)', *Grotiana* 11 (1990), p. 8.

[20] For a couple of other prominent late nineteenth-century examples, see Travers Twiss, *The Law of Nations Considered as Independent Political Communities* (Oxford: Oxford University Press, 1861), pp. iii–iv, and Thomas Alfred Walker, *The Science of International Law* (London: C. J. Clay & Sons, 1893), p. 91. Nevertheless, Lawrence's interpretation was

Indeed, international lawyers had already been making essentially the same point for at least fifty or sixty years. In the early 1840s, for instance, Henry Wheaton had described Westphalia as marking 'the epoch of the firm establishment of permanent legations, by which the pacific relations of the European states have been since maintained; and which . . . contributed to give a more practical character to the new science created by Grotius and improved by his successors'.[21] Another prominent international lawyer of the early nineteenth century, William Manning, similarly argued that Grotius 'had the happiness of being exactly adapted to the times in which he lived, for had he lived much earlier he would have found Europe unfitted for the reception of his doctrines; and his times required a mind like that of Grotius, the new relations of the European powers needing reference to settled principles for their guidance'.[22]

There is a certain synchronicity between the publication of *De Jure Belli ac Pacis* (in 1625) and the signing of the Peace of Westphalia (in 1648), but it is hardly obvious that the two events should be linked together as the founding of the modern era in international law. Grotius himself was, of course, profoundly affected by the Thirty Years War, but it is surely more plausible to suggest that a subject closer to his mind, even when he wrote *De Jure Belli ac Pacis*, would still have been the Dutch revolt against Philip II of Spain and their struggle against the Portuguese, with which his earlier works on the law of nations had principally dealt, anticipating prominent themes in his later masterpiece as they did so.[23] The Dutch war with Spain ended in 1648 with another Treaty, signed in January rather than October (when the Peace of Westphalia proper was finally agreed), but one hears relatively little about it in

an influential one for twentieth-century international theory, especially in its impact on Wight's thinking. I have discussed this elsewhere, both in *Beyond the Anarchical Society*, and, more fully, in 'The Reception of Hugo Grotius in International Relations Theory', *Grotiana* 20/21 (1999/2000), 137–60.

[21] Henry Wheaton, *History of the Law of Nations in Europe and America, from the Earliest Times to the Treaty of Washington, 1842* (New York: Garland Publishing, 1973), pp. 71–72. Although I make the point only tentatively in this context, it is at least worth noting that in this earlier account we begin to find traces of Grotius' importance framed in terms of his contribution to the development of international law as a *science*. I will return to this in a moment.

[22] William Manning, *Commentaries on the Law of Nations* (London: Sweet, 1839), p. 21.

[23] Hugo Grotius, 'Commentarius in Theses XI': an Early Treatise on Sovereignty, the Just War and the Legitimacy of the Dutch Revolt, trans. Peter Borschberg (Berne: Peter Lang, 1994); and Grotius, *De Jure Praedae Commentarius*, trans. Gwladys Williams (Buffalo: William S. Hein, 1995).

conventional legal histories on Grotius' work, and certainly less than one hears about the other Westphalian treaties between France, Sweden and the Emperor.[24]

Similarly, why should so much importance be vested in the Peace of Westphalia as such a pivotal legal instrument? The Peace did not proclaim the Augsburgian principle of *cuius regio eius religio*, which is often supposed to lie at the heart of the modern practice of toleration in the society of states; the bulk of its text was taken up with accommodations for the various parties who had been engaged in the war, often with little demonstrable significance for the further development of modern international relations; and, Lawrence's claims on its behalf notwithstanding, the Westphalian recognition of the principle of 'territorial sovereignty' was specific to the internal constitution of the Holy Roman Empire, defining a limited set of privileges held by the German states that fell well short of outright independence from imperial authority.[25] In a host of ways, Westphalia is an odd choice of starting-point from which to date the origins of the modern era, and that applies *a fortiori* to the Grotian-Westphalian conjunction.

How, then, have we come by the ideas that the Peace of Westphalia was not only the origin of the modern international society, but also that it served as the practical realization of Grotius' theoretical scheme of the law of nations? To answer this question, we need to take a quick look at three distinct literatures on international law and politics that emerged in the two centuries after Grotius' death. As I suggested in the introduction, by shining a spotlight on Grotius, historians of ideas have left many of these other authors in shadow. What follows, then, is an exercise in trying to recover a proper sense of the various ways in which people thought and wrote about international politics and international law in the hundred or hundred and fifty years after Grotius' death, during which time the conventional image of him as the father of an international legal theory suited to the 'Westphalian system' very gradually began to take shape.

---

[24] A notable exception is Wheaton, *History of the Law of Nations*, p. 70.

[25] An entertaining broadside against the absurdity of the orthodox view on the importance of Westphalia can be found in Stephen Krasner, 'Westphalia and all that', in Judith Goldstein and Robert Keohane (eds.), *Ideas and Foreign Policy* (Ithaca: Cornell University Press, 1993), pp. 235–264. An earlier source, containing an excellent discussion of Westphalia's implications for the imperial constitution is Johann Stephan Pütter, *An Historical Development of the Present Political Constitution of the Germanic Empire*, trans. Josiah Dornford, 3 vols. (London: 1790).

Forms of early modern international political thought

First, as most historians and International Relations theorists are well aware, there was a great deal of work that explicitly sought to develop Grotius' own system of the law of nations, whether by refining his conception of natural law, developing his theory of the role played by state volition, or building on his own eclectic method to produce an updated version of the content of contemporary natural and volitional legal rules. The classic references here are, in turn, Samuel Pufendorf, Cornelis Bynkershoek, and Christian Wolff and Emmerich de Vattel. Discussions of these authors as the successors to Grotius can be found in almost any textbook on international law, and in many on international political thought as well. These authors tended to be rather abstract philosophers of the law of nations. Although some, notably Pufendorf, did engage in empirically detailed historical studies of quasi-international legal systems such as the imperial constitution, in the theoretical juristic works for which they are most famed they typically engaged in only marginal analyses of treaties as a source of law. Little in their work, in other words, explains the Grotius-Westphalia connection which is so central to modern international law.[26] Their subsequent development of some Grotian ideas was crucial to the elaboration of the positivist-naturalist dichotomy as an organizing device for the history of international legal thought, but that alone is insufficient to grasp the origins of the conventional image of Grotius.

Quite distinct from this, however, was a more strategically-inclined, and far less legalistic, literature on the balance of power, worked out by seventeenth- and eighteenth-century commentators like Slingsby Bethel, John Campbell, James Howell, Francois-Paul de Lisola and Henri de Rohan.[27] The last of these was one of the real celebrities of the genre, having acted as the leader of the Huguenot faction during the

[26] For a good recent survey, see Tuck, *Rights of War and Peace* (which, incidentally, illustrates the lack of direct attention that these scholars paid to the content of European treaties, including the Peace of Westphalia).

[27] For a survey of thought on this topic from the relevant period, see Michael Sheehan, *Balance of Power: History and Theory* (London: Routledge, 1996), pp. 29–52. See also Keene, *International Political Thought: A Historical Introduction* (Cambridge: Polity Press, 2005), Chapter 4. In my view, one of the most interesting texts here, which has moments where it anticipates current International Relations theory to a remarkable degree, is John Campbell, *The Present State of Europe, Explaining the Interests, Connections, Political and Commercial Views of its Several Powers*, 3rd edn, (London: Longman, 1752). Other references are James Howell, *Lustra Ludovici, or the Life of the Late Victorious King of France, Lewis the XIII (and of his Cardinal de Richelieu)* (London: Humphrey Moseley, 1646); François Paul de

religious wars in France, before writing a classic treatise on reason of state: *The Interest of the Princes and States of Christendom*.[28] Rohan eschewed the time-honoured philosophical methods of enquiry into the law of nations, whether rationalist or theological. Understanding the interests of the state, he argued, was not something that could be done through abstract speculation about the eternal, divinely-sanctioned laws of nature, nor even through the historical study of examples of statesmanship from the past: 'one cannot establish an immutable rule for the government of states, because revolutions in world affairs change the fundamental maxims of policy'.[29] According to Rohan, the only way to survive was to pay constant attention to one's immediate political environment, and above all keep track of the activities and interests of other powers (*puissances*).

Thus, for example, he suggested that all rulers should keep a close eye on the two mighty states of Spain and France, which dominated Christendom 'like two poles'.[30] Rohan concluded that the true interest of France lay in thwarting Spanish ambitions. If France could match Spanish military power in this way, not only would it serve its own interests, but it stood to win the gratitude of all the other princes and states of Christendom by preserving a balance (*contrepoids*) that was essential to the continuing survival of the lesser powers.[31] Gradually, in the works of other authors, this was developed into a general thesis that European princes should unite to resist projects of 'universal monarchy' in order to preserve their individual 'liberties'.[32] Grotius, like other jurisprudential scholars, seldom figured in this literature as an important influence.

At the same time, and even more important for our purposes here, there was a third literature, written by international lawyers but not so much concerned with the doctrinal discussions of Pufendorf et al., nor with pragmatic advice about how to preserve the balance of power *à la* Rohan, as with the need to provide for practising diplomats a sketch of the current state of play in agreements among European rulers. The main work of these authors was to produce compendia of major treaties, often with detailed commentaries on the negotiations leading up to them and an analysis of their implications for what rulers could

---

Lisola, *The Buckler of State and Justice* (London: James Fisher, 1667); and Slingsby Bethel, *The Interest of Princes and States* (London: John Wickins, 1680).

[28] Henri de Rohan, *De l'intérêt des princes et des états de la chrétienté*, ed. Christian Lazzeri (Paris: Presses Universitaires de France, 1995).

[29] Rohan, *De l'intérêt*, p. 159.   [30] Ibid., p. 161.   [31] Ibid., pp. 171 and 173.

[32] Lisola, *Buckler of State*, is an excellent example.

or could not legally do. Amidst all the attention that has been paid to celebrities like Grotius, this literature has been almost completely neglected by both International Relations theorists and international lawyers, which is shameful in view of its considerable importance for modern international legal thought. Probably the most respected work at the time was Jean Dumont's *Corps universel diplomatique du droit des gens*.[33] Other noteworthy texts are Frederic Leonard's *Recueil des traitez de paix*, and Jean-Yves de Saint-Prest's *Histoire des traités de paix et autres négotiations*.[34] Interestingly, in view of the importance that Westphalia has since acquired, although all recognized the Peace as important, only a few treated it as a really distinctive breaking point in the history of the European legal order.[35]

Initially, while one or two of these texts paid tribute to Grotius, they were quite explicit about the fact that they were engaged in a substantially different kind of enquiry, one that was more empirically-based than his abstract reflections.[36] Later in the eighteenth century, however, the pretensions of treaty-historians grew to the point where they proffered their work as an alternative to the general systems of the natural lawyers. They began to argue that, 'by comparing the treaties that the powers of Europe have made with one another, we discover certain principles, that have been almost universally adopted by all the powers that have made treaties on the same subject'.[37] And, as they made this larger thesis, they increasingly began to invoke Grotius' name as an authoritative source for their approach, claiming him 'as the father of this science'.[38]

During the eighteenth century, and especially under the pressure of the French Revolution, the once-distinct lines between these literatures

---

[33] Published in Amsterdam (for Brunel) in1726.

[34] Published in Paris, 1693 and Amsterdam (for Bernard) in 1725, respectively.

[35] See 'S.W.', *A General Collection of Treatys, Declarations of War, Manifestos and other Publick Papers, Relating to Peace and War among the Potentates of Europe, from 1648 to the Present Time*, 4 vols. (London: Andrew Bell, 1710–1732), and Fr. Bougeant, *Histoire des guerres et des négociations qui precederent le traité de Westphalie*, 6 vols. (Paris: P. J. Mariette, 1751).

[36] Dumont, *Corps universel*, vol. I, pp. i–iv.

[37] G. F. von Martens, *Summary of the Law of Nations, Founded on the Treaties and Customs of the Modern Nations of Europe, with a list of the Principal Treaties Concluded since the year 1748 down to the Present Time, Indicating the Works in which they are to be found*, trans. William Cobbett (Philadelphia: Thomas Bradford, 1795), pp. 3–4.

[38] Ibid., p. 8. A similar point can be found in Robert Plumer Ward, *An Enquiry into the Foundation and History of the Law of Nations in Europe*, 2 vols. (London: Butterworth, 1795), especially the final two chapters. (But note also that, even at this late stage, little explicit reference is made to the Peace of Westphalia as the founding instrument of the European order.)

became blurred.[39] Bull partially captured this development in his observation that, in Grotius' time, theories on the law of nations and the balance of power had originally been

> held by different groups of persons and in their respective contexts were largely antithetical. But in the eighteenth century the two streams converged, as in the writings of Vattel international law came to take account of the balance of power, and in the writings of [Edmund] Burke and later [Friedrich von] Gentz the political maxim enjoining the preservation of a balance of power came to be defined in a more legalistic way.[40]

What this misses, however, is the importance of the third literature based on the legal analysis of European treaties. This, rather than Vattel's doctrine on natural law and the law of nations, formed the real bridge across which the counter-revolutionary theorists like Gentz pursued their effort to define the balance of power system in more legalistic terms. The doctrine that emerged treated European public order as founded on a series of treaties between dynastic rulers, and pointed to the balance of power as its defining institution.

A key work here was Cristophe-Guillaume Koch's *Short History of Peace Treaties*, which made extensive, one might even say liberal, use of the provisions in the Peace of Westphalia on the 'territorial sovereignty' of the constituents of the Holy Roman Empire to argue that the balance of power and the liberties of sovereign princes had been legally established as the basis of the European political system.[41] This line of argument was then picked up by the extraordinarily influential historians at the University of Göttingen, most notably A. H. L. Heeren, to produce a general account of how the modern states-system had developed out of the ruins of medieval Christendom. Understandably, given his desire to impugn the Napoleonic imperial system as a tyrannical abuse of the traditional rights of other European states (including, of course, his own), Heeren laid overwhelming emphasis on the principles of 'internal

---

[39] I have also discussed this development in *Beyond the Anarchical Society*, especially Chapter 1.

[40] Hedley Bull, 'Society and Anarchy in International Relations', in Herbert Butterfield and Martin Wight (eds.), *Diplomatic Investigations: Essays on the Theory of International Politics* (London: George Allen & Unwin, 1966), p. 39, and see also his similar, but even more general comment in *The Anarchical Society: a Study of Order in World Politics* (London: Macmillan, 1977), p. 33.

[41] Cristophe Guillaume Koch and Maximilian Frederic Schoell, *Histoire abrégé des traités de paix, entre les puissances de l'Europe, depuis la paix de Westphalie*, revised edition (Paris: Gide, 1817).

freedom' and dynastic monarchy as the established and lawful pillars of order in modern Europe.[42]

After 1815, then, when international lawyers began to write new textbooks on the post-revolutionary law of nations, what they had to go on was a pre- or counter-revolutionary literature that seemed to be built on two prominent claims: Martens' statement that Grotius was the 'father' of the modern science of studying international law through the historical analysis of treaties; and Heeren's proposition that the fundamental principles of the modern European system, especially relating to the equality and independence of territorially sovereign states, had been established by the Peace of Westphalia. Rather than abandon one or the other of these cherished doctrines, they reconciled them through the now-familiar thesis that Grotius' theory had anticipated Westphalian practice. Grotius' theory of the law of nations was, it was now argued, based on the doctrine of the equality, independence and territorial sovereignty of states: precisely the principles, in other words, that their histories told them had been enshrined in 1648.[43]

This doctrine rested on rather flimsy evidence, and several lawyers noted that much of Grotius' actual discussion of *summum imperium* and so forth did not really correspond to their version of him. They dealt with the problem, however, in a way that reinforced their claims about the structure of the modern international system: Grotius' theory, they argued, was imperfect because he had not yet fully liberated himself from the shackles of medieval theory and practice. He still hankered after the religious and political unity of Christendom, and his grasp of the new dynamics of the states-system was understandably defective, since the system had not yet been fully established.[44] At a stroke, the awkward details of Grotius' actual writings could not only be explained away, but could actually be used as further evidence to colour in the differences between the medieval and modern patterns of international political and legal order.

The result was an interpretation of Grotius as the 'father' of a science of international law predicated on the method of treaty analysis, and as the purveyor of the substantive doctrine that the legal order

---

[42] A. H. L. Heeren, *A Manual of the History of the Political System of Europe and its Colonies*, trans. from fifth German edition, 2 vols. (Oxford: D. A. Talboys, 1834). On the influence of the 'Göttingen school' see Herbert Butterfield, *Man on his Past* (Cambridge: Cambridge University Press, 1955), and Herbert Butterfield, *The Origins of History*, ed. Adam Watson (London: Eyre Methuen, 1981).

[43] See, for example, Twiss, *Law of Nations*, p. v.

[44] A good early example is Manning, *Commentaries*, pp. 21ff.

was founded on the principle of the equality and independence of territorially sovereign states, subsequently to be realized by the Peace of Westphalia. This interpretation flowed from the counter-revolutionary historical and legal scholarship of the early nineteenth century; it gradually made its way into the textbooks between 1815 and the 1840s; and by the 1860s it had, to all intents and purposes, achieved the status of an axiom. The masterstroke was that any potential difficulties that might have arisen from the fact that the conventional interpretation bore scant resemblance to Grotius' actual description of the law of nations was not just defused, but was turned into a positive blessing for orthodox thinkers by being used to illustrate the backwardness, incoherence and idealism of medieval scholarship, in contrast to the systematic and practical rigour of the moderns.[45] 'Eclecticism' became the last piece in the jigsaw of the conventional legal wisdom, placing Grotius neatly at the Westphalian turning-point when the modern age was presumed to be beginning.

Imagining Grotius today

The textbook legal interpretation of Grotius that I have just outlined is, of course, still alive and well today.[46] The problem we face in unpacking how International Relations theorists currently think about Grotius is more complicated than can be understood simply in terms of the version of his work presented by nineteenth-century international lawyers. It is not an exaggeration to say that most students of International Relations, even experts on the history of thought about International Relations, are unfamiliar with the legal textbooks in which the conventional wisdom on Grotius was developed.[47] Nowadays, Grotius' work is seldom

---

[45] I should acknowledge that there were a few exceptional international legal scholars who pointed out the inaccuracies of this interpretation. Henry Sumner Maine, *International Law: The Whewell Lectures of 1887* (London: John Murray, 1915) is tantalizing, but tends to skirt the central point a bit; P. J. Baker, 'The Doctrine of Legal Equality of States', *British Year Book of International Law* 4 (1923–24), p. 7 is spot on, but also serves to reveal the enduring dominance of the conventional wisdom. To the best of my knowledge, the point that the Peace of Westphalia also did not fit its appointed role was not seriously developed by any nineteenth-century international lawyers, but that is a sweeping claim, and I could easily be wrong.

[46] Bull's work is replete with examples: see *The Anarchical Society*, pp. 27–38, and 'The importance of Grotius in the Study of International Relations' in Hedley Bull, Benedict Kingsbury and Adam Roberts (eds.). *Hugo Grotius and International Relations* (Oxford: Clarendon Press, 1992), pp. 65–93, especially pp. 75–78, 79, 87 and 89–91.

[47] Historical surveys of International Relations theory after Grotius usually draw their material instead from the canons of social and political theory: see, for instance, Kenneth

studied in conjunction with the works of scholars like Martens or Koch, but rather is placed alongside the treatises of thinkers who are presumed to be of equivalent stature, like Machiavelli, Hobbes and Kant. Grotius has become, in other words, a political philosopher of international society rather than a jurisprudential theorist of the law of nations.

This change has largely happened through the efforts of members of the so-called 'Grotian tradition' in International Relations theory, notably the 'English School' of Martin Wight and Hedley Bull. I have discussed how they constructed their interpretation of Grotius elsewhere,[48] and will not repeat that analysis at length here. The key move was Wight's decision to frame a new category of 'international theory' that combined legal and political thought in one historical scheme.[49] Legal traditions, like Grotianism, thus mingled with, and gradually acquired the characteristics of, political traditions of thought. This was carried even further by Bull, who, unlike Wight, almost completely erased the original legal context of the Grotian tradition and much more unequivocally located Grotius within the context of international political thought.[50]

One effect of this slippage within the English school's image of Grotius is the reinforcement of the rather questionable interpretation of his account of the law of nations as an anticipation of the Westphalian system. Indeed, in some respects the more narrowly legalistic interpretation of Grotius has gained some authority because it may be used as an apparently more authentic reading, in comparison with the stretch involved in Bull's equation of Grotianism with Wightian 'rationalism'.[51] As even more far-fetched invocations of Grotius' name appear in international political thought, so the English school's version comes to acquire a seeming authenticity in its own turn.[52] A further effect has been that the intellectual origins of the classic legal interpretation of Grotius have been

Thompson, *Fathers of International Thought: the Legacy of Political Theory* (Baton Rouge: Louisiana State University Press, 1994), and Torbjørn Knutsen, *A History of International Relations Theory* (Manchester: Manchester University Press, 1992).

[48] *Beyond the Anarchical Society*, Chapter 1; and 'The Reception of Hugo Grotius'.

[49] Wight, *International Theory*.

[50] As well as Bull, 'Martin Wight and the Theory of International Relations', see my analysis of debates about Grotianism within the English School: 'The Development of the Concept of International Society: an Essay on Political Argument in International Relations Theory', in Michi Ebata and Beverly Neufeld (eds.), *Confronting the Political in International Relations* (London: Macmillan, 2000), pp. 34–37.

[51] See, for example, Cutler, 'The "Grotian tradition"'.

[52] See, for example, Martha Finnemore's criticisms of the description of regime theory as 'Grotian' in *National Interests in International Society* (Ithaca NY: Cornell University Press, 1996), p. 19n. As Finnemore notes, Wight's and Bull's interpretations of Grotius (she seems

concealed, or at least obscured, since few theorists of International Relations look beyond Wight or Bull in trying to understand how Grotius should be understood. Wight and Bull are therefore often seen as having created this interpretation of the Grotian tradition rather than, as was really the case, merely having given the traditional story one or two novel twists.

Conclusion

We have seen how Grotius first became identified as the 'father' of something that its exponents called the 'science' of 'modern international law'. We have seen how this science came to be associated with the 'Westphalian' rejection of universal monarchy and an endorsement of the balance of power. And we have seen how these origins of the 'Grotian tradition' have been cloaked by a relocation of that tradition in the context of political philosophies of International Relations rather than jurisprudential debates about the law of nations. All of this explains why the real origins of the idea of a Grotian tradition in international law have become obscure. It also indicates the range of early modern international political thought that has been masked by the excessive attention that International Relations theorists have paid to Grotius. To the extent that Tuck's new interpretation returns Grotius to a tradition of enquiry grounded in moral philosophy, this may perhaps even liberate historians of international political thought to escape from the fixation with Grotius, and begin instead to adopt a more open-minded approach to the early modern period.

This would be valuable because the conventional image of Grotius reinforces one particular way of thinking about international relations in the sixteenth and seventeenth centuries. It highlights the emergence of the 'Westphalian system' in western Europe, and treats both the theory and practice of early modern international politics as a gradual leading-up to the establishment of this modern states-system. Alternative dimensions of international political thought and practice, such as republicanism or imperialism,[53] are thus overlooked. Moreover, whole

to see no significant difference between them) are 'more faithful' to Grotius than regime theory. True enough, but it should not lead to the conclusion that their interpretations are unimpeachable.

[53] On the former, see Nicholas Onuf, *The Republican Legacy in International Political Thought* (Cambridge: Cambridge University Press, 1998); on the latter, see Keene, *Beyond the Anarchical Society*.

literatures, most importantly the treaty collections of Dumont and others, have been systematically neglected, in favour of a concentration on a small group of thinkers who are seen as having anticipated the subsequent development of a system of sovereign states. We might use these historical examples drawn from the early modern period to illustrate other forms of international interaction than anarchic inter-state relations, and thus give ourselves a better sense of the peculiarity of certain aspects of our world. By interpreting the sixteenth and seventeenth centuries in the conventional terms of eighteenth- and nineteenth-century international legal thought, however, we merely give the latter a timeless quality that makes them seem like unalterable fixtures. When we fail to locate the conventional image of Grotius in terms of its own ideological origins, we allow it to be part of an ideological conception of world politics that persists today.

11 The Hobbesian theory of international relations: three traditions

Michael C. Williams

Describing International Relations (IR) as a realm of 'Hobbesian anarchy' remains one of the most popular shorthand descriptions of the nature of world politics. To invoke Hobbes is to call forth the image of a world of conflict and perpetual danger, a 'Realist' vision of international politics as a 'state of nature' defined by continual insecurity, competition and potential or actual conflict. As is often the case with the use of classical political thinkers in IR, these references tend to be cursory, with declarations of world politics as a condition of 'Hobbesian anarchy' or a 'Hobbesian state of war' serving more as rhetorical or metaphorical markers than as full analytic accounts of either Hobbes' vision of international politics or its historical validity and contemporary relevance. This chapter has two goals. First, I provide a reading of Hobbes' vision of international relations that highlights its relationship to his political thinking as a whole, and especially to his concern with the relationship between knowledge and practice. I argue that Hobbes was concerned with what we would today perhaps call the social construction of politics, and that his work can be read as an attempt both to explicate the foundations of politics and an attempt to reconstruct politics in the light of them. Hobbes' vision of international politics can only be properly reconstructed and understood in the light of his concerns with the nature of political order as a whole and with the constitution of domestic political orders.

In the second section of the chapter, I briefly examine the implications of this understanding for different appreciations and appropriations of Hobbes' legacy in IR today. The understanding of Hobbes' view of international politics I develop here challenges fundamentally those positions which view him as a rationalist theorist of international anarchy, as well as presenting challenges to the much more subtle and sophisticated view developed within the English School of international society. At the same time, it also allows for a broader reassessment of his legacy in IR. Uncovering this legacy requires stepping outside the confines of contemporary IR theory, to examine (albeit only briefly and suggestively in this context) perhaps the most striking engagement with Hobbes' thinking in the twentieth century: the revival of Hobbes in Weimar Germany. Examining the debates over Hobbes that took place in this period – particularly between Carl Schmitt and Leo Strauss – provides essential elements in understanding the intellectual context within which Hans Morgenthau developed the theory of political realism that was to have such a profound impact on the development of IR. Perhaps even more intriguingly, these debates also provide insights into the origins of contemporary American neoconservatism.

Foundations

As has often been noted, Hobbes' specific reflections on international politics are rare, and nowhere does he develop systematically his views on the subject. As a consequence, it is necessary to try to reconstruct his vision of international relations from his broader understanding of the foundations of politics. At the heart of this position is an analysis of the relationship between knowledge and politics.[1] As numerous philosophical treatments have argued at length, the central intellectual context in which Hobbes' thought must be located is the 'crise pyrrhonnienne' of the sixteenth and seventeenth centuries.[2] Knowledge of the truth about empirical and moral questions, he argued, is purely knowledge of things as they *appear* to us as conditioned by our individual appetites and aversions. As Richard Tuck has noted, in this regard Hobbes' 'crucial idea . . . was simply to treat what is perceived by man – the images and so on which are immediately apparent to an internal observer – as bearing no

---

[1] This section draws upon the analysis in Michael C. Williams, *The Realist Tradition and the Limits of International Relations* (Cambridge: Cambridge University Press, 2005).

[2] See Richard Tuck, 'Optics and Sceptics: the Philosophical Foundations of Hobbes's Political Thought' in Edmund Leites (ed.), *Conscience and Casuistry in Early Modern Europe* (Cambridge: Cambridge University Press, 1988); Richard Tuck, *Hobbes* (Oxford: Oxford University Press, 1989); Richard Flathman, *Thomas Hobbes: Scepticism, Individuality and Chastened Politics* (London: Sage, 1993); and also Richard Popkin, *A History of Scepticism: from Erasmus to Spinoza* (Berkeley: University of California Press, 1979). However, as Quentin Skinner has argued, it is important not to overstate the sceptical dimension of Hobbes' thinking, since Hobbes retains a strong commitment to the role of reason, however powerful scepticism and rhetoric may be. Quentin Skinner, *Visions of Politics, Vol.3: Hobbes and Civil Science* (Cambridge: Cambridge University Press, 2002), pp. 79 and 88.

relationship of *verisimilitude* to the external world. Man is effectively a prisoner within the cell of his own mind, and has no idea what in reality lies outside his prison walls . . .'[3] Empirical knowledge is always hypothetical and conjectural; there is no way to get behind the appearances to the thing itself.[4] *Rational* knowledge, by contrast, is like a language: it consists of a set of formal definitions and relational rules. For Hobbes, truth is not an objective characteristic of things, but rather resides in a set of accepted and logically related frameworks of definitions and referents. Or, to put this another way, in Hobbes' philosophical nominalism truth is a function of logic and language, not of the relation between language and some extralinguistic 'reality'.[5]

This view extends to the question of moral knowledge as well.[6] That which we view as good, or beneficial, is not so in itself, but is so only because it appears to us as such. And since these perceptions are inescapably conditioned by the different appetites and aversions of each individual, there is no natural harmony or order amongst them. In *Leviathan*, for example, he puts the point this way: 'whatsoever is the object of any man's appetite or desire that is it which he for his part calleth *good*; and the object of his hate and aversion, *evil*; and of his contempt, *vile* and *inconsiderable*. For these words of good, evil, and contemptibel are ever used with relation to the person that useth them, there being nothing simply and absolutely so, nor any common rule of good and evil to be taken from the nature of the objects themselves . . .'[7] In *De Cive*, he phrases the issue more simply still, holding that: 'Wherever *good* and *evil* are measured by the mere diversity of present desires, and hence by a corresponding diversity of yardsticks, those who act in this way will find themselves still in a state of war'.[8]

This helps explain the extraordinary stress which Hobbes places on the definitions and relations of words throughout his political philosophy, a stress clearly linked to his thinking on the question of moral and practical judgment and action. Words and concepts are not pale reflections of an 'objective' reality – they are fundamental constituents of the

---

[3] Tuck, *Hobbes*, p. 40.
[4] As Jan Blits has argued, the generalized fear that Hobbes sees as the prime motivation for action is not reducible solely to a fear of the potential actions of others. It is constituted by a more fundamental fear of the unknown – and in some basic ways unknowable – nature of reality as a whole. Jan Blits, 'Hobbesian Fear' *Political Theory* 17 (1989), p. 425.
[5] I am thankful to Ross Rudolph for stressing the importance of this point to me.
[6] See particularly, Quentin Skinner, 'Hobbes on Rhetoric and the Construction of Morality' *Visions of Politics, Vol.3*, pp. 87–141.
[7] Hobbes, *Leviathan* (Indianapolis: Hackett, 1993), p. 28.
[8] Quoted in Skinner, *Visions of Politics, Vol.3*, p. 20.

reality of the agents that use them to make sense of their worlds. In this sense, the social world is fundamentally constructed out of the beliefs that individuals have about themselves and their world. As Andrej Rapaczynski has insightfully noted, for Hobbes: 'Acting on those beliefs that they actually have about themselves, men, being authors of their own actions, *create* the truth of their own beliefs . . . Political science is, more than any other, concerned with postulates and definitions, because what men postulate with respect to the relations of power among themselves they very often *ipso facto* bring about'.[9] Or, as Hobbes tersely expressed it: 'the Actions of men proceed from their Opinions'.[10]

This view of Hobbes' state of nature differs considerably from those who portray it as the outcome of materially self-interested rational actors competing for the same scarce goods within a condition of epistemic agreement. In the view that emerges from an engagement with Hobbes' philosophical nominalism, by contrast, the state of nature derives from precisely the *lack* of any such commonality. In the state of nature, individuals construct their own realities, their own understandings of what is good and bad, desirable and undesirable, threatening and unthreatening, and act on the basis of these beliefs. Lacking agreement on what the world *is*, as well as over what it ought to be, the state of nature is anarchic in a sense far deeper than that captured by the 'security dilemmas', or 'coordination problems' or logics of 'relative gains' so beloved by rationalist thinkers.

What is more, beliefs themselves can represent important elements of conflict. Insult, for example, is not a threat to an individual's material wellbeing, but as an assault upon a person's idea of 'honour'; and insults may well provoke reactions in which the dread of dishonour outweighs fears of death or physical harm. This is an essential aspect of the pride and 'vainglory' that loom so large in Hobbes' thinking. Precisely because they are *beliefs* these commitments are not susceptible to rational discussion or determination, and they may have little or no relation to material interests. Indeed they frequently overwhelm material interests, and are at the heart of the dynamics of fear, distrust and animosity.[11] The modern jibe that it is difficult to convince people to go to war to protect

---

[9] Andrezj Rapaczynski, *Nature and Politics: Liberalism in the Philosophy of Hobbes, Locke and Rousseau* (Ithaca NY: Cornell University Press, 1987), p. 109.
[10] Hobbes, *Leviathan*, p. 233. See also the excellent discussion of 'Hobbes's Irrational Man' that is Chapter 3 of Steven Holmes' *Passions and Constraint* (Chicago: University of Chicago Press, 1995).
[11] Holmes, *Passions and Constraint*, p. 84.

a market is one that Hobbes was more than familiar with. His worry, by contrast, was that the centrality of belief and the remarkable power of rhetoric to mobilize action made it much easier to convince people to kill and die for considerably less tangible goals – be they creed, religion or honour; in short, for beliefs.[12]

In the state of nature, even the fear of death which Hobbes considers universal is unable to create order. For even if all agreed on the desirability of physical self-preservation above all else (which, as will be discussed in a moment, Hobbes doubts), this would not mean that all could agree on what the threats to that preservation were, on how to react to them, or how best to secure themselves against them. Conflict is not simply intrinsic to humanity's potential for aggression, nor can it be attributed to (or resolved by) straightforward utilitarian calculations of competing and conflicting interests. The state of nature is defined not just by a lack of trust, but much more fundamentally by a condition of epistemological indeterminacy which renders even the universal fear of death at best a partial remedy, and the existence of conflict and mistrust endemic.

A central goal of Hobbes' state of nature is to demonstrate to individuals (in a context dominated by the Thirty Years War and the English Civil War) the importance of the relationship between knowledge claims, political authority and social peace. A return to the state of nature is a metaphor (and a warning) illuminating the dynamics of social conflict arising from the absence of both cultural consensus and a sovereign authority to fix meanings, determine contested facts and the like. By demonstrating the foundations of the state of war that is the state of nature, Hobbes seeks to convince individuals of the need for a sovereign authority, and of their need to obey it. Moreover, he seeks to provide a rational foundation for political authority that would supplant the now unstable and unsustainable beliefs of traditional political authorities. In the escape from the state of nature that Hobbes proposes, the individual does not simply alienate the 'right to all things' to a political authority. More fundamentally, what is granted to that authority is the right to decide upon irresolvably contested truths: to provide the authoritative criteria of what is, and thus to remove people from the state of epistemic and ethical indeterminacy that is the basis of the state of nature.

---

[12] Ibid., p. 81. For a contemporary exploration of this theme, see Judith Butler, *Excitable Speech* (London: Routledge, 1996).

Hobbes uses his scepticism both to show the necessity of his solution and to destroy (what he views as dogmatic) counter-claims to political authority based upon unsupportable (individual) claims to truth. In arguing against individual claims against the authority of the sovereign in *De Cive*, Hobbes puts it in the following way: '*the knowledge of good and evil belongs to each single man*. In the state of nature indeed, where every man lives by equal right, and has not by any mutual pacts submitted to the command of others, we have granted this to be true; nay, [proved it] . . . [But in the civil state it is false. For it was shown . . .] that the civil laws were the rules of *good* and *evil*, *just* and *unjust*, *honest* and *dishonest*; that therefore what the legislator commands, must be held for *good*, and what he forbids for *evil*'.[13] Earlier in the same work he had phrased the argument even more unequivocally, noting that since 'the opinions of men differ concerning *meum* and *tuum*, *just* and *unjust*, *profitable* and *unprofitable*, *good* and *evil*, *honest* and *dishonest*, and the like; which every man esteems according to his own judgement: it belongs to the same chief power to make some common rules for all men, and to declare them publicly, by which every man may know what may be called his, what another's, what just, what unjust, what honest, what dishonest, what good, what evil; that is summarily, what is to be done, what to be avoided in our common course of life'. It follows that for Hobbes: 'All judgment therefore, in a city, belongs to him who hath the swords; that is, to him who hath the supreme authority'.[14]

For Hobbes, epistemic claims and political claims are clearly connected. A fundamental reason why the Sovereign must be unchallengeable in definitional matters is that to rebel against this authority is to return to the subjectively relative claim to know and the conflict which, for Hobbes, this inevitably entails. This is why the Sovereign ultimately must control language (definitions of what is), and explains his repeated stress on the importance of education (and sovereign control over its institutions) rather than straightforward coercion as the essential element in a successful Sovereign's rule.[15] For Hobbes, mistaken claims about the foundations of knowledge were a source of mistaken political beliefs and were thus at the heart of the conflict he saw around

---

[13] Hobbes, *De Cive*, (Indianapolis: Hackett, 1993), p. 244.

[14] Hobbes, *De Cive*; see also *Leviathan* p. 28, and the rendition in Tuck, *Hobbes*, p. 65. As Skinner has noted, for Hobbes if we wish to fix 'our moral language unambiguously onto the world, we can only hope to do so by fiat. His conclusion is sceptical, and does little to uphold the dignity of moral philosophy. For all that, however, he may be right'; *Visions of Politics, Vol. 3*., p. 141.

[15] Hobbes, *De Cive*, pp. 262–263.

him. Interpretive dissent leads potentially to political dissention and to conflict. In the words of Hobbes' patron, the Earl of Newcastle, 'controversy Is a Civill Warr with the Pen which pulls out the sorde soon afterwards'.[16]

In his endeavour to avert this situation, Hobbes does not rely primarily upon the coercive capacities of the sovereign. More fundamentally, he undertakes what David Johnston has described as a 'politics of cultural transformation': an attempt to reconfigure political order by demonstrating to individuals the nature and limits of their knowledge, and convincing them of the political consequences of these limits.[17] At the heart of this project lies his attempts to limit the claims of knowledge through the promulgation of an ontological materialism, and the assertion of a materialist understanding of the self and self-interest. Limiting knowledge to the material world marginalizes beliefs in non-visible or immaterial realms and powers – whether these be knowledge of God's will or claims about its power. As such, materialism is an essential element in his attempt to marginalize destructive influence of beliefs in 'some *power*, or agent *invisible*'. In the same way, the fear of pain, and particularly of death, on which he bases so many of his claims and pins so many of his hopes will not operate if individuals believe in an afterlife which transcends and justifies any form of suffering (or the infliction of suffering) in this world.

By limiting knowledge claims (as opposed to private belief or faith) to the material realm, a *public* arena of discussion concerning truth could be secured.[18] Even more importantly, in this way a degree of liberty and security from the 'enthusiasm' of others could be achieved.[19] Hobbes' limitation of the grounds of knowledge is spurred by, if not reducible to,

---

[16] Quoted in Steven Shapin and Simon Shaeffer, *Leviathan and the Air-Pump: Hobbes, Boyle and the Experimental Life* (Princeton NJ: Princeton University Press, 1985), p. 290.

[17] David Johnston, *The Rhetoric of Leviathan: Thomas Hobbes and the Politics of Cultural Transformation* (Princeton NJ: Princeton University Press, 1986). See also the insightful treatment in Noel Malcolm, 'Hobbes's Theory of International Relations' in *Aspects of Hobbes* (Oxford: Clarendon Press, 2002), pp. 454–455.

[18] For treatments of this broad movement, see Steven Shapin, *A Social History of Truth: Civility and Science in the Seventeenth Century* (Chicago: University of Chicago Press, 1994); G. Oesterich, *Neostoicism and the Early Modern State* (Cambridge: Cambridge University Press, 1982); James Tully, *An Approach to Political Philosophy: Locke in Contexts* (Cambridge: Cambridge University Press, 1993). As Holmes has insightfully argued, successfully banishing religious strife from politics was also an important means of strengthening the state, and this contribution to state power was part of its attraction. See also Cornelia Navari, 'Knowledge, the State and the State of Nature' in Michael Donelan (ed.), *The Reason of State* (London: Allen and Unwin, 1978).

[19] In Blits' formulation: 'In order to establish and maintain civil society, men's common fear of a sovereign must be made to overpower their mutual fear of one another . . . yet

a concern with religious toleration and a desire to remove the destructive conflict engendered by irresolvable questions of religious truth from the political realm.[20] The reduction of knowledge of the world – including the self – to materiality does not reflect an unexamined epistemic commitment, a naive vision of scientific practice[21] or the influence of nascent forms of capitalist ideology.[22] A material understanding of the self (and self-understanding) would make possible a new set of political practices based on the (now rationally, *not* naturally) universal fear of pain and death which provided a basis for a legitimate theory of sovereignty (the social contract) and obedience to the sovereign and the laws of nature. The transformation of theory was intimately linked to an attempt to transform practices.

While Hobbes has often been portrayed as basing his political vision on the *assumption* of materially self-interested actors, and while this has often been taken as one of the core defining assumptions of Realist thinking, the reality is quite different: Hobbes actually seeks the *creation* of such actors, hoping to limit the basic irrationality of human action through the adoption of practices of material self-interest. The kind of individuals that Hobbes seeks to promote (one might even say create) are those who have literally *learnt* to think of themselves and their worlds in terms of objective material calculation, and who thus provide the foundation upon which a stable politics can be built. The epistemic materialism that he advocates is thus not an abstract methodological assumption, as 'ontological materialism' has come to be understood in

---

even if men fear the sovereign more than they fear one another, they will not enjoy lasting peace unless in the first place they fear "powers visible", that is, death at the hands of other men, more than they fear "powers invisible", that is, hellfire or damnation'; 'Hobbesian Fear', p. 427.

[20] The role of the 'Independency crisis' concerning the relations between church and state in Hobbes thought has been highlighted by Tuck, *Hobbes*.

[21] Indeed even Hobbes' specifically scientific claims – such as his (materialist) denial of the possibility of a total vacuum which marked his long controversy with Robert Boyle – were informed by his concerns with the politics of knowledge. See the fascinating treatment in *Leviathan and the Air-Pump*.

[22] Perhaps most significantly, it was linked to new understandings of 'property' as a 'juridical concept of self-ownership' whose main agenda was "moral, political and military, not economic". It is not concerned with the alienation of labour power but with political power (the power of self-defence). The individual as well as the state are concerned with preservation not consumption'; Tully, *An Approach to Political Philosophy*, p. 82. On this theme see also J. G. A. Pocock *The Machiavellian Moment* (Princeton NJ: Princeton University Press, 1985), Chapters 3, 6 and 11, especially; and Albert O. Hirschman, *The Passions and the Interests* (Princeton NJ: Princeton University Press, 1977); and in International Relations, Kurt Burch, *'Property' and the Making of the International System* (Boulder CO: Lynne Rienner, 1999).

International Relations: it is a political commitment, a central element in his attempt to establish new intellectual and practical foundations for authority in a culture wracked by violence and conflict.

As Malcolm importantly notes, this was not a purely 'domestic' agenda; it had an important international dimension since it provided a counter to the supranational claims of the Catholic church (that 'Confederacy of Deceivers') to the temporal authority of sovereigns that Hobbes viewed as a key source of 'rebellions within states, and wars between them'.[23] As a principle linking domestic and international orders, Hobbes' theory of sovereignty delimits the realm of political disputation and conflict, creates a sphere of politics in principle separate from religion, and allows for religious faith largely unconstrained by politics. In this way, it would provide the foundation for a stable sovereign authority, and a relatively stable system of sovereigns, based upon the rational self-interest that Hobbes identifies as the 'Laws of Nature'.

To this end, Hobbes undertakes the tricky task of mobilizing the most basic, powerful and yet unstable element of his vision of human motivation: fear. Rational (Hobbesian) citizens will accept the rule of the Sovereign in part out of fear of its power. They may also accept it as an outcome of ratiocination. But, finally and significantly, they will accept this rule because of the powerful link which Hobbes draws between the two: because they understand the foundations of the Sovereign authority and learn to fear both its power and the disastrous consequences of its dissolution: a return to the warlike state of nature. The extraordinarily powerful, evocative and metaphorical language of *Leviathan* reflects Hobbes' recognition that the construction of his rational political order required an *affective* element if it was to be effective.[24] Logic alone was insufficient to this task. Nor were the coercive powers of the Sovereign alone sufficient to construct and maintain such a political order. No government is powerful enough to regulate totally the lives of recalcitrant citizens, or continually to compel them to obey.[25] Only if the people

---

[23] 'Hobbes's Theory of International Relations', p. 453.

[24] Evidenced as far back as Hobbes' translation of Thucydides' *History of the Peloponnesian War*. On this see again Johnston, *The Rhetoric of Leviathan*, and Quentin Skinner, *Reason and Rhetoric in the Philosophy of Hobbes* (Cambridge: Cambridge University Press, 1996), and *Visions of Politics*, Vol. 3., pp. 1–141 especially.

[25] Drawing again on the analysis of religious affiliation in *Behemoth*, Holmes has insightfully noted that 'Hobbes stresses the self-defeating character of attempts to change people's minds by brutal means: "Suppression of doctrine does but unite and exasperate, that is, increase both the malice and power of them that have already believed them." This is a

understand why the polity must be ordered as it must, and only if they continue to view the sovereign as a legitimate authority and trust in its judgment, can a political order be secure. *Leviathan* is an attempt to create precisely this understanding, acceptance and support, and through it to legitimize and strengthen the political order of the state.

Fear and reason, logic and affect, are thus linked in Hobbes' attempt to foster an 'enlightened'[26] citizenry and political leadership. However, Hobbes does not seek constantly to invoke fear as a means of limitation. Though he recognizes the political utility of fear, his political sensibilities are far too subtle to rest with the idea that fear – the most basic and potentially destablizing of passions – provides a simple or straightforward resolution to the difficulties of constructing and maintaining a political order.[27] Rather than valorizing fear as the basis of a rigid absolutism, or denying it in the name of a politics of transparency, he seeks to manage a politics of fear in order to construct a political order which can minimize its necessity and to create a recognizably liberal political society in which fear plays a minor but positive role in a politics of self- and sovereign-limitation.

Hobbesian international political theory

Examining the foundations of Hobbes' thinking shows that 'natural' human aggressiveness, vanity and the like are not the sole or fundamental bases for his analysis of the state of nature. Nor does that foundation lie in the assumption that utilitarian individuals are equally rational in competitive pursuit of the same things, or that they are objectively determined by the (scientifically discernible) structure within which they find themselves. Rather, the dilemma is that human beings have no *natural*

---

stunning admission from a champion of unlimited sovereign power. Indeed, it sounds more like Locke than Hobbes'. *Passions and Constraint*, p. 93; the quote is from Hobbes, *Behemoth or the Long Parliament* (Chicago: Chicago University Press, 1991), p. 62.

[26] Blits, 'Hobbesian Fear', pp. 426–429.

[27] In an insightful reading, David Campbell has stressed this aspect of Hobbes' thinking, using it primarily to stress the negative disciplining role of otherness in Hobbes. I here largely pursue the alternative reading that Campbell notes as possible: discipline is not an end in itself for Hobbes – it is limitation in the name of a strategy of autonomy and pluralism, and an attempt to construct a liberal politics on the basis of the recognition that epistemic pluralism (as embodied in this scepticism) cannot be straightforwardly translated into political pluralism. In this regard, Hobbes can be seen as a profound if somewhat discomfiting exponent of what Judith Shklar called the 'liberalism of fear'. See David Campbell, *Writing Security*, 2nd edition (Minneapolis: University of Minnesota Press, 1998), pp. 53–60, and fn. 19; and Shklar, 'The Liberalism of Fear' in Stanley Hoffmann (ed.), *Political Thought and Political Thinkers* (Chicago: University of Chicago Press, 1998).

way of agreeing upon what things are – what the reality of the world *is* – in either an empirical or a straightforwardly moral sense. Perceptions of what is good as well as bad, potentially beneficial as well as threatening, are at the most basic level inescapably relative. This is the source of Hobbes' portrayal of the state of nature. It is not simply authority or coordination which is lacking. For Hobbes it is *truth* in the conventional sense which is absent.

Through a combination of shared beliefs and the political power they make possible, particular political orders represent specific resolutions to this situation. The sovereign is not just a structure for the coordination of individual interests. It is also (and much more fundamentally) the agency which provides stability in conditions of epistemic disagreement, underpins social structures of epistemic concord, provides authoritative (and enforceable) interpretations and decisions in contested cases, and creates conditions of predictability that minimize fear and allow rational cooperation. Seen in this light, the role and capacity of sovereigns to solve these dilemmas domestically creates – by virtue of their necessarily authoritative role *internally* – a condition in which political orders are necessarily limited and relations between sovereigns 'anarchic'.

But Hobbes is not content merely to demonstrate these underpinnings of political authority. He does not view all resolutions to this situation as equally viable or desirable. Indeed in the context of the chaotic and conflictual breakdown of previous forms of order – and the understandings of the self, society and sovereignty upon which they were based – he feels it imperative that the foundations of sovereignty and its requirements be reconstructed. To this end, he articulates a politics of limits: a vision based upon a reasoned understanding of the limits of reason, a materialist ontology and understanding of the self and self-interest, and a finely balanced practice of sovereign authority drawing upon rational understanding, fear of the sovereign and fear of its dissolution.

A corollary to this individual recognition of limits is that the rational (Hobbesian) sovereign will recognize the *practical*, if not juridical, limits upon its authority and will moderate its actions accordingly.[28]

---

[28] As he put it in an early and recently authenticated discourse: 'For it is a great misfortune to a people, to come under the government of such a one, as knows not how to govern himself'. 'Discourse Upon the Beginnings of Tacitus' in Hobbes, *Three Discourses*, edited by Noel B. Reynolds and Arlene W. Saxonhouse (Chicago: University of Chicago Press, 1996), p. 57. See also Malcolm's incisive treatment of these issues in 'Hobbbes's Theory of International Relations', pp. 446–48.

This puts considerable practical limits upon the sovereign for Hobbes, and given its implications for state action it is important to understand fully the rather complex argument he makes in this regard. Hobbesian individuals never give up their right to judge situations for themselves in the sense that if they believe their self-preservation to be threatened they retain (via the right of nature) the right of rebellion against the sovereign. If an individual judges her life to be in danger (and in this realm the individual's judgment remains supreme), or has committed an act which is a capital crime, then even if she is juridically wrong she has by nature the right to defend herself. Equally, should a group come to feel that the sovereign is not protecting their lives adequately, or should they come to judge that the sovereign constitutes a threat to their lives, they have the right to band together in mutual defence. As Hobbes puts it: 'But in case a great many men together have already resisted the sovereign power unjustly, or committed some capital crime for which every one of them expecteth death, whether have they not the liberty to join together, and assist, and defend one another? Certainly they have; for they but defend their lives, which the guilty man may as well do as the innocent.'[29]

Ultimately, by this logic, if this group should become strong enough that it threatens the ability of the sovereign to guarantee the security of other subjects, or they feel that to obey the rebels is necessary to their survival (in their judgment), then these individuals are at liberty to do so. In this way, Hobbes tries to show how on the very basis of the principles of its foundation and within its own logic, civil order can break down and (civil) war emerge. The fragility of this order, and the disastrous consequences of its breakdown become a lesson to both citizens and the sovereign to understand the practical/prudential limits upon their claims and activities. Rational beings should not challenge the sovereign, Hobbes believes, but this does not mean they will not, and the 'Negligent government of Princes', he argues in characteristically dire terms at the conclusion to Part II of *Leviathan*, is naturally attended by 'Rebellion; and Rebellion, with Slaughter.'[30]

The sovereign should assiduously avoid policies which make rebellion likely. It must educate subjects so that they understand and accept the principles of sovereign authority, and it must maintain sufficient coercive power to 'convince' them if they do not. But even in this latter case, Hobbes accentuates the importance of acceptance and legitimacy,

[29] Hobbes *Leviathan*, p. 143.   [30] Ibid., p. 243.

for the coercive capacities of the Sovereign themselves depend upon it. If the people rebel, the Sovereign must, Hobbes argues, have recourse to arms to enforce civil order. But the possession of this coercive power and the ability to wield it is dependent upon the prior and continuing legitimacy of the Sovereign's authority in the eyes of those who will act on its behalf. The problem, as he pointedly asks in *Behemoth*, is that 'if men know not their duty, what is there that can force them to obey the laws? An army you will say. But what shall force the army?'[31] Without the social legitimacy which makes it possible, the Sovereign's coercive power is likely to prove chimerical. While the Sovereign thus has *in principle* the right to act in any way it chooses, Hobbes argues that a correct understanding of politics will lead not only to obedient citizens, but to prudential self-limitation of activity by a rational sovereign. Since, as he states clearly, again in *Behemoth*, that 'the power of the mighty hath no foundation but in the opinion and belief of the people',[32] the sovereign will avoid actions which too obviously threaten the interests of the citizens for fear that it will lose their acceptance of its authority and foment dissension and rebellion.[33] This places considerable limits (again rationally, not juridically) on state action both domestically and internationally.

In Hobbes' view, Sovereigns cannot act toward each other as individuals might because as a corporate body the Sovereign must consider the relationship between its external relations and relations with its own citizens. The Sovereign, recognizing the foundations of its authority, must be careful not to lose the trust of the citizens, or to tip the balance of fear to such an extent that the citizens come to see obedience to the state as a greater threat to their survival than disobedience. Even though the Sovereign has the right to treat its citizens in virtually any way it sees fit, Hobbes believes that it should not, and he believes he has given convincing reasons why it should not. These considerations put limitations on the external actions of the sovereign beyond those of simple caution or restricted material 'capabilities'. Hobbes' analysis is not simply that an adventurous foreign policy is imprudent. Rather the question of knowledge and social consent is once again key here. Since aggression is not innate but arises in part from uncertainty, Hobbes' Leviathans are not necessarily aggressive towards one another. More importantly, since

---

[31] Hobbes, *Behemoth*, p. 59. Again, my thanks to Ross Rudolph for alerting me to this passage.
[32] Ibid., p. 16. Holmes makes this revealing quote the centrepiece of his treatment.
[33] On this theme, see especially Flathman, *Thomas Hobbes*, pp. 121–125.

they must ultimately convince the citizens to obey their judgments of threats (and thus convince citizens themselves to go to war or support preparations for it) the prudent sovereign will be cautious in engaging in the practice, for fear of losing the trust of the citizens in its judgment (just as it should not oppress the citizens unnecessarily for the same reason) and by so doing push them to dissension or rebellion.[34]

Since the Sovereign's authority rests not just on coercive power or the ability to manipulate utilities, but also depends upon its ability to retain legitimacy in the eyes of its citizens, the Sovereign should always weigh the implications of its actions on the lives and opinions of its citizens, and keep these issues clearly in mind. In its external relations, the same logic applies. The Sovereign should not unnecessarily do things which would push the citizens too hard, threaten them or their livelihoods too much, or cause them to question their belief and trust in the judgment and actions of the Sovereign. Indeed in external relations this logic may be even more imperative. For since the Sovereign may be asking (and potentially compelling) the citizens to put their lives at risk in war (and thus potentially allowing them to rebel on the grounds of self-preservation which is their right by nature) it can only do so if the vast majority of the population continues to trust in its adjudication of the situation (threat) and the necessity of risking their lives. It is in war that the continuance of the sovereign's rule is potentially most in jeopardy, not just from the power of other sovereigns, but from domestic dissention. Hobbes, of course, believes that the Sovereign is justified in forcing citizens to go to war, but he nonetheless feels it would be unwise and unreasonable to force them to do so too often or in situations where the judgments of threat decided upon by the Sovereign are shaky enough and risky enough potentially to erode its legitimacy in the eyes of the citizens.

Scepticism about the limits of human knowledge leads Hobbes to great caution in human affairs, especially regarding the relationship of theory to practice. He warns that to act as if we can know (predict) and control the future is to court disaster. Knowing the limitations of human knowledge, and the inability to know God's will or other visions of ultimate human fulfilment, Hobbes believes that rational sovereigns will not act in an unnecessarily aggressive manner. His vision of foreign

---

[34] In relation to taxation, and especially the Monarch's demands for 'Ship Money' for the building of a larger navy, which Hobbes helped collect despite the objections of many citizens, see Johan Somerville, *Thomas Hobbes: Political Ideas in Historical Context* (New York: St. Martin's Press, 1992), p. 18.

policy is cautious and essentially pacific, a position which, as Flathman has illustrated drawing upon a passage from the *Elements of Law*, is conditioned by – or perhaps founded in – his scepticism: 'Hobbes is far from a supporter of bellicose or expansionist policies. Because no preparation can assure victory, "such commonwealths, or such monarchs, as affect war for itself . . . out of ambition, or of vain-glory, or that make account to avenge every little injury, or disgrace done by their neighbours, if they not ruin themselves, their fortune must be better than they have reason to expect".'[35]

The hubris engendered by religious dogma, political fanaticism, pride, vanity or (social scientific?) claims to political wisdom will most likely lead to disaster. This fits clearly with both Hobbes' strictures on the claims to religious knowledge and his attacks on militaristic or destructive ideologies of honour.[36] Scepticism leads to a suspicion of, and attack against, dogmatism and (in Hobbes' sense) irrationalism. A transformation of epistemic practice was seen as a means of transforming social and political and ethical practices both with and between sovereigns.

In principle, sovereigns exist in the same situation of sceptical indeterminacy toward one another as individuals in the state of nature. But there are crucial differences between states and individuals which render this a much different situation. The first of these concerns the different physical capabilities of states and individuals. In *Leviathan*, Hobbes argues that: 'Nature hath made men so equall, in the faculties of body, and mind; as that though there be found one man sometimes manifestly stronger in body, or of quicker mind than another; yet when all is reckoned together, the difference between man, and man, is not so considerable, as that one man can thereupon to himself any benefit, to which another may not pretend as well as he.'[37] There is no natural hierarchy in the state of nature upon which order can be based. Characteristics advantageous in the struggle are diversely distributed: some are strong, others quick, still others clever. Moreover, this relative equality of capacities is tied to the existence of these individuals *as* solitary individuals. Even the strongest must sometimes sleep, and all are subject to disease, age and ultimately death, circumstances which make any continuing exercise of domination impossible.

[35] Flathman, *Thomas Hobbes*, p. 110.
[36] See especially Keith Thomas, 'The Social Origins of Hobbes's Political Thought' in K. C. Brown (ed.), *Hobbes Studies* (Cambridge MA: Harvard University Press, 1965), pp. 96–98 especially.
[37] Hobbes, *Leviathan*, p. 74.

Between Hobbesian sovereigns, however, the most destructive and fearful aspects of the state of nature have been ameliorated, lessening the radical insecurity and conflict which dominates the state of nature. The Leviathan never sleeps and (except in specific circumstances) it never dies. Ever-alert and immortal, it transcends the limitations which simple individuals encounter in their attempts to survive in the state of nature. As a corporate body, its strength is the strength of all its members. The result is that the radical equality which defines the state of nature composed of individuals is not present in the relations between states; they are qualitatively different orders. And since states are not subject to the same conditions as individuals – equality, sleep, mortality – they can transcend some of the more anarchic qualities of the state of nature and create, via the Laws of Nature, more stable forms of co-existence among themselves.[38]

Yet it is important to note that, from a Hobbesian perspective, the fact that states are corporate bodies is not in itself enough to secure an acceptable international order. Just as individuals in the state of nature must come to understand themselves and their world in a rational manner in order to live by the cooperative dictates of the 'laws of nature', so states would also need to adopt rational (i.e. Hobbes') maxims of internal organization and external behaviour for the international realm to be any more than a contingent and fragile form of order or domination. Hobbes' argument is not that such an order is natural, or that its norms would simply evolve through time. On the contrary, he feels that political orders must be willed and constructed in accordance with the dictates of rationality and with a clear view of its limitations. Other forms of international order certainly can exist – medieval Christendom being perhaps the prime example. But in light of his concern with the violence that attended the breakdown of that order, Hobbes would likely have regarded such orders as unacceptably fragile and prone to conflicts as 'irrational' as the principles upon which they were founded.

These considerations point to the ways in which Hobbes' commitment to the absolute nature of sovereignty is by no means incompatible with international order and with shared understanding between rationally constituted sovereignties.[39] Based upon the same principles,

[38] As discussed momentarily this theme has been most fully explored by the English School.
[39] Again, see the excellent treatment in Malcolm, 'Hobbes's Theory of International Relations', pp. 451–55; and the discussion of Hobbes' views on trade in David Boucher, *Political*

Hobbesian states will share the same understanding of political order, the same commitment to a politics of limits and the same constraints on their actions. Moreover, the materialist and empiricist practices that are essential in the constitution of a rational Hobbesian order could provide a common framework of understanding between sovereigns. The materialist and empiricist practices of knowledge that Hobbes advocates would, if adopted, allow for mutual knowledge and calculation and a partial overcoming of the basic sceptical situation within which different sovereignties encounter each other.

These mediating practices of material interest lack the order provided by the authoritative decision-making, cultural legitimation and coercive capacities that characterize the state. But the international realm is not a state of nature. Materialist and rationalist practices allow the shared construction of concepts of interest, power and action, and provide the basis for common calculation and adjustment even when sovereigns are at odds with each other. In short, a materialist balance of power could become a mediating structure of practice between sovereigns. Finally, and admitted more speculatively, it is possible to conceive how the principles of legitimacy upon which the practice of sovereignty is based – that is, legitimate action in the eyes of *citizens* – might become transnationalized to a point at which juridically absolute sovereigns would nonetheless be *practically* constrained by their limits. The issues this raises are highly complex, for Hobbes would undoubtedly continue to insist on the absolute necessity of the sovereign as a locus of decision in an inherently indeterminate world. But be this as it may, absolute sovereignty and cosmopolitan constraints are not necessarily opposed in Hobbes' vision of the *practice* of sovereignty, however much they may seem precluded by his definition of it.

The Hobbesian legacy in international theory

Beyond doubt the most common and influential use of Hobbes in IR is that which sees him as a theorist of international anarchy. Treating states as the equivalent of Hobbesian individuals (who are themselves reduced to rational pursuers of material interests, fearful egoists or calculators of relative gains), Hobbes' treatment of state of nature as a 'war of each against all' is treated as a compelling metaphor, or perhaps even

Theories of International Relations: From Thucydides to the Present (Oxford: Oxford University Press, 1998), pp. 160–161.

a model, capturing and conveying the logic of an anarchic international system. In fact, it is precisely this image that made his thinking such a popular touchstone within many neorealist declarations about international politics – with the image of individuals simply elevated to the world of states.

As the foregoing analysis has sought to demonstrate, however, despite its popularity this image does little justice to Hobbes' thinking or to understanding a 'Hobbesian' vision of international relations.[40] Far from seeking to develop either a straightforward rational-choice theory of social life (and an analogous account of international relations), or a theory modelled on some vision of modern science, Hobbes begins from a profound scepticism toward both. His vision of politics (and the 'science' of it) is, as Richard Flathman has vigorously argued, a highly 'chastened' one, both in its epistemological claims and its practical recommendations. While some scholars continue to call for a discipline constructed along the lines of positivist science, this is not a stance which Hobbes would have supported, nor can it be sustained by a reference to the 'Hobbesian' analysis of international relations. Indeed as Flathman notes, to the extent that Hobbes' ideas in this realm were 'In important respects anticipating views now prominent in the philosophy of science, it is not an account that is likely to warm the hearts of the apostles of science – whether natural or the so-called science of politics'.[41]

Similarly, the interpretation of Hobbesian individuals in the rationalist view, and the transposition of this vision into a model of state action, is fundamentally misleading. Whereas rationalist positions take for granted a world of rational-actors calculating in the context of material gains, Hobbes did not *assume* the existence of such actors; to a significant degree he sought to *create* them. William Connolly has nicely summarized the point made earlier

> Hobbes is often held to believe that most human beings are self-interested most of the time and that a sovereign power must be devised that is able to contend with these self-interested beings. But this interpretation exaggerates and misleads. It exaggerates by treating human beings who are to become both self-interested and principled as if they were secure agents of self-interest prior to the education they receive in civil society, and it misleads by pretending that the self-interested

[40] For an analysis of other shortcomings in attempting to read Hobbes in this way see Don Herzog, *Happy Slaves* (Chicago: University of Chicago Press, 1989), Chapter 3 especially.
[41] Flathman, *Thomas Hobbes*, p. 29; see also p. 49.

individual is the problem when it comes closer to being the solution Hobbes offers for the problem he identifies.[42]

The main competitor to the rationalist-realist view of Hobbes has come from theorists of international society. This position begins from a basic paradox in the rationalist view: why, if Hobbes felt the solution to anarchy in the state of nature lay in the creation of the Leviathan, did he not extend the logic of this solution to the international level? In short, if Hobbesian individuals were able to contract in the state of nature, why are not Hobbesian states capable of doing so in the international anarchy? In the words of John Vincent, 'it is even reasonable to ask why, if Hobbes' view of international politics was really as the Realists take it to be, he did not seek to bring the international anarchy to an end in the same way as *Leviathan* ordered relations among individuals?'[43]

Rather than building its analysis upon the supposed affinities between the state of nature and an international state of war, the case for viewing Hobbes as a theorist of 'international society' emerges in part from an attempt to resolve the question of why Hobbes fails to make the apparently obvious logical extension of the contract from the relations between individuals to those between states. The answer, according to these members of the English School, lies in Hobbes' stress on the relative equality which characterizes individuals in the state of nature and thus differentiates these relations from those of states.

The key to Hobbesian international theory, in this perspective, becomes a support for a stress upon rules and norms and rationally-derived understandings of mutual interest in the constitution of 'international society'. As Bull notes, the Hobbesian 'laws of nature' provide a common, if imperfect, foundation for the coordination of inter-state relations. Rational self-interest provides a common foundation for the coordination of action, the conduct of behaviour and the creation of relatively stable international orders. In Bull's view, 'imperfect though they are, these laws of nature, 'the articles of peace' as Hobbes calls them, are the lifeline to which sovereign states in the international anarchy must cling if they are to survive'.[44] Although the embodiment of

---

[42] William Connolly, *Political Theory and Modernity* (Oxford: Basil Blackwell, 1988), pp. 26–27. Indeed in its concern with language, and with the relationship between knowledge, belief and action, Hobbes' thinking resonates much more clearly with the concerns of contemporary constructivism than with rationalist approaches.

[43] John Vincent, 'The Hobbesian Tradition in Twentieth Century International Thought' *Millennium* 10 (1981), p. 85.

[44] Hedley Bull 'Hobbes and the International Anarchy' *Social Research* 48 (1977), p. 728.

these precepts in practice is difficult and contingent, and certainly different from the realm of domestic politics, these laws of nature form a common foundation of political order at both levels. As Bull argues: 'The articles of peace contain within them most of the basic rules of co-existence on which states have relied in the international anarchy from Hobbes's time and before it to our own'.[45] And as he concludes, a clear understanding of Hobbes' ideas yields results almost directly contrary to the Realist interpretation, forcing us to recognize 'how deeply pacific Hobbes's approach to international relations was, at least in the values from which it sprang. There is no sense in Hobbes of the glorification of war, nor of relish for the game of power politics as an end in itself, nor of willingness to abdicate judgment in favour of the doctrine that anything in the international anarchy is permissible'.[46]

There is little doubt, as Malcolm has argued, that this position provides a more adequate appraisal of Hobbes' views than those which reduce his vision of IR to an anarchic state of nature. A stress on the laws of nature, on reciprocal limits and on shared notions and norms of sovereignty as basis for international order capture many aspects of his thinking. However, there are also serious challenges presented to the English School by a closer examination of Hobbes' thinking. Taking seriously Hobbes' focus on the construction of agency, for example, raises issues that until fairly recently the English School has generally ignored.[47] For Hobbes, rationally calculating states were not natural. While it is intriguing to speculate about whether he might have viewed them as capable of learning to be so (and certainly he felt that fear and insecurity could act as spurs in this direction) he was also convinced that this vision of politics was a result of knowledge and will – a conscious choice and effort on the behalf of individuals that then needed to become the basis for political understanding and action in both the state and society. Grasping this element of the Hobbesian legacy would contribute to pushing theories of international society further along the road to engagements with issues of culture and identity, and of critical judgments about the status of norms (and the role of fear) than its traditional formulations have tended to allow, while Hobbes' fundamental

---

[45] Ibid.

[46] Ibid., p. 729. Here again, however, the dividing line between the contrasting schools of analysis becomes somewhat blurred, for Smith argues that 'realists' have also developed this theme; see Michael J. Smith, *Realist Thought from Weber to Kissinger* (Baton Rouge: Louisiana State University Press, 1986), pp. 13–14.

[47] For a move in the latter direction, see Timothy Dunne, *Inventing International Society* (London: Macmillan, 1998).

stress on the importance of decision as a condition of domestic order certainly calls into question the ease with which his thinking fits English School attempts to think about the possible emergence of transnational orders.[48]

Yet perhaps the most challenging aspect of stressing the role of the social construction of action and decision in Hobbes' thinking lies in its connections to the origins of post-war classical Realism, and to contemporary neoconservatism. The most direct means of examining this dimension of the Hobbesian legacy is to turn to what John McCormick has termed the 'revival of Hobbes in Weimar and National Socialist Germany'[49], and the pivotal role that Hobbes played in the thinking of a number of influential figures but particularly, in this context, Carl Schmitt and Leo Strauss.

Significantly, both Schmitt and Strauss understood that Hobbes' theory of 'human nature' as 'evil' was far from a reduction of human beings to material interests or simple aggression, or even calculating insecurity. The Hobbesian understanding of evil, they recognized, was founded in his broad epistemic claims and philosophic appraisal of the conditions of human knowledge and action.[50] But for both Schmitt and Strauss (albeit in different ways) Hobbes' appeal to instrumental-material calculation as the form of discipline most likely to allow individuals to restrain their actions and develop common modes of conduct reflects a fundamental instability in his vision of political order, and state survival in the international order. The difficulty, in the eyes of both Weimar thinkers, is that the more successful Hobbes' reconstruction of subjectivity and action is, the less individuals will see the *need* for such discipline, and the less they will understand the fundamental role of the state in the production of social order and its necessary capacity for decision. In Schmitt's view, for example, Hobbes fails in his attempt to secure the state, because his

---

[48] For a criticism of the English School's notions of norms and values that stresses its often uncritical nature, see Nicholas Rengger, *International Relations, Political Theory, and the Problem of Order* (London: Routledge 2002).

[49] John P. McCormick, 'Fear, Technology and the State: Carl Schmitt, Leo Strauss, and the Revival of Hobbes in Weimar and National Socialist Germany' *Political Theory* 22 (1994), 619–652.

[50] Carl Schmitt, *The Concept of the Political* (Chicago: University of Chicago Press, 1996), p. 61. Or as he also phrases it, any 'genuine political theory' must presuppose humanity as 'evil', not as perfectible or angelic. Strauss' most extended, if early, appraisal of Hobbes is his *Political Philosophy of Hobbes: Its Basis and Genesis* (Chicago: University of Chicago Press, 1952). The relationship between Schmitt and Strauss is discussed in Heinrich Meier, *Carl Schmitt and Leo Strauss: The Hidden Dialogue* (Chicago: University of Chicago Press, 1985).

balanced creation of self-interested actors removes the *fear* necessary to get individuals to obey decisions that are not in their interest. Equally importantly, it makes it impossible for the state to mobilize individuals to put their own lives in mortal danger (pre-eminently in case of war) in defence of the state.

This, for Schmitt, is the ultimate failure of the Hobbesian Leviathan. Beginning from a clear understanding of what Schmitt famously termed 'the political', Hobbes ultimately contributed to the development of a modern liberalism and rationalism that systematically misunderstood it. While politics remained in its essence defined by Hobbesian sovereignty – by the capacity to make authoritative decisions, and to have them accepted by the society – this insight had been lost, covered over by liberal conceptions of self-interest in which the state was reduced to pluralistic mechanism at the mercy of individual interest groups that would either attempt to capture it for their own ends, or refuse to obey and defend it if it was not in their interest to do so. In a way, Hobbes had been all too successful in seeing rational self-interest as a potential aid to the solution, but paradoxically the state was now weakened in the face of adversaries both inside and outside, and its capacity to play the vital role that Hobbes reserved to it was – as to Schmitt (and Strauss) conditions in Weimar Germany amply illustrated – reduced almost to nothing.

In response, Schmitt argued for the need to recover the Hobbesian essence of sovereignty as decision. The basis of this, he argued, again like Hobbes, was *fear*. Recognition of the foundation of politics in the fear of death, and of primary obedience to the sovereign as a result of its ability to secure the individual needed to be recovered. The essential means that Schmitt invokes for doing so is a renewed stress on the fear of the Enemy as a means of cementing solidarity between Friends and securing the authority of the state. By heightening fear, defining politics as the distinction between friend and enemy, and using fear to mobilize the society – in part through myth, an aestheticization of violence and a glorification of war – Schmitt sought to restore the Hobbesian Leviathan to its rightful and necessary place in the constitution of political order. A radical, perhaps the most radical, understanding of international politics as constituted by a fundamental antagonism between Friend and Enemy was, at least on some readings, the ultimate result of this ambition.

This reading of the Hobbesian legacy is thus at the centre of Schmitt's radical form of *Realpolitik*, and the most complex philosophic lineage in

IR theory. It also set the context for the development of Morgenthau's thinking. Morgenthau's famous critique of liberalism clearly bears the mark of his engagement with Schmitt, and the debt that both owe to a sophisticated engagement with Hobbes. As Morgenthau once argued, 'There is a profound and neglected truth hidden in Hobbes' extreme dictum that the state creates morality as well as law and that there is neither morality nor law outside the state'.[51] Yet, as William Scheuerman has pointed out in an important treatment, Morgenthau's thinking can be read as an ongoing dialogue and critical engagement with Schmitt, seeking to oppose the radical (and, in Morgenthau's view, reactionary and destructive) conclusions to which it could lead.[52]

The critique of liberalism that emerged from the Weimar engagement with Hobbes is equally essential in coming to terms with one of the most controversial forms of thinking about international politics today, that of neoconservatism. While neoconservatism has a number of diverse sources, one of its most important inspirations lies in the political thought of Leo Strauss.[53] Although Strauss did not ultimately accept Schmitt's attempt to resolve these dilemmas, his Weimar critique of liberalism (and Hobbes) shares many of the points articulated by Schmitt, and constitutes an important theoretical basis of contemporary neoconservatism's claim that modern liberalism confronts a crisis that it cannot resolve, and that it cannot provide a basis for either domestic or foreign policy.

The connections between Strauss and neoconservatism are more complex than can be entered into here.[54] However, they suggest that opening up these oft-ignored dimensions of the 'Hobbesian' tradition in IR demonstrates the depth, complexity and continuing relevance of

---

[51] *In Defense of the National Interest* (New York: Knopf, 1951), p. 34. As Malcolm, 'Hobbes's Theory of International Relations', pp. 437–438, has importantly pointed out, taken on its own there is a vital flaw in this formulation. Hobbes does not deny the existence of rational moral principles (the Laws of Nature) arising from the goal of self-preservation, and reducing Hobbes' theory to an existential fear undercuts his crucial stress on rationality and the role that self-interest could play as a check on state power. It is, however, by no means clear that Morgenthau was as obtuse on this question as Malcolm implies.

[52] William Scheuerman, *Carl Schmitt: The End of Law* (New York: Lexington, 1999), Chapter 11. I have explored some of these themes in 'Why Ideas Matter in International Relations: Hans Morgenthau, Collective Identity, and the Moral Construction of Power Politics' *International Organization* 58 (2004), pp 633–665.

[53] For an exploration see Shadia Drury, *Leo Strauss and the American Right* (London: Macmillan, 1998). On Schmitt, Strauss and Hobbes see again the excellent treatment in McCormick 'Fear, Technology and the State'.

[54] See Earl Shorris, 'Ignoble Liars: Leo Strauss, George Bush and the Philosophy of Mass Deception' *Harpers Magazine* (June 2004).

Hobbes' thinking today. Whether in terms of the nature and adequacy of rationalist and materialist approaches to state action, of the lineages and consequences of constructivism, of the nature and limits of political community or of engagements with 'the political' and the role of myth and culture in constituting the relationship between society, the state, foreign policy and the international realm, an engagement with the traditions of Hobbesian thinking in IR hold considerable resources for contemporary inspiration well beyond a simple concern with a more adequate appraisal of the intellectual history of International Relations.

12 Re-appropriating Clausewitz: the neglected dimensions of counter-strategic thought

Julian Reid

The art of war deals with living and with moral forces.[1]

Carl von Clausewitz's *On War* is widely regarded as the most influential text for the traditions of military-strategic thought and practice that have attended the development of modern State power. Colin Gray declares it the only truly classical theory of war written in the modern era.[2] Clausewitz's statement that war is to be understood as 'nothing but the continuation of policy with other means' remains the most influential definition of the concept not only for military-strategic thought but for the major traditions of thinking about international politics in which the study of war continues to be a central preoccupation.[3] While the ontological veracity of the definition of war as a continuation of politics is increasingly debated, theorists of war still tend overwhelmingly to assume Clausewitz's dictum as a recommendation for the management of its instrumentality.[4] Ensuring the subordination of war to the political ends of sovereignty remains the central tenet of neo-Clausewitzian military-strategic thought.[5]

Yet Clausewitz's thought has played as important a formative role in the development of a tradition of thinking about war for which sovereignty is political anathema. That tradition is what I call

[1] Carl von Clausewitz, *On War*, trans. Michael Howard and Peter Paret (London: Everyman's Library, 1993), p. 97.
[2] Colin Gray, *Modern Strategy* (Oxford: Oxford University Press, 1999), pp. 113–119.
[3] Clausewitz, *On War*, p. 77. For an excellent recent account of the importance of Clausewitz's dictum for understandings of war in military-strategic thinking see Anthony Burke, 'Iraq: Strategy's Burnt Offering' *Global Change, Peace & Security* 17 (2005), 191–210.
[4] See Martin van Creveld's critique of the relevance of Clausewitz to problems of war in the contemporary era in *The Transformation of War* (New York: Free Press, 1991).
[5] Beatrice Heuser, *Reading Clausewitz* (London: Pimlico, 2002), pp. 179–194; Gray, *Modern Strategy*, pp. 56–68.

counter-strategic thought. Counter-strategic thought is a tradition of thinking concerned with intensifying critical understandings of the depths and modalities of relations between war and modern formations of power. The concept of war figures within this tradition not firstly as an instrumental tool of political sovereignty or simply as a spatio-temporally discrete activity engaged in by sovereign bodies. War, here, is reconceived primarily as an immanent force invested within forms of modern political order that exceed the boundaries of traditional models of State power. Concomitantly, this tradition reconceives war in essence not simply as a means to be employed in defence of sovereignty, but as a condition of possibility for the development of new forms of political subjectivity that exceed the disciplinary and control capacities of sovereign power. As such, it is as much concerned with recovering the practice of war from its colonization by the State and the military-strategic discourses and institutions on which State power is founded as it is with demonstrating the hitherto veiled roles that war plays in the development of modern societies and in the shaping of modern forms of subjectivity. It incorporates a complex genealogy of thinkers, involving Friedrich Nietzsche, Michel Foucault, Gilles Deleuze and Felix Guattari, Paul Virilio, Jean Baudrillard, and Antonio Negri, but its first architect is Clausewitz. Each of the other authors within this tradition, where they have been concerned with thinking through the problem of war and its relations to sovereign power and political order, have been inspired in one way or another by him.

The counter-strategic tradition for which Clausewitz is a crucial thinker is important in particular for its contributions to the broad revision and critique of social-strategic thought that has occurred since 1968. One of the least recognized but nevertheless central elements of this revision has been a reconceptualization of war as a generative principle for the formation of social relations in the composition of modern political orders. The concept of war is integral to the counter-strategic tradition in ways that are as essential as, but by no means exclusive of, the ways in which the concept of labour helped constitute counter-capital traditions of social struggle pre-1968. This reconceptualization of war as a generative principle of social relations has been achieved via an ongoing interrogation of the limits as well as the political and social potential of Clausewitz's *On War*. Rather as Marx began by grappling with the works of Smith and Ricardo, so today's counter-strategists have begun by reading and critiquing Clausewitz. In the works of Foucault, Deleuze and Guattari, Virilio, and Negri especially, can be found a substantial engagement with Clausewitz which has never been given satisfactory attention in the secondary literatures on Clausewitz, and only passing reference in theoretical works on the broader philosophical and political problems posed by the concept of war to date. The main task of this chapter, then, is to address that lacuna. I am going to focus, for the sake of brevity and clarity, on the specific engagements with Clausewitz to be located in the works of Foucault and Deleuze and Guattari respectively. Constituting a debate within itself, the conversation that runs through the thought on the nature of war and its relation to political power between these two counter-strategists is useful to focus on for the extent to which it demonstrates the seminal roles of Clausewitz for the theorizations of problems of counter-strategy that each of them offers.

Pure war vs real war

For counter-strategic thought the importance of Clausewitz lies in his fourfold definition of war. Firstly he defines war as 'an act of force' to which 'there is no logical limit'.[6] Secondly as a 'conflict of living forces'.[7] Thirdly as 'commerce'.[8] And fourthly as 'nothing but the continuation of policy with other means'.[9] None of these definitions of war developed by Clausewitz can be understood exclusive of the others. Rather, he urges us to grasp how each of these definitions of war operates within a holistic system in which each definition places specific compromises upon the other. Interpreters of Clausewitz who attempt to reify one or other of these different definitions for the purpose of critique fail to comprehend the intricacy of his thought.[10] Likewise, critics who attempt to explain Clausewitz's differing definitions of war as a vacillation produced by the contradictions in the lines of influence exerted upon him by different philosophical thinkers fail to appreciate the distinctiveness and complexity of his account of war. When W. B. Gallie, Raymond Aron or Azar Gat, for instance, dispute the merits of the Hegelian versus the Kantian Clausewitz they obscure the irreducibility of his ideas to philosophical currents.[11] In contrast, within the counter-strategic tradition

---

[6] Clausewitz, *On War*, p. 85.   [7] Ibid., p. 174.   [8] Ibid., p. 173.   [9] Ibid., p. 77.

[10] As, for example, in van Creveld, *Transformation of War*, pp. 148–149.

[11] W. B. Gallie, *Philosophers of Peace and War: Kant, Clausewitz, Marx, Engels, and Tolstoy* (Cambridge: Cambridge University Press, 1978); Raymond Aron, *Clausewitz: Philosopher of War* (London: Routledge, 1976); Azar Gat, *The Origins of Military Thought: From the Enlightenment to Clausewitz* (Oxford: Clarendon Press, 1989).

we find Clausewitz's conception of war being engaged with precisely at the expense of both Hegel and Kant. Clausewitz, rather than being either Hegelian or Kantian, is the first figure within a tradition that is both expressly anti-Hegelian and anti-Kantian in its pertaining to wage war upon the limitations for political being established by those philosophers of duty.

Discussions of Clausewitz's definition of war too often privilege his dictum that war is 'nothing but the continuation of policy with other means'. Those interpretations of him emanating from the domains of military-strategic thought are especially inclined to start from this perspective. The dictum is read either as an ontological statement or as a recommendation to policy-makers for the instrumentalization of war to the political ends of sovereign power. Yet Clausewitz's discussion of 'what war is' takes place at a level of abstraction and in a vein of theoretical sublimity that defies such interpretations. In posing the question of what war is, Clausewitz is asking the fundamental question of ontology. The question of 'what is war' is the question for Clausewitz of the essence of things. In being so, the question of war cannot, for Clausewitz, be limited to or start from the problem of war as it is understood and dealt with from the instrumental perspective of the State. The question of what war becomes in a world of States is a problem that can only be understood and dealt with when one takes into account what war is in a world without States.

Clausewitz argues that in abstraction 'war is an act of force' to which 'there is no logical limit'.[12] In its purest form, war is a force he defines as a movement 'toward extremes'.[13] This 'abstract' or 'pure' concept of war exists in complex antagonism with the forms that war assumes in the 'real world'. In being a movement toward extremes, pure war tends to be subject to political modification in the real world. As he argues,

> in the field of abstract thought the inquiring mind can never rest until it reaches the extreme, for here it is dealing with an extreme: a clash of forces freely operating and obedient to no law but their own. From a pure concept of war you might try to deduce absolute terms for the objective you should aim at and for the means of achieving it; but if you did so the continuous interaction would land you in extremes that represented nothing but a play of the imagination issuing from an almost invisible sequence of logical subtleties. If we were to think purely in absolute terms, we could avoid every difficulty by a stroke

[12] Clausewitz, *On War*, p. 85.   [13] Ibid., p. 84.

of the pen and proclaim with inflexible logic that, since the extreme must always be the goal, the greatest effort must always be exerted. Any such pronouncements would be an abstraction and would leave the real world quite unaffected.[14]

In reality the movement toward the extreme that defines war in its purity is always mitigated, for Clausewitz, by the existence of other living forces. In the real world war is not 'the action of a living force upon a lifeless mass (total non-resistance would be no war at all) but always the collision of two living forces'.[15] While war in its purest conception is an act of force that searches for its most extreme expression as life, in the real world this search is thwarted by the existence of other living forces with which it enters into interaction. Instead of allowing for the realization of this innate tendency toward the extreme, real war is defined by a condition of interaction that imposes limits on the pure act of force. War becomes not a singular act of force but, instead, a force relation conditioned by an interaction with other life forms that establishes the limits within which war itself can be expressed as life. Pure war, defined as a movement toward the extreme, is conceptually comparable to the 'movement of infinity' which Søren Kierkegaard's 'knight of faith' attempts and which expresses his 'power to concentrate the whole content of life and the whole significance of reality in one single wish'.[16] The movement of pure war emits of a passion which is immune to the resistance of the wills of others because it is driven by a search for expression bereft of relation to others. 'It is only the lower natures which find in other people the law for their action.'[17]

It is this basic distinction that Clausewitz draws, between the pure form of war understood as a movement toward the extreme expression of living forces and real war understood as a force relation conditioned by limitation imposed in relation with others that I want to focus on in looking at the influence Clausewitz exerts on the counter-strategic thought of Foucault and Deleuze and Guattari. For there we find an account of this basic distinction of Clausewitz's between pure war and real war as well as the logic of their relation in application to the problem of power within modern societies that is distinct from any other interpretation of Clausewitz's work. In the work of Foucault and Deleuze and Guattari we discover the development of an account

[14] Ibid., pp. 86–87.   [15] Ibid., p. 86.
[16] Søren Kierkegaard, *Fear and Trembling and the Sickness unto Death*, trans. Walter Lowrie (New York: Anchor Books, 1954), p. 53.
[17] Ibid., p. 55.

of modern society as a complex field of force relations in which war is generative of life. In turn we discover an account of the sovereign power of the State as that which seeks to modify this generative force through the imposition of its political objects upon the movements of war as life. For sure, this is a radically different conception of war from that found in most other existing theoretical works about war. Yet it is, without doubt, an enduringly Clausewitzian one. Through Clausewitz, Foucault and Deleuze and Guattari reconceive war not simply as a spatio-temporally discrete practice of States or State-like actors but as an immanent force investing each and every social relation. Understood in such a manner, war does not simply serve a function for the State. It threatens, with the prospect of its rupture, to destabilize the organization of relations in which power itself is invested. The founding goal of counter-strategic thought becomes, then, that of disinterring this pure power of war from its capture within the strategized relations of State power.

Foucault's Clausewitz: war, society and force relations

It is in *The History of Sexuality* that Foucault most significantly develops his thesis as to the relations between war and modern social relations. Modern Western societies are composed, Foucault argues, of a 'moving substrate of force relations which, by virtue of their inequality, constantly engender states of power'.[18] This substrate of force relations can be said to exist 'not out of a speculative choice or theoretical preference, but because in fact it is one of the essential traits of Western societies that the force relationships which for a long time had found expression in war, in every form of warfare, gradually became invested in the order of power'.[19] Modern societies, while bearing witness to an increasing civil peace, are made possible, Foucault argues, by an investment of forces deriving from war.

This observation, the argument that the forms of society ordinarily identified with peace and civility are, upon closer inspection, riven by war is a standard feature of leftist political thought. One need only think of Marx's argument that modern societies are defined by a 'more

---

[18] Michel Foucault, *The History of Sexuality, Volume 1, An Introduction*, trans. Robert Hurley (London: Penguin, 1990), p. 93.
[19] Ibid., p. 102.

or less veiled civil war'[20] or of Gramsci's account of the wars of position and movement that structure the relations between civil society and the State.[21] What distinguishes Foucault's position, a position that plays a large role in the constitution of the counter-strategic tradition as a whole, is the expressly Clausewitzian nature of its conception of the typology of that war. While many argue that the entire tradition of leftist thought owes too much to Clausewitz, such arguments rest, like those interpretations of a military-strategic persuasion, on a very narrow understanding of Clausewitzian thought, more often than not on a simplistic reduction of it to the dictum.[22] One of the many contributions of Foucault as well as Deleuze and Guattari to the transformation of leftist political thought has been their development of a Clausewitzian account of the typology of war that underlies the organization of power relations within modern societies in ways that exceed and challenge such orthodoxies.

Here we are mainly concerned with the ways in which leftism has traditionally operated upon a dialectical understanding of the 'civil war' that takes place at the heart of modern societies. Ordinarily war is conceived within this tradition as a form of relation that defines the division of society into two distinct camps. War also figures within this tradition as a principle of opposition that describes the mode of antagonism assumed between those two camps upon recognition of the existence of this relation. War distinguishes, in turn, a form of decision that is taken and a temporal process that is entered into upon the establishment of the political irreconcilability of the motives and wills of the two camps involved. The form of war involved here within this dialectical tradition is that of a parameter of interaction between two sets of forces that are sent into collision by the raising of the awareness of their irreconcilability and the experience of the decision that follows. These forces are then presupposed as entering into the parameter of war in the full possession of an array of strategies and tactics designed as instruments for the fulfilment of their contradictory political wills. The basic principle of being able to define 'the left' in diametrical opposition to 'the right' is reliant upon precisely such an imaginary. Marx's idea of a 'civil war' raging at the heart of modern societies composed

---

[20] Karl Marx, *Capital: Volume 1* (London: Penguin, 1990), p. 412; Karl Marx and Frederick Engels, *The Communist Manifesto* (New York: Norton, 1988), p. 66.
[21] Antonio Gramsci, *Selections from the Prison Notebooks* (London: Lawrence and Wishart, 1996), pp. 229–235.
[22] Ernesto Laclau and Chantal Mouffe, *Hegemony & Socialist Strategy: Toward a Radical Democratic Politics* (London: Verso, 1985), pp. 69–70.

of two more or less discrete competing classes of social forces is the ultimate expression of this dialectical conception of war.[23] Understood in such light, the history of modern societies describes a development of alternating periods of relative dominations and liberations in which the political wills involved are variably repressed, incited, released and realized.

Against this dialectical conception of war as a principle of intelligibility for historically founded divisions that structure antagonisms within society, Foucault develops a neo-Clausewitzian account of war as an active force that disrupts existing divisions, constituting social relations anew and allowing for the composition of new forms of political subjectivity. He utilizes Clausewitz to redefine a leftist conception of war as an active force of creation rather than a historically sedimented form of antagonism. Dialectical models, where they seek to reduce our understanding of the role of war in the constitution of modern societies to that of a formalized structure of antagonism, play into the hands of State power. On the other hand it is the generative potentiality of war, its essential dynamism and instability that offers the possibility of forms of society that exceed the disciplinary and control capacities of sovereign powers. The problem that war poses, for Foucault, then, is less that of exposing hidden wars or reactivating forgotten or historically sedimented lines of social division than it is of seeking out future war, pursuing war as a condition of possibility for new forms of subjectivity. This Foucauldian interpretation seeks to utilize Clausewitz both to reinterpret the role of war in the organization of power in modern societies as well as to disturb that organization by accentuating the movement of the force of war toward its extreme.

In order to understand how Foucault develops such a Clausewitzian conception of war it is necessary to contextualize its development within Foucault's broader theory of power. In his later works Foucault is concerned with challenging traditional accounts of power that construe their definitions around the exercise of the right to kill. Such 'juridical' models of power Foucault challenges with his conception of a 'strategic model'. According to Foucault's strategic model, power is identified with the making and shaping of life rather than the right to take it.[24] Power according to this strategic model does not reside in specific subjects as a latent capacity to be exercised at will over others but is, instead, a force that functions in relations that makes subjects.

---

[23] Marx, *Capital*, p. 412.   [24] Foucault, *History of Sexuality*, pp. 135–159.

Traditional models of power presume the formation of subjects to be extraneous to the coming into being of power relations. Foucault's strategic model, in contrast, construes power 'not on the basis of the primitive term of the relation but starting from the relation itself, inasmuch as the relation is what determines the elements on which it bears; instead of asking ideal subjects what part of themselves or what powers of theirs they have surrendered, allowing themselves to be subjectified, one needs to inquire how relations of subjectivation can manufacture subjects'.[25]

As Foucault describes in greater detail in his recently translated *Society Must Be Defended*, more traditional accounts of power tend to construe modern social order as a resolution of the problem of war through which preformed subjects confer sovereignty upon a transcendent State; the 'right of making warre' being chief among those powers surrendered to the State.[26] Other dissident accounts of modern society, from the advent of early modern revolutionary tracts on politics onwards, construe social order simply as a continuation of specific wars in which the terms of a historical defeat by one social group over another are inscribed and preserved in the uneven distributions of power that prevail.[27] In brief, contract versus conquest theories of the State. Foucault's account is distinctive insofar as he conceives a more complex process through which war is neither removed from society in order to provide greater security to preformed subjects nor simply disguised in the form of unjust social contracts between historically sedimented groups of subjects. Along with other counter-strategic thinkers, Foucault conceives modern societies forming not out of a resolution of the problem of war, nor as a continuation of specific historically defined wars, but as a product of a refinement of the role of war in the constitution of relations. Rather than simply removing war from relations or disguising them within relations, modern societies operate dynamically through the inculcation and dissemination of the force of war throughout relations. Here Foucault's work dovetails with other counter-strategic thinkers who

---

[25] Foucault, 'Society Must Be Defended' in Michel Foucault, *Ethics: Subjectivity and Truth*, ed. Paul Rabinow (London: Allen Lane, 1997), p. 59. This text was a summary of a course of lectures Foucault gave at the Collège de France in 1975–1976. The lectures are now published in full as Michel Foucault, *Society Must Be Defended*, trans. David Macey (London: Allen Lane, 2003). However the translation of the shorter course summary is in specific instances more erudite which is why I choose to quote from it here rather than the fuller lectures.

[26] Thomas Hobbes, *Leviathan* (London: Penguin, 1985), p. 234.

[27] Foucault, *Society Must Be Defended*, pp. 87–111.

similarly understand modernity as a process made possible by the release of immanent forces of life over and against the newly transcendental power of the State.[28] The transition to modern societies is affected not simply by the concentration of war-making powers within the State apparatus, for Foucault, but by what he describes as the 'investment' of 'force relations' deriving from war within the order of political power.[29] Arguing so, Foucault challenges not only the idea that modern societies are peaceful in the simplistic terms in which peace is construed as antithetical to war in both realist and liberal theories of international relations, but also those critical traditions in which war is understood simply as a principle of intelligibility for historically founded divisions within society. For Foucault, in contrast, the distinctiveness of modern societies is born not from the ways they preserve certain historically constituted divisions and generate social antagonisms in accordance with those divisions, but from the fact that war plays an active role within their political orders. Neither socially homogeneous nor dialectically polarized, modern societies develop according to a Foucauldian analysis through the generation of a series of differential divisions, of increasingly complex lines of antagonism. A certain force of war functions actively within all social relations, allowing for the decentring of new forms of subjectivity that lay claim to their own particular conditions of possibility. The subject that emerges among these force relations, that is subjectified in accordance with their generative force, is a polemical subject; forever fighting to survive, waging a war in pursuit of the truth that he or she is. As he describes,

> It is the fact of being on one side – the decentered position – that makes it possible to interpret the truth, to denounce the illusions and errors that are being used – by your adversaries – to make you believe we are living in a world in which order and peace have been restored. The more I decenter myself, the better I can see the truth; the more I accentuate the relationship of force, and the harder I fight, the more effectively I can deploy the truth ahead of me and use it to fight, survive and win.[30]

A war continues to rage at the heart of modern societies, then, for Foucault. Not a war that simply preserves inequalities established in the past, at the origin of the birth of society. Rather, a war that intervenes

---

[28] Michael Hardt and Antonio Negri, *Empire* (Cambridge MA: Harvard University Press, 2000); Gilles Deleuze, *Pure Immanence: Essays on a Life*, trans. Anne Boyman (New York: Zone Books, 2001).
[29] Foucault, *History of Sexuality*, p. 102.   [30] Foucault, *Society Must Be Defended*, p. 53.

in the constitution of the present, subdividing existing social relations, creating new lines of activity that incite the formation of different forms of political subjectivity that in turn reinvent their relation with the past; a force of war activating mobility within power relations rather than the reactivation of a form of war the lines of division of which were long ago decided upon. Here, then, Foucault is deploying Clausewitz's conception of war as an 'act of force' against the more traditional leftist conception of war as a dialectical form. We are to conceive the role of war, if we follow Foucault, as an operator rather than a parameter. War is less the product of a historical decision than it is an active, divisive and productive capacity moving within social relations, conditioning their mutability. Echoing Clausewitz, Foucault offers us a conception of war as 'a pulsation of violence, variable in strength and therefore variable in the speed with which it explodes and discharges its energy'.[31]

Reconceptualizing war thus allows for a significantly different understanding of the subject of social relations. More traditional leftisms conceive of war as an outcome of politically defined oppositions that constitute the subjects of conflict. Constitution within any such dialectically defined opposition requires each opponent as Gramsci describes, 'to seek to be itself totally and throw into the struggle all the political and moral "resources" it possesses, since only in that way can it achieve a genuine dialectical "transcendence" of its opponent'.[32] Clausewitz himself recognizes the logical link between such a dialectical conception of war and the tendency toward the extreme. In being an act of force with no logical limit war dictates the maxim 'if you want to overcome your enemy you must match your effort against his power of resistance'.[33] Such a dialectical conception of war must necessarily lead to a strategy of extremes.

Yet what is of crucial importance for Clausewitz is that in dialectical conditions of contradictory opposition this logic always breaks down. The dialectical conception of war presupposes two parties whose political subjectivities assume the form of a contradictory relation. 'Force to counter opposing force' as Clausewitz describes.[34] Each experiences, as a condition of their war relation, a force of decision that produces a tendency toward the extreme where the extreme is defined as the 'rendering powerless of the enemy'.[35] Yet, the movement toward the extreme of one dictates, because of the specific condition of contradiction, the

---

[31] Clausewitz, *On War*, p. 98.   [32] Gramsci, *Selections from the Prison Notebooks*, p. 109.
[33] Clausewitz, *On War*, p. 86.   [34] Ibid., p. 83.   [35] Ibid.

annihilation of the other. 'If one side uses force without compunction, undeterred by the bloodshed it involves, while the other side refrains, the first will gain the upper hand. That side will force the other to follow suit; each will drive its opponent toward extremes.'[36] The upshot of this inference is that this condition of contradiction compels, Clausewitz argues, a movement away from the extreme. The fact of being constituted within a relation of war in which such a strategy of the extreme is a mutually shared principle dictates to each party concerned a methodological caution. The result is that dialectical war is never witness to the realization of a maximum display of force but always involves weakened expressions of the wills that comprise such force relations. Constituted in biopolar contradiction, the subject is incapable ever of, as Gramsci would say, 'seeking to be itself totally'. It is, instead, forced by dint of war into a degenerative movement of compromise by which it becomes less like itself, only more similar to the other.

The brunt of Clausewitz's argument, then, is that the dialectical conception of war never produces dialectical results. The logic of the dialectic is such that it compels the parties that constitute such a war relation to enter into a process of barter. This is precisely why Clausewitz chooses to further define war as 'commerce'.[37] Once war is recognized as an act of exchange its logical tendency toward an expression of the extreme is thwarted. The very nature of war as an act of exchange prevents the full concentration and expression of force as 'anything omitted out of weakness by one side becomes a real, objective reason for the other to reduce its efforts, and the tendency toward the extremes is reduced by this interaction'.[38] Rather than forging the full expression of a contradictory opposition in production of transcendence, dialectical war imposes a perpetual condition of limitation amid the reduction of possibilities. The parties that constitute such a war relation are, in this condition, overwhelmed by the 'political object of war'.[39] The political object reduces the condition of war to one of increasingly negligible barter. 'The smaller the penalty you demand from your opponent, the less you can expect him to try and deny it to you; the smaller the effort he makes, the less you need make yourself. Moreover, the more modest your own political aim, the less importance you attach to it and the less reluctantly you will abandon it if you must.' The logic of war relations is one of a movement towards indifference rather than the forms of transcendence afforded by the tendency of pure war toward the extreme.

[36] Ibid., p. 84.   [37] Ibid., p. 173.   [38] Ibid., p. 89.   [39] Ibid., p. 90.

For Foucault it is precisely this Clausewitzian logic of war that explains the strategy of modern sovereignty and the ways in which social relations form in the production of modern political orders under the duress of the power of the modern State. This logic of war is not a feature only of international relations between States. It is a feature of the force relations that compose societies within States. In *Society Must Be Defended*, Foucault depicts 'a battlefront running through the whole of society, continuously and permanently . . . a battlefront that puts us all on one side or the other . . . (where) there is no such thing as a neutral subject. We are all inevitably someone's adversary'.[40] Yet, the structural conditions for this war are substantially different from those portrayed by more orthodox leftisms. While traditional leftisms ordinarily construe dialectical war in terms that are determined by the existence of inequalities ineradicable by anything other than war itself, Foucault depicts a society permeated by a war determined principally by the existence of equality. This war, he argues is 'a war born of equality and takes place in the element of that equality'. This war is the effect not of inequality or difference, but 'the immediate effect of nondifferences, or at least of insufficient differences'.[41] 'If there were a difference, there would be no war. Differences lead to peace.'[42]

What, then, is that form of equality which, for Foucault, defines a war relation? Again, Foucault takes his leave from Clausewitz. War in its essence is defined as an act of force without limit. Yet in a relational context where force meets with counter-opposing force this tendency of the extreme is displaced, Clausewitz argues, by a movement towards indifference conditioned by the experience of fear. Each, in spite of their tendency toward the extreme, fears the consequence of being unable to realize that movement towards the extreme. If we suppose war to take place in a dialectical context in which the act of force is never pure but a collision with other living forces, so the subject of the act must calculate upon the mutually opposing movements of other forces. What if the resisting movements of those forces exceed one's own? The experience of this fear and the forms of calculative caution that then ensue determines, Clausewitz argues, an essential equality within the war relation which in turn initiates the circumscriptive movement toward indifference that displaces the pure tendency toward the extreme.

War becomes descriptive, then, from this Clausewitzian perspective, of specific types of force relation in which equality of fear is the

---

[40] Foucault, *Society Must Be Defended*, p. 51.   [41] Ibid., p. 90.   [42] Ibid., p. 91.

determinate condition. Without that shared condition of fear, war would realize its essence as an act of force tending toward the extreme. This mitigation of the war relation by the experience of fear is crucial for Foucault insofar as it establishes a condition upon which war becomes amenable to the sustenance of life. War relations, when understood in this light are defined not simply by the risk of death but more crucially by a preference for the preservation of life. Each party to a war relation shares this basic experience of equality before the risk of death and a concomitant interest in the sustenance of life. This equality before death and shared commitment to life renders war into a productive kind of force. The shared risk of death in which the possibility of death is determined by the potential of a movement toward the extreme produces another, different form of movement: a movement toward circumscription and modification.[43] War relations in which the potential of the tendency toward the extreme carries with it the risk of death are in turn productive of new forms of life defined by their negligible differences. This Clausewitzian logic is precisely what allows Foucault to argue that it is the investment of force relations deriving from war within political order that make the modern power of the State productive rather than disabling of life. The form of logic that Clausewitz describes in definition of the war relation is what Foucault otherwise describes in definition of strategic power relations. As Foucault argued, 'relations of power are strategic relations. Every time one side does something, the other one responds by deploying a conduct, a behaviour that counter-invests it, tries to escape it, diverts it, turns the attack against itself, etc. Thus nothing is ever stable in these relations of power.'[44] This 'strategic model' of power, while made possible by the investment of force relations deriving from war, is distinct from other models of power in that it is 'bent on generating forces, making them grow, and ordering them, rather than being dedicated to impeding them, making them submit, or destroying them.'[45] Modern forms of power are 'strategic' by definition of the ways in which they incorporate and function through force relations derived, in Clausewitzian terms, from war. Yet these are forms of war relations that are, as Foucault argues in extraction of Clausewitz's principle of modification, amenable to the (de)generation of circumscribed life forms.

---

[43] Clausewitz, *On War*, p. 84.
[44] Michel Foucault, 'Talk Show' in Michel Foucault, *Foucault Live: Collected Interviews 1961–1984*, ed. Sylvain Lotringer (New York: Semiotext, 1996), p. 144.
[45] Foucault, *History of Sexuality*, pp. 102, 136.

The war that permeates modern societies is, then, from this neo-Clausewitzian perspective of Foucault's a productive war. Constituted in essence by the tendency toward the extreme, but mitigated by the experience of fear, this form of war does not foster great inequalities, vast cleavages or significant differences between the forms of life that emerge from it. Rather what takes place in the birth of modern societies is the subordination of the pure essence of war to the political object of a sovereign power concerned with the governance of difference itself; a subordination which serves to reduce differences, imposing limits on the forms of life that war produces. War becomes, in turn, a machine for the circumscription of life. The problem of war is, seen in this light, not so much its being active in the constitution of the force relations that compose modern societies. The problem lies in war's capture; its surrender to the instrumental requirements of State power. For Foucault, then, Clausewitz's further definition of war as 'nothing but the continuation of policy with other means' describes the strategy of modern State power. On this point Foucault could agree with any number of neo-Clausewitzian military-strategic theorists. Yet in detailing the processes by which war becomes the continuation of politics Foucault considerably dislocates prevailing conceptions of war and politics in ways that compromise those more traditional interpretations of Clausewitz. The form of war that enters into subordination to politics describes that primitive entity that Clausewitz pinpoints as 'an act of force with no logical limit'.[46] The subordination of war to politics leads to a modification that in turn compromises the potentialities of the forms of war realizable under conditions of modern State power. What emerges from this manoeuvre is a strategy of power that functions by securing, governing and optimizing the forms of life that war realizes. Strategy becomes the process of ensuring the continued subordination of war to politics.

Deleuze and Guattari's Clausewitz: the nomadic movement of war

If it is Foucault who utilizes Clausewitz to reinterpret the relation between war and modern societies it is Deleuze and Guattari who employ him to respond to the problem of how to (dis)engage that relation politically. There is a sense that in his account of modern

---

[46] Clausewitz, *On War*, p. 85.

societies Foucault over-emphasizes the ease with which power strate-gises the pure force of war within power relations. Foucault's engage-ment with Clausewitz is in this vein a somewhat tragic reading in which war is never able to realize the pure force that defines it in abstraction because it is 'in the real world' destined to be captured and compro-mised within a network of relations designed to mitigate its tendency toward the extreme. Yet, in reading Clausewitz there is a crucial ambi-guity and tension in his depiction of the relation between pure war and the form it assumes under the duress of State power. As he states, war 'is an act of policy', because 'were it a complete, untrammelled, absolute manifestation of violence (as the pure concept would require), war would of its own independent will usurp the place of policy the moment policy had brought it into being; it would then drive policy out of office and rule by the laws of its own nature, very much like a mine that can explode only in the manner or direction predetermined by the setting'.[47]

This is not, as is often confusedly supposed, an argument for an onto-logical understanding of war as a continuation of policy. The rendering of war as an act that fulfils policy is a contingent political requirement for the defence of State power. Were war to realize its 'absolute man-ifestation' it would 'drive policy out of office' he argues. The suste-nance of State power relies, in this sense, on its ability as Clausewitz describes, to 'trammel' war: like a fisherman who employs a trammel net to trap his prey without slaughtering it; to enmesh it, hinder its movement, contain its freedom, subjecting it to the political purposes of sovereignty. Foucault pursues the same conception of the investment of war within political order affording 'networks of power relations' that form 'dense webs' of social relations traversing and manufactur-ing individual subjects as an affect of power.[48] Yet in Deleuze and Guattari's conceptualization of the war/power relation we find a sig-nificantly different account of the potentialities of war in its subjection to the State. Deleuze and Guattari, like Clausewitz, depict a State power that captures, enmeshes and 'throws its net' over war.[49] However this relation of capture is never assured. 'The man of war, in his exteriority, is always protesting the alliances and pacts' achieved by sovereignty, as well as severing its bonds. War is, for Deleuze and Guattari, 'equally an unbinder and a betrayer: twice the traitor' as much as it is a force

---

[47] Ibid., p. 98.   [48] Foucault, *History of Sexuality*, p. 96.
[49] Gilles Deleuze and Felix Guattari, *A Thousand Plateaus: Capitalism & Schizophrenia*, trans. Brian Massumi (London: Athlone Press, 1999), pp. 424–425.

for the equalization of power relations.[50] There is then, in Deleuze and Guattari's account of power a much more Clausewitzian insistence on the indeterminacy of war's capture by the State. For Foucault, we can say, the utility of Clausewitz lies in his codification of the strategy of power that informs the growth and development of the modern State. For Deleuze and Guattari, on the other hand, Clausewitz provides not only an outline of the strategy of modern State power but a means with which to theorize its destruction. That is to say Deleuze and Guattari follow Clausewitz in his leading us toward the idea of the disinterment of war from its subordination to political sovereignty and the reassertion of its tendency toward the extreme.

If, in its subjection to sovereignty, war becomes a continuation of politics, then the aim of countering State power must involve the disinterment of war from that state of subordination. Indeed, in spite of his tragic rendering of the circumscription of war by State power Clausewitz himself is clear on this necessity of pursuing the absolute ideal of war when he argues in book eight that:

> The origin and the form taken by a war are not the result of any ultimate resolution of the vast array of circumstances involved, but only of those features that happen to be dominant. It follows that war is dependent on the interplay of possibilities and probabilities, of good and bad luck, conditions in which strictly logical reasoning often plays no part at all and is always apt to be a most unsuitable and awkward intellectual tool. It follows, too, that war can be a matter of degree. Theory must concede all this; but it has the duty to give priority to the absolute form of war and to make that form a general point of reference, so that he who wants to learn from theory becomes accustomed to keeping that point in view constantly, to measuring all his hopes and fears by it, and to approximating it when he can or when he must.[51]

Contrary to those interpretations of Clausewitz, Michael Howard's for example, which theorizes his development of the concept of absolute war as an extension of a theory of wars conducted by and for the State, Deleuze and Guattari account for it as an assertion of the irreducibility of war to State power.[52] Ultimately, Clausewitz's concept of absolute war makes sense for Deleuze and Guattari as a war not for the State, but a war 'directed against the State and against the worldwide axiomatic expressed by States'.[53] The extremity of absolute war is not that of a

---

[50] Ibid.   [51] Clausewitz, *On War*, p. 702.
[52] Michael Howard, *Clausewitz* (Oxford: Oxford University Press, 1983), pp. 47–58.
[53] Deleuze and Guattari, *A Thousand Plateaus*, p. 422.

concentrated military violence as Peter Paret interprets it, but another kind of violence, the violence of a movement against the State.[54] That is to say, not a militarized violence committed against a specific State, its governmental institutions, leaders or representatives; rather, the violence of a movement that breaks from the distribution and strategization of forces that compose existing social relations.

Foucault follows Clausewitz's logic of war to render an account of the development of modern social relations that involves the gradual circumscription of life potentialities. The investment of war within modern social relations incites processes of life's degeneration in which the existence of differences are gradually countermanded by powers that seek firstly the management of difference, and secondly their eradication, for the purpose of securing peaceful civil societies. The limitation of life possibilities are, then, the defining feature of this form of power and society born of the investment of war. Deleuze and Guattari, on the other hand, pitch their faith in the incapacities of the State to suborn war. Whereas in Foucault's reading of Clausewitz real war always prevails over pure war, Deleuze and Guattari insist on the failures of the State to capture the pure force of war in the social relations it manufactures. The State, according to Deleuze and Guattari's reading, is formed on the basis of an 'appropriation' of the war machine which nevertheless fails to realize the 'essence' of war provoking the escape of that pure force and its redirection against sovereignty.

The concept of the warrior has, then, for Deleuze and Guattari, significant symbolic value. Whereas for Foucault war relations are always degenerative power relations in which the life of the subject is gradually being closed down, Deleuze and Guattari provide a conception of modern societies in which the potential to wage war, to accentuate movements within the fields of force relations that compose power, to seek out new forms of truth, establish new forms of social practice and political subjectivity, are vital and expansive tasks. This ability to wage war, to locate and explore its pure force, is not a question of privilege. In theory, anyone can be a Clausewitzian warrior in the 'strange war' that Deleuze and Guattari urge upon the State. The late modern era, involving as it has the decline in the power of nation-states, the collapse of dialectically organized social struggles, the proliferation of offensives against socially encoded power arrangements, the diversity of forms of subjectivity, suggest the flowing forth of that pure force of war from out

---

[54] Peter Paret, 'The Genesis of *On War*' in Clausewitz, *On War*, pp. 3–28.

of its capture by the State. And Clausewitz, that paragon of the military-strategic tradition that has informed the development of State power, is heralded the architect of its destruction.

Conclusion

Clausewitz's *On War* is a sublime text. It has proven, unquestionably, the most influential text in the consecration and development of the military-strategic power of the modern State. It has likewise been influential in the development of orthodox Marxist-Leninist theories of revolution and insurgency. This much is well known. The purpose of this chapter has been to detail its influence upon a tradition of counter-strategic thought that seeks to critique and undermine both the power of the State as well as to redevelop those traditions of leftist thinking in which the principle of opposition to State power was born. This counter-strategic tradition, represented here in the works of Foucault and Deleuze and Guattari, adapts Clausewitz's logic of real war in order to provide a radical account of the strategy of power that informs the development of social relations under the duress of the modern State. In this vein Clausewitz's portrait of the dynamics of real war in which relations reduce to contradiction and opposition is productive of a limitation of life potentialities was fundamental. The counter-strategic tradition exposes the ways in which this conception of war as a dialectical form only serves to reproduce the methods by which the State governs the force of war, bringing its movements within its control, and countermanding it to its own degenerative purposes. In turn, this counter-strategic tradition develops Clausewitz's concept of a force of pure war as a new principle of opposition to the dialectical forms of contradiction that inform more orthodox leftisms. Clausewitzian war, in this tradition, is reconceived neither as the continuation of policy by other means nor as the mere inversion of that formula, but as an active force of subversion by which the substance of the relation between war and politics is reconfigured.

Index

Foucault's theory of 284
in inter-state relations 69
of modern State 289, 291, 292–294, 295
and right (lawfulness) 79
strategic model of 290, 292
use of 31, 48, 75
see also balance of power; coercion;
   political authority; sovereign
   authority
preliminary articles, for perpetual peace
   (Kant) 59, 65, 69–71, 190
presentism, in use of classical authors 3, 6,
   15
'problem-solving' 15
progress
   concept of human impetus to 136–137
   revolution and 220
property
   community rights to 168–169
   and distribution 169
   importance of 161–163
   limits to accumulation of 172
   Locke's chapter on 158–161
   Locke's theory of 169–175
   as moral quality 167, 168
   Pericles' exhortation to sacrifice 34–35
   private (Rousseau) 103
   use right over 167, 170
   see also land
property laws
   dependent on public claims 166
   in European states 157, 160
property rights 156, 160, 260
   and notion of just war 163, 175
   Pufendorf's view of 166–169
prudence, and realism 46–48
Prussia 186
   and religion under Frederick William II
   217, 219
   see also Germany
Pufendorf, Samuel
   and absolute monarchy 101
   and development of Grotius 244
   French translations of 100
   Kant's criticism of 70, 77, 215
   and property rights 166–169, 174
   and sovereignty 176

rationalism, Hobbes and 255, 257,
   269–271, 275
Rawls, John 70, 71
Realism
   and chance 35
   Hobbes and 253, 254, 260, 272
   and international norms 44

and moral norms 46–49
origins of 1
and prudence 46–48
Rousseau and 1, 96, 113–114, 119
timelessness in 10
and war 7
see also Hobbes; Rousseau
reason
   and experiential world (Kant) 213, 215,
   217, 220, 221
   and fear 261–262
   in German Enlightenment 213
   Kant's faith in 68, 183, 214
   and liberalism 199–200
   as moral guide 214
   see also moral principles; rationalism
reason of state theory 238, 245
rebellion
   forbidden by Kant 218
   in Hobbes 264
Recht, principles of (Kant) 66
reciprocity
   in Athenian democracy 33
   in Kant 60
reform
   international political 68
   'natural' (teleological) track to 65, 68–69,
   91
   obligation to 85, 90, 190
   potential for 64, 216
   of states 55, 64, 182, 190
religion
   separated from political sphere
   (Hobbes) 259, 261
   and war 256–257
   see also belief; Christianity
religious toleration 260
Rengger, Nicholas 10, 15
republican constitutions
   identification with modern liberal
   states 181
   imperfect 61, 64
   Kant's requirement for 8, 11, 58, 61,
   81
   as lawful 66
   and perpetual peace 67, 185
   rights and freedoms under 218
   and rule of international law 64
   see also liberal states
revolution, as process 220, 221
rights
   community 168–169
   dynamic creation of (Hegel) 222
   of indigenous peoples 165, 167
   settlers' 164

Index

Tesón, Fernando
  and Democratic Peace 80–81
  interpretation of Kant 75, 78, 82–83, 84, 93
  on lawful coercion 90
  and liberal enforcement 86
  on nature of non-liberal states 88
Test Act (1673) 159
Third World, and conditional aid 188
Thirty Years War 237, 238, 242, 257
  see also Westphalia
Thucydides 17, 18–19, 233
  account of Corcyraean civil war (*stasis*) 39, 40–41
  Archeology 46, 47
  and historical forces 46
  History of the Peloponnesian War 27
  and moral norms 28
  on Pericles 28, 30–35
  and Realism 1
  scepticism 38, 49–50
  use of antithesis 28–30, 47
time
  and human development theory 125, 143–144, 147–148
  and space 143, 144–145
'time-shifting' 131, 134, 142
trade
  and equality of states 110
  free 193
  Kant's limits on 187
  right to 187
  and transnational relations of states 54, 181, 187–189
traditions, invented 10
treaties, early modern analyses of 245–248
trust-building 70
Tuck, Richard
  Philosophy and Government 239
  re-interpretation of Grotius 234, 237–240
  The Rights of War and Peace 239
tychê (chance), power of 35–38, 44

unilateral judgments 75, 85, 91
United Nations 56, 158
  Charter 77
  legal shortcomings of Charter 78–79, 94
  and sovereign equality 78, 79
United States of America
  application of *terra nullius* doctrine 157
  Declaration of Independence (1776) 156, 211
  'Hobbesian' world view 2, 9

modern imperialism 196
  and Nicaragua case before ICJ 90–91
  see also American Indians; Virginia
'unjust enemy'
  defined 65, 87
  legitimate defence against 92–93

Vattel, Emmerich de
  and Grotius 237, 244, 247
  Kant's criticism of 70, 77
  and obligation to cultivate land 163, 175
  and *terra nullius* doctrine 157, 174
Venice, Rousseau's observations on 99
Virginia
  Declaration of Rights (1776) 156
  settlement of 164, 172
Virilio, Paul 278
visible hand, political intervention 148, 151
Vitoria, Francisco de 132, 165, 238
Voltaire 100, 101
  and Lafitau 130

Walker, R. B. J. 234
war
  as 'act of force' (with no logical limit) 287, 289
  as act of policy 292
  and beliefs 256–257
  between liberal and non-liberal states 189
  Clausewitz's definitions of 277, 279
  as 'commerce' 288
  concept of absolute war 293–294
  dependent on trust of citizens 265–266
  in dialectical models 283–284, 287, 288
  effect on norms of rational action (Thucydides) 40
  and equal experience of fear 289–290
  as generative principle in social relations 278, 282, 285–287
  Hegel's view of 223, 227
  Kant's analysis of 185, 216
  and *kinesis* (motion, instability) 40, 41
  logic of relations of 288
  norms of (Greek) 45
  popular support for 185
  pure vs real 279–282, 295
  and Realism 7
  as right of sovereign states 77–78
  role in formation of modern societies 285–287
  and state power (Deleuze and Guattari) 292–294, 295
  subordinated to political ends 277, 288, 291

CAMBRIDGE STUDIES IN INTERNATIONAL RELATIONS